Plate 1. Sen Tantansai Sōshitsu, master of Ura Senge, 14th generation from Rikyū, from a portrait taken at the Daitokuji, December 1, 1924, when he performed Cha-no-yu before Her Majesty the Empress Dowager.

CHA-NO-YU

THE JAPANESE TEA CEREMONY

by A. L. SADLER, M.A.

CHARLES E. TUTTLE COMPANY
Rutland, Vermont & Tokyo, Japan

Representatives

Continental Europe: BOXERBOOKS, INC., *Zurich*

British Isles: PRENTICE-HALL INTERNATIONAL, INC., *London*

Australasia: BOOK WISE (AUSTRALIA) PTY. LTD.
104-108 Sussex Street, Sydney 2000

Published by the Charles E. Tuttle Company, Inc.
of Rutland, Vermont & Tokyo, Japan
with editorial offices at
Suido 1-chome, 2-6, Bunkyo-ku, Tokyo, Japan

© *1962 by Charles E. Tuttle Co., Inc.*

All rights reserved

Library of Congress Catalog Card No. 62-19787

International Standard Book No. 0-8048-1224-1

*First edition, 1933 by
J. L. Thompson & Co., Ltd., Kobe and
Kegan Paul, Trench. Trubner & Co., Ltd., London
First Tuttle edition, 1963
Sixth printing, 1982*

PRINTED IN JAPAN

INTRODUCTION

For the last four hundred years there has existed in Japan a very definite point of view or way of life associated with the ceremonial drinking of tea. It is called Cha-no-yu, literally Hot Water for Tea, or Chado, the Way of Tea, and those who follow it are known as Chajin or Tea-men. It might be described as a household sacrament of esthetics, economics and etiquette. It has been and still is practised by a very large number of the most cultivated people in the land, by statesmen, soldiers, artists and men of business, as well as by artizans and ordinary people. And so its influence has penetrated deeply into the details of the everyday life of the community and has taken a large part in forming its tastes and habits. It is little known outside the country because nothing much has been written about it by Europeans with the exception of short descriptions by Kaempfer and Brinkley and some pictures of Tea gardens in the works of Morse and Conder.* But the importance of its contribution to the civilization of the country would hardly be gathered from these writings.

By far the best description of its spirit is the short essay of Okakura Kakuzo entitled ' The Book of Tea,' a composition of great charm of style very suitable to the elegance of the subject, but rather stimulating interest in ' Teaism,' the word he coined to describe it, than giving a detailed account of it. Therefore this book may be considered as an attempt to supply further information from Japanese sources for those whose curiosity and interest Okakura has aroused. Cha-no-yu does not owe so much as might at first appear to China and India, for, as usual in such cases, the national spirit of Japan soon asserted itself, so that what was at first an imported taste became in the course of time so completely naturalized and transformed that it now seems perhaps the most Japanese of all institutions. China only supplied the stand and utensils imported with the tea and the method of grinding and infusing it, and these things still survive, associated with and almost hidden by their purely Japanese surroundings and adjuncts, and yet also quite consciously distinct from them, and as such used on occasions of special ceremony or when otherwise considered fitting. But the Chaseki or Tea-room and its special garden or Rōji are entirely Japanese, partly inspired though they may be by ancient India through the Buddhist Sutras.

Indeed Cha-no-yu may be considered an epitome of Japanese civilization, for it is a well-blended mixture of elements drawn from the two most ancient cultures of the East eclectically acquired by extremely able and critical minds capable of discerning exactly how they could best use it for the convenience and education of their people. And very completely were the Tea Masters justified of their

* Since this went to press in 1930 there have appeared two works dealing with the subject, that of Mr. Y. Fukukita in English, and A. Berliner's *Der Teecult in Japan*, both of them well illustrated.

creation, for it has kept the national taste more sensitive and healthy and potent than that of perhaps any other country, and this I submit is now being demonstrated by what is called ' Modernism ' in the art, architecture and interior decoration of Europe. This movement may be called Modern only in Europe, for it appears to a great extent to be, where it is not influenced by machinery of some kind, a copying of the national outlook and taste of Japan in these spheres, for though it may only lately have dawned on continental artists and decorators that a house is a machine to live in and from which all superfluous and irritating ornaments should be banished, the contact between this part of Europe and Japan has been too close of late to allow of the discovery being entirely an independent one. The necessity for strict economy in life and the lack of means for ostentation which post-war conditions have brought about, combined with the impulse to simplicity inspired by militarism, may supply the reason for the departure from previous traditional standards. These conditions were also responsible for a similar feeling in Japan of the sixteenth century, for this too was the end of an epoch of exhausting civil wars. To this extent simplicity in both East and West may spring from the same cause, but there is so much in the details* of this Modernism that is identical with what has long been characteristic of Japanese idiosyncrasy that it might not unsuitably be described as the Rikyu style, for Sen Rikyu perhaps did more than any other artist to stimulate and standardize that sort of architecture and interior decoration or lack of it, and to expound the creed on which it is based, as may be seen by a perusal of the things that he said and occupied his life in doing.

To those who claim that this feeling is more ancient in Europe and might better be termed Attic, seeing that it has been so concisely stated in the famous claim of Pericles that his countrymen ' loved beauty with economy and culture without softness,' there may be pointed out the strange truth that Japan has preserved this spirit up to the present time though without a trace of influence from Greece except for a few details in the Hōryuji, the folds of the Buddha's garments and possibly the word for wine, whereas, in spite of the continuous and persistent teaching of the Greek texts in our schools for centuries and an assiduous aping of the Parthenon and Hellenic statuary in our monuments, we are only just beginning to realize what it means. Similar economic and geographical conditions, the same lack of other-worldly sentiment and a cult not very unlike, are no doubt the causes of what Japan and Greece had in common. Had Greece been an island ruled by the Spartans and decorated by the Athenians there would have been an even greater likeness.

What has not been sufficiently emphasized is that the men of Athens, like the Japanese, were most distinguished by what they had the sense to omit, and it would be well if the modern designer would

---

* E.g., plain walls, one picture, sliding doors dividing one room into two or more, cupboards along one side of room, straight lines with perhaps one arched door or a round window, plain unpainted wood, square lighting fittings, sideboards and tables like ' chigai-dana,' windows and sliding doors barred like Shōji. See, for examples, the *Studio* Supplement of Decorative Art for 1930, pp. 17, 43, 44, 76, 79, 107 etc.

keep some of the admonitions of Rikyu and his followers in mind, that they may be saved from those tendencies that already begin to show as a result of that attempted originality of the commonplace mind, to discourage which the Tea Masters always needed all their powers of restraint.

Through the teaching of Sen Rikyu it was that Teaism, from being a diversion of the wealthy and of retired people, came to be a point of view and a way of life. It became the control of everyday affairs, the making of a dwelling and living in it according to the dicta of the most eminent Masters. It is therefore a kind of ancestor worship, for these men are the esthetic ancestors of the nation, and their traditions have been handed down by their various disciples and schools to this day and are still alive and vigorous.

Under these schools the country was organized under Teaism as as it was under autocracy and bureaucracy, and the result has been successful enough, for life is principally composed of the details that the Tea Masters have studied and arranged and refined, and if harmony and etiquette are lacking in the meal that is taken three times a day, and in entering and leaving the room, and making up the fire and so on, there is not much likelihood of their being found elsewhere. What Teaism has done for Japan may be seen from the contrast in other lands where any such disciplined estheticism is unknown. Lack of taste and balance in decoration, a confused ostentation and want of any system of etiquette permeating all classes of society have been and still are very noticeable in the West and in America, and practically all visitors to Japan seem to be struck by the strange phenomenon that good manners are as natural to the peasant and workman as to the leisured classes. No doubt this is partly due to the antiquity of the civilization and its experience in the best way to live, since we find the same thing to some extent in the more ancient countries of Europe, but equally at least it would seem that direct teaching in taste and etiquette is responsible. And of course the teaching was not the less effective in a society where a breach of manners might put life or limb in jeopardy. At any rate Japan has held, apparently, that if you wish ethics and politeness to be understood, you should teach these things and not a system of theology of a more or less hypothetical kind, or the ways of people whose enthusiasm often led them to forget the consideration due to their neighbours. It must not be forgotten that Confucius some 500 years B.C. gave the golden rule in its negative form in such a way that even Shaw could not take objection to it. For he said that all his doctrine could be summed up in the one ideograph Shu, consideration or sympathy.

And it was the strong and centralized administration of the Tokugawa Shoguns that made the esthetic control of the Empire possible and easy. Japanese historians observe in commenting on the culture of the Tokugawa period as distinct from those that preceded it, that in this era it was not the monopoly of any special caste, noble or priest or soldier, but was diffused through all classes both in town and country. For more than two hundred and fifty years the land was without war, foreign entanglement or serious misfortune, and so, prosperous under a strong government, it had leisure and moderate means to devote to the quest of the most interesting way to live. Even without being able to read any of the large mass of literature of the Edo period, Europeans can see this in the profuse illustrations of the manners and customs in books and prints of the seventeenth and eighteenth centuries. Without the severe and restrained taste of those whose standard was that of Cha-no-yu these popular masterpieces might have been somewhat different.

If Teaism had only taught people that any display is vulgar and undesirable it would have been justified, for this is no easy thing to instil into any nation, since man is acquisitive by nature and inclined to hoard and show off, so that the most troublesome problems in the social and political spheres proceed from these egoistic qualities. Here its Buddhist basis is evident, for the main theme of Buddhism is the repudiation of the ego. An institution that made simplicity and restraint fashionable and at the same time kept itself accessible to all classes, providing a ground on which all could meet on terms of equality, thus combining the advantages of a Muhammedan Mosque and a cricket-field, and some may add, also, those of a Freemasons' Lodge and a Quaker Meeting-house, was well qualified to temper the disruptive forces of society. And how much it came to represent the standard of the ordinary man is suggested by the common expression ' Mucha,' or ' It isn't Tea,' used in Japan in almost the same way as we are accustomed to declare, ' It isn't cricket.' And in this connexion it is very apparent from the various anecdotes of the great Japanese generals that they regarded their battles as won in the Tea-room both literally and figuratively, for not only was it a first-rate training place for the disciplined mind and resourceful observation so needed in a strategist, but it was also a very convenient spot for a quiet discussion of the plans of a campaign.

Art, says Sir W. R. Lethaby, in *Form and Civilization*, is service and labour, and all admit that these are fine things, but practical demonstration is not so common. If the common domestic duty of serving a meal is shown to be not inferior to any other act by the highest class of people performing it with their own hands quite naturally and without affectation, it is not likely to be regarded as humiliating ; and the custom of going into domestic service for a few years before marriage to learn etiquette, which is usual in Japan, is as much part of the spirit of Teaism as is the wearing by his Majesty the Emperor of the insignia of the lowest as well as the highest class of the Imperial Orders. Tokugawa Japan was organized entirely on a basis of labour and service. One rank served that above it, and all ranks served the elders in the family and their ancestors who are their seniors in the history of the nation. So it is not remarkable that Teaism should often be described as only another version of Loyalty and Filial Piety. It is something like an artistic presentation of these sentiments. And since Teaism was the art of making a house as well as living in it, the Tea Master was the architect in many cases. There was not exactly such a profession in those days, for temples and mansions were designed by Buddhist monks and craftsmen, and built, like the houses of the rest of the population, by artizans, much as they were in earlier days in Europe. Chōgen Shonin and Eisai Zenji in the Kamakura age, for instance, introduced Sung architecture to Japan, and built and designed temples, much as Herbert de Losinga, Alan of Walsingham and Hugh of Lincoln did in England, and later on in the 16th century we find Mokushoku Shonin, the monk of Koya, appointed to design Hideyoshi's many palaces and temples, though Hideyoshi, himself a Tea Master and amateur architect, played no small part in this himself. The views of the Tea Master as esthetic advisor were naturally very influential in their effect on the design of both house and garden, especially the latter, and Kobori Enshu, to whom many such works are attributed, was the most notable example of an artist, architect, decorator and connoisseur who was a professional Tea Master and ennobled and salaried as such, though Honami Ko-etsu, who was an amateur of Tea, was perhaps more versatile.

It may be observed that Chinese styles of architecture have affected the ordinary Japanese dwelling very little, if at all, for this has always preserved the ancient way of building of a much simpler order that we see exemplified in the Shinto shrines of Ise, undoubtedly the Imperial Palace of earlier times before the residence of the sovereign was modelled on that of the T'ang Emperor. This Chinese flavour was most evident in the mansions of the Court Nobles of Kyoto, whereas the military aristocracy preferred the more Japanese simple thatched house, more in accordance with their principles of frugality, self-discipline and restraint.

But it was under the rule of Toyotomi Hideyoshi, with Rikyu as his esthetic advisor, that there was worked out a blending of the two styles for ordinary dwellings, the finest examples of which are the residence called Hi-un-kaku which was part of the Taiko's mansion of Juraku, and that exquisite building the Daigo Sambo-in, designed with its gardens by Hideyoshi himself. It was to the military class and their liking for Zen Buddhism that the Japanese house owes the type of room called Sho-in so characteristic of it since the era of Higashiyama. This arrangement of the reception room with Tokonoma or alcove and window beside it was introduced by the Zen monks for greater convenience in their studies. The buildings of a Zen temple differ from those of the other sects, being more for residence and meditation and less for ceremony and show. Whether the Japanese house would have developed differently if there had been no Tea Masters it is not easy to say, but at any rate in all things that pertained to the house and everyday life and behaviour their principles of restraint and simplicity as exemplified in the Tearoom and its Roji usually acted as a corrective to any tendencies to extravagance and ostentatious originality on the part of commonplace people whose only object was to obtain a little advertisement. Though there were times when the Way of Tea became luxurious itself.

Since the Japanese house is and has long been a standardized

one, it is easy to design and comparatively economical to build. The
rooms are multiples of one unit, the mat of six feet by three, the
space between two pillars being the length of the mat, and the width
of the sliding door the half of this, three feet. The length of the
building is described in ' ken ' of six feet. The house is therefore
fitted to the mats and this standardization began when the floors,
which were originally, before the Ashikaga period, of bare wood with
a mat here and there, came to be competely matted over. The house
is arranged so that it can be worked in the most effective manner
both for ordinary convenience and the reception of guests, and particularly so that it fits in harmoniously with the plan of the garden,
which should be first considered. There is no concealment of construction or unnecessary ornament.

Nor is this standardization confined to the house, but extends to
the clothing of the occupants, for just as the building is assembled
of materials of fixed dimensions and labour thereby saved, so kimonos
are made from bolts of stuff of unvarying length and breadth, and
their shape is practically uniform so that it is within the power of
everyone to make their own clothes, and they are normally put together by the women of the family. Hence it is not easy for any commercial combine to dictate to the population what kind of costume it
shall wear for the next six months.

And yet, though there is this uniformity of pattern in both house
and costume, there is also an infinite variety of detail and arrangement that avoids monotony, and the evident judgment of discriminat-
ing European critics both in previous centuries and now is that the
Japanese house and garden are beautiful and harmonious, and the
costume pleasing and dignified and well suited to set off the wearer,
of whatever age or figure, to the best advantage. A group of Japanese in their own costume is more pleasant and restful to the eye
than one of Europeans, though in the latter case individuals may look
well enough if the fashion happens to suit their style.

It is a special artistic mercy in Japan that only children and
young people are permitted by convention to wear bright colours,
and since few houses are without them they supply the occasional
touch of colour that varies the quietness of the monotoned interior.
Does it require the development of a more delicate sense of values
to convince Western women that they look better against the background of a self-coloured room like the flower in the Chaseki?

Now this comparatively universal good taste in life could hardly
have come about without an organized education in what was to be
considered admirable and what eliminated, and it was the Tea Master
who in the main had charge of this, the best kind of education, perhaps, because it could be imparted and practised in the home under
the ordinary conditions of life. Okakura calls it ' moral geometry,'
in that it puts man in his proper place in the universe, giving him
the Zen outlook according to which one must get outside oneself and
regard life as a spectator, finding plenty therein to make merry over.
The more resourceful the mind the less does one need outside stimulus
to enjoyment.

' How supernatural and how miraculous !
I draw water and I carry brushwood,'

said the Zen monk, and so the most ordinary thing in life, the preparation of the fire and taking a simple meal and drinking tea, was
chosen as the best way of inculcating good manners and that economy
of movement lately re-discovered by psychologists. When we consider
how ridiculous is a considerable part of modern education, which
teaches what a large proportion of the taught neither wish to learn
or will ever get an opportunity of practising, while neglecting the
simple appreciations that make life, we can perhaps perceive how
much this natural way of educating the Japanese has contributed to
the clear-sighted practical and sane outlook on life that they have
undoubtedly come to possess. If they appear to anyone who lives
among them as distinctly lacking in that sentimentalism that is the
cause of so much inconvenience to us, though also a source of
amusement to many, the extra-logical common-sense of Zen can supply
a reason, and it is through the teaching of Teaism that Zen became
diffused among the ordinary people. Belief in or obsession with a
future life seems no very good foundation for order or fastidiousness
in this one, according to Zen, and it is instructive to read Father
Frois's description, in his *History of Japan*, of Nobunaga, that very
enthusiastic Teaist, as ' one who with Zenshu did not believe in the
immortality of the soul or in reward or punishment in the hereafter,
but who was very clear-minded and no holder of any kind of super-
stition, and at the same time exceedingly cleanly, courteous and
orderly in his way of living.' To very few in contemporary Europe
would the latter part of this sentence apply.

Sir W. Fergusson, writing in 1891, considers that in the Far East
there is hardly anything that can be called architecture, just as there
is 'no poetry, properly so called, and no literature worthy of the name.'
Ideas as to what constitute architecture have changed since then, but
there may be some truth in this part of the statement though not in
the sense this authority meant. It may be that the best architecture
is no architecture, just as the best colour scheme is no colour scheme.
The house and garden built and laid out together simply for use and
satisfaction ought to be the exact expression of the way of life of the
inmates without any ostentation or affectation.

This is what the Japanese house is, to a greater extent perhaps
than that of any other country, when all classes of people are considered. And this because it had to be, for the Tokugawa laws for-
bade all classes to have dwellings and furniture any more elaborate
than their position and occupation required, from Daimyo to peasant,
and these laws were the product of an official world educated in Cha-
no-yu, for much of the detailed legislation was the work of the third
Shogun Iemitsu, an enthusiastic Tea Master himself and pupil of
Kobori Enshu, whose influence in matters of taste was then supreme.
And Enshu knew how to use the Way of Tea to beggar the rich as
well as Rikyu had known how to employ it to comfort the poor.

And these Japanese houses that so accurately express the ways
of their builders are not very much unlike the simple types of Tudor

and Georgian days in our own country. These are constructive and efficient and fit on their sites naturally without making themselves conspicuous, and their plainness is relieved by perhaps one decorative feature that is quite in place, such as a door, chimney or window. These moderate sized residences are far more attractive and in better taste for a human being to live in than the immense mansions built almost entirely for display, up to whose grandeur no one ought to have been able to stand the strain of living for long. Of course there were some such buildings in Japan too, but they were for ceremonial, that is occasional use, or else they were political architecture intended to impoverish the feudal lords who were granted the honour of constructing them, that their purses might remain too lean for them to be a menace to the Shogun's government.

Actually the great noble preferred to live in a number of simple wooden buildings scattered round a fine garden, and the light nature of these made it easy to vary the monotony of things by shifting them at any time. This may be seen in the surviving feudal residences at Hikone, Kanazawa, Okayama and Kagoshima, formerly occupied by the Daimyos of these places. There is nothing pompous or consciously impressive about them.

It is evident that this quality of the Japanese residence is not entirely due to the Tea Masters, for the mansion built round and into a garden antedates them and was known in Fujiwara days as the Shinden style, probably originating in the idea of the Vihara or garden monastery of Indian Buddhism, but it is the influence of the Chajin that has made both garden and house what they have come to be in detail. One of the most unpleasant features of our own interiors has been the attempted imitation in the living room of the ordinary house of the salon of the mansion, without considering that decoration which may be tolerable and even diverting when seen for an hour once a week, is, or ought to be, intolerable when before the eyes every day. In restaurants and inns in Japan striking details and eccentric decorations are often seen which nobody would think of having in a private house. Cha-no-yu emphasizes the enlightening value of the need for economy so that it is more stimulating to be poor than rich, for if the wealthy man merely acts as such he is only a dull study in the obvious. Moreover he is likely to lose his sense of proportion, which is the sense of humour, and to forget that man is, after all, only a forked radish between five and six feet long. The well-known incident of Hideyoshi's quick change from taking the part of principal figure in the stately ceremony of welcoming the Korean envoys to strolling in on the same scene as a spectator nursing his baby in ordinary dress is probably an exercise in this discrimination, as is also his famous garden-party in a melon plantation at which the gardener was host, and all the great nobles and generals masqueraded as itinerant tradesmen, mendicant priests and beggars, and he himself played the part of a melon-hawker.

It may seem a little affected for the noble to mimic the ways of the fisherman or hermit, but it is only viewing existence from a different angle, just as the house is arranged to look on various aspects of the garden from different rooms. Things being as they are, few can spend their life sitting under a tree thinking themselves into the universal like Buddha, but they can keep as near the trees as possible and reflect that they are themselves only just such another phase of nature. So to have a detached cell at the end of the garden where you can play the hermit for a while when you feel inclined, as Japanese do when they indulge in Cha-no-yu, is a very refreshing change, and unlike a private oratory is not associated with any particular sect or dogma.

' It is difficult,' says Tokutomi in his great work, *The History of the Japanese People in Modern Times*, ' to understand the Momo-yama age without a knowledge of Cha-no-yu. It was not only the amusement of the noble, but almost a necessity of life for the ruling class of this time. It was used as a pious device to win over men's minds. And of those who handled the Empire by means of it Hide-yoshi is the most prominent example. Nobunaga too had an almost uncontrollable enthusiasm for Tea, and he sprang upon a Tea-bowl or Kettle like a lion on a hare. Just where Cha-no-yu ceased to be an amusement and became a practical affair is a little difficult to determine, *and it is this difficulty that makes it the more interesting*.'

And since Tokutomi had to go back to the Momoyama age in order to explain the phenomena of modern Japan, some knowledge of Cha-no-yu is evidently necessary to an understanding of the development of the nation, its ideas and its taste. It may seem strange, therefore, that so little has been said about it in European works dealing with the civilization of Japan. This may partly be accounted for by the fact that very much historical matter now available in Japanese has been published or reprinted comparatively recently. This explains probably why even Murdoch's volume dealing with the age of Hideyoshi does not so much as mention Sen Rikyu, which is like writing of Nero and omitting Petronius or of eighteenth century English society without Beau Nash, though Rikyu had greater in-fluence on his country than either of these. It is true that Murdoch does not profess to deal with Japanese culture to any extent, but a very prominent part was played in politics and economics by the great Tea Master and his seven disciples, some of whom, curiously enough, were Christians, as well as by the great merchant esthetes, Shimai Sōshitsu and Kamiya Sōtan, from whose diaries as well as those of the nobles, much of our knowledge of the time is derived. There is a short note in Dening's life of Hideyoshi dealing with Cha-no-yu, but as this was written twenty years ago it was hardly possible to realize its importance. He concludes his account by the surmise that ' the Tea cult is not likely to survive long in the go-ahead Japan of to-day.' Certainly Japan is not less go-ahead now, but Cha-no-yu, like Nō and similar institutions, continues to flourish more vigorously than ever.* Should it cease to do so the soul of Japan will have depart-ed from her, and that is hardly thinkable. Such evidently is the view

---

* There is a fortnightly magazine called *Miyali no Tomo* or ' The Friend of Elegance,' treating of everything of interest to those who like Cha-no-yu, published in connexion with the house of Sen.

of Japanese critics of to-day. For the rest, since the average English writer on Japanese civilization or art has not the knowledge of the language possessed by Brinkley, Dening or Murdoch, or in fact any knowledge of it at all, his neglect of the subject is natural.

In England the two Beaux, Nash and Brummel, are in certain aspects the nearest approach to a Japanese Tea Master, though their interests were more limited, and on the ethical side they fell rather short. They seem most comparable to such an one as Furuta Oribe, who was particularly a specialist and connoisseur, and whose defects of character brought about a collision with Tokugawa Ieyasu which caused his destruction. Brummel's severe taste in clothes might have received the approval of the Japanese esthete, while one can imagine even Rikyu walking the streets of Bath with satisfaction. There is a distinct similarity in the aims of Nash and Rikyu too, if the former is regarded as having done a unique service to society by providing and supervising a place where the various classes could meet in decorous intercourse, drinking with some ceremony too a bitter liquid.

But these men were isolated phenomena and left no school. There was no family system to hand down their taste and adapt it and relate it to the life of the people. For they were arbiters of fashion for the upper classes only, and the defect of confining the sense of fitness to the few is that when any change in society throws up plutocrats from the people these will have no conceptions but those of banality and ostentation. During and since the end of the Tokugawa period this acquisition of wealth by the masses went on too, and it is owing to the spirit of Cha-no-yu and the existence of the Tea Master and the Flower Master and their standards that the result has not been worse. Wherever these teachers exist, and there is no town, however small, that does not hold at least one of them, there oil is being quietly poured on the fire of pure Japanese taste, and though superficially there may seem to be a large injection of European influence of the commercial type, more mature consideration will show that this is not anything like so great or widespread as it might be. As Lafcadio Hearn pointed out some considerable time ago, such a city as Kobe, which has grown up entirely since, and as the result of, trade with Europe, is yet entirely Japanese.

And now that the taste of Europe has come under the influence of these principles in architecture and decoration which are so strangely identical with those of the Japanese esthete, foreign buildings and furniture in Japan will not be so incongruous as they have been hitherto. Since the destruction of the central part of Tokyo there has been an opportunity which its citizens have taken, of reconstructing it in this ' Modern ' style, for little traditional work is to be seen in the new buildings, and here one can see Japanese feeling interpreted in steel and concrete instead of wood. So far this is mostly confined to commercial and public buildings and structures, and it does not look as though the home would be much affected for some time to come. But if it is, it may remain as Japanese in spirit as ever, the material merely becoming fire-proof. Since the matted floor is comparatively modern a return to a wooden one with some sort of low chair or divan would only be a return to the style of Kamakura days. So principles retrace their steps, as in machinery the reciprocating engine gives way to the turbine.

We may agree that in many ways the Japanese preference for wood as a material for building is justified, for apart from its more interesting texture and restfulness, even the frail Tea-rooms of the sixteenth century have survived unimpaired, while the massive timbers of the great temples, gates and mansions have weathered the centuries as effectively as the stone buildings of Europe, though permanence was not to the same extent their object, since restoration in the same style was always easy. And the buildings that have survived have not suffered from the doctrinaire restorer whose hand has done so much damage in Europe, owing to the freedom from conflicting architectural styles, due apparently to the greater emphasis on function.

'Never make anything of metals that can be made of wood or earthenware because you think you can make money by it. Only make of metal what cannot be made of anything else,' said Akishino Yohei, and it is a fair summary of Japanese culture. It has been a wooden and non-commercial one on the whole. And yet no people have surpassed or perhaps equalled the Japanese in the metalwork they undertook. The Samurai carried swords of matchless forging and temper, but apart from the essential parts of his pipe and purse, he had nothing else of metal about him. He seldom carried money on his person, and his house, which needed no nails, only boasted a few bronze flower vases and sometimes a water-basin of the same material, though these were as likely to be of wood or stone. His wife's hairpins and the kitchen knife were the only other metal objects. With so little of this material of commerce and militarism the world of art was hardly the worse, and daily life scarcely inconvenienced.

Modern communication, said, especially after dinner, to foster international friendship, depends on metal, but so do the battleship and submarine. A better case might be made out for the cricket bat and tennis racket as instruments of the amity of peoples, or that admirable institution the cask, which Japan, by the way, makes with bamboo bands instead of iron, thus greatly improving its appearance.

In connection with present-day feeling, Brinkley's criticism of Japanese eclecticism in pottery, written some two decades ago, is rather significant. He writes: 'From the catalogue of objects of *vertu* offered by China and Korea, her implicitly trusted preceptors in so many matters, Japan made a strikingly narrow choice. Instead of taking for porcelain utensils the liquid dawn reds, the ripe grape purples, the five-coloured egg-shells or any of the glowing monochromes and half-tone enamels of the Chinese ceramist, she confined herself to the ivory whites, delicate celadons, comparatively inornate specimens of blue *sous couverte*, and blue full-bodied, roughly applied over-glass enamels such as characterized the later eras of the Ming dynasty. It has astonished many students of Japanese manners and customs to find that the objects which Europe and America search for to-day in the markets of China with eager appreciation are scarcely represented at all in the collections of Japanese virtuosi made at an epoch when such masterpieces were abundantly produced within easy reach of their doors. The explanation is to be found in the conservatism of the Tea clubs. But, he adds, 'the Japanese adopted to a certain extent the standard set by the Chinese themselves. For a Chinese art critic of the sixteenth century, one Hsiang, compiled a set of illustrations of eighty *chefs d'oeuvre* approved by the art critics of the day, of which fifty were celadons.'

Now it is these celadons and ivory whites that are sought by Europe and America, and that our present-day potters of France, Germany and England are striving very earnestly to imitate. As taste improves the rather childish love of polychrome is disappearing, and there is a closer approximation to the preference for quiet monochrome and sparse unemphatic designs that has always been the rule in Japan. And it should be observed that the reason why such a system of esthetics could be made to penetrate so deeply into society was because the government of Japan has always been of the oligarchic and bureaucratic type, and the average man has had no opportunity of interfering. The ordinary man in any country is lacking in the self-restraint and mental energy that make the effective ruler or artist, and is naturally inclined to prefer the art and architecture that require no thought to appreciate and the manners that call for the least exertion. What he likes is something to flatter his vanity and stimulate his emotions. Only by severe pressure imposed from above can he be brought to appreciate anything but the highly coloured and obvious, and beauty seems to be a by-product of Spartan qualities.

Sen Rikyu was not by birth a member of the military class he came from a trading community, but men of outstanding ability and energy have always been able to win a place among the rulers.

However, the process of rising was not made easy for them, and, much as elsewhere, the Buddhist priesthood was probably the best ladder. Since Italy, whether by accident or design, is now under exactly the same system of government as was Japan in the days of the Shogunate, and her administration is not dependent on the votes of the average citizen, with a similar inheritance of great art in the past there should be a hopeful outlook towards making more beautiful again the every-day life of her people.

Of those endowed with the Cha-no-yu spirit in our own time and country, the late Ernest Gimson will occur to many, for his furniture and buildings have all that simplicity and fitness that the Japanese masters prize so highly. If one looks, for instance, at the small house designed by him and carried out by another architect acting as builder (a very fine thing to do), illustrated in *Small Country Houses of To-day*, this is very evident, and its distinction for these qualities marks it out as rarely satisfying among the many other works in the same volumes by some of the foremost names in the world of architecture.

And in glancing through such a set of representative examples of exterior and interior designs, it seems evident that the fashionable artist is not improved by commissions for large and expensive and necessarily ostentatious creations. Dulness and dreariness are so much more apparent in big things than small, and the small house is more likely to be free from them than the mansion.

Another, very much alive this time, of the same school is evidently Mr. Clough Williams Ellis, whose writings as well as his designs possess in full measure the same insight into the essential of fit and fair living in the world as it is.   It is hardly probable that he has studied the ways of the Japanese Chajin, and it is therefore the more interesting to see that he has produced an exact western edition of the Chaseki villa in the small week-end cottage designed for his own use of just the nearest material that lay to hand, even allowing the trees to remain and enter into it.   Contrast this with the laboured imitation Japanese garden, usually further spolit by a Chinese summer-house equally conscious of itself, that is occasionally to be seen in extensive grounds, and there is indeed a 'difference of clouds and mud.'

The problems worked out by the Tea Masters as to how best to move and place the utensils and so on are the same as have just begun to be considered in America lately, for in the *Architectural Record* (N.Y.) of March 1930 is a study by a lady efficiency engineer, with accompanying plans, of how to act and the best positions to take up in a kitchen to perform the ceremony of making a cake, a thing naturally of daily occurrence in millions of homes there and elsewhere. If it be true, as Mr. Curle observes, that 'at any given moment in Australia a thousand Irish publicans are drawing beer,' it is no less so that where this is not permitted or has become for economic reasons increasingly rare, these manipulations of the kitchen are likely to assume a correspondingly important part in life.   And by taking thought in this particular case and by a suitable arrangement of the room and furniture, the movements necessary for making this cake are reduced from fifty of an unimproved lay-out to twenty-four in an improved one

These adaptations correspond to that part of the Tea ceremony that concerns the arrangement of the hearth and Mizuya, and position of the utensils, and only omit consideration of the most efficient and satisfying way of holding and handling the various implements and utensils so as to avoid fatigue and breakage.

These efficiency movements in America started in the sphere of industry and are known as Taylorization or simplified practice, and now appear to be spreading to domestic life in the order of importance presumedly, while in Japan they started in the everyday life of the Zen monastery and then spread to the homes of the people and also almost simultaneously to militarism, for this economy of effort is very noticeable in Japanese fencing which has too drawn its inspiration from Zen thought, and even more so in its accompaniment Jujitsu, or the art of overcoming an opponent with the least exertion.   This was in substance introduced by a Chinese about the middle of the seventeenth century, but owes its development and organization entirely to Japan.   The connection between these rather different types of movement comes out in the statement of one Master that ' the main object of Cha-no-yu is to brace and invigorate both mind and body (lit. the abdominal region).   When one makes Tea, unless the muscles and diaphragm are held tense, all natural rhythm will be lost and all that will result will be mere conscious imitation.'

If some enthusiasts in Japan speak of Chado as a religion and declare that their civilization may be called a Tea civilization, it may at least be admitted that it is as much so as European civilization is a Christian one, since it looks as though their everyday life has been as much influenced by the teachings of the Chajin as has ours by those of the Church Fathers. It may seem to some not to go far enough, but it makes life less monotonous and people less dependent on that rather doubtful factor their fellow-man, as well as being a great comfort to the declining days of many. And there is nothing in it to conflict with the reason of the normally intelligent.

> But if at church they would give us some ale
> And a pleasant fire our souls to regale,
> We'd sing and we'd pray all the livelong day
> Nor ever wish from the church to stray.

Blake's picture suggests something like the atmosphere of the Tea-room, and as he is more admired in Japan than most English writers it must be for his Zen sentiments. Perhaps if any life is ever restored to churches and chapels it will be along these lines.

The first part of this work, consisting of the details of the ceremony and of the construction of the Tea-room and Roji and of the utensils, may appear dry and trivial to many. Compared with what might have been given they are not very full, and would be hardly sufficient for anyone, should there be such, who might wish to learn Cha-no-yu, though they might be of some assistance. But they may be of interest to students of architecture, anthropology and social customs. The second part consists a series of stories illustrating the Tea experiences of representative men of all types during the Muromachi, Momoyama and Tokugawa periods from the days of Ashikaga Yoshimasa to those of Ii Kamon-no-kami. They throw light on aspects of these periods not treated in any European works dealing with the time, and may make more familiar some distinguished personalities famous enough in their own country, but so far strangely little known outside it. For these I am largely indebted to the excellent collection in the *Chawa Bidan* of Kumata Sojuro, which I have supplemented and collated from other sources such as the *Koji Ruien*, the *Hankampuden*, and *Matsudaira Fumaiden*. Though these stories are not without value to the historian it is chiefly as descriptions of manners and customs that they are given here, and it does not follow that the motives they suggest and the facts they present are always accurate statements, for the discourses of Tea Masters might be more concerned with the esthetically satisfying than the real. But at times they undoubtedly do give a clue as when, for example, the meeting of Ieyasu and Hosokawa Tadaoki in the Tea-room is recalled, a connexion that made the victory of the former at the critical battle of Sekigahara less of an uncertainty than is often supposed.

Not the least diverting of these anecdotes are those about comparatively unknown people like Shibayama Motoaki, Doi Toyotaka and Akishino Yohei.   Such characters exist in all countries and ages, but in Tokugawa Japan one feels that conditions would be exceptionally favourable to them.   They were of the company of the poet Basho, who was so pre-eminent in the expression of the impermanence of things and fellowship with nature.   For that matter one cannot sufficiently admire the resource with which the weather and the seasons are used to give variety to the entertainment by Chajin. Snow, rain, moon, dawn, mid-day heat and winter cold all equally supply sensations to the adept, who still contrives to extract as much enjoyment from them as did Kamo no Chōmei in his hut on Toyama hill.

In conclusion I wish to express my sincere thanks to Sen Tantansai for his kindness in allowing me to see his Tea rooms and to reproduce his portrait, and to Professor A. R. Radcliffe-Brown for reading through some of my MSS.   I am also greatly indebted to Mr. A. Morgan Young for his scholarly assistance in reading the proofs and making several valuable suggestions, as well as to Miss M. E. Lake for making the index.   The book has also had the advantage of the skilled supervision of Mr. H. J. Griffiths.

A. L. S.

Sydney: October 1933.

CONTENTS

CHAPTER I

CHAPTER II

TEA-MASTERS

CHAPTER III

LIST OF PLATES

CHA-NO-YU

THE JAPANESE TEA CEREMONY

Simplification of life, except from the voices of ascetics and fanatics, does not mean either sordidness, uncleanness, bareness or ugliness. It simply means the reduction of life to beauty instead of letting it be overloaded with luxury.

Mrs. Havelock Ellis, " Democracy in the Kitchen."

Art is many-sided and manifold: it is not only a question of high genius; that is only the crest of a great wave rising from gifted peoples, and without the flood of common art you cannot have the crest of genius. This common art is concerned with all the routine things of life, laying the breakfast table and cleaning the doorsteps of our houses, tidying up our railway stations and lighting the High Streets of our towns.

Sir W. R. Lethaby, " Form in Civilization."

Oyobazaru wa sugitaru yori masareri. The insufficient is better than the superfluous.

Maxims of Tokugawa Ieyasu.

In Japan the whole tone of the social organization is permeated by a gracious artistic temperament which endures all sorts of discomfort and even resorts to all sorts of ruses, rather than destroy the beauty of nature or the beauty of social intercourse.

Ellsworth Huntington, " West of the Pacific."

The Way of Tea lies in studying the ceremony, in understanding the principles, and in grasping the reality of things. These are its three rules.

Hosokawa Tadaoki.

CHA-NO-YU

THE JAPANESE TEA CEREMONY

CHAPTER I

ORIGINS

Tea drinking began in China among the Zen monks, who used it as a method of preventing sleep, and from that progressed to the Cha King or Tea Gospel of Luh Wuh in the period of T'ang, but it was the Sung and Yuan ages with their devotion to philosophy on one hand and sentiment on the other that combined Tea and Zen to produce that characteristic culture that aimed at a life of calm and simplicity. This was brought to Japan and developed in the brilliant and luxurious days of Higashiyama and Momoyama and became the diversion of the military and wealthy classes, and passing through the eclectic hands of Shukō and Shō-ō it finally took shape under those of Sen Rikyu as that " Way of Tea " which is peculiar to Japan and which may be described as the mixture of Tea and Zen again blended and reinforced by the code of rigid self-control, Spartan simplicity and enthusiastic loyalty created by the military class and now known as Bushido. Later on the influence of Sen Sotan is especially noticeable in the development of the taste for neatness and detachment in all that pertains to the building of the Tea-room and the arrangement of its garden, while Kobori Enshu brought Teaism into harmony with the love of Waka, that Japanese verse that so entirely expresses the mind of the people, and which, like Tea, is the common possession of all classes of society. Among the three hundred aphorisms of Katagiri Sekishu we find it stated that " Tea includes both Buddhist philosophy and poetry, and just as poetry makes new verses from old words so does Tea use old materials for new interests." And the reason that writing is preferred to painting in the Tokonoma of the Tea-room is that Ikkyu Osho observed to Shukō, when he presented him with a scroll by Engo Zenji, that the contemplation of the words of a profound thinker leads to enlightenment. And because Teika expressed the sentiment about using the old to create the new, his poems are appreciated by Tea Masters above all others. Thus Teaism may be called the religion of daily life in Japan since it combines in itself the essence of Zen, Poetry and Bushido.

As to etiquette, in early days Japan adopted the ceremony of the T'ang Court of China for her own state uses, but when the age of military rule followed there grew up a new code of behaviour that was a compromise between that of the Court Nobles and that of the

Feudal Lords, and this is embodied in the two systems of deportment that go by the names of the Ise and Ogasawara Styles. But
these were no more than rules for ceremony, and it is to Teaism that
we must go for the rules for eating and drinking and entertaining
guests. Eating and drinking are the fundamentals of life and if there
is no proper etiquette in regard to them, people are no better than
animals. There are, of course, rules of this sort in other countries
too, but Japanese etiquette, embracing as it does not only the way
of holding chop-sticks and ladles, the handling of the covers of vessels,
taking up the cup and drinking, but also the correct things to say
and the desirable thing to think, is far more elaborate and complete
than any other, more advanced in complex simplicities. So it may
not be far from the truth to describe Teaism as a religion, and one
that is both spiritual and satisfying, for its chief aim is contentment
with one's lot, and on its teaching of Urbanity, Respect, Cleanliness
and Imperturbability the manners of the country are founded. In one
sense Japanese civilisation is Tea civilisation, for the life of the people
is coloured by Tea as it is permeated by Zen, and these two influences
are likely to endure as long as the Empire they have so largely formed.

Arrangement of Utensils on Board   Daisu or Stand for Tea Utensils

The Utensils shown are, from left to right, the Furo, the Ladle-stand with ladle and
Charcoal tongs, the Slop bowl with lid-stand inside it and the Mizu-sashi or "water-
vessel." On top of the Daisu is the Tea-caddy.

The origin of the ceremonial serving of Tea is described by the
priests as being based on the Hyakujo Seiki of Toku-ki (Te-hui) of
Sung. When the temple of Myoshinji at Shiojiri was rebuilt an
inauguration festival was held and after it a meal was served. Then
cakes were eaten and Koicha offered to the guests. There was a
large number of priests present and they made the tea in one bowl
and served it to five or six at a time, and these then went out and
made room for others. The tradition is that Nambo Shomei, the
founder of the Sufukuji temple in Chikuzen, went to Sung in the era
Shogen (1259), studied Buddhism under Kyodo of the Keizanji,
and came back in the 4th year of Bunei (1286) bringing with him a
Daisu which he used at the Sufukuji. And this was the beginning
of the Tea-ceremony in Japan. This Daisu was afterward taken to
the Daitokuji at Murasakino, Kyoto, and given to Muso, the founder
of Tenryuji. Muso began Cha-no-yu with this utensil and handed
down rules for its use. (*Ki-yu-sho-ran.*) When Shuko was about thirty

he became a Zen priest and went and lived at the Shinju-an Hall of the Daitokuji. Now they had a Daisu there, but no one knew what it was. It was, of course, the one brought from China by Shomei. When Shuko saw it he at once recognised what it was and proceeded to use it for serving Tea. With it were also the Furo and Water-jar and Slop-basin.

But the Teiyo-shu says that in the days of Ashikaga Takauji, Musō Kokushi made gardens and water-gardens, and also made Tea with the Daisu, that the military class imitated his taste and built Tea Arbours in their gardens, and that this use of the Daisu was handed down among them till the days of Yoshimasa, so that if this is correct there was nothing for Shuko to rediscover.

The Daisu called Kyudaisu was so called from its likeness to the tablet over the gate by which the scholars who had graduated (Kyudai) entered the T'ang Court. It was copied by Oribe. It was like a book stand and was lacquered.

The Daisu was modified by various Tea Masters, and a board also was used instead, the utensils being then arranged in a different manner. Yoshimasa used this board with Furo and Slop-bowl and Ladle-stand and Lid-rest. Both this and the Daisu can be used in an ordinary room or out of doors, and the Daisu ceremony still remains the most formal style. It is also handed down that in the time of Ashikaga Takauji, Zekkai Osho, pupil of Musō Kokushi, went to China about 1340, and when he came back Musō began to perform Cha-no-yu with the Daisu that had been long disused, and the custom spread, but not to the ordinary people. Ashikaga Yoshimitsu and Yoshimasa were both addicted to it. When the latter Shogun appointed Shukō as Tea Master (Cha-no-yu-shi), Nō-ami used to sit in the chief place, but afterwards Shukō took it.

Cha-no-yu was originally called Cha-e, as for instance in the *Taiheiki*, but Shō-ō and Rikyu began to use the expression Cha-no-yu. This they took from the Buddhist phrase Ten-cha-ten-tō shortened to Cha-tō or Sa-tō, and meaning the Tea-offering made before Buddha, ancestral spirits, or the dead. This was altered to Cha-no-yu to avoid confusion of the two institutions by the simple expedient of using the Japanese reading Yu for the Sinico-Japanese Tō. But in the *Ryuteiki* it is said that the expression Tea Hot-water means just what it says, the hot water in which Tea is boiled, and quotes the *Kissa Yoseiki* of Eisai Zenji, where the phrase is paralleled by that of Kuwa-yu or Mulberry Hot-water, which Eisai thought also very salubrious. The expression Cha-no-yu was probably transferred to the ceremonial making of Tea as being longer and therefore more dignified than the simple Cha. The ceremony from which much of the detail of Cha-no-yu was taken was that of Incense Comparing (Ko-awase), which had grown up at Court from the use of incense at the Buddhist temples in the same way as had the various other "comparing" pastimes (Mono-awase) such as Cock-comparing or Cock-fighting, Flower, Plant, Fan, Shell, Armour Comparing, accompanied usually by the making of suitable verses. This Incense Ceremony was very fashionable in the Ashikaga period, and Yoshimitsu and Yoshimasa were both addicted to it, the latter especially being credited with finalising its form. It is noticeable that most of the early Tea-masters are also quoted as teachers of Incense, for as the ceremony became more elaborate schools and teachers had also appeared. So in the wake of Sanjo Sanetaka, the founder of the main school, are found Shino Sōshin, Botankwa Shōhaku, Sōgō, Sōgi, Shukō, Shō-ō, Oda Yuraku, Rikyu, Oribe and Honami Kōetsu.

Evidently taken from the Incense Ceremony is the number of guests, which is just half the ten of Ko-awase, the style of the pro-gramme, the use of the terms Jo-kyaku, Chief Guest, Tsume and Batsu, Last Guest, Ko-no-mono or Incense things, for pickles, since nothing stronger than these was allowed before incense sniffing for fear of blunting the power of smell. There are descriptions of this Incense ceremony in Brinkley's *Japan and China* and also in Laf-cadio Hearn's *In Ghostly Japan*.

The original Tea Ceremony was a competition for Tea Com-paring of the same kind as the Incense Ceremony, to distinguish between Hon-cha or Real Tea, i.e. that of Toga-no-o, and Hi-cha or Non-Tea, i.e. that of other places. On this the Daimyos and great merchants would stake fine incense, gold dust, valuable silks and brocades, and armour and swords, though when they won these things they thought it beneath them to keep them, but gave them as presents to the Dengaku players and dancing girls.

EARLY USE OF TEA

It is recorded that in the era of the Three Kingdoms in China (221-265 A.D.) Wei Yao* of Wu used Tea instead of liquor at entertainments, and that Wang Mêng† of Tsin also offered it to his guests. In the days of Hsuan Tsung of T'ang (713) lived Luh Wuh who wrote the Cha King, which contains all the lore of Tea vessels, Tea making, quality of water, and methods of infusing in vogue in his day, for which he himself was perhaps largely responsible. Evidently Tea was a fashionable amusement of the T'angs as well as liquor, for this was the great era of the tipsy poets. It became more so still under the Sungs when the custom of drinking Powder Tea came in.

In Japan Shomu Tenno (724-749) was the first to offer Tea ceremonially, for it is written that he entertained a hundred priests with it after they had chanted the Sutras for him in the palace. Hiki-cha is the expression used here, and it is uncertain whether it was imported or not.

From the era Enryaku (782) to that of Konin (810) Tea is mentioned in the Anthologies of Chinese poems called Shin-shu and Ryoun-shu, and again in those of the period Ninna (885) to Engi (901). Sugawara Michizane also refers to it in one of his poems. In the second year of Engi (903) when the Emperor Uda retired the Emperor Daigo visited him at Ninnaji and was offered Tea. In

---

* 韋曜 cf. Giles Biographical Dictionary p. 870.   † 王蒙.

the Manyoshu appears the expression Usucha-no-setchie.* It seems evident that from these days right through the Kamakura period Tea was a luxury for the Court and Nobility and was not in use among the ordinary people. And it was not made in the way afterwards practised. There is mention of " Japanese tea of Ureshino," a special kind called " Kanime-gata " or " Crab's eye shape " evidently of the brick tea variety used by the Sungs, which seems to have been the sort made by Eisai Zenji from the shrubs that he planted at Seburiyama.

Eisai also sent some seeds to Myoei Shonin, Abbot of Toga-no-ō in Yamashiro in a jar called " Kogaki " or " Little Persimmon," and this jar is now one of the great treasures of that temple. The seeds he planted at Fukase at Toga-no-Ō and afterwards some of the plants that came up were transferred to Uji, where the soil was found to be extremely suitable. So more and more tea came to be planted there and the methods of treating the leaves by steaming and roasting were studied and improved, with the result that the Tea of Uji is the finest in the country.

Tradition has it that the seed was first sown in the footprints of a horse that was ridden between the old plants in the garden, and that it is for this reason that one of the oldest gardens of Uji, that belonging to Matsui of Kobata, is called Koma-no-Ashikage or Colt's Hoofprint.

After this, tea was planted at Ninnaji and Daigo, at Takarao in Yamato, at Tanabe in Kii, at Hattori in Iga, at Kawai in Ise, at Hongo in Totomi, at Kiyomi in Suruga, and at Kawagoe in Musashi.

Uji also received attention from the Shogun Ashikaga Yoshimitsu, who ordered his minister Ouchi Yoshihiro to have plantations of tea made there, and the five gardens of Asahi, Kambayashi, Kyogoku, Yamana and Umoji, which were then established, are still in existence. Then the Governors and Jito of all provinces were ordered to plant tea in their domains, and it was probably at this time that they discovered the existence of the Japanese wild tea.

Tea is plucked about the fifth month, and as some is early and some later it is distinguished as First, Second and Third crop. The early plucked leaf is called Cha 茶 and the later Bei 茗. It is prepared in various ways, but in all it is first steamed and then cooled and roasted. When the leaves are infused with water it is called Ha-cha 葉茶, Dashi-cha 出茶 or Sen-cha 煎茶. When however it is powdered and mixed with water it is known as Mat-cha 抹茶 or Ten-cha 碾茶, Ground or Grated Tea. There is another kind called Kawara-cha 瓦茶 or Tile Tea, made of leaves pressed into a hard flat mass some seven or eight sun long by seven bu thick. The kind exported is put into a damp place before roasting and the leaves allowed to ferment. This is known as Ko-cha 紅茶 or Red Tea.

When the leaf germinates it is covered up with straw to remove

---

* A festival called Hiki-cha-no-sechie or Powder Tea Festival is mentioned as having taken place at Court in ancient times, but the Mokuga-setsu considers that had there been such a festival, details of it would have been found in the Court records, and that probably what is meant is the giving of Powder Tea to the priests on the occasion of the reading of the Dai-hannya-kyo or Maha-prajna-paramita Sutra at Court in spring and autumn.

the astringency if the tree is intended for powder tea, but if it is for Sen-cha this is not done. The leaf is then plucked and dried and winnowed with a fan, and the lightest that flies off first from the tops of the leaves is classified as Superior, Medium and Inferior Thin Tea Usu-cha 薄茶. What remains after this process is called Koi-cha 濃茶 or Thick Tea. The stems and stalks that remain at the last are used for Sen-cha. Sen-cha is classed as Orimono 折物 Broken, Taka-no-Tsume 鷹の爪 Hawk's Talons and Kashira-ha 頭葉 or Top Leaves. Koicha is classed as Hatsu Mukashi, Ato Mukashi etc.

KAKOI AND SUKIYA

The Tea-room is called sometimes Kakoi and sometimes Sukiya. Of these words the former has the meaning of " Enclosure," and signifies a portion of a larger room enclosed by a screen in a square form of four and a half mats or more in which Cha-no-yu was given according to the original manner. This is still done in a house where there is no regular Tea-room. Sukiya, on the other hand, denotes a special room separated from the main house, or sometimes attached to it as a lean-to, and its meaning is more complicated.*

---

* Takasaki Danjo said that a certain Murakami Gen-no-jo of Shikoku related the content of some conversation he had with Shō-ō as follows :—There are two kinds of people interested in Tea. We may call them Cha-no-yu-sha and Suki-sha. The former are those who know all about the ceremony of serving Tea and cooking meals, and are very capable of officiating in the Tea-room, but Sukisha are those who are quite content with the simplest meal, say one soup and one vegetable course, and have a real understanding of things and are enlightened. The word Suki comes from Zen Buddhism like most of the other terms in use in Tea, and the Sukisha lives in accordance with its philosophy.

Before the Ashikaga period and its consequent adoption by the Tea enthusiasts the word Suki was used of poetical taste, to which we have seen Tea compared. The Nihon Kissa Shiryo quotes the Kiyu Shoran of Kitamura Shosetsu as declaring : " Mukashi wa Suki to ieba, Uta no koto ni kokoroe haberi," i.e. " In olden days when one spoke of Suki it was understood to mean poetry," and in support of this he adduces the passage of the Heike Monogatari concerning Taira Tadamori, which runs ; " Tadamori mo suitarikereba kono nyobo mo suitari " (or Yu nari keri, according to another reading), " Tadamori was fond of verse as this lady was also fond of it," though Utsumi in his note on this passage regards the word as equivalent to Fūryu or fine taste generally (Suki, sunawachi Fūryu no Michi wo kononde iru no imi).

Of those who are given to Teaism the words " Wabi " and " Suki " are used above all others. It is because they delight in what is elegant (Fuga), and take pleasure in quiet simpli-city. And in their enjoyment of this quality of " Wabi " there is mingled a love of the mellow-ness of antiquity that leads them to amuse themselves by indulging in the connoisseurship of old utensils. This is what is called Suki. This admiration for the natural rhythm and quiet grace of things is what the Zen devotee considers most desirable and tries to attain in his monastery. (*Fude no Susabi*). As to the words " Fuga " and " Furyu " they have no exact equivalent in English. The Japanese-English Dictionary gives " Taste " and " Elegance " for both, but Taste is the Japanese " Shumi," while Elegance is represented by " Karei," and these have a meaning quite different. Fuga and Furyu suggest an intermingling of Man and Nature, an entering into the confines where the Human blends with the Universal. So the writers of the short verses called Haiku and Waka that deal with nature as it varies according to the seasons are called Furyu-jin. Takahashi thinks that though such poetry is not non-existent in China and Europe, it is comparatively rare, for the writers of these lands are so very much taken up with the performances of man. European poetry especially, he considers, cannot forget this everyday world for a moment. He quotes Natsume Soseki, the famous novelist, who, in commenting on a Chinese poem by Toemmei (T'ao Yuan Ming) which runs
Picking a chrysanthemum under the eastern fence,
Calmly I look at the southern hills,
observes, " In European verse even a real poet cannot detach himself from the ordinary sub-jective outlook. He cannot forget sympathy or love or right or freedom or some other aspect of the workaday world. But in this verse there is no allusion to it. There is no word of the girl next door looking over the fence of one's friend working on the southern hills."

風雅, 風流. In Chinese 風人 means an inspired person. Chinese 風月 dissipation, Japanese, the beauties of nature. So in Chinese 風流人 means gay, dissipated or elegant, but in Japanese only the latter.

Taking it in the plain sense of the characters used to write it namely, "Kazu wo yosuru (to bring together a number of objects)," it may be explained as referring to the acquisitive collector spirit of the early Tea Masters. Ikkyu, however, takes the second character Ki in the sense of Kimyo (wondrous), when it would mean "Many wondrous things," according to an observation that he made to Shukō that "Cha-no-yu is in harmony with the Wondrous Way of Buddha, for it utilises the marvellous workings of the Universal Mind." By others this syllable Ki is taken to mean "Odd," in the sense that Teaism is associated with what is odd and not even, since it dislikes the complete and prefers the imperfect. Again the word Suki may be regarded as the equivalent of "Tashinami," "Taste," thus signifying those who have a tasteful feeling generally, then applied in a particular manner to those who liked Tea. This is the view of an older work on the subject, the Rōji Chōsho, but a more modern writer thinks the sense of "Oddness" is best, and certainly "Suki" is explained as meaning "Uneven" in passages where it occurs in the Chinese classics. So the Tea devotee is one who finds his interest in spheres that are apart from the ordinary spheres of life and "remote from the dust of this world." There is a certain oddness about him as well as his Tea-room. Its situation should not be specially chosen, neither should any roughness in its eaves or windows, or lack of symmetry in its posts cause the owner any uneasiness. All he should think about is the equilibrium of his mind, and however great or distinguished his visitor may be, he must forget all his magnificence and put off for the time the fetters of the world to which it belongs and become a "guest above the clouds." Rikyu would not permit those in a humble position to show any deference in the Tea-room for he said, "In the Sukiya and its garden (Roji) there are but Host, Guest and Tea."

Shukō's Tea-room called Shukō-an is termed the "Formal" style to distinguish it in the usual way from the "Informal" and "Intermediate." It was of four and a half mats and the walls were covered with egg-shell coloured paper, the ceiling being of narrow boards of knotless cedar and the Tokonoma six feet wide. It was roofed with boards. Later on a hearth a foot and a half in diameter was cut in the floor and a kettle called "Flat Spider" used with it, the shelf called Kyudai Daisu holding the utensils. On the walls of this room there are said to have been black-and-white sketches by Engō Zenji, while in the Tokonoma either a single picture or a set of two was displayed. In front of this was a stand with an incense burner and a flower vase, either one of the ordinary sort or a small one with a single flower. Boxes for stationery and Tanzaku or poem-slips, inkstone and bookstand, a tray-garden and jars for leaf-tea are also mentioned, so that it is evident that this Tea-room was much like an ordinary study in its furnishings and not specialised as afterwards.

Shō-ō went a step further and made a Tea-room of the same size but had the walls plastered instead of papered and used bamboo for the lattice window instead of wood. Hence it was that Shukō's

style was called Formal and Shō-ō's Informal. The latter used a
kettle suspended by a chain and arranged his utensils on a Fukuro-
dana or Tea-cabinet. So he may be said to have come nearer to the
unadorned simplicity of Vimalakirti in his meditation hut.

The next impulse was due to Rikyu, who
was dissatisfied with the air of luxury and com-
plexity that had come to surround the Tea-room
and its furnishings, and who therefore designed
a two-mat Tea-room after consultation with his
master Shō-ō. This was the beginning of " Rōji
Teaism," as it was called from the guests entering the Sukiya by way of the " Rōji " or Dewy
Path. In these days, however, there was no
Machiai or Arbour for the guests to rest in
before entering the Tea-room. The first Machiai
was that built by Kanamori Izumo-no-kami Ari-
shige to entertain Hidetada at his mansion opposite Tora-no-mon.

After the death of Rikyu the direct tradition
of his house came to an end for a while, since
when the master is under a cloud the disciples
generally go elsewhere. But Sōkei handed it
on and it is to him that we owe our knowledge
of what Rikyu taught. Sōkei was a priest of
the Shu-un-an at the temple of Nansoji at Sakai,
hence his usual designation Nambo Sōkei. Of him Rikyu said, " If,
after my departure, there is anyone among my descendants who wishes
to understand Teaism let him become the pupil of Sōkei." His
work the *Nambo Roku* in which the traditions of the Sen house are
recorded together with the diary of Rikyu's Cha-no-yu meetings for

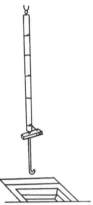

Jizai or Kettle Hanger.
Length 4 ft. 7 in.
Made of 1 inch bamboo
with 7 knots.

a year, has lately been reprinted in
six volumes, and is a most valuable
text.

Since the Tea-room is modelled
on the pure and spotless ideal world
of Buddhist meditation, all luxury
and ostentation must be avoided,
and especially expensive straining
after simple rusticity and sending to
distant provinces to get adzed wood
irregularly worm - holed. Costly
affectation of simplicity is as bad as
obvious display of wealth, and will
certainly elicit the smiles of the
enlightened. Rikyu used red pine
with the bark on for the pillar of the
Tokonoma and weathered square timber for the others. Kobori Enshu
liked a frost-mottled cryptomeria pole showing the adze marks for the
former and dead chestnut wood for the latter. Ordinary pine, cryp-

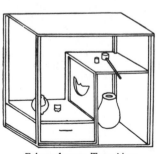

Fukuro-dana or Tea-cabinet

tomeria, hinoki or plum in the round with the bark on will do quite well for the pillars, while for the thresholds, sills and lintels cryptomeria with a reddish tinge is very suitable. The same wood may be used for the outside shutters and entrance hatch. Rare woods like Bonin palm are quite out of place. The important thing about building a Tea-room is that the owner and the carpenter should think out how best to make use of and fit in any ordinary wood that happens to be available. It is the suitability to its purpose that is to be considered, and not the material.

The measurements and dimensions of floor, alcove, window and door openings, etc., have been fixed by the great Tea-Masters because of their practical convenience and it is best to follow them. Any attempt to change them for the sake of individual whim or because "it would look better" or "seem more quaint" is not to be countenanced.

Similarly the plaster on the walls is to be plain grey, and put on in a manner suitable to the size of the rooms. There is no need to use various colours or do the work in a fussy and elaborate way. It should be rendered with simplicity and vigour so as to give a good texture, and then left alone. Too much finish is on the vulgar side. All round the bottom of the plaster the wall should be papered to the height of nine inches. Mino paper laid inside out should be used. By the entrance from the Mizuya a skirting of light grey Minato paper is put on one foot eight inches high. This skirting paper is a survival of the days when the Tea-room was built of wood simply papered over without any plaster. The "fitments" (shoji and fusuma) should be as light as may be, for a tea-room is not built for strength. The small window openings should have cross pieces of bamboo, the horizontals with the bark side uppermost, and the vertical rods with the bark side inwards if there is only one, and the middle one bark side inwards and the two others with it outwards if there

Arrangement of Four-and-a-half Mat Tea-room

are three. Rikyu and his school used fusuma with black lacquer frames, but ordinary wood is common.* The fusuma in a tea-room

---

* Rikyu was very fond of a certain shape called Tsubo-tsubo, and used it as a pattern for shoji and on the wall as well as for open work carving. It was originally the shape of a children's toy called Dembo sold at Inariyama near Kyoto, and people used to take it home and present it as an offering to the God Kōjin. It was made of dried clay pressed into the shape of a round jar, whence its name. It was called Dembo Tsubo-tsubo or Ricefield Treasure because it was considered that if the clay of Inariyama was taken and scattered on ricefields they would be fertile that year

are papered in the manner called Fukuro-bari, i.e. they are like shoji
but with white paper pasted on both sides instead of on one side
only. A Tea-room should neither be too light or too dark inside.
A room that is too light is not suitable for concentration, for the
mind is likely to be disturbed, but on the other hand if it is not
light enough a sense of gloom and melancholy may be felt, which
is worse. The outer windows and overhung shutters must be arranged
according to the position of the sun so that a happy medium can
be obtained. When the Tea-room does not form part of the main
building but is built separately there must always be a garden between
it and the main house. This must have a fence round it, and inside
this fence will be the waiting arbour and the privy. Beside these
will be a wash-basin. From this a small gate through another fence
leads to the Tea-room. This small gate which is known as " Sarudo "
or " Monkey gate " has also a low water basin beside it on the
inside.

THE VARIETIES OF TEA-ROOM

Tea-rooms are classified according to the position of the hearth
as well as according to the number of mats. There are eight kinds
called the " Eight Hearths " besides some other modifications. These
Eight are, the Four-and-a-half mat, the Daime, the Muko-giri or
Opposite Hearth, and the Sumi-giri or Corner Hearth, each in two
styles, Normal and Reverse.

The Four and a half mat is the ordinary or original style, and
is said to have been so proportioned because the eighteen mat room
in the Ro-ei Mansion at Kamakura was divided into four and this
quarter screened off for Cha-no-yu.

Daime is the name given to a mat cut smaller by about a quarter
than the usual size, and so used for a Tea-room in which the
hearth is cut beside a mat of this dimension which is used as the
Utensil Mat. The third variety, or Opposite Hearth, is so designated
because the hearth is cut at the opposite end of the room instead
of in the middle as in these former cases; and the last one, or Corner
Hearth, because it is cut in the outer corner rather than on the inner
side of the mat. Since each of these may be made in the " Normal "
style, i.e. with the hearth on the left side of the room and the host
sitting in front of it so that the guests are to his right, or in the
„ Reverse " style with the hearth to the right and the guests on his
left, they are classified as the Eight Hearths. There are quite a
number of others that are less common, but on the whole they are
only modifications of these. These varieties are explained by the
authorities as originally owing to lack of space, or to the necessity
of entrance from a different quarter. Afterwards they became
stereotyped as interesting variations or opportunities for complication,
thus leading to a greater liability to mistakes, which they consider
regrettable, seeing that both host and guests are apt to become
hypercritical and to watch for a slip on the part of one or the

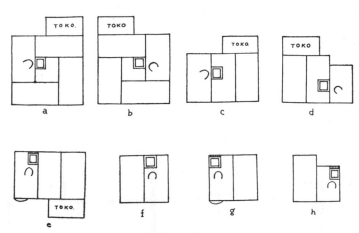

The Eight Hearths.

(a) Four-and-a-half Mat   (b) Ditto Reversed.   (c) Daisu
(d) Ditto Reversed.   (e) Opposite Hearth   (f) Ditto Reversed
(g) Corner Hearth   (h) Ditto Reversed

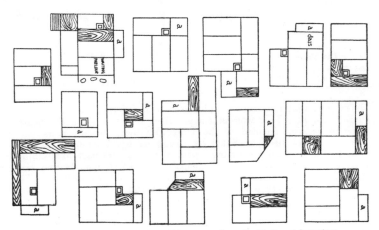

Some Less Common Styles of Tea-room, Several with Board Insertions.

(a) Tokonoma

the other.   This difficulty is due to the different positions that the
host must be prepared to take up according to the location of the
hearth.

Shō-ō and Rikyu together devised the two mat Tea-room. Shō-ō's
Yamasato and Rikyu's Myōgi-an are the first two specimens, and
also the first in Rōji style with a separate garden. They are of the
variety called Two Mat Corner Hearth. It was afterwards enlarged
to three mats and further varied by other Tea Masters. Sōkei made
a three mat room called Shu-un-an. In Shō-ō's day a two and a
half mat room seems to have been considered best.

A Daime is attached to two mat, three mat, or four-and-a-half
mat rooms. The word Daime means the space taken up by the

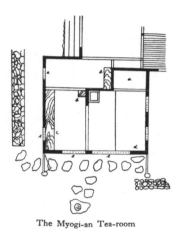

The Myogi-an Tea-room

(a) Tokonoma   (b) Shelf   (c) Board
Floor   (d) Wriggling - in Entrance
(e) Window

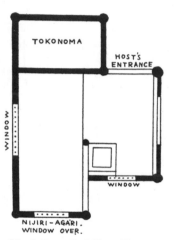

Rikyu's One-and-a-half-mat Tea-room

Daisu (one foot four inches) plus one inch for the low screen that
surrounded it. This was subtracted from one mat when the hearth
came to be used instead of the Daisu. Others explain it as from
Daime, a word used at Sakai by druggists for three-quarters of a
pound of drugs and so coming to mean the greater part of anything.
Furuta Oribe popularised it, especially the three mat Daime size.
As being larger than half a mat it has a desirable asymmetry. The
middle pillar is erected by the hearth of the Daime. It was suggested by Dō-an the son of Rikyu.

Rikyu liked a one-and-a-half mat room, and when he lived in
Yoshiya Machi in Ichijo, Kyoto, he did so in a one-and-a-half mat
room attached to a four-and-a-half. It was at the Jōdōji at Sakai
that Rikyu first made a Kakoi or enclosure of three mats by cutting
off that amount of verandah with a screen.

Up to the time of Shō-ō the four and a half mat room was used with " Kagami " ceiling and square pillars. There was a one mat Tokonoma and the walls were papered. But Rikyu introduced round pillars of natural wood and plastered walls with a papered skirting (koshibari), while only one part of the roof was ceiled and the other left with the tiles showing. He made a push-up window or skylight* and devised the " Wriggling-in " entrance. There was a two-and-a-half and a one-and-a-half mat size, and it was his pupil Oribe who invented the term Daime. Till Rikyu's day there had been no hearth cut in the floor, but the Daisu only had been used, and when Oribe ceased to use it he cut away that part of the mat on which it stood and made the hearth in the remaining part, diminishing also the size of the Tokonoma. Oribe also introduced the Naka-kuguri or middle entrance.

From ancient times to the days of Shō-ō the room for Cere-monial Tea was eight mats or six. There was a verandah also. It was built of finely wrought pine scoured with " muku " leaves, and the pillars were square, of stained wood, the walls boarded and the Tokonoma papered with white paper. A lacquered Daisu was used and a caddy of Chinese ware on a tray. The Tea was served in a Temmoku bowl on a ceremonial stand.

Rikyu made his Tea-room with round poles with the bark on and had the interior plastered as well as the Tokonoma. The plaster was mixed with long straws four or five inches long that had been allowed to rot and then mixed with soft clay and applied over reeds in the natural state. The windows were plastered up to the edge without woodwork and the ceiling made of rushes plaited like a hurdle with green bamboo applied round the edges. Instead of reeds slightly stained laths of cedar or Japanese cypress an inch wide might be plaited in the same way. The verandah was floored with bamboos and the eaves thatched with reeds. Part of the ceiling of the room was formed by a lean-to in which was the push-up window.

The Chō-on-do is an example of a Tea-room made from part of a temple. When the Great Buddha of the Tōdaiji at Nara was restored, Nakai Yamato-no-kami thought the Mieido of Shunjo Shonin a very charming little building, so he took it away and rebuilt it as a Tea-room. It was only seven feet square and had a cupboard and Mizuya. He put an image of Amida Buddha into the cupboard and made it into a shrine, and though small it was quite a good Tea-room. He observed that Kamo-no-chōmei had retired to a ten foot square hut like that of Vimalakirti and there found pleasure in solitary meditation and prayer to Amida, and though his hut was not as large as this, yet as he could and did entertain a number of people in it for Cha-no-yu he thought himself not inferior to Vima-lakirti and his host of Bodhisat guests, much less to Chōmei. The figure of Amida was, he considered, quite in keeping, as the hut

---

* This push-up window in the roof was especially devised for the Dawn Tea, so that the early sunbeams could illuminate the room, but it was also used to get more light for examining the utensils.

had been Shunjo's shrine and so he had installed it, but personally he did not rely much on this Buddha; still, as Shunjo had been a disciple of Hōnen of the Amida sect, he kept it there as a matter of etiquette. And when Kogetsu Osho went to Edo as this Tea-room was being built, Nakai wrote and told him about it and appended to the epistle this comic verse:

> Though it's very small
> It's quite big enough for me
> And Amida too.
> But I don't disturb his rest
> To get into Paradise.

And in reply he got this:

> It is rather odd
> To live at such close quarters
> With Amida Butsu
> Though it is not quite unknown
> With the Goddess Kwanzeon.

Some time after Kobori Enshu was asked to write a tablet for this Tea-room, and he selected the name " Chō-on-do." When asked to explain it he said, " Chō refers to Chōmei since you compare yourself to him. The second character of his name ' mei ' (clear or apparent) was suitable enough for him, for his learning could be so described, but not for you. ' On ' means obscure, like your mind." This was considered a good joke and the name was adopted.

Dimensions of the hearth.—1 ft. 4½ in. square outside and 9¾ in. square inside rim. But Rikyu prefers 1 ft. 5½ in. outside and 1 ft. inside. The rim is usually of chestnut or mulberry wood or it may be of persimmon, keyaki, cherry, or even pine. Plain wood is used in the summer and lacquered in the winter. Though Rikyu first used the square hearth, in the days of Shuko and Shō-ō there was a round copper cauldron let into a board in the floor, and the round make-up of the ashes in the hearth is said to recall this.

Tokonoma.—The Finished style has a raised dais and rim and this may be either plain wood or matted. A simpler kind on the same level as the mats, without dais, is called Fumikomi Toko or Walk-in Toko. Other varieties are the Muro Toko, that is, plastered all round inside, and Earth Toko which has the floor also plastered and papered. There is also the Hora Toko, that is, deep like a cave.

The middle of the Tokonoma is called Jiku-mae, or in front of the Kakemono, the front of it Jiku-saki or facing the Kakemono, and the part opposite to the chief guest's seat Jiku-waki, or at the side of the Kakemono.

Dimensions of Tokonoma are from 6 ft. wide and 2 ft. 3 in. to 2 ft. 9½ in. deep. 4 ft. 4 in. wide and 2 ft. 4 in. deep; 4 ft. 6 in. wide and 2 ft. 4 in. deep; 4 ft. wide and 2 ft. 4 in. or 3 ft. 3 in. deep. The Tokonoma for a four-and-a-half mat room was originally 6 ft., but Sen Dō-an made one 4 ft. 3 in. which Rikyu approved, and this is now the usual size.

Windows.—The "plaster window" (Nuri-nokoshi mado) *lit.* window made by leaving the bamboo rods of the wall unplastered, finishing it without any frame, dates from Rikyu's time.

A poem of Fujiwara Teika refers to this kind of window:

On the plastered wall,
Through the bamboo window bars
Of the simple hut.
Shining with a steady light
Autumn's evening moonbeams fall.

The window in the Tokonoma is attributed to Oribe and the one opposite the Furo (Furosaki Mado) to Rikyu. Dōchin perhaps invented the Tsukiage Mado or Push-up window to view the snow on the main building from the Tea-room.

Nijiri-agari or Wriggling-in entrance. — The expression dates from the days of Oribe and was originally a slang word used by carpenters. It was first called Kuguri-guchi or Crawling-in entrance. Dimensions 2 ft. 2 in. 5 bu high, and 1 ft. 9 in. 5 bu wide according to the Izumi-gusa. Rikyu introduced it after noticing the small opening through which fishermen crawled into their cottages.

The host's entrance is called Katte-guchi or Cha-tate-guchi, i.e. Back entrance or Tea-maker's entrance. When rounded in arch form at the top it is termed Kato-guchi. Another entrance from outside is the Kayoi-guchi, planned by Rikyu for the entrance of a servant who might have to come into the Tea-room without disturbing the host by using his door. Through it are brought the tobacco-tray, cakes, etc. It gives on to the verandah. Its dimensions are the same as the Katte-guchi, 2 ft. 5 bu wide and 5 ft. 6 in. 7 bu high.

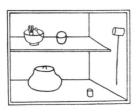
Dōkō

Dōkō.—A built in cupboard for Tea-utensils either in the Tea-room itself or in the Mizuya. The name Dōkō was taken from the box in which the strolling puppeteers kept their dolls and which hung from their neck. It was the name of the puppeteer transfered to his box, and was borrowed by Rikyu. It stood on the floor, and then was promoted to hang on the wall, and then built in. It is made of cedar and has a shelf of bamboo grating. The Nambo Roku describes it as having sliding doors above and a shelf below. On the shelf the water-jar is placed and the other vessels above it. According to the Izumi-gusa it was used in a very small room for convenience.

TEA UTENSILS

Lamps.—Those used in the Tea-room are of the simplest kind, consisting only of a stand, either of wood or bamboo, to which is attached a horizontal projection to hold the wick saucer of rough pottery. This saucer has a small bamboo ring to hold the wick threads in place. Vegetable oil is used. They are called Tankei and are of various styles. That called Yahazu or Arrow-notch was a favourite of So-on, the wife of Rikyu. The Andon is the same type of light but enclosed in a papered lantern of square or oblong or tapering shape.* It may be for outside or indoor use. The dimensions of these lamps should be in proportion to the size of the room.

The Furo or furnace is made in various shapes. There is the Nara Furo, the Bronze Furo, the Cheek-plate Furo, which is like the cheek-plate of a helmet, the Devil Furo and the Jujube Furo.

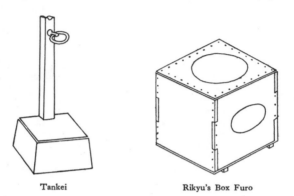

Tankei　　　　　　　　　Rikyu's Box Furo

The Furo has three feet and according to the shape of these is called Teat-foot or Spindle-foot, and there are fenestrations both in front and behind.

The first Furo came from T'ang. It was called Devil-face Teat-foot. It was destroyed in the Onin wars. (*Chado Zentei.*)

Rikyu made a Furo of wood for Hideyoshi when campaigning at Odawara. He thought it rather suitable for Cha-no-yu in the field. It was of cedar, lacquered and shaped like a box, so called Odawara Furo or Box Furo.

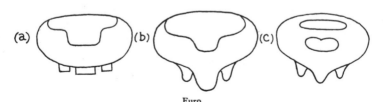

Furo

(a) Wheel Shaped without Rim　　(b) Teat Foot without Rim　　(c) Ditto with Rim

---

* The round Andon or Night-light is the invention of Kobori Enshu, who first made it in this shape, and also suspended the light-stand in the middle instead of having it on the floor of the lamp as formerly.

Konoe Iehiro had one made from one of the "Giboshi" or bosses of a pillar of the long bridge of Seta that had been thrown away when the bridge was rebuilt. It had a very fine patina, for it was quite old, and the shape was interesting. This was in 1727.

The Furo is used only in the summer, though in a place where no hearth is cut in the floor it is permissible to use it for winter Tea. The months reckoned as summer are May to October inclusive, while from November to April the hearth is used. It is said that the Furo should be used as soon as a red bud is seen on the Kaname or Chinese hawthorn tree, and the change made to the hearth when the Yuzu or citron begins to yellow. But if the Furo is used in winter or, as may sometimes happen, the hearth in summer, the proper use of the season should always be preserved: in the case of the Furo it should be treated as though it were a hearth if used in winter, so that the correct distinctions may be preserved.

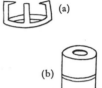

(a) Gotoku or Trivet
(b) Bamboo Lid Rest

The Gotoku (Five Virtues) or Trivet used to support the kettle on the hearth or Furo was in use from the time of Shō-ō.

A board is used as a stand for the Furo. The large one measures 1 ft. 4 in. square and the small one half this. The small one is used with a large size Furo, and a large one with the small size for the sake of asymmetry.

Kettles were of various shapes,* some round and others square, some square ones having a round mouth and vice versa. Bag shape and Fuji shape are also common. They were named from some

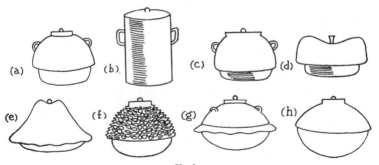

Kettles

(a) Jobari or Ordinary Shape (b) Unryu or Cloud Dragon (c) Minakuchi or All Mouth (d) Ubaguchi or Hag's Mouth (e) Fuji Shape (f) Arare or Hail-stones (g) Ha-gata or Winged Shape (h) Waguchi or Ring Mouth

---

* Echigo-no-kami Moroyasu was a worthless fellow. He confiscated the endowment of the light that had burned before Buddha in the Tennoji for seven hundred years, so that it went out, and made the Kurin or bronze pinnacle of the pagoda into a Tea-kettle, so that it became the fashion among the samurai, and few pagodas were left intact. (Taihei ki.)

peculiarity or association. Thus Mozuya, Amida-do, Daruma-do are from places, Shiribari, Koshi-manji and Kikusui are from their peculiar shape or the design embossed on them, while Raisei (Thunder-voice) and Ubaguchi (Hag's mouth) are comic designations.

The Kettle-stand (Kamashiki) is made of Mino paper or bamboo. The King of Luchu sent a bamboo flower vase to Sen Sotan and he cut off part of it and used it as a kettle-stand.

The Kettle-hanger (Jizai) was adapted from the farmhouse kitchen like the hearth. It is very suitable in a small room of one-and-a-half or two-and-a-half mats.

Tea-jars (Cha-tsubo) for leaf tea. The Sen family possesses three of these that are well-known, two from Luzon and one of Shigaraki ware. The first two were brought to Japan in Hideyoshi's time. One is called Renge-ō because it has the character O (King) on it and a lotus flower (renge), the other Seiko (Pure Perfume) because it is thus inscribed. Some of the best of these jars are said to have been dredged up out of the Western Lake at Hang-chow and are no doubt Sung.

Mizusashi.—The Mizusashi or Cold water vessel is made in many shapes, usually of porcelain, celadon or pottery, or it may be lacquer. The wooden variety seems to have been invented by Rikyu. The origin of the square well-bucket variety is thus described.

Rikyu was giving a Cha-no-yu on a very hot day in summer and as he drew the water from the well it seemed so cold and fresh in the bucket that the happy thought came into his mind to unshackle

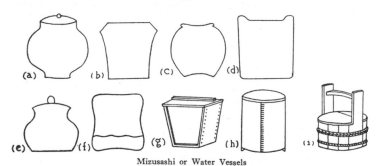

Mizusashi or Water Vessels

(a) Fushiki   (b) Akazutsu   (c) Imogashira   (d) Sashigae   (e) Shakin-bukuro
(f) Owakizashi   (g) Well-bucket   (h) Round Wood   (i) Bucket

the bucket from the rope and take it into the Tea-room and use it as a Mizusashi as it was. This so delighted one of the guests that he had a Mizusashi specially made in this shape for use in summer, and as the square shape went particularly well with the round Furo it has become one of the conventional styles and is known as Rikyu's Well-bucket. But it is also sometimes used in the winter as well and the sanction for this is the experience of Sen Sotan who once went to draw water on a morning that was so cold that it froze immediately, before he could pour it into the Mizusashi, for he had put down the bucket for a moment beside the well, and so he took it into the Tea-room and broke the ice with the ladle and used it instead of the Mizusashi. So in memory of this occasion its use is justified even with the square hearth.

THE RŌJI*

Roji is the name given to the garden of the Tea-room. It means Dewy Path or Dewy Ground according to the spelling. It differs from the ordinary garden in being only a passage, and is made as simple and unornamental as possible. No feature in it should be particularly prominent, and it should have a natural unostentatious appearance. It is now generally divided into two parts, the Outer and Inner Rōji. In the Outer Rōji is the Machiai or Waiting-arbour and the Setsuin or Privy, while the Inner, separated from this by the middle Gate, is the garden of the Tea-room. There are various styles of Rōji, but in all the introduction of ornamental trees, artificial grouping of trees or stones, the use of stones of a peculiar shape or anything suggesting prettiness or expense are out of place. The feeling should be of a simple mountain path of some character, made of ordinary trees and stepping stones in an interesting manner. It symbolises the pure Buddha world where host and guests may meet in frank and quiet friendship. " Thick green moss, all pure and sunny warm,"† was Rikyu's answer when asked to describe the ideal Rōji. His own Tea-room at Sakai was so placed that he could get a glimpse of the sea between the trees when he stood by the water-basin. This was arranged in accordance with the verse of Sogi, which he very much admired, " A glimpse of the sea through the trees, and the flash of the stream at my feet."‡ And the feeling

---

* The word Rōji comes from the Hokke Hiyu-bon, one of the Seven Parables of the Hokke-kyo or Lotus Sutra, where it occurs in the phrase, "Escaping from the fire-stricken habitations of the Three Phenomenal Worlds they take their seats on dewy ground." The expression came to be used of part of the grounds of a Buddhist Temple but never of an ordinary garden. Hence it was that Rikyu selected it to denote the enclosure surrounding the Tea-room. The Sado Dokugan says: "The word Rōji in this sense does not originate with Shūkō or Nō-ami, neither does it come down from the Tea Classic of Luh Wuh. It is entirely the invention af Rikyu."

Originally there was no Rōji, according to the Izumi-gusa; one entered straight into the room. It was all rather simple and severe. Ikei said "the outer Rōji and Arbour is a complication. and not according to the simple style. It did not originally exist and the guests came when they pleased and entered the Tea-room directly. In the days of the Shogun Hidetada, Kanemori So-un first had one made and now they have become common. There is a difference between the outer and inner Rōji. The outer has no special character but is narrow and dark, but when one opens the Naka-kuguri and enters the inner the scene should change. The outer gate of the outer Rōji is left a little open when ordinary guests are expected and they come in and enter the Arbour.

Hosokawa Sansai says in the *Chadansu:* the Rōji should be natural, and so it is not easy to lay down any rules about it. All depends on the situation and one may gauge the character of the host from its appearance. It shows want of taste if it appears short and shallow and as though made to lead straight to the Tea-room. The best feeling would be as though it seemed to lead round to the back of the house or somewhere else so that you come on the Tea-room accidentally. It should have a sense of depth and remoteness.

† 青苔日厚白無塵.
‡ Umi sukoshi
Niwa ni izumi no
Ko no aida ka na.

that is to be aimed at in the Rōji is very well expressed by his own verse :

> *Since the Dewy Path*
> *Is a way that lies outside*
> *This most impure world*
> *Shall we not on entering it*
> *Cleanse our hearts from earthly mire?*

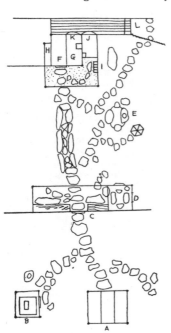

Conventional Arrangement of
Tea-room and Rōji

(a) Machiai for changing clothes (b) Setsuin (c) Middle gate and seat (d) Ornamental Setsuin (e) Crouching Basin (f) Wriggling-in Entrance (g) Tea-room (h) Tokonoma (i) Sword-rack (j) Chadoguchi (k) Kado-guchi (l) Mizuya (m) Stone Lantern

On entering the Inner Rōji the aspect should be quite different from that of the Outer, where no particular impression need be made but one of absolute cleanliness. The path across it to the Tea-room does not go straight through the centre, but divides it into two unequal parts. Here it is usual to emphasise certain points by the arrangement of trees and stones. The number of these will differ according to the size of the Rōji : five may be the average, but for a smaller space three will be enough, while if large seven or even nine may be used. These points are the Nakakuguri or Middle Gate, the Stone Lantern, the Water-basin (either one or two), and the entrance to the Tea-room. The Outer Rōji is generally sanded, while the Inner is mossy.[*] Rikyu liked his Rōji to suggest a mountain path after rain, and used pebbles o get this effect. He preferred pine-trees and bamboos and the eleagnus pungens, while Oribe has a liking for firs, since he liked the sombre dignity of those ancient trees at Sojo-ga-dani.

Water may in some cases be introduced, so as to suggest, for instance, a mountain valley with its cascade, or the path by the side of a lake, but it should not be elaborated to the same extent as in the ordinary landscape garden. Since the Rōji is a garden composed almost entirely of stepping-stones,

---

[*] Sen Sōjun in Cha-zen Dōitsu Mi states that Rōji was originally only a name for the Tea-room and means that place where the real mind is revealed and all attachment put away. In this case Rō = arawasu, to reveal (as in rōkotsu and rōken) and ji is equivalent to Kokoro, mind. So it is also called Haku-roji, Haku, white, signifying clear or pure. Its application to the garden of the Tea-room he considers a mistake that crept in later. This would easily lead to the spelling ji = michi, path.

there is seldom any need for the groups of stones found in an ordinary garden. But should these be required they are to be in accordance with the same rules. What these are may be seen very well in the excellent " Gardens of Japan " by Jiro Harada, published by the *Studio*. The same three kinds of stones too are to be avoided : " Diseased stones," i.e. those distorted at the top : " Dead stones," or horizontal ones that look like vertical ones that have fallen down : " Pauper stones," or those that stand about by themselves without any relation to others. Thus the Rōji may be regarded as in some sort the original form of the Japanese domestic garden, modelled on

Conventional plan of Rōji and Tea-room from the Shin-sen Teisaku Den. To the left the Waiting Arbour and Setsuin, and to the right the Tea-room with Nijiri entrance and Sword-rack, while on the wall hangs the wide Rōji hat and umrella combined for use in the rain. In front is the Tsukubai with its lantern, and the well with another to the left of this by the middle gate.

that of the Zen temple and apart from the larger Island and Lake form attached to the residence of a noble. Its small size and harmonious proportions and simple suggestiveness have therefore supplied a model that can be employed to lend simple distinction to the smallest space. It is just this that European gardening lacked, for everything had to be the cut-down version of the mansion pleasance, except that charming specimen the cottage garden, which owes its excellence to its having been simply for use.

As to the stepping stones of the Rōji they should be laid so that they are easy to walk upon, but not in a straight line, for that would be uninteresting. At the same time they must not be so

Rōji entrance and Waiting Arbour with Tea-room in rear, arranged in a small space and screened with high " Numazu " bamboo fence. From Shin-sen Teisaku Den.

irregular as to appear artificial. They should look as though they led naturally through the trees with which the Rōji is planted. The stones themselves are not selected or valuable ones, but rather the reverse, for in making the Rōji the aim is to obtain an interesting effect by the skilful arrangement of intrinsically valueless things. If the stones are large enough to receive the foot that is sufficient. Rikyu has laid it down that the arrangement of these stones should be on the principle of six points for use and four for appearance, but Oribe would reverse the proportion. Stepping stones are usually laid in groups of three and four, but abbreviated groups of two and three are not inadmissible. Stones of the same size are not laid in succession, nor are any ever laid lengthwise in the line of the path. There is no rule about the distance between them except that it should allow of comfortable walking. Opinions differ among the different schools as to their height above the ground. The Sen school says two inches, Oribe an inch and a half, and Enshu one inch. Label stones or flat slabs laid side by side partly overlapping are often seen in a Rōji. They are generally one foot two inches wide by three feet long. Another way of varying stepping stones is to use a long step occasionally made of stones set in mortar. Sometimes these stones are flat ones of different sizes or large ones varied by insertions of pebbles. These long steps were first used as paths inside the gate of the Daitokuji, and from this Rikyu took the idea and adapted them for the Rōji. It may sometimes improve the scenery of the Rōji to lay a stone of interesting appearance in a spot where something seems to be needed and where a tree cannot be planted. Especially if a stone that will not fit in anywhere else can be found.

Beside the stepping stones there are the three other groupings to be considered. Those at the Middle Gate and those at the Wriggling-in Entrance of the Tea-room, and those in the Waiting-arbour in the Outer Rōji.

Outside the Middle Wicket there is a stone big enough to stand on, so placed that its surface is about a foot below the level of the threshold of the gate. This is called the Guest Stone. On the inside is another similar flat stone, slightly larger and higher, called the Crossing Stone. These should be separated from the gate by a space of four or five inches and three inches respectively. It does not matter which is the nearer as long as the spaces are not equal. Next to the Crossing Stone is another like it, but a little smaller and one inch lower, called the Host Stone, and beside this is placed a small stone known as the Lantern Stone, for the hand lantern carried when Cha-no-yu is given at night.

At the Wriggling-in Entrance of the Tea-room there is a group of three stones. The one nearest the room, set six inches from the skirting-board, is large enough to stand upon comfortably and is four inches high from the ground, leaving a distance of one foot two inches from its upper surface to the top of the lintel of the entrance. This is called the Treading Stone. Next to it comes the Falling Stone, an inch and a half lower, and then the Mounting Stone, again an inch lower, so that these two will be two-and-a-half and one-and-a-half inches high respectively. Some say that the stepping stones in the Rōji should all be either five inches and six-tenths or four and seven-tenths apart.

In the Waiting-arbour stones are arranged according to its shape, and suitably dissimilar flat-topped ones are chosen.

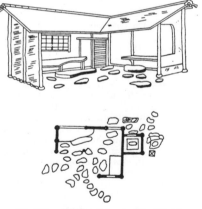

Machiai or Waiting Arbour of the Hitotei Tea-room at Ninnaji, Kyoto, with Setsuin and Tsukubai and Lantern on the right.

One of them should be larger and higher than the others and from its upper surface to the top of the seat one foot two inches is measured, the height of the seat above the ground being given as one foot seven or eight inches. This is known as the Chief Guest Stone.

The Arbour (Koshikake) to which the guests retire in the Interval is furnished with an Andon, a tobacco tray and paper and inkstone for the guests to write their names. In winter, a hand-warmer is provided. In Rikyu's day tobacco was not used, so he laid down no rules for it. The Arbour in the outer Rōji is called Machiai and not Koshikake. Oribe and Enshu developed the Dō-Koshikake or Arbour for Distinguished Guests so that they could change their clothes in it and it was styled therefore Ishō-dō or attiring room. Their retainers could enter also and assist them.

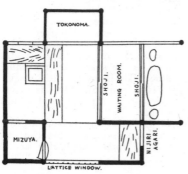

Fuhaku style Tea-room of two mats with board floor insertions, and waiting room built in.

"Under the shade of an ancient grove a bamboo thicket is planted and a narrow path made. A bamboo gate (Take no shiorido) or a plain wooden wicket (Sarudo) leads into it. All is silent and calm. The stone lanterns and water-basin are mossy, and the stepping stones quite natural and untouched. Under the trees bamboo-grass is growing and the leaves of the trees lie as they fall. Oak and pine leaves lie thick on the ground but unmixed with dirt as though blown there by the wind so that the ground is covered everywhere. Only the path is swept. Such was Rikyu's idea of the Rōji. Like a hermit's cell."* (*Cha-fu.*)

Oribe's Rōji was much like that of his master Rikyu but a little less rough. He thought Rikyu went too far in this direction. He liked a spacious Rōji planted with great pines and fir trees and a reed-thatched hut visible in the distance. In both outer and inner enclosure there was a seat, the outer one in a square tiled arbour of six mats. Here the guests met and changed their dress if necessary. He used long flat stones interspersed with the stepping stones and grouped with smaller ones set in plaster. Some of these large stones were four or five feet long. Under the verandahs and in the Setsuin the earth was beaten hard. The lanterns were carved, and for the water-basin he liked an old square box-shaped stone hollowed out at the top. On the ground he carefully strewed pine needles so that it was quite covered. He did not like the leaves of any other tree. The view from the Water-basin or the Arbour should be as of the hills in the distance, and the stones round these two features should, he thought, have a smart and bright appearance.

A certain Goto in Kyoto had a Tea-room in Oribe style and

---

* Rikyu had a Rōji without any stones. There was a little verandah of boards and bamboo and on this the guests sat and took off their footgear before entering the Sukiya. This Rōji was all covered with grass.

there was a large lake drawn from the Kamo river across which the guests were ferried to the Arbour of the outer Rōji by a boy dressed as an acolyte.   On the way he would make them hand over their upper garment (Kataginu or Juttoku) as fare and they would have to enter the Arbour in Hakama only.   *Cha-no-yu Koji-dan.*

Rikyu always carried water in a bucket to the water-basin in the Rōji.   He said that the first business of the host in the Rōji is water carrying, and of the guest washing his hands.   That is what it is for.   It is to cleanse oneself from the dust of the world.   So in hot weather water gives a sense of freshness, and in winter too one must carry it and wash in it, caring nothing for the cold.

Originally guests did not wash in the morning since they had already done so and because there was then no waiting arbour, but now it is always done.   Also a bucket of hot water is now set by the side of the water-basin in winter.

THE MIZUYA

This is the Tea-room kitchen where the utensils are kept so as to be brought in readily, and where they are washed and stored. It is first found in Rikyu's Tea-room the Fushin-an.   A special room is not absolutely necessary, since part of the adjoining room or of the verandah may be utilised, but a properly constructed Mizuya next to the Tea-room is usual, especially where it is detached.   The Dōko is the Mizuya of a very small Tea-room.   Formerly Chajin preferred to make tea with the water of the Uji River or some other famous stream, and drew it and let it settle for a while in the

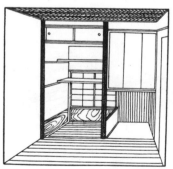

Mizuya of Shogetsu-tei at Daigo Samboin

big water-jar kept in this place. Where this cannot be obtained well-water is used still, for it is far better than any drawn from the tap.   Wells are still found in nearly every Japanese house. Hence the name Mizuya or Water house.

There are very many styles of Mizuya made to suit the space at the designer's disposal, and the various schools of Tea have their traditional models, but the commonest form is a recess three or four feet wide by a little over two feet deep, with a space of a mat or so in front of it.   At the bottom of this is the bamboo grated sink for washing the vessels, with the water jar beside it, and a board with pegs on which to hang the ladles and towels.   Above this are two or more shelves seven or eight inches wide for the other requisites.   There grew up during the Tokugawa period

Mizuya-kazari or Arrangement of
utensils in Mizuya

Three styles of Mizuya

a method of arranging the utensils for the inspection of the guests, but this is quite optional. The tea-things may be placed in the manner most convenient according to the size and shape of the Mizuya.

TREES AND SHRUBS

The planting of trees in a Tea-garden should be such as to suggest some quiet spot in the woods where all the fresh purity of nature abides in an air of solitary detachment. But the plantation must not be thick enough to produce any feeling of stuffiness or restraint. There should be sufficient trees and shrubs to give an impression of depth, but all must be quite natural, and rare or peculiar specimens or those that bear bright flowers should be omitted.* It is best to have only those that are common in the neighbourhood.

Three trees of the same shape standing in a row are to be avoided, as are trees exactly opposite each other or one behind the other. Neither must one be placed exactly facing the entrance to the inner Rōji as one enters, or opposite the water basin. Trees and shrubs that grow in the mountains are most suitable, and they

Water-basin, Stepping-stones and Nijiri-agari

should not be chosen particularly for their shape as in a more formal garden but planted naturally as they grow, and the leaves be allowed to lie on the ground beneath them as in the forest.

To vary the effect and prevent monotony deciduous trees such as the different varieties of Maple and Oak, Willow, Mimosa, Melia Japonica, etc. may be planted, but a Tea-garden must never be without evergreens, and the Pine, Cypress, Cryptomeria, Ilex, Palmyra Palm, Tamarix Chinensis, Viburnum, Aucuba, Fatsia Japonica, Cercidiphyllum and Japonicum, and Aegle Sepiaria with firs and bamboos are the most suitable. Bright-coloured trees such as the Wistaria, Clove, Pyrus Spectabilis, Camellia, Tea tree, Magnolia, Cucumber and Orange are out of place in a Rōji.†

---

* It is perhaps hardly necessary to emphasize the Japanese preference for black-and-white, or rather the varying shades of black, to colour. Just as in music their taste is for the simple and unsophisticated, so in decoration their most favoured hues are Ash colour, Tea colour and Mouse colour, though there are a very great number of shades of these.

† Furuta Oribe was the first to plant Fir trees in the Rōji. Till then Pines and Bamboo with grass or Eleagnus Pungens underneath was the rule.

It is because of their high regard for flowers that Chajin do not care for flowering trees or any blossom in the Rōji. For these would catch the eye before entering the Tea-room and the mind might be distracted and exercised by comparisons so that it would not be easy to maintain that quiet concentration on the flower in the Tokonoma that Tea taste requires.

The exception is the Cherry tree, which may be permitted, though not exactly recommended. Where there is one the host may invite guests when it is in blossom, and then a picture may be hung in the Tokonoma without any flower arrangement, or an empty flower vase may be put there and beside it a flower tray with a pair of scissors on it. This is sufficient to suggest the presence of the Queen of flowers in the Tea-room while she holds her brief court outside.

Rikyu held that a Tea-garden should be arranged with the tallest trees in the foreground and the lower in the background, but Furuta Oribe preferred the reverse, while Sen Dōan thought the ideal Rōji a very small neat garden broadening out into a landscape of unlimited extent toward distant hills. It is well to keep in mind the principle laid down by Katagiri Sekishu in this as in all other matters concerning Cha-no-yu that the best taste lies in not showing it, and that a house or garden should be made not with the intention of showing the taste of the owner, but because it is fit for its purpose. Conscious estheticism is always bad.[*]

The sweeping and cleaning of the Rōji must not be overdone,

Grouping of Stepping-stones

(a), (b) and (c) Groups of three, four and five stones used at turnings (d) Straight path (e) Group at middle gate (x) Host's stone (y) Threshold crossing stone

---

[*] There is a good story to the effect that a certain host who was very proud of his house and furnishings said to his guest, "As you see, my things are of no consequence at all, so if you think there is anything that does not harmonise, just say so and I will take it away at once." "Well," replied the guest, who happened to be a plain-spoken fellow, "I find no fault at all with the furnishings, the only improvement I can think of would be your own absence."

It may be instructive to compare this with the anecdote of Castruccio Castracane, Lord of Lucca, quoted by Machiavelli, which relates how that warrior being invited to supper, by Taddeo Bernardi, a very rich and splendid citizen of Lucca, he went to the house and was shown by Taddeo into a chamber hung with silk and paved with fine stones representing flowers and foliage of the most beautiful colouring. Castruccio gathered some saliva in his mouth and spat it out on Taddeo, and seeing him disturbed at this, said to him, "I knew not where to spit in order to offend thee less." The difference between European and Japanese civilisation here seems to be one of words and spit rather than of "clouds and mud."

though it should not, of course, be at all neglected.   The ideal to be aimed at is that it should be naturally clean like a forest glade, but not aggressively neat.   Therefore the Tea Masters considered that a boy or an old man, or at least someone other than the owner was best entrusted with the task, because they would not be too painstaking.   Leaves that have been blown about under the trees and between the stones look interesting and should not be disturbed.

Rikyu laid it down that the Rōji should be swept overnight for a morning Cha-no-yu, and in the morning for one at midday, so that the leaves would have time to fall in the meanwhile.

THE WATER BASIN

The Water Basin or Chōzu-bachi is the symbol of purity both in the physical and also the spiritual sphere, for here in the inner Rōji in which it is placed all the " dust of the world " is finally washed away and the devotee of Cha-no-yu enters another atmosphere.   Hence it is the central point of this part of the garden. Moreover the Water Basin of a Tea-room is of a different kind from that used in ordinary gardens, in that it is placed low on the ground instead of on a pedestal.   Hence its name " Tsukubai " or " Crouching Basin."   It is the conventionalised form of a pool in some secluded valley into which run the mountain brooks.   Here it is probably also a suggestion of the parable of Taoism concerning the greatness of a kingdom which says : " it is like a down-flowing rill, the central point toward which all the smaller streams under heaven converge."   And to use this Tsukubai it is necessary that all, even the greatest of men, must stoop low on the ground, for it is by humility that the true Sage is known.*

The Water Basin is set on a supporting stone that should be visible above the surface of the ground if the basin is a low one, but should be flush with it if it be high.   Its purpose is to give a firm base for the Water Basin which should be and appear perfectly steady and immovable.   Though one usually finds a large Basin in a large Rōji and a smaller in a more circumscribed one, there are cases where a large one looks well in a small garden and vice versa, so that it is difficult to lay down any exact rule.

In front of the Basin and about two feet and a half from it,

---

* The cavity of the Water Basin should be seven inches across by six deep in the case of round openings.   Other shapes are the Senkata or round with a square hole, Hyotan-kata or Gourd-shaped and Ichimonji-kata or Character-one-shaped.   If a bucket be used instead of a Stone Basin, one made of Chamaeparis Pisifera is best with a Pine lid and a dipper of Hinoki.

The water in the Chōzu-bachi is called Pure Water.   Another receptacle is provided for washing the hands after using the Setsuin.   This is called Not-pure Water.

Rikyu's Water Basin is now in Kiyomizu-dera.   It is called the Owl Water Basin.   It is square with Buddhist figures carved on the four sides hence also called Shiho-Butsu or Four-sided Buddha Basin.   The water is led to it by a bamboo spout.   It was made by Rikyu on the model of the famous Basin now in the Imperial Museum at Tokyo that was placed in the Ginkakuji at Kyoto by Soami when this palace was built for Yoshimasa.   It is 2.3 feet high by 3.1 feet wide, and has Four Buddhas carved on it in low relief.   It is said to have come originally from the Hōshoji (founded 1148) for the founder of which, the Kwampaku Fujiwara Tadamichi, it was made.   When this temple was pulled down it got buried in rubbish and was resurrected by Soami.

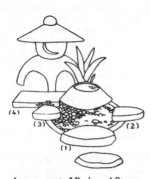

Arrangement of Basin and Stones
(1) Front Stone (2) Hot Water Vessel
Stone (3) Candlestick Stone (4) Lamp-
lighting Stone

Chinese Junk Shaped Basin
Oribe Style Lantern

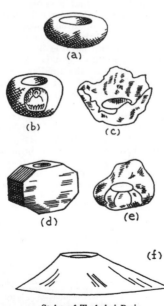

Styles of Tsukubai Basin
(a) Iron Pot Shape (b) Wakidama Shape
(c) Shiba Onko Shape (d) Nambaji Shape
(e) Fishing-frog Shape (f) Fuji Shape

centre to centre, is the Front Stone, and to the left of this and about midway between the two is a rather small stone called the Candlestick Stone, while on the right side opposite is a larger one, the Hot Water Vessel Stone.   The space between these stones and the Basin is cemented or pebbled and enclosed with an edging of stones or little stakes as is usual in water basins, and in the middle of this space a group of five round pebbles is to be placed as a splash breaker.   Should the Water Basin be round then the Front Stone should be rather square in shape and vice versa.

The water basin is not well placed if it is too much in the shade, but it is even worse if there is none at all.

A stone lantern is often placed behind the Water Basin to illuminate it.   Various shapes are used, as for instance the Enshu shape, the Oribe shape, the Michi shirube or Mile post shape or a variety of the Yukimi or Snow Viewing shape with the legs replaced by a low stone base, a simple rustic type of natural stone being preferred.   In front of the lantern is a stone called the Lamp-lighting Stone.

A rather uncommon setting for a Water Basin is that called Koke Shimizu or Mossy Spring, in which a bamboo fence shaped like an opened two-fold screen is placed behind a Crouching Basin with a small shelf in the angle on which the dipper is placed.

A well with its attendant stones, the Water-drawing Stone in front and the Bucket Stone at the left side, may sometimes be found behind the water basin, and behind this again there may be a screen fence known as Yoroi-gata Sodegaki or Armour pattern screen fence.   In other Tea-gardens the well forms a separate feature by itself beside the gate of the Inner Rōji.

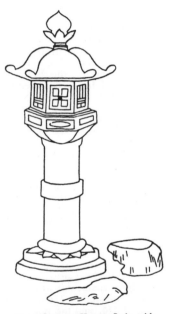

Stone Lantern, Kasuga Style, with Lamp-lighting Stone

The use of the Tsukubai or Crouching Water-basin was evidently not general at first, for when Ieyasu made one at Sumpu, Honda Masazumi remonstrated with him, saying that most people made their ablutions standing.   Ieyasu replied that even the Shogun (Hidetada) would have to crouch down at this, much more any lesser person.   (*Tokugawa Jikki*.)

At the same period Oribe made a high basin in the garden of

the Tea-room of the Shogun called Yamasato at Edo Castle. But in the days of Iemitsu the third Shogun, Kobori Enshu was ordered to remodel this garden and made the basin low. Iemitsu enquired why he did so and Enshu said that it was made during the li etime of Ieyasu so it was made high for his special convenience when he came to Edo. But since then all the Tokugawas have had low ones like anyone else. This answer pleased Iemitsu who was a great worshipper of his mighty grandfather.

THE SETSUIN OR PRIVY

Setsuin, the classical word for privy, has its origin in Zen Buddhism and came into the language through the Tea Masters. It is composed, according to one view, of the first character of the name of a certain Zen monk named Seppo Gison Zenji, of Fuchow in China, and In, the Sinico-Japanese reading of the first character of the word for privy, because this monk set himself the task of cleaning the monastery privies and thus obtained enlightenment. According to another opinion it derives from the name of the monk Setto Zenji who undertook the same task at the temple of Reiin, the second syllable of the name of the temple forming the last character in this case.*

There are two privies attached to a Tea-room, one for use called Kafuku Setsuin, and the other called Kazari Setsuin or Ornamental Privy, which is not used. Though it is customary to use old timber or bamboo in Tea-rooms to produce a feeling of mellowness, yet in the Setsuin only new and clean wood is employed. And the reason why the guests at Cha-no-yu always inspect the Privy with the rest of the Rōji is because in a Zen Monastery† cleaning it has always been regarded as part of the discipline of the sect and is often undertaken by famous priests, and it is in this spirit that it should be approached. Moreover the host bestows special care on keeping it spotless and in proper order so that it is natural that the guests should view it to appreciate this.

The Ornamental or Sand Setsuin was first made by Sen Dōan at the command of Hideyoshi when he was campaigning at Odawara against Hōjō, and the manner in which he made it has been followed

---

* Seppo and Setto are contracted forms of Setsu-ho and Setsu-to. Setsu means snow, while In means to hide or conceal, and read with its Japanese Kun, kakureru is the first syllable of Kakure-dokoro, Place of concealment. The other ancient and classical word for this place still in use is Kawaya, by some explained to mean River-house from Kawa river, from the custom of making it over a stream, as in the monasteries of Koya San (9th century) where it may have originated. But others derive it from Kawa side, so Side-house, from its position in a building.

† In a Zen monastery it is called Seijōshō or Clean Place, because since it is naturally unclean especial care is taken to keep it scrupulously pure and spotless. Cf. the statement in the Jataka Tale No. 16. The excellent Rahula went neither to the Buddha as being his father, nor to Sariputta, Captain of the Faith as being his preceptor, nor to the great Mogallana as being his teacher, nor to the elder Ananda as being his uncle; but betook himself to the Buddha's jakes and took up his abode there as in a heavenly mansion. Now in a Buddha's jakes the door is always closely shut: the levelled floor is of perfumed earth; flowers and garlands are festooned round the walls: and all night long a lamp burns there. Jataka, Vol. I. translated by R. Chalmers.

ever since. Up till the time of Rikyu, since it was a period of civil war, the Setsuin was sometimes used a hiding place from which to make a surprise attack, so especial care had to be taken about it, especially at twilight or evening Cha-no-yu.

Katagiri Sekishu considers that the Setsuin is best placed behind a few trees or bamboos planted so that it is half concealed. If at a little distance from the other buildings especially it looks well if it shows just the roof and the window or part of it. Where there is no waiting arbour trees should be planted so as to conceal it completely.

After a Cha-no-yu the Setsuin should be cleaned with the most scrupulous care and spread with fresh sand, because cleanliness and purity should be its outstanding feature.

That the inspection of this place was, at any rate in early days, also intended to make certain that no one was lurking there with evil intent is indicated by the story of Hariya Sōshun who invited three guests to an evening Cha-no-yu, among whom was Toda Mimbusho. In the interval one of the

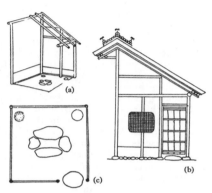

Sand Setsuin
(a) Interior   (b) Exterior   (c) Floor plan

three, Naraya Sansuke, went and examined the Setsuin while the other two proceeded to the Koshikake. He found a man hiding there and asked him who he was. The other said that he had a grudge against Toda Mimbusho and was waiting to attack him, and suggested that Sansuke should entice him that way so that he could do so. But Sansuke was the Batsu or junior guest, and thought that if any harm came to Toda he would be failing in one of his duties. So he refused, and told the man to go away quietly and he would see that he was not molested. The man declined to do, so Sansuke drew him into the Setsuin as though to discuss the matter further and there stabbed him at once. The others then came up on their way round, and Toda examined him with the *andon* and recognised him. They then returned and finished the ceremony without saying anything to their host until the end of the party, when Toda apologised profusely to him for the unfortunate pollution of his Setsuin. He also commended Sansuke and gave him a new name and promoted him to the rank of Samurai as a recognition of his quick resource. They agreed that the inspection of the Setsuin was most important at Evening and Dawn Cha-no-yu. (*Memoirs of Hosokawa Sansai.*)

The result of the inclusion of the Setsuin in the sphere of Zen

and Tea has been very well described by the famous writer Nagai
Kafu in one of his charming studies of old Edo :

"Consider how much esthetic value has the privy of the ordinary
Japanese family as it stands in the position ordained for it by ancient
custom, forming part of the composition of the verandah, the reception rooms and the garden.   With its low shingled roof detached
from the main building, its delicate door of cedar and its bamboo-
barred window, and especially the water-basin that stands always
near it by the edge of the verandah, with its ladle for pouring the
water over the hands, and the aspidistra or other broad-leaved plant
growing round its base to catch the drops, how elegant it looks.

"In front of the brushwood fence that inevitably forms the
background of this basin we have the Nanten bush or the flowering
plum tree, and in the early morning in spring we may see the
bush-warbler perch on the handle of the ladle as he sips the water.
On hot evenings in summer a great cool-looking toad may very
likely drag himself slowly out from under the verandah and on to
the damp green moss that gathers on the stones at the foot of the
Chōzu-bachi, and if the master of the house keeps gold-fish or grows
water plants in bowls, it is in this part of the garden that they are
put.   Here the ladies may hang up their wind-bells or the cages of
singing insects in which they delight.

"And how often does the door of the privy and the water-basin
with its patterned cotton towel hanging up daintily above it figure
on the insides of the covers of our old block-printed books or
elsewhere.   Certainly in our country only does one find that such a
thing as the privy and its surroundings can be thus associated with
poetic fancy and esthetic taste.   In a European home it is so concealed that you don't know where to find it, and even the artists of
France, with all their quaint and unconventional disregard for custom
and convention, have not so far been able to make it the subject of
a serious artistic composition.

"Contrast this with the Ukiyoe painters of Japan and their
delightful grouping of women with this background.   How daring
and yet how quite successful they are!   Standing by the basin and
pouring some water over her delicate fingers from the ladle, her
figure loosely clad in her sleeping kimono with its narrow obi, and
holding her paper handkerchief in her mouth, there is an indescrib-
able grace in her willowy poise.

"And then you get a glimpse of the garden with the evening
rain falling gently and scattering the petals of the drooping Kaido
blossoms in the light of the lantern she has put down on the
verandah beside her, which throws those rather exaggerated but
effective shadows that are the characteristic of this school.   A subtle
silent poem that we cannot resist."   (Shotaku.)

And how many pictures of this kind are now to be found in
conventional European sitting rooms, where their subtle appeal is
quite lost, though if understood it would reveal a point of view as
unique as this eminent novelist asserts.   Possibly many claims made
for Japan in other directions may be based on slighter foundations

than that which distinguishes her as the only people to make the Kawaya a work of art.

"A strict regard for cleanliness is the first principle in entertaining guests. And this love of purity and hatred of dirt was certainly not derived from Tea and Zen, but has always been a part of our national character." (*Takahashi.*)

THE STONE LANTERN

The use of the stone lantern in gardens seems almost certainly to be owing to the Tea Masters, who adapted it from the Buddhist temple where it originated. This may be seen from the names of the various shapes which are almost all taken from temples or from

Stone lantern in the Tachibana-dera near Nara, the birthplace of Shotoku Taishi. It is said to be the oldest stone lantern in the country.

Bronze lantern before the Todaiji at Nara. Tempo period (728–746). Evidently the oldest specimen of a standing lantern and the ancestor of those of stone.

Stone lantern in Count Matsuura's garden at Asakusa. Tradition says it was presented by Shizuka Gozen to the Shrine of Hachiman at Kamakura in the 12th century.

the Tea masters who designed them. Thus we have "Kasuga," "Nigatsudo," "Uzumasa" and "Daibutsu" shapes associated with the most ancient Buddhist architecture of the Nara age and decorated moreover with lotus and jewel motif on the cap. These lanterns most probably developed from the hanging lanterns of bronze or wood which were originally used about temples and are a good example of Japanese eclectic taste, for they have not envolved in this way in China whence the temple artitecture was brought. A further simplification is seen in the Miya-gata or Shrine Shape, which follows the severer lines of a Japanese Shinto Shrine. Practically all the others, designed for garden use by the Tea Masters, are of even simpler form, and for the Tea-garden especially lanterns made of natural uncut stones are preferred. So there are Shukō, Shō-ō

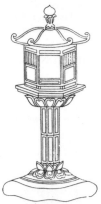

At Kitano, presented by
Yorimasa (12th cent.)

Naniwa Daibutsu shape

Genkoji dated 1336

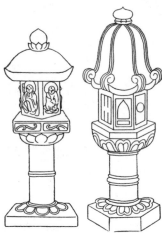

Six Jizō lantern at
Asakusa
(Said to have been
presented by Kamada
Hyoye Masakiyo 12th
century)

Rikyu shape

Yuraku shape

Oribe shape

Sōwa, Sōeki, Rikyu, Oribe and Enshu shapes, to mention only the most famous names, and these were afterwards modified and made in various styles. The type called Snow-viewing lantern is much appreciated in the Rōji both in the more formal as well as in the rougher shapes made of natural stone.

Lanterns are placed by the gate of the Rōji, by the Water Basin, beside the entrance to the Tea-room, by the Waiting Arbour and by the Setsuin, but it is not good taste to put them at all these places, for they will look monotonous like street lamps. So if, for instance, one is placed by the Tea-Room, those by the Water Basin, the Waiting Arbour or the Gate are better omitted, and if the Gate and Water Basin have them it is well to leave them out at the other points.

Moreover, a tree should always be planted beside the lantern so that one branch hangs over or in front of the top. This branch is called the Hi-sawari or Light-obscuring Branch. This is specially important in the case of the Snow-viewing class of lantern, for it adds very much to the effect. Since these lanterns are not used to illuminate the garden but to lend an added charm and interest to the scene they must not on any account be overdone.* Three at most will be sufficient according to the size of the Rōji, one as an addition to the scenery of a grouping and the other two at places where light

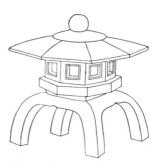

Snow viewing lantern in the temple of Sentsuji, Kyoto, selected as a model of fine proportions.

would be required as by the Water Basin or Gate. Or two or even only one will often be quite sufficient. According to some Tea Masters where a stone lantern has a " New Moon " shaped opening in its top this should always be turned toward the west, while a Full Moon shaped one should be turned toward the east, but others consider this of no great importance and prefer to turn the lantern so that the light looks best in the garden.

Lanterns are always arranged with stones according to the usual rhythmic order of grouping, the lantern taking the place of the Upright Torso Stone as the principal element in the group. There may be two or three other stones in the group and the Lamp Lighting Stone at one side is often stepped.

Concerning the earliest history of the Stone Lantern there is the following record in the temple of Tachibana in Unebi in the province of Yamato : " Irihi-no-ko-no-O-kami after he had made a lake in the hills in Nii-gori in the province of Kawachi, heard that bandits often frequented the road by the side of it, which was a particularly

---

* They are not useless ornaments, however, for they are necessary at dawn and evening Tea to indicate the position of the various points in the Rōji and guide the guests in the dark, and it was for this reason that they were first introduced into it. A lantern is never placed where light would not be needed.

lovely place, and attacked travellers at night and despoiled them
of their goods and sometimes of their lives, so he had a lantern
made of stone and placed it there, and this work he entrusted to
his younger brother Ishizukuri-no-kami, saying that stone was strong
but did not crush benevolence and fire was positive and conquered
darkness, and by this means he did away the evil. And this is the
first lantern to be made of stone in Japan. And since the Mausoleum
of his son Miyaku-no-kami is in this temple according to tradition,
this lantern has been removed and erected here." Now this temple
was built by Shotoku Taishi, son of the thirty-third Sovereign
Suiko Tenno. Now concerning this Irihi-no-ko-no-kami, the eleventh
Earthly Sovereign Suijin Tenno named Ikume-Irihiko-Isachi-no-
mikoto, who reigned in the palace of Shiki Tamagaki, married the
younger sister of
Saho - hiko - no -
mikoto and had
a son Ha-mutsu-
wake - no -mikoto,
and he married
the daughter of
Tamba - no - ushi -
no-o and begot a
son Inishiki-no-
iruhiko-no - miko-
to, who is the
Prince referred
to above. And
in the Kojiki it is
recorded that Ini-
shiki - no - irihi-ko-
no-mikoto made
the lake Chinuma
and also the lake
Sayama, and so
it seems that this
lake Sayama is
the one referred
to in the temple

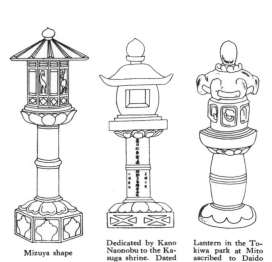

Mizuya shape

Dedicated by Kano
Naonobu to the Ka-
suga shrine. Dated
1647.

Lantern in the To-
kiwa park at Mito
ascribed to Daido
era. 806–809 A.D.

annals. And moreover his younger brother Ishizukuri-no-kami may
be identified with Iwatsuku-wake-no-mikoto, and his son Miyaku-
no-kami, whose mausoleum is in the Tachibana temple, may be that
Mio-no-kami, who is referred to as Hagui-no-kami, ancestor of the
lords of Mio and descendant of Ishizukuri-no-kami.

The only objection to this tradition, says Tamaki Issai, in
quoting it, is that it seems that this lantern bears on its head something that looks like a Buddhist figure, and also has what appears
to be a lotus design on its base, whereas Buddhism was not introduced into Japan till the time of Kimmei Tenno some five hundred
years after the period of the Emperor Suijin (about 50 B.C.) to which
it is referred. It certainly does not seem so likely that stone lanterns

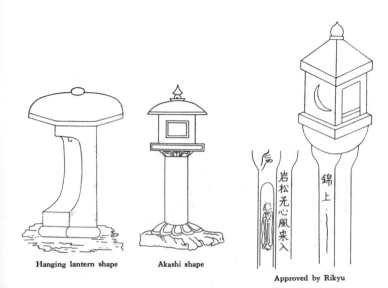

Hanging lantern shape

Akashi shape

Approved by Rikyu

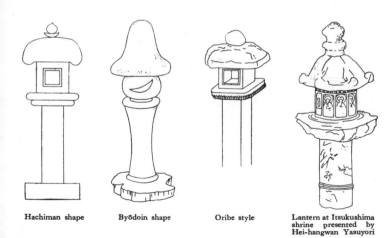

Hachiman shape

Byōdoin shape

Oribe style

Lantern at Itsukushima shrine presented by Hei-hangwan Yasuyori

of any kind were used before the introduction of Buddhism, since the oldest specimens show these signs of Buddhist influence. The case of the Torii is somewhat similar, for this seems to have been originally of wood, though it is not in Japan connected with Buddhist edifices, in spite of which some derive it from the Indian Torana. In the mansion of Count Matsuura in Mukoyanagiwara, in Tokyo, there is a stone lantern that is said to have been set up originally by Shizuka, the consort of Yoshitsune in the 12th century, and there is also another in the precincts of the temple of Kwannon at Asakusa, in the same city, engraved with the Six Jizo, which is referred to Kamada Hyoye Masakiyo in the same century. There is also another in the Hōzenji temple at Kawajiri Mura in Tsukui district

Lantern in the garden of Mr. Akaboshi. Oribe style

in the province of Sagami, with the date Second year of Kenkyu (1192). It is written in the Heike Monogatari also that Taira Shigemori, in the 12th century built forty-eight temples on Higashiyama in Kyoto, and lit forty-eight lanterns in them, and on account of this he got the nickname Tōrō Daijin, or Lantern Minister, just as Soga Umako got that of Shima-no-Omi or Island Minister because he made a lake in his garden, with an island in it ; but it is most likely that these lanterns were hanging ones.

The earliest form of standing lantern was evidently that formed by mounting the hanging shape on a bronze stem as in that formerly before the Todaiji at Nara, which is thirteen feet high and beautifully cast and wrought in openwork. It is of the early part of the 8th century. Later stone and wood were preferred in accordance with Japanese taste, which admires the delicate effect of the weather and age on these materials. When the Tea masters brought Zen feeling into their little gardens it was natural that they should introduce these lanterns for convenience at Cha-no-yu at dusk or dawn.

But now from examples illustrated by Eckardt in his excellent *History of Korean Art* it is apparent that the stone lantern was in use in Korea in the 8th century. It seems there to have developed from the incense burner in the style of the pagoda and has beside it the stone known as the Lamp-lighting stone in Japan. The forms of the oldest Korean specimens given in Eckardt figs. 127 and 128, if these dates are exact, are just those of the lanterns at Tachibana-dera and Nara, said to be the most ancient in Japan, while that in the Tokiwa park at Mito is very reminiscent of the pagoda of fig. 115. Compare also Eckardt fig. 113 with the Mizuya shape and fig. 121 with that in Count Matsuura's garden. Some were evidently brought to Japan in the course of Hideyoshi's Korean campaign, for there is a characteristic pagoda-shaped example said to have been brought by Kuroda Josui, and now at his mortuary shrine of Ryuko-in

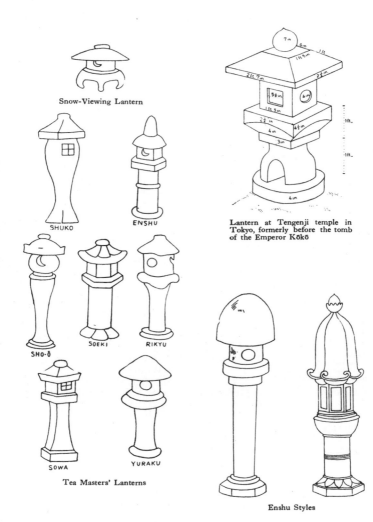

Snow-Viewing Lantern

SHUKO

ENSHU

Lantern at Tengenji temple in Tokyo, formerly before the tomb of the Emperor Kōkō

SHO-Ō

SOEKI

RIKYU

SOWA

YURAKU

Tea Masters' Lanterns

Enshu Styles

at Daitokuji, Kyoto. Hosokawa also brought one of the foundation stones of one of the gates of Seoul for a water-basin, and the Fusen water-basin at the Kō-hōan looks like another. Such things, and Korean potters, were the souvenirs most preferred by the Japanese generals. Since very many lanterns found in the Rōji and favoured by Chajin have the foot buried in the ground without any base, it is sometimes said that only this kind is correct, but this is not necessarily so. Only the inclination to avoid anything elaborate and imposing and to maintain the proper proportion in a small space has tended to eliminate the base.

TIMES FOR CHA-NO-YU

Midday may be said to be the proper time for the full ceremony with Kaiseki, but some speak of the Five Times for Tea and others

of Seven. The Five Times are Midday, Morning, Dawn, Evening and Odd Times, while the Seven include one Guest Tea and After-meeting.

Yō-banashi or Evening Tea.—This follows the evening meal, and was not originally given in summer because of the discomfort caused by mosquitoes. But on cool summer evenings it was often given.

Asa-cha or Morning Tea.—This follows the morning meal, and if a meal is served both at this and also at the evening tea it is a lighter one than at midday.

Akatsuki or Dawn Tea.—Also called Uzumibi Cha-no-yu or Buried Embers Tea. This is because old people, who wake early in the morning, would rake out the glowing embers from under the ashes and make tea at this time. This, like the Evening meeting, was not originally given in the Winter.

Lantern in front of the Tsukubae of the Tanko-an Tea-room of Kamiya Sōtan at the residence of Hiraoka Ryosuke Fukuoka.

Toki-hazure or Tea at Odd Times.—This is given between meals, either morning, afternoon or evening. It is usual not to serve any repast with it, but only tea and cakes. Though if the meeting be much prolonged vermicelli or any other light dish is often brought in.

Ikkyaku Isshu or One Guest and One Host.—The usual number is five, and the correct is three, but in special cases two may make a Cha-no-yu meeting.

Atomi or After-meeting.—After one party of guests have been entertained another guest or guests may come, and the same utensils, picture and flowers are used a second time, and the food that remains is also consumed. In this case either the host may invite the guests or they may ask to be allowed to come and see the utensils.

Until the days of Rikyu people had only two meals a day, the first or morning meal at the hour of the Snake (9 o'clock), and the

Lanterns of natural stone favoured by Mizuho school.

Stone lanterns from illustrated books of the 18th century.   Yukimi or Snow-viewing lanterns.

evening meal at dusk. So originally morning Cha-no-yu was at the former hour, but now there are three meals it is held after 12 noon. Evening Tea was subtitle, as above.

According to Furuta Oribe, Shō-ō used to say that evening was not a very suitable time for entertaining distinguished guests or people one was particular about at Cha-no-yu, since it was inconvenient and not good for digestion. Moreover one could not see the dust or dirt, and that also was bad. (*Cha-no-yu roku-sō-denki.*)

At night water should not be sprinkled in the Rōji. The host should go out with an Andon to meet his guests. He puts the Andon down on the seat, and the chief guest takes it up and sets it down by the water-basin while he washes his hands. Inside the Tea-room a "Tankei" or lamp on a stand is used. It may be put in various places, and if the Tokonoma be dark one may be placed there. If the Kakemono be a famous one it is better to inspect it with a hand candlestick.

At an evening Cha-no-yu the lanterns that stand by the path of the Rōji should all be lighted, and those in the shade of the trees should be lighted too, for that gives an interesting effect. On the seat of the Arbour there should be a lighted Andon and by the sword-rack on its proper stone a lighted candlestick (Teshoku.) On the floor of the Tea-room the Tankei with an oil lamp is used, and there should be five or seven threads in the wick, the length of which should be one and a half to two inches. (*Korobi Enshu.*) But with stone lanterns three or five threads are proper in the clay saucer, according to the size of the lantern. (*Nambo Roku.*)

Sometimes a Kakemono is used at evening meetings and sometimes not. Rikyu and Oribe are both of the opinion that a formal evening Cha-no-yu is not a thing to be given frequently. Cha-no-yu given in snow or rain has special features. A large straw hat like an umbrella of which the wearer forms the stick, is provided for each person and also a pair of clogs. The sojourn in the arbour is as short as may be in the cold weather, and a water basin in this arbour is substituted for the one in the open.

Uzumasa shape   Byōdō-in shape

In very snowy provinces a path may be made beside the stepping stones owing to the difficulty of walking on them.

At meetings for snow scenery and also for those when the moon is to be viewed, paper and writing brushes are provided in the arbour for the poems which guests will be moved to write in celebration of these beauties, and on the latter occasion lights are naturally not put in the lanterns, except perhaps where heavy foliage may cast a deep shadow.

At a Moon-viewing Cha-no-yu no flowers should be used. The expression Setsu-gek-ka (Snow Flowers Moon) is the conventional phrase for beautiful things and a man of taste prefers to break such a cliché. A Flower Tea for some special flower is known, but rare, as might be expected.

When the guest has finished inspecting the Kakemono with the candlestick (Teshoku), he should put it down on the utensil mat with its handle turned to the host. The host comes out and takes it with the proper salute and trims the wick, and then proceeds to make up the hearth. The Teshoku should be held by the two feet and not by the third, which is sometimes called the handle, because so it is less likely to tilt and spill the grease. The Teshoku should be placed where it is convenient to illumine the hearth.

The Tankei is to be placed on the 11th or 12th line of the mat from the hearth, or, according to some, on the 9th. It must be understood that the Tankei is to give light to the room generally and so is to be put where it will best do so and not get in the way of the guests. The Teshoku, on the other hand, is to light the hearth and not the room. A Kakemono with large characters of a definite type that is easily seen without special lighting is to be used. It is objectionable if the picture is cut in half by a shadow and so the light should be arranged so that it is either all in the light or entirely in shadow. In the matter of food also, dishes with small bones and so on should be avoided. (Konoe Iehiro in *Kwai-ki*.)

Cha-no-yu at Dawn.—The Rōji must be sprinkled with water the evening before and the lanterns and Andon lighted and then put out, and then lighted again at about four o'clock in the morning. The kettle is also prepared the night before, and when the guests appear in the Waiting Arbour one or two sticks of charcoal are put on and the water changed in the basin. When the guests arrive Saké and Zenzai or soup of red beans with rice-cake in it, and Mochi (rice-cake) are offered to them. The Usucha is made in a leisurely fashion to the accompaniment of quiet conversation. This over, the kettle is taken out and filled up and brought back wet and put on again. Only a part of the water in it should be changed or it will boil too slowly. When the hearth is made up and the meal served the window is opened and the Andon put out, for it will now be growing light. But one should not be in too great hurry to do this, or the proper effect will not be gained. It is rather interesting to serve the meal just when the light is still dim, and for the host to call out to the guests the name of the dish. If it is not easy for the host to get to the window to open it, the junior guest may be asked to do it. If the Tea-room has no push-up window then the Shoji may be opened instead.

The opening and shutting of the windows is a thing that reveals an experienced host. Sometimes the upper windows should be opened, and sometimes the lower. It depends on the moonlight. When the moonbeams shine in there should be no light visible inside the room. (Konoe Iehiro.)

Between Meal Tea, or Cake Tea.—This is a Cha-no-yu without any meal. Also called Impromptu Tea. The ceremony is much the same with the necessary abbreviations. There is no Interval (Nakadachi), though the garden and utensils are inspected by the guests as usual.

It is related that Abe Shinano-no-kami, though very fond of Cha-no-yu, never gave any but this abbreviated form. And to indicate this fact he called his Tea-room Han-go-an, or Between Meal Hut.

Tea with only one guest is much the same, but here the host takes care not to leave his guest by himself for long. When he goes out for a while into the Mizuya he may ask the guest to arrange the flowers to keep him occupied.

Lantern of extremely simple form, presented in 1761 by Matsudaira Yoritaka, Lord of Takamatsu in Shikoku to the house of Sano, a samurai of that clan, where it still remains. Height of head 2 ft. 5 in., of pillar 2 ft. 2 in.

Twilight Tea is given when a guest happens to drop in about dusk. *Water Tea* is that given when the host has got some specially famous water such as that of Uji, Yanagi, Amadera, Samegai, Akuoji, Kiyomizu in the Kyoto district, or Tennoji at Osaka or Ocha-no-mizu at Edo.

Rustic Tea (Yagake or Fusube Cha-no-yu).—This is Cha-no-yu given out of doors, the kettle being hung on a pine tree and pine needles kindled beneath it.   Hideyoshi often had his Tea Masters perform it in this way.   It was rather informal and a mat was spread for the guests, while the utensils were used from the box in which they were carried.   This box is like a small Doko or Utensil Cabinet.   Of course the utensils are taken out and used according to the usual order.   In fact the treatment of the kettle is the most informal part of it, for the host merely makes a heap of pine needles and puts them under it and fans them to keep the fire going.   The kettle may be suspended on a bamboo tripod.

A *Censer Tea* is one in which the Censer together with the Incense Box is passed round on a tray and each guest burns a piece of incense and inhales it in turn.

There is a special Cha-no-yu for Farewell to the Hearth at the end of the cold season and another for Welcome to the Furo.   The exact time for beginning to use the Furo, according to Rikyu, should be determined by the warmth of the season.   If it was not warm enough to be comfortable with the Furo, but too warm for the hearth, some Chajin made a compromise by covering the hearth with its lid and putting the Furo on top of it, instead of in the usual place.   As the Furo was thus in the middle of the room it gave more heat.   In this case the kettle was suspended over it.

At the end of the eighth month, according to the old calendar, or the beginning of the ninth, is held the Nagori-no-Chaji or Farewell to the Old Tea, while the next party after this is called Kuchi-giri or Inauguration of the New.   On this occasion the Tea-jar is exhibited in the Tokonoma.   Parties for Cha-no-yu given from the first day of the year to the fifteenth are called Dai-fuku-cha or Tea of Great Good Fortune.   After this period until the summer they are known as Haru-cha or Spring Tea.

DRESS FOR CHA-NO-YU

No special dress is required, but in former days the material called Kachin, dark blue Harima coarse cloth, was not worn, and

also care was taken by the host that the colour of his dress was not the same as the mounting of the Kakemono.   The garments called Dōfuku, Hattoku and Jittoku were much worn.   The Haori was removed when entering the Tea-room.   Full dress is not worn, for if it were people could not get through the narrow wriggling-in door with any comfort.   Tabi were worn on the feet.

Rōji Geta.   Rikyu style

They were originally made for the Tea-room, since before Rikyu's day only leather footgear was used, and it was impossible to enter the Sukiya in these.[*]

Dress must be quiet and not gaudy.   Konoe Iehiro says that when a Cha-no-yu was given to cheer the Shogun Ietsuna, who was

---

[*] The use of cotton Tabi or socks as now worn is attributed to the mother of Hosokawa Tadaoki, who made them for her son because he suffered from coldness of the feet when he took part in Cha-no-yu.

indisposed, Inaba Mino-no-kami appeared in crested costume of bright colour and Kamishimo. When Katagiri Sekishu was asked what he thought of this he said it was permissible as an interesting departure from custom to amuse the Shogun, but when Iehiro reported this decision to Teikyo Ho-Shinno, he dissented from it, for he thought some other better variation could have been devised for this purpose than a rather childish breach of the basic principles of Tea, for gaudy dress was always in bad taste at such a time.

When a meeting is to be given invitations are issued by the host not less than three days before. If Koicha is to be offered the formula of invitation is " Sō-cha Ippuku kenjitashi "—" I wish to offer you a cup of coarse tea," whereas if Usucha, the shorter expression " Sō-cha kenjitashi,"—" I wish to offer you some coarse tea," is sufficient. The day before the meeting the host should see to the cleaning of the Inner and Outer Rōji and especially to that of the Setsuin. The tea-whisk, the swab and the ladle should all be new, while the cookery-chopsticks and the spittoon of the tobacco-tray should be made of green bamboo. The lid-rest ought properly to be made of it also but it is often of other materials. The tatami should be new also and the shōji freshly papered.

On the day of the meeting the host gets up rather earlier than usual and again cleans everything that was done the day before,* sweeps out the Mizuya and then carefully inspects everything that is to be used, orders the menu for the meal, puts fresh water in the water-basin, moistens the ashes, cuts the charcoal, puts the incense into the incense-burner and arranges the flowers. The incense differs according to the season of the year, Neri-ko being used in winter, the kinds called Jin or Byakudan in summer, while at the end of spring and beginning of autumn that called Koku-kobei or Ume-ga-ko is most suitable.

About nine o'clock in the morning, if the meeting is to be at noon, a low fire is made in the hearth or Furo, and the kettle put on with the lid slightly raised to let out the steam, so that the air of the Tea-room does not get too dry.

The waiting-arbour is to be swept carefully, and smoking-tray, hand-warmer, writing-paper, Tanzaku paper and tinted paper for verse-writing and a writing-box placed ready. There should also be a kettle with hot water and hot-water cups, but no tea. In the Arbour should be laid out copies of the programme of the meeting and also of the menu of the repast. Sandals are provided here for the guests and also high clogs and a wide umbrella-like hat if it rains.

At about ten o'clock water is thrown over the stepping-stones and sprinkled in the Inner and Outer Rōji to give a cool appearance.

---

* In the *Chaso-kenwa* Oda Yuraku says in the course of a chat that Takayama Ukon suffered from a malady in his Teaism, and that was the disease of overcleanliness, though he was able and resourceful in the ceremony. Cleanliness was such a disease with him that he did not understand what it meant. Not only the Rōji but every possible place, even under the verandah, he was always cleaning in season and out of it.

Konoe Iehiro observes that the custom of spreading pine needles in the Rōji arose in the time of Oribe, who had them spread one very bleak morning to hide the inhospitable coldness of the ground and make it look more cosy.

This is not necessary to any extent in the winter.* It is well, too, to see that the lanterns are ready for lighting, for one never knows how long the meeting may last, and nothing should be left to chance.

When the preparations are complete the host changes his clothes and waits till the guests have all arrived.† This is announced to him by the chief guest, whereupon he again goes into the Tea-room, puts the lid of the kettle right on, and sweeps the room. He then takes the feather brush and dusts the lid of the kettle and the edge of the hearth. The kettle lid is then slightly lifted as before. If a Tea-shelf is used this also is dusted. Then the Kakemono is straightened and anything else that may have been overlooked is put right, after which the water in the Basin is again changed and the ladle put properly in place, while if it is very cold weather a covered bucket of hot water is also provided. The host then goes out to meet the guests.

THE GUESTS

The guests should take a bath and make a careful toilette and put on their dress of ceremony. They should wear fresh tabi and be careful not to forget to take a napkin (Fukusa) and paper and a fan, as well as a towel.‡ They should not forget the trouble the host is taking to entertain them, but should remember how they feel when acting as host and put themselves in his place. When they reach the house they go to the Waiting-arbour and there remain till all are assembled. Since at a Cha-no-yu meeting it is the chief guest who is the important person while the others are regarded as merely accompanying him, great care should be taken that no mistake is made on this point, otherwise the host would be seriously embarrassed. Should by any chance the chief guest not be specified distinctly in the invitation, then he may be chosen in the Waiting Arbour by mutual agreement. In the Arbour deportment should be quiet and dignified. There should be no loud talking on the one hand, or whispering together on the other.

---

* The Rōji is watered from the second to the tenth month, but in winter it is only cleaned, But the stone by the Wriggling-in entrance must never be wetted.

Watering is done three times during a Cha-no-yu: before the arrival of the guests, in the Interval in the middle when they go out of the Tea-room, and when they leave. It should, of course, be done gently, and it is very bad to throw a lot of water about just when the guests are arriving, wetting oneself and making the trees and everything else look soaked.

† The number of guests must not exceed five, and two or three are best. The fewer the better if the host is at all inexperienced, for there may be some confusion if he does not remember how to direct matters. The great object of both host and guests is that everything shall go simply and smoothly. (*Nambo-roku.*)

In the case of a very distinguished guest of high rank the host is to watch for his coming and go out to meet him some distance, and so bring him in. He must also escort him some considerable part of the way back and call on him the next day to thank him for coming and enquire after his health.

‡ Guests bring with them toothpicks with which to pick up cake, towels and paper handkerchiefs. These latter are used to wrap up cakes and also to handle the clogs when taken off. The left sleeve is kept as the receptacle of soiled paper after such use, the right being only for what is clean.

When the guests enter the Rōji the host wipes the bars of the gate with a duster he carries with him and also the edge of the Kuguri.

When the host comes in to greet the guests and ask them to come into the Tea-room, it is the chief guest who answers and gives the return salutation* while the others only bow and otherwise keep themselves in the background. They then make their way very leisurely to the Tea-room, those who feel inclined to do so smoking a pipe or paying a visit to the Setsuin by the way, the reason for this dilatoriness being to give the host an opportunity of rectifying anything he may possibly have forgotten in the Tea-room. The last guest puts things straight in the Arbour before leaving and shuts the door after him. When the chief guest has reached the Water Basin the second should be at the Rōji gate, and when the chief is at the entrance of the Tea-room the next will be at the Water Basin and the third at the Rōji entrance.† Then when the chief guest has entered the room and seated himself in front of the Kakemono, which is the first thing he does on entering, making a bow to it and admiring it, the second guest will be at the door and the third at the Water Basin. The chief guest then goes and sits in front of the hearth to admire that, and the next takes his place in front of the Kakemono. The chief guest then returns to his proper seat and the others take theirs in order next him. Should the seat of the chief guest be in front of the Tokonoma, then he must sit out of the way somewhere else for a while until all the guests have looked at it, and then take his proper seat. The foot-gear are deposited outside, leaning up against the skirting under the Wriggling-in Entrance and beside the " Shoe-removing Stone." In order to prevent soiling the hands the thong of the sandal is grasped with a piece of paper, which is kept in the left sleeve, since the right is the receptacle of paper for clean purposes, such as wrapping cakes and so on.

When the last guest enters the Tea-room he shuts the door of the entrance with a slight noise. The sound of the shutting of this door is not easy to get exactly right, as it ought not to be too loud or excessively soft. It is to let the host know that all the guests have come in, and should not be obvious to the others. When the host hears this sound he goes round through the middle gate into the Inner Rōji and puts some more water into the basin there, not so much because it is necessary as to let the guests know by the splashing that he will soon make his appearance in the Tea-room. So when the guests hear this they should finish their inspection and sit down in their places.

The host then enters by the door leading from the Mizuya and makes his bow and salutation which is returned by the chief guest,

---

* In complimenting the host on the stones or other objects in the garden the guests should not put on an authoritative air or be too loud in their praise. Discrimination is always necessary.

† Before washing the hands at the basin the towel should be taken out of the sleeve and tucked into the girdle so that there may be no need to search for it with the hands wet.

A certain countryman who liked Tea sent Rikyu one ryo in money with a letter requesting him to buy with it whatever utensil he thought best. Rikyu spent some of it on a long roll of towelling and sent this to him with the remainder of the money and the comment that as long as you have a clean towel you don't need anything else for " Simple Tea." (Wabi-no-Cha-no-yu.)

who then proceeds to compliment him on the Kakemono and also
on the Tea-room itself should it happen to be a new one,

The Tea-ceremony begins with the " Sumi-temae " or " Making
up the fire," and this is followed by the serving of the meal where
the full ceremony is given, after which the host prepares the room,
while the guests retire again to the Arbour for a short rest, after

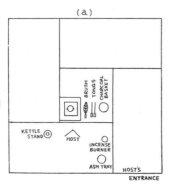
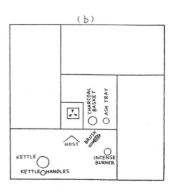

Making up the Fire.
(a) First Position.   (b) Second Position.   Four-and-a-half Mat Room.

which they again enter the Tea-room and are offered first Koicha
and then Usucha.   Then comes the inspection of the " Three
Utensils," i.e. the Tea-caddy, Tea-scoop and Caddy-bag, after which
there may be a second attending to the fire, like the first except that
the incense burner is not passed round, and last of all an inspection
of the boxes in which the utensils are kept and of their inscriptions.

The ceremony of making up the fire begins by the host appearing
at the door of the Mizuya and making a bow, after which he brings
in the necessary utensils,* i.e. the charcoal basket with the various
kinds of charcoal in it, some thick, some long and narrow, and
some small sticks, with the feather brush on the right side and the
Hibashi or fire tongs stuck in front, the two rings that form the
handles of the kettle being hung over them.   In winter these fire-
tongs should have handles of mulberry wood, but in summer they
should be of metal or bamboo.   The kettle-stand is also carried in
this basket.   The host brings in this basket and sets it down midway between the edge of the hearth and the border of the mat in
which it is cut.   He then goes out again and brings in the tray
with the ash scoop, which he carries with the left hand under it
and the right holding it, and deposits on the floor behind his seat
to the right.   He then takes the brush and puts it beside the hearth
with the fire-tongs next it and between it and the basket, and the

---

* In the utensils care is taken that a round vessel does not stand on a round base or
square on square and also that the colours differ should there be any.

kettle handles find their place in front of the basket. The incense burner which was brought in on top of the kettle-stand in the basket is put on the right between the ash tray and the charcoal basket. In some cases the incense burner is brought in on a tray of its own separately. Then the ring handles of the kettle are taken in the right hand, passed to the left, and the kettle lid put on with the right, when the handles are slipped through the ears on each side of the kettle that are made to receive them. Then the kettle-stand is placed to the left of the host, the kettle lifted off the trivet and put on it and the ring handles removed and laid down to the left of it, whereupon the host takes up the feather brush and proceeds to dust the edges of the hearth in a conventional manner while the guests edge up nearer to look on, bowing as they do so, the chief guest complimenting the host on the fire. The brush is then placed beside the incense burner in what is called the Hachimonji or Figure Eight style, i.e. two lines inclining to each other. The host then takes the Hibashi or fire-tongs and stirs up the fire (and there are four different ways of doing this), then puts them back on the charcoal-basket, after which he takes the ash tray in his right hand, then applies his left and so brings it to the front of the hearth and smooths the ashes up round the glowing charcoal in a formal pattern. The chief guest then compliments him on the smoothing of the ashes. The ash utensils are then laid in the left palm and with the right hand the charcoal basket is brought close up to the hearth, while the ash tray is put down on the right of it. The edge of the hearth is again dusted with the brush and the chief guest compliments on this also. The trivet is then dusted, and again the chief guest bows in acknowledgment. The host returns the bow and taps the handle of the brush on the right side of the hearth sharply to shake off the dust and replaces it beside the incense-burner. The next thing for the host to do is to put fresh charcoal on the fire which is now glowing. To do this he takes certain kinds of charcoal from the basket

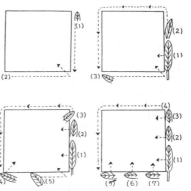

Methods of brushing the Hearth.

and with the Hibashi puts it into the ash tray whence it is transferred to the fire. This done, the chief guest praises the charcoal and all the guests shift back to their original places. The host then puts the Hibashi back into the charcoal basket and then replaces first the ash tray and then the charcoal basket in their original positions, again dusts the hearth with the brush and puts that to the left of the charcoal basket. The host then takes the incense burner and transfers it to his left hand, while with his right he takes off the lid, puts it down in front of him, and then takes the Hibashi and with them inserts two pastilles of incense, afterwards placing the Hibashi on the charcoal box.

FEATHER BRUSH

ASH BASKET

The chief guest then asks if he may be permitted to examine the incense burner, and the host pushes it slightly towards him in front of the feather brush. He then turns to the left and puts the ring handles back on the kettle, lifts it on to the hearth and puts the kettle-stand on the charcoal-basket face downwards. The kettle is then adjusted so as to be straight on the trivet, and the handles removed and placed on top of the stand. This done, the lid of the kettle is dusted with the feather brush in the form of the letter E in the Hiragana script and the figure one, and the brush is put on top of the charcoal basket and the host goes out first with the ash tray and then with the charcoal basket and shuts the door behind him. Mean-

while the guests are examining the incense burner, and when they have done so the chief guest replaces it where the kettle stood before it was put on the hearth. When the host thinks they have finished examining this he comes out again, and, sitting down before the kettle, shifts the lid into a partly open position and bows to the guests. They may then ask about the incense burner and he gives them its history if it has one, and then takes it into his right hand, shifts it into his left and goes out, supporting it in his left hand and steadying it with his right. He then comes to the door and announces that as it is now lunch-time he wishes to offer them a little simple refreshment and again goes out and shuts the door. In a minute or two he opens it again and proceeds to bring in the trays for the Kaiseki.[*]

ORDER OF MEAL

(a) Serve principal dishes on tray. Retire and shut door of Mizuya.

(b) Bring in either pickles or side dish (hirazara) whichever is included.

---

[*] Kaiseki is the word used in Cha-no-yu for the light meal which is served. Literally it means "warming stone," the stone used in Zen monasteries to put in the breast in cold weather. Then it came to mean a simple meal just sufficient to stay hunger, and so was borrowed by the Tea Masters.

Originally in the Zen temple they had a table that was used by from two to four monks, but the Tea Masters Shō-ō, Rikyu, and their contemporaries in the Daitokuji preferred a small one for each person.

(c)   Change soup bowls.

(d)   Bring in Saké and pass cups round. Then take away bottle.

(e)   Serve broiled fish or side dish if there is none.

(f)   Change the other bowl on the tray.

(g)   Hand Saké to chief guest. Here the host's assistant, should there be one, comes to the door of the Mizuya, makes a bow, retires and shuts the door.

(h)   Serve soup course and take away side dish.

(i)   Bring in Saké bottle and writing box and offer liquor again. Bow and retire.

(j)   Bring hot water. Take away soup bowl and shut door.

(k)   Take away trays, retire and shut door.

(l)   Bring cakes, retire and shut door.

Originally rice was not served, but only cakes. But the lovers of simplicity did not care to provide elaborate cakes, and thought it more convenient to serve cold rice warmed up again. In summer the dishes should be cold but in winter warm. A meal is most enjoyable served in a small room in this way, because the few guests can be quickly attended to and the courses brought in exactly the right condition. Strange things are objectionable because the guests do not know whether they will like them or not, and so may be in a quandary. But if a guest knows a dish and doesn't like it he will leave it and so all will be satisfied. Moreover it is the way of people to say a strange dish is good, whether they like it or not, simply because they do not wish to be thought ignorant.

Rikyu considered that the meal should consist of no more than a bowl of soup, one, or at most two dishes of vegetables and some cakes. Later on the dishes evidently increased in number, for we find it stated that there should not be more than three soup or broth courses and five other dishes. A good average is two soup bowls and three other dishes, or one soup and three other courses. Cha-no-yu cookery should have no bones or fins or dishes that are difficult to eat or that cause any crunching with the teeth. There should be no sign of profusion, and anything startling or novel is not in good taste.*

Katagiri Sekishu was famous for the elegance of his light repasts. When asked the secret he said : " If you begin by intending to prepare something light you will probably fail. You must prepare a large variety of things and from them select a few of the best. Then you will have a meal fit to give anyone."

---

* The meal is served on plain wooden stands of the simplest shape with the edge of the wood only lacquered, called " Handai " or " Food-stand " and not " Zen " as usual. The bowls on it are of porcelain or celadon. Laquered wooden bowls are not used. For the chop-sticks, also of plain wood, a small rest is provided, since the stand has no rim. They are placed on a paper napkin.

There is an amusing work called " Shushoku Ron " or " The Argument of Gourmand versus Drinkhard." The advocate for the case of the drinker is one Zoshu-no-Sho Kasuya Ason Nagamochi or Lord Stronghead Dreghouse of Bunghole Castle, Maltshire, and for that of the eater Hanshitsu Risshi Kohan or the Reverend Dean Trencherman Cakebread, the Arbiter being Chuzaemon no Taiyu Nakahara Chusei or Sir Gallio Middleton.

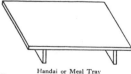

Handai or Meal Tray

The guests on their part observe certain prescribed rules as to the way of handling the bowls and their covers, saké cups, etc. These rules are devised with a view to facilitating the task of the host in serving and removing the trays and bowls with the least possible number of movements, and having them, when removed to the Mizuya, as clean and handy for washing up as may be. This is why it is not good to leave any food in the bowls.

There should be complete freedom for both host and guests, in that it is not necessary for the host to press the guests to eat, while they on their part can leave what they do not like without offence. Only it is well that they make up their mind whether they will eat or leave any dish, and do not touch it unless they mean to finish it. For then it can be eaten by someone else and will not be wasted. It is correct to finish the meal feeling somewhat unsatisfied.

Covered Bowls (Wan) for Kaiseki

(1) Ichimonji. (2) Ami-wan. (3) Yoshino-wan.
(4) Goke-wan.   (5) Maru-wan. (6) Noboriko-wan. (7) Enchu-wan. (8) Omote-oke.

The Kaiseki ended, the guests go out again to the Arbour to stretch their legs and smoke, after saluting the hearth and the Tokonoma as on entering. Here they wait till summoned by the sound of a gong.*

In the interval the host removes the Kakemono and substitutes a flower vase. There is no special way of arranging the flowers in it. They should be put in quite artlessly and there should never be more than two colours. Any flower or grass that has an unpleasant smell or that is not in season is inadmissible.

Then follows first the serving of Koicha and then of Usucha and the inspection of the utensils and afterwards of their bags and boxes. This over, they salute the host again and depart.

Koicha was originally made with one bowl for each person, but as this took a long time and was tedious for the guests, Rikyu introduced the custom of passing the bowl round.

Usucha came to be used later in the ceremony, partly because some did not like the strong variety and partly because Koicha alone did not quench the thirst.

Since, according to Rikyu, Koicha is to be regarded as the Finished Style, and Usucha, if taken after it, as Informal, the corresponding type of utensil should be used. But there should be a proper balance between them, lest the former be so exquisite as to put the latter into the shade, like a fine gentleman followed by a rustic, as he put it.

Cha-no-yu for Daimyos and Imperial Abbots and Great Court Nobles is somewhat different from the ordinary. It is always in the

---

* Striking a gong to recall the guests comes from the custom of the Zen monastery.

Finished Style. It may be called Highly Finished, perhaps. It is in accordance with their way of life. A six mat room or larger is proper with an ante - room for attendants. The Daisu is used and the Water Jar and Ladle as well as the Furo are of metal. The Kaiseki and Tea making are carried out with the ceremony proper to a Court Noble. But it did not follow that such personages were always treated thus. It was only when they were officially entertained.

In this case

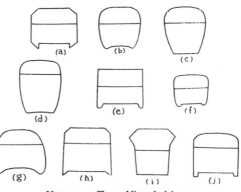

Natsume or Tea-caddies of plain or lacquered wood for Usucha†

(a) Fubiki-kata. (b) Ko-natsume. (c) Naka-natsume. (d) O-natsume. (e) Nakatsugi. (f) Ippuku-iri. (g) Shiri-fukure. (h) Mencha-oke. (i) Yaku-ki. (j) Chaoke-zunkiri.

a hearth is never used ; always a Furo and Daisu. And Tea is served in a Temmoku on a stand.[*]

Such guests are ushered into the reception room connected with the Tea-room with their two or three retainers, and their swords are deposited on the sword rack in the Tokonoma. A guard of the host's retainers should be posted outside the outer gate of the Rōji. The sandals of these important guests should be put by themselves, and not beside those of the host. The Tea-bowl and stand used should be new.

Temmoku on stand

Tea-bowl with Natsume and Napkin arranged to carry into Tea-room.

Konoe Ōzan once went to a Cha-no-yu with Sen Sōtan, and though Sōtan had a very proper appreciation of the high rank of his guest, for Ōzan was then Kwampaku, he yet entertained him

---

[*] Temmoku Tea-bowls are so called from the mountain range of that name called in Chinese T'ien-mu-shan. It lies west of Hangchow and has two lakes on it whence the name "Heavenly Eyes Mountain." On it is the famous Zen monastery of King-shan-ssu or Keizanji to which the monks from Japan went to study and where was the great priest Kyōdō. Since they brought back Tea-bowls in which the Tea was there drunk before Daruma, this name stuck to them, and as they were thus ceremoniously used they were set on the stand which always accompanies this type of Tea-bowl. They also have a rim of silver or gold because, as they were fired upside down resting on their mouth, this part was bare of glaze and therefore rough, and though later on the mouth also was glazed the rim continued to be used.

† The Natsume for Usucha is so called from its likeness to the Natsume or jujube berry which was considered auspicious because reputed to be an antidote to poison.

in the Informal Style in a small Tea-room as usual. In the course of it Ōzan enquired when the Temmoku Tea-bowl on a stand was used, and Sotan explained that an old or interesting specimen might be used among equals, but that a new one was only used when entertaining guests of high rank. On Ōzan asking what he meant by guests of high rank his host replied that people like himself should be so treated, but as he had come purposely to this humble Tea-room, and as he was known to be one enlightened in the real meaning of Tea, which does not regard rank, he had not departed from the ordinary simple ceremony. Sōtan then asked him to step into the reception room adjoining, where he served Usucha in a Temmoku on a stand. Ōzan admired his understanding and resource, which revealed the real value of Teaism.

THE KAKEMONO

The writings of great Zen priests are preferred to all others in the Tea-room since they suggest the feeling of drinking tea with

Way of Handling the Ladle

reverence in the presence of these sages. Next comes old Japanese poetry such that of Teika-Kyo, Shunzei, Tsurayuki or Saigyo. Calligraphs (Bokuseki) either old or new are equally suitable, and good modern ones or the writings of one's friends are preferable to some spurious antique. Then come old paintings. They should have little or no colour and are best if they look faded and indistinct. Black and white landscapes of a rough type of the Nangwa school are very pleasant and modern specimens will do if old are not available. Figure subjects and brightly coloured birds and flowers are of course out of place in the Tea-room. The Haiku of Basho are quite suitable, but this does not apply to other poets of this school who lack the necessary flavour of " Sabi." Poems that treat of love or sentiment are quite inadmissible, however ancient they may be, though " Waka " that describe the seasons or have merely an esthetic appeal may be hung. Similarly didactic sentiments such as those taken from the texts of Confucianism are incompatiable with the spirit of Tea, for besides being concerned with everyday affairs they have a minatory air and smack of conscious pedagoguery and so hardly conduce to calmness of mind.

Both writings and paintings should be naive and unsophisticated rather than a display of finished technique, and it is the preeminence of the Zen priests in this quality that makes their writings so desirable.* The writing considered most valuable, as it is one of the oldest, is the famous letter of Tokko Zenji of the Ikuozan or Asoka Temple in Che Kiang, written to Taira Shigemori to acknowledge the receipt of a hundred ryo of gold which he had sent to that monastery in the twelfth century, and so called the " Kane-watashi no Bokuseki " or " Writing of the handing over of the money." It is in the possession of Prince Tokugawa Iesato who also owns another great treasure of the kind, the autograph of Engo Zenji, the compiler of the Hekigan Roku which Takahashi calls the " Zen Bible." It is hardly proper for Zen to have a bible, but even these sages are not quite consistent in their contempt of scriptures, and it may be this that makes their bible and its compiler interesting. Moreover it is quite unintelligible. Other eminent Zen monks whose writings are favoured are Eisai, Dōgen, Daito, Muso, Nambo, Ikkyu, Kōkei, Takuan, Kōgetsu, etc.

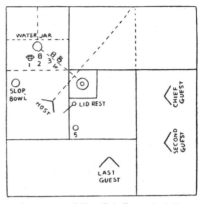

Arrangement of Utensils in Four-and-a-half Mat Tea-room

(1) Tea-bowl and Whisk. (2) Tea-caddy. (3) Tea-caddy. (4) Whisk. (5) Place where Tea-bowl is put for guests.

FLOWER ARRANGEMENTS FOR CHA-NO-YU

Flowers arranged according to the conventional styles of the various schools such as Ikenobo, Enshu, etc., are not suited for the Tea-room. It seems that the very formal types of arrangement now called the Enshu and Sekishu schools are much later than these masters, and only derive from later pupils of their schools of Tea, if indeed they have any connexion with them at all. The earlier Tea Masters only taught the simple natural style called Nage-iri (Thrown-in flower).

---

* With regard to the Kakemono, if it is a writing it may be used at any time that suits its sentiment, but if it is a painting summer scenes can only be hung in winter and winter ones in summer.

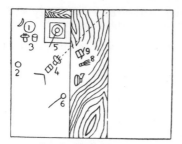

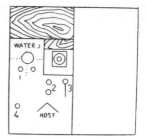

Opposite Hearth, Two Mat
with Middle board

(1) Water-jar. (2) Slop-bowl. (3) Tea-bowl Whisk and Tea-caddy. (4) Do. second position. (5) Ladle resting on Kettle. (6) Ladle on lid-rest. (7) Tea-bowl offered to guests. (8), (9) Tea-caddy Tea-spoon and Tea-whisk do.

Opposite Hearth. One mat
and Daime with board.

(1) Tea-bowl and Tea-caddy, first position. (2) Do. second position. (3) Ladle on Lid-rest. (4) Slop-bowl.

Only a single blossom is placed naturally in the vase, or at most one or two more may on occasions be added.[*]

At evening Cha-no-yu the flower vase is used first and the Kakemono afterwards. Only in a room larger than four-and-a-half mats may both be set out together.

At an Evening Tea coloured flowers should never be used for they cannot be seen properly. Yellow is the most undesirable since it is the most invisible. White flowers should be used at night if any are needed.

It is related of Tokugawa Hidetada, the second Shogun, who was fond of Cha-no-yu, that he was once presented with a peony that had blossomed in the winter as a rarity. He looked at it and praised its beauty, but ordered that it should be thrown away and not put in a vase, because unseasonable things are unnatural and should never be displayed. Chajin prefer bamboo flower vases to either pottery or bronze ones. Their preference is in that order. The first was made by Rikyu for Hideyoshi when on the Odawara campaign against Hojo in 1590. Hojo is said to have given Hideyoshi a present of three pieces of bamboo in return for one of three bales of rice which the Taiko had sent to his castle as a joke. Of these Rikyu made three flower vases, one single, one two-storied and one flute-shaped. The first was named Enjōji, because, like the bell of that temple, it was cracked. This fact seems to have given it the greatest reputation of the three. It passed to Sen Sotan and once when some one commented to him on a slight leak from the crack that moistened the Toko, he replied that this was its life. But it would have been reprehensible in any other. These three are the Great Meibutsu of bamboo vases and Takahashi informs us that the Shakuhachi or flute-shaped one was sold at the Akaboshi sale in 1918 for £ 8,600.

[*] The height of the flower above the vase is only one-third of the height of the latter, compared with the one and a half times of the ordinary arrangements.

Should the guest be asked by the host to arrange flowers in the Tea-room, as for instance when there is one guest only, so that he will not be lonely while the host is preparing the utensils in the Mizuya, he should always request the latter to pour in the water, for this is considered a very delicate operation, since it varies according to the flower and the vase, while to put the finishing touch is the prerogative of the host.

ORDER OF TEA CEREMONY

(1) Bring in separately (a) Water-jar; (b) Tea-bowl, Tea-spoon and Tea-caddy; (c) Slop-bowl and hot-water ladle.

(2) Wipe (a) Tea-spoon; (b) Ladle.

(3) Take napkin from girdle and put it in the slop-bowl. Remove the lid from the Kettle and place it on the Lid-rest.

(4) Take one ladleful of water from Kettle and put it into the Tea-bowl.

(5) Wash Tea-whisk and replace Ladle on top of Kettle.

(6) Empty Tea-bowl.

(7) Wipe Tea-bowl with Swab.

(8) Put Swab on lid of Kettle.

(9) Take up Tea-spoon and Tea-caddy.

(10) Put lid of Tea-caddy in front of Water-jar.

(11) Take up two spoonfuls of Tea and put into Tea-bowl.

(12) Put lid on Tea-caddy and place in front of water-jar with spoon on top.

(13) Remove lid from Water-jar and place beside it.

(14) Put a ladleful of hot water into Tea-bowl, replacing ladle on Kettle.

(15) Whisk Tea and replace Tea-whisk to right of Tea-caddy.

(16) Take Tea-bowl in left hand and present with right hand. Bow.

(17) Replace napkin in girdle.

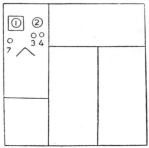 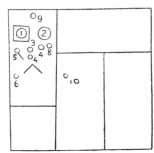

Positions for Furo

(1) Furo. (2) Water-jar. (3) Tea-bowl whisk and spoon. (4) Caddy. (5) Ladle. (6) Slop-bowl. (7) Lid-stand. (8) Tea-whisk. (9) Caddy-bag. (10) Place where Bowl and Utensils are offered to guests.

(18)   Take another ladleful of hot water and put in returned Tea-bowl.
(19)   Replace ladle on Kettle.
(20)   Empty hot water into Slop-bowl.
(21)   Take up swab and wipe Tea-bowl.
(22)   Replace Tea-bowl and put swab on top of Kettle-lid. (Repeat from (11) if required.)
(23)   Take a ladleful of cold water from Water-jar.
(24)   Put cold water into Tea-bowl and wash Tea-whisk.
(25)   Empty cold water into Slop-bowl.
(26)   Put swab into Tea-bowl with whisk on it and replace in position.
(27)   Take napkin and wipe Tea-spoon and put this also on top of Tea-bowl.
(28)   Put Tea-caddy by side of Tea-bowl.
(29)   Refold napkin and replace in girdle.
(30)   Take up ladle and put cold water into Kettle.
(31)   Change ladle to left hand. Take Kettle-lid in right and replace it.
(32)   Put ladle on rest.
(33)   Replace lid on Water-jar.
(34)   Take ladle and lid-rest in right hand and Slop-bowl in left and withdraw.
(35)   Return and take Tea-caddy in right hand and Tea-bowl in left and withdraw.
(36)   Return and take Water-jar in both hands and withdraw.
(37)   Come back to door of Tea-room and bow to guests from threshold.

Cha-no-yu should be performed in complete silence. But there are the Three Sounds of Tea. The first is the clink of the lid on the Kettle. The second is the tap of the Tea-bowl on the mat. And the third is the clink of the Tea-spoon on the Tea-bowl.

It is hardly possible to describe the proper way of handling each utensil. Every movement is exactly prescribed, but must be seen for its inevitability to be appreciated.

TEA FOR THE EMPEROR AND THE TOKUGAWA SHOGUNS

In the ninth year of Kwan-ei (1633) the third Tokugawa Shogun Iemitsu appointed eleven Cha-shi or Tea Officers ; four from the house of Kambayashi of Uji, this family already having been made chief of the Tea growers, and one each from the houses of Nagai, Sakata, Ozaki, Nagara, Hoshino, Tsuji and Hori. These had to superintend the preparation of three jars of the finest tea for presentation by the Shogun to the Imperial Palace. For this purpose ten tea jars were used, named Fuku-kai 福海, Tabi-goromo 旅衣, Sodesema 袖狹, Umoregi 埋木, Higurashi 日暮, Torasaru 寅申, Tarogoro 大郎五郎, Fujikobu 藤瘤, Niji 虹, and Shiga 志賀, and every year in the fourth month three of these were sent up in turn to Uji. A lucky day was selected within three days of the eighty-eighth night

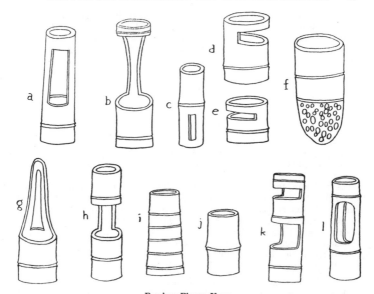

Bamboo Flower Vases

(a) Double pillar. (b) Stork's neck. (c) Bridge pillar. (d) Wayfarer's pillow. (e) Lion's mouth. (f) Stone mallet. (g) Begging monk's bag. (h) Pestle. (i) Flute. (j) One knot. (k), (l) Two story.

and the jars were filled.   Meanwhile a proclamation was posted up in the village of Uji to the effect that: " No new tea may be sent out before the August Tea jars have departed."   Twenty half bags of Hatsu Mukashi and Ato Mukashi Koi-cha were first put into the jars (one bag=20 momme), and then the remaining space in them was filled up with Usu-cha.   They were then sent to Otagiyama in the Capital, and after staying there three months the Chief Tea Room Official (O-Sukiya-gashira) and the Lower Tea Officials (O-Bozu-shu) took charge of them and sent them to Edo in charge of fifty O-kachi or guardsmen under command of an O-kachi-gashira. Each of the jars was first wrapped in silk Habutai and then in a thickly wadded outer covering.   It was then put into a box, and the box into a small specially made palanquin with long handles borne by several bearers, so that, whatever happened, the precious jar could not come to any harm.   The posting charges were borne by the Daikwan or Local Governor where the Territory belonged to the Shogun, but where it did not the Feudal Lord had to provide it.

As the procession went along the guards called out " Get Down! Get Down !" and the common people had to prostrate themselves on the ground, while even a great Feudal lord had to get out of his palanquin and make obeisance if the tea jars met his train. Consequently Feudal Lords on the march gave them a wide berth if they could. Moreover, if any ford happened to be impassable for a time any waiting Daimyo must give way and allow the jars to go over first, and this applied even to special messengers on government business. It seems that not infrequently on these occasions a present given on the quiet to the guards made them look the other way. It was also the custom for either the Daimyo or one of his Karō to come out to meet the jars when they entered his domains and to bring presents and feast the officials who accompanied them. All this respect was on account of the tea being not only escorted by the Shogun but being intended as a gift for the Emperor.

When the jars arrived at Edo the Shogun himself sampled the tea and decided which jar was the finest and this was set aside for presentation to the Emperor. Of the other two jars one was kept by the Shogun for his own use and the other was divided between the Sanke or Tokugawa Lords of Kii, Mito and Owari. The value of this tea was set down as 35 Oban or 335 Ryo of gold.

But after a while the Shogun's government found out that this elaborate escort caused the inhabitants of the territories through which it passed unnecessary trouble and expense, and also gave opportunities for extortion on the part of the accompanying officials, so in the eleventh year of Kambun (1671) the following decree was published:

> Though so far the pack horses for the August Tea from Uji have not been included under the Red Seal (i.e. paid for by the Shogun), from this time on thirty horses will be provided at government expense. This is because when they were provided by the people too many were exacted, and this became a grievous burden to the dwellers in those parts.
>
> (signed) ITAKURA DAIZEN NO SHO.

Again in the period Teikyo (1684-88) another order was issued that the jars should proceed from Edo to Uji by the Tokaido road, but from Uji to Edo by the Nakasendo, so as to divide the troublesome necessity of entertaining the officials between the two roads. It was ordered also that they should not be put up in temples but in small " Dō " or chapels and shrines that they might be safe in case of fire.

Again in the fourth year of Shōtoku (1715) the seventh Shogun Ietsugu ordered that they should not be taken to Otagiyama as heretofore, but be lodged at Tanimura in the Tsuru district of Kai.

Then the eighth Shogun Yoshimune decreed that, to save expense, the services of the O-kachi and O-kachi-gashira should be dispensed with, but that one O-go-ban of the Nijo Castle should superintend them instead, and moreover that they should no longer be deposited at Tanimura but taken direct from Uji to Edo by the Tokaido and there lodged in the Fujimi tower of the Chiyoda Castle.

In the Shogun's household there were three O-sukiya-gashira who had control of the Tea-rooms and of all the artizans who were necessary for their upkeep, paperers, bag-makers, kettle-makers and

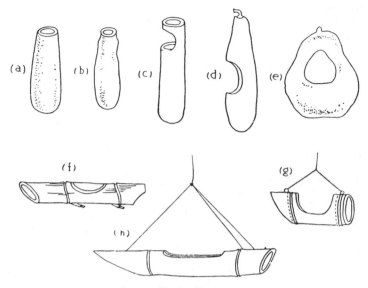

Hanging Vases

(a) Fishing-frog. (b) Incense stand. (c) Shrike's nest. (d) Long gourd.
(e) Flower window.

Ship-shaped Vases

(f) Standing ship. (g) Stirrup shape. (h) Anchored ship.

wood-workers of various kinds. They also superintended the landscape
gardeners in charge of all the Shogun's gardens. Their salary was a
hundred and fifty Hyo of rice. Under them were a hundred and twelve
" Bōzu " or " Tea Pages " under eleven Bōzu-gashira whose services
were valued at forty Hyo. These Pages were called " Bōzu "
because at the Ashikaga Court Tea was served by shaven Bōzu or
priests, and the custom continued since then, though these pages
were not priests but only shavelings.

The tea of Uji was classified as Hatsu Mukashi and Ato
Mukashi. These words mean literally Early Ancient and Late
Ancient. This was because the former was gathered during the ten
days before the eighty-eighth evening of the year and the latter
during the ten days after that date. Since these periods are reckoned
together as twenty-one days, and the signs for this written as one
make the Chinese characterf or Mukashi 昔, or Ancient, the tea was
thus styled. Matsuura, lord of Hirado, had a tea similarly named
Number One White Ancient, for the character for White is an
abbreviation of that for Garden (Hatake), and this is the tea from
Garden Number One. There is also in use the curious name

Grandmother Ancient for a certain tea. And this is because the grandmother of Kamibayashi Kamon-no-suke of Uji picked some tea with her own hands and presented it to Tokugawa Ieyasu, and since he liked the flavour very much he jokingly gave it the name of Grandmother Ancient. He also presented the tea-garden from which it came to the family. And so the name Grandmother Ancient became a privileged one in the house of Kamibayashi and no other might use it.

The Koicha called Hatsu Mukashi and Ato Mukashi was not for sale, even to Daimyos. The only way to get it was to put in a request to the On-mono-chashi or August Tea Officials, to the effect that such and such a lord desired some, and if granted it was usual to send a piece of gold for each jarful as a thank-offering. This custom continued right up to the Restoration of Meiji.

The special protection of the Tea-gardens of Uji dates from the 14th year of Tensho (1587), and the privilege of providing tea for the Emperor and Shogun was strictly limited to them, but in case of fire or earthquake or other such calamity there was a sub-official in charge of the gardens of Okura and Kobata, which would in such emergencies be able to take the place of those of Uji.

Besides the tea presented every year by the Shogun, the Imperial Court obtained more from Uji direct for the use of the Emperor, and this amount was by no means small. Then some thirty odd jars were contributed by Rinnoji-no-Miya, the Imperial Abbot of Nikko, and the Six Branches of the Tokugawa family called Sanke and Sankyo.

REGULATIONS FOR THE SUKIYA OF THE SHOGUN

DRAWN UP BY THE SHOGUN IETSUNA IN THE NINTH MONTH OF
THE SECOND YEAR OF MANJI (1659) IN THE ERA OF THE EMPEROR GO-SAIIN

(1) When the Shogun himself attends a Cha-no-yu the greatest care must be taken.

(2) When Cha-no-yu is given in the gardens of the Castle they must be given a special Cleaning.

(3) The head of the attendants of the Castle Tea-rooms and those under him (Go-katte Bozu) must be on duty there day and night to do what is required.

(4) Concerning the cleaning of the Apartment called Kuro Shoin the greatest attention shall be paid to it, not only on days of Ceremony but at all other times, and when the attendants go off duty those who relieve them shall again see that nothing is overlooked.

(5) In the two sets of Tea-rooms in the Outer Castle the Tea pages (Bōzu) shall be always on duty and ready to serve tea at any moment. But Cha-no-yu performed with the Daisu shall be prepared from the hour of the Dragon (10 a.m.) and served after the hour of the Ram (2 p.m.) Cha-no-yu

shall always be given after the hours of duty.   Neither shall this tea be on any account carried to any other room.

(6)   The Chief Tea Master shall go round and inspect the Tea-rooms twice every day, but not at any fixed time, and the chiefs of the pages under him (Kumi-gashira) shall do the same three times during the day and night, also at odd times that there be no negligence.

(7)   The chief officials in charge of the Rōjis shall also go round every day and superintend the cleaning of them, and shall see that all the duties pertaining to the buildings in them are properly performed.

(8)   The greatest precautions must be taken against fire, not only in the Tea-rooms but also in the rooms in the Rōji by all the Tea Officials.   Fire pages shall make their rounds by night and day and shall exercise all vigilance.

(9)   The Chief Tea Master shall see to it that at no time is there any unceremonious deportment on the part of the least of all those who are employed in any part of the apartments where Cha-no-yu is performed.

(10)   When the following members of the Sanke visit the Castle and Tea is served the officers down to the Metsuke shall be presented and then those in attendance.   Kii Dono, Mito Dono, Owari Dono, Sama-no-kami Dono, Kii Saisho Dono, Mito Chūjō Dono, and Owari Uemon Dono.

(11)   On the Five Festivals, and the first, fifteenth and twenty-eighth days of the month when the Daimyos come to pay their visits of ceremony Cha-no-yu is to be performed with the Daisu in the Tea-rooms adjoining the Great Hall of Audience, but on no account is Tea to be taken to any other apartment.

(12)   With regard to the visits of the Daimyos Tea is not to be served to them without orders from those in charge, and the Chief Tea Master and the chiefs of the pages shall go round and inspect the Daisu and utensils and shall see that the greatest care is exercised.

(13)   Let all be very particular to see that no tea or any utensils or anything of any kind in use in the Sukiya department is lost.

(14)   No official of the Sukiya is to visit any of the Daimyos without some good reason.   Should there be any question about the matter report should be made to the Chief and his order awaited.

(15)   Concerning the hours of duty those employed in the Rōji as well as Tea pages (O-Sukiya-gashira) shall be on duty in their respective watches every day.

(16)   Should any member of one watch be ill, some one off duty shall immediately offer assistance.

(17)   There shall be no loud talking about the Tea-rooms.   Particularly shall voices not be raised when on duty in the Great Hall of Audience and in the Reception rooms known as

Kuro Shoin and Haku Shoin, and care must be taken that those employed in the Rōji and any others who have business there are warned not to speak loudly.

(18) Should there be by any chance anyone who plots to do anything reprehensible, not only should no countenance be lent him, but, without losing the least time, material information should be given to Izu-no-kami and to the Chief Tea Master. In such case lands, rice and money will be given to the informer to the extent of double that which he would gain by agreement.

THE POTTERY OF CHA-NO-YU

A few words may not be out of place on this subject, rather in explanation of matters referred to elsewhere than as an attempt to deal with it adequately, which could only be done by a separate work, well illustrated, in the style of the *Kwan-kō-zu-setsu* of Ninagawa.

The most important pottery of Cha-no-yu is first the Cha-ire and then the Cha-wan. It is said that among the military class the most precious possessions were first Tea-caddies, second writings and third swords. For this was the order in which they were presented by the Shogun to one he desired to honour. Consequently it was the ambition of all Daimyos of over a hundred thousand koku to possess all three, without which they considered their household treasures to be incomplete.

Tea-caddies were put in the first rank because they were impossible to counterfeit owing to their characteristic feature being something that was the fortuitous result of the action of the fire, while at the same time they were not liable to damage by rust or moth and so needed no special attention.

Chinese specimens are considered the most valuable. They were originally bottles used in China in the Sung period for oil or drugs, and were only imported into Japan for use as caddies up to the end of the Ashikaga or beginning of the Tokagawa era. Tea-caddies are thus classified :

JAPANESE

Provincial Ware.	Later Kilns.	Original Kiln.	Heiji Kiln.
Karatsu. Satsuma.	Maemon. Rikyu.	Tojiro II.	Old Seto.
Shigaraki. Takatori.	Genjuro. Oribe.	„ III.	Tojiro I.
Omuro. Tamba.	Kichibei. Sohaku.	„ IV.	
Bizen.	Shidoro. Zeze.		
	Moemon. Shimbei.		

CHINESE

Nasu. Bunrin. Katatsuki. Marutsubo. Taikai. Tsurukuki. Shirifukure.

The Japanese go by the names of the potters and kilns, the Chinese by those of their shapes.

Tea-bowls are divided into three classes, Chinese, Korean and Japanese. The Chinese varieties were always used for tea, but those of Korea were rice-bowls adapted for tea in Japan just as the Chinese oil-bottles were used as Tea-caddies. The Korean wares were admired by Rikyu and his followers since their rough naiveté was just what their standard demanded. Here also Matsudaira Fumai's work *Ganka Meibutsu-ki* is considered the criterion, and those described in it are regarded as Great Masterpieces, while all others are styled Later Treasures. They are arranged thus.

JAPANESE		KOREAN
Provincial.	Raku.	
Karatsu. Asahi,	Chojiro I.	Kaki-no-heta. Kinsan. Ido.
Oku-gorai. Iga.	Kōetsu.	Gōki. Goshō Maru. Mishima.
Hagi. Seto.	Nonko.	Totoya. Katade Komogai.
Izumo. Shigaraki.		Kohiki. Amamori. Hageme.
Oribe. Shonzui.		Sōhaku. Gohon. Tamagote.
Gempin. Shino.		Sōba. Unkaku. Wari-kodai.*
Satsuma.		Iraho.

CHINESE

Temmoku. (Haikatsugi. Yohen. Kensan. Yuteki. Taihisan.)
Celadon. (Seiji.)
Blue-and-white. (Sometsuki.)

The glaze of the old Chinese Tea-caddies is more brilliant than that of the early Japanese specimens, but as they are of persimmon, or Ame colour (reddish yellow), or sometimes very dark brown, their brilliant glaze does not give them a glittering appearance. Moreover their being made for ordinary purposes prevents them having the conscious air of the Japanese pieces, which were specially made to contain tea by professional potters. But though they have not quite the natural dignity of the Chinese specimens they certainly have a very definite quality of "Wabi," and seem to be suitable for a more easy-going and intimate style than the former, which demand that only a great Tea Master shall handle them.

Owing to their brilliance they are kept in a bag of very quiet type to quench it a little, while the Japanese caddies should have a bright covering of gold brocade to set them off.

Chinese Temmoku and celadon Tea-bowls are artistically fine and pleasing to look at but they are not good for tea drinking on account of their hardness. The best of the Korean bowls have a pleasant softness to the touch as well as an interesting unevenness and lack of symmetry. They were originally made as rice-bowls by some quite unknown village potters and so have the required quality of unsophistication. Even now in Korea this kind of vessel may be found combining traditional quality with artless elegance. It was after the decline of the Li dynasty of Korea that some of the best work was done in kilns roughly constructed on the hill sides to supply the everyday wants of an impoverished population. Hageme, Mishima and Iraho ware is of this kind. It is unnecessary to say,

---

* Cf. Eckardt, *History of Korean Arts*, Chap. V. for descriptions of these types of pottery.

perhaps that the Koreans themselves, as well as the Chinese and also Europeans, who do not understand the Cha-no-yu point of view, have little or no interest in these wares. Satsuma has become famous in the world as a gaudy ware well suited for export, but the real Satsuma that is sought after in Japan is this rough Korean ware make by the artizans of that country who were brought over by Shimazu. At the same time, as these Korean bowls were made for rice, they are rather too wide and flat in shape for the ideal Tea-bowl. Therefore the Raku type made in Japan is more effective.

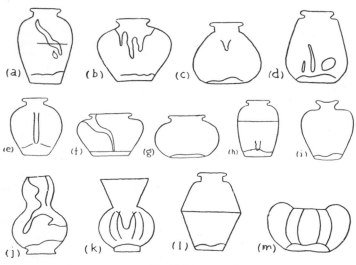

Tea - Caddies.
(Cha-ire)

(a) Katatsuki or Shouldered caddy. So called from its shape.

(b) Bunrin or Bunrinro. This name was given because it resembles an apple (Ringo). It is said that Li Kin presented an apple to Kao Tsu of Han and received from the Emperor a salary and an office entitled Bunrinro, hence this word was used henceforward as a nickname for an apple.

(c) Nasubi or Egg-plant. Also from its shape.

(d) Shiri-fukure. Bulge-bottom.

(e) Bunna. Hideyoshi gave it this name which is composed of the first syllable of Bunrin and the first of Nasubi because it partakes somewhat of the shape of both.

(f) Taikai. Great Ocean. From its wide mouth. It was originally used as an intermediate receptacle for the Tea as it came from the mortar before it was transferred to one of the smaller sizes. Hence it was never put in the Tea-room but kept on a shelf in the Reception Room.

(g) Utsumi. Inland Sea. A smaller variety of the above.

(h) Hitachi-obi. On the tenth day of the first month it is the custom to present an obi or girdle to the shrine of the god Kashima in Hitachi, and since this caddy has a girdle the name was suggested.

(i) Ass's hoof. From the resemblance of the mouth to the hoof of an ass.

(j) Gourd shape.

(k) Anko or Fishing-frog. Kobori Enshu gave it this name because it had a wide gaping month like that of this fish.

(l) Efugo. Name of the utensil in which hawk's food was kept.

(m) Uri or Melon. The shape of the mouth here is that called Uba-guchi or Hag's mouth.

It has the requisite thickness and quiet feeling, is pleasant to handle and soft to the touch, while it is wide at the bottom and rather cylindrical so that the Tea-whisk can be used freely and the contents are not likely to spill. The thickness of a Tea-bowl is a very important matter, for if too thick it does not get warm enough, and if too thin it becomes too hot to hold comfortably.

Raku ware is very successful in fulfilling all these conditions and moreover is inexpressibly pleasing to the touch. This sense of touch is highly developed among devotees of Cha-no-yu, and they obtain very great satisfaction from the mere feel of the Tea-utensils, just as others do from handling jade or ink-stones, quite apart from any use they may have.* Then also the taste of tea from Raku bowls far surpasses that of the same liquor drunk from the celadons of China and Korea. And when connoisseurs wished to judge of the quality of water for making tea, it was from Raku Cha-wan they used to taste it. The most unsuitable wares for Tea-bowls are the gilt types of Satsuma and Kutani, quite lacking in the necessary quality of reticence, and Kenzan and Ninsei bowls with their colour decoration, which although, by virtue of the vigour in them, not entirely to be rejected, are only suitable for very occasional use and for the delectation of lady guests.

The Tea-caddies of Japanese make that were so much valued in the days of Hideyoshi and afterwards in the Tokugawa era were mostly the early wares of Seto made by Kato Shirozaemon called Toshiro, who went to China to study ceramics in 1223, and who made the first Tea-caddies for Myōei Shōnin at the very beginning of the first period of the popularity of the herb then lately imported. Some of these pieces were made of earth brought from the continent, and some with mixed Chinese and Japanese clay. What are called Kara-mono or Chinese wares were sometimes pieces actually brought from that country and sometimes these works of Toshiro. Afterwards, so much was Toshiro's work appreciated, pieces that he made before he went to China, some of them very rough and imperfect and incompletely glazed about the mouth because he fired them standing on this part, were much sought after also, and even faulty work that he had thrown away was dug up and eagerly acquired. These two varieties are known as " Kuchi-hagete " or " Bare mouth ware," and " Hori-dashite " or " Disinterred ware." The ware made by Ito Gorodayu of Ise in China, or made by Shonzui and brought home by Gorodayu, or made at Karatsu by the Hizen potters under his direction, whatever may be the truth about it, is also much valued, but it is not till the time of Rikyu that the potters began to work essentially for the Cha-no-yu taste, and so it is that the Japanese histories of ceramics call this period by his name. This

* Cf. the verse :

> Who's the biggest fool
> In this witless world of ours
> But the connoisseur,
> Dropping heartfelt tears of joy
> As he feels a Raku bowl.

But the folly here is that Zen simplicity without which one does not enter the kingdom of enlightenment.

enthusiasm on the part of the potters was the natural result of the great encouragement given them by Nobunaga, Hideyoshi and even Ieyasu, for Nobunaga went round the potteries of Seto and appraised the products of the kilns, giving special honour to six craftsmen whom he designated the Six Masters of Seto, while Hideyoshi gave a golden seal bearing the second character of the name of his Palace of Juraku to Chōsuke, son of Sōkei, hence the name Raku applied to the ware he made. It is a soft pottery only fired to red heat, easy to make compared with the harder wares, and lending itself well to amateur efforts.

Chōjiro* is famous for his Seven Tea-bowls (Chōjiro shichi-shu) called Daikoku, Toyobō, Hachibiraki, Kōmori, Hayabune, Kengyo and Rinzai. Daikoku was named from its black colour, the characters of the Deity's title being Great and Black, while the second was given by Rikyu to the Toyobō Hall of the Shinnyōdō Temple. Both of these have Rikyu's inscription on their boxes and belong to the family of Kōnoike.

Kōmori or Tree Warden gets its name because it was left over when Rikyu showed his pupils ten bowls and told them to chose which they liked from them, thus showing their lack of appreciation. The word Kōmori is used of a single fruit purposely left on a tree to " guard " it when it is denuded of all the rest.

Hayabune or Swift Ship is so called because when in Osaka Rikyu sent a swift ship specially to fetch it from Kyoto. He once served tea in it to Hosokawa Tadaoki who asked what ware it was, whereupon Rikyu laughingly replied that he had sent a swift ship all the way to Korea for it. On his return home Tadaoki sent a retainer to ask for it but apparently did not get it.

Kengyo or Blind Minstrel was named on the same principle as Kōmori. Rikyu once went to see Chōjiro and asked him if he had any Tea-bowls. The potter replied that he had only one left which the connoisseurs who had taken his others had not appreciated. " They are like Kengyo," he observed. So Rikyu gave the Tea-bowl this name. It is in the possession of the Lord of Satsuma. Rinzai is called after the great Zen monk of that name, because it was as preeminent in its way as he. Hachibiraki or Bowl Inauguration was a black one, and Rikyu was going to use it for the first time at a Tea to Hideyoshi, but the Taiko objected because he had been told that the black glaze had some impurity in it. So Rikyu went through the form of inaugurating it, but did not actually use it. The Chōjiro family has continued to the present day and is now

* Chōsuke or Chōjiro I. was received in audience by Hideyoshi and given an income so that he did no more commercial work. He was formally appointed Tea-bowl Maker (O-Chawan-ya) to the Taiko to work under Rikyu, who gave him his own surname of Tanaka. His father was a Chinese who had become naturalized and was known as Ameya (Rice-jelly seller) and afterwards took the title Sōkei. He died in 1575 and his widow carried on his work, and since she became a nun in order to pray for his happy rebirth her pottery is termed " Nun's ware." It was by her name of Sasaki that Chōjiro was known until he was given that of Tanaka. Sōkei was really the founder of the Kyoto wares, for until his day nothing of any importance had been made there. The Chinese character Raku with which Chōjiro's ware was signed was written by Honami Kōetsu.

When Hideyoshi built the Juraku-tei he brought Chōjiro to live there and had him make tiles and Tea utensils. And since the character " Raku " was stamped on the tiles his ware came to be known as Raku ware. (Tokutomi, *Kinsei Nihon Kokuminshi*.)

in the twelfth generation.* It produced many famous potters especially the third of the line named Dō-nyu, usually known as Nonko, also renowned for his Seven Bowls. Then there were the potteries started by the Korean craftsmen brought back after the campaign in that country by Nabeshima of Hizen and Shimazu of Satsuma and other Daimyos.

Their purpose was to make Tea vessels, and it is curious that the name of Satsuma especially should be so widely known in Europe and America in connexion with a ware of a very different type. Hideyoshi with his usual shrewdness was not slow to seize the opportunity offered by Cha-no-yu of encouraging the fashion for things of no intrinsic value among his vassals the great Daimyos, for since this value was created by his own connoisseur Rikyu and soon soared to a huge extent, he found it an easy matter to reward services to himself with Tea vessels instead of fiefs in many cases, an example which Tokugawa Ieyasu and his successors were naturally very pleased to follow.†

Japanese pottery benefited greatly by the importation of both craftsmen and specimens from the continent, and the potteries founded or encouraged by Rikyu produced fine work, but at the same time the comparatively rare imported utensils came to be valued at such huge prices that the Master's dictum that the standard of criticism for these things should be only that of their fitness for the purposes of Cha-no-yu itself and should have nothing to do with rarity seemed likely to be forgotten. This tendency Kobori Masakazu did something to correct by insisting that Japanese pottery was far superior to Chinese for these utensils, and by investigating the possibilities of the material of various districts and encouraging them to produce suitable wares which he himself patronized; he was able, owing to the commanding position he occupied as Tea Master to the Shogun Iemitsu and acknowledged chief esthete of the Empire, to stimulate and maintain a powerful interest in the native craft. Moreover as the land was now at peace under the Tokugawa rule, and all the feudal lords had to spend so much time in Edo under the Sankin Kotai system, the fashion for Cha-no-yu caused them to set up kilns first in their own mansions and then in their provinces, and the

---

* The generations of the family are as follows. (1) Sōkei. (2) Chōjiro, d. 1592. (3) Jōkei, d. 1636 aet. 100, younger brother of Chōjiro. (4) Dōnyu or Nonko, d. 1658, son of Jōkei. (5) Ichinyu, d. 1697, younger brother of Dōnyu. (6) Sōnyu, d. 1725, pupil of Ichinyu. (7) Sanyu, d. 1740, adopted son of Sōnyu. (8) Chōnyu, d. 1769, younger brother of Sanyu. (9) Tokunyu, d. 1775, son of Chōnyu. (10) Ryōnyu, d. 1835, son of Tokunyu, who retired in his old age to Ishiyama and there signed his work " Gwandō Rōjin " or " The old man who plays with clay." (11) Tannyu, d. 1854, son of Ryōnyu. (12) Keinyu, d. 1893, son of Tannyu. (13) Kichizaemon.

† That these rewards were not always appreciated is evident from the story told of Matsudaira Tadanao, Lord of Echizen, who was presented with a Tea-caddy by Hidetada as a mark of appreciation of his victory in a fight at Osaka, the Shogun telling him that his exploit was worth a million koku. Tadanao called his men together and announced the receipt of the Tea-caddy to them, thanking them for their loyal help to which his success was entirely due. Unfortunately, he continued, he had nothing to give them but this piece of pottery, and since it was obviously unfair that they should not share in his prize he smashed it to pieces and offered to distribute them.

Under the Tokugawa Shoguns a gift of a Tea-caddy was only for life, and on the death of the recipient it had to be returned. And this rule sometimes applied to retirement. The treasure might be granted to the heir or it might be issued again to some other person the Shogun wished to honour. So it is with the more modern Orders of Merit, which must be sent back on the death of the possessor and cannot be sold.

rivalry that sprang up among them in the production of ware for presents to the Shogun and each other gave a further impetus to ceramics, and during this era fine work was done in all parts of the Empire, in which undoubtedly the Seven Kilns of Enshu may be regarded as pioneers.*

THE CONNOISSEURSHIP OF TEA VESSELS

Tea Masters are supposed to be connoisseurs of these things by the majority of people, perhaps, but it is not part of the real Tea Spirit to bother about questions of genuineness or otherwise, if only because it is difficult or almost impossible to do so. According to Tamaki the number of " genuine " works of Ōkyo " painted by his spirit after death " as he puts it, certified by connoisseurs, has been reckoned by some assiduous investigator as requiring an output of thirty pictures every day of the painter's life, beginning from the day that he was born. He does not give the number of those " Country Ōkyos" that are not so certified. And there may be others more copied even than Ōkyo. The same writer gives a good story of

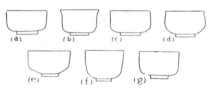

The Seven Tea-bowls of Chōjiro.
(a) Daikoku. (b) Hachi-biraki. (c) Toyobō. (d) Kōmori. (e) Hayabune. (f) Kengyo. (g) Rinzai.

another great painter who has not long been dead, Tanomura Chokunyu (d. 1908. aet. 94). While Chokunyu was living at Suma a friend brought him one of his own pictures and asked him to examine it to see if it was indeed quite right. The artist did so, and after studying it very carefully for some time, declared that it was certainly one that he had painted some years ago when he was living at Ōsaka. But this was denied by a pupil who was there with him and who was certain that it was a forgery. Chokunyu, however, maintained his opinion and pointed out that the vigour of the style as well as the colour of the medium and the correct seals all distinguished it as his own work. But when the pupil, with a smile, pointed to the date on it and asked him to consider whether that did not happen to be the time when he had been ill and unable to paint at all, the master suddenly remembered and became lost in admiration of the skill of the forger and his work, which he declared to be if anything better than he could do himself. This is not an isolated case either, for another living artist is quoted as having certified a copy as his own work. And while people buy the name rather than the work there will be no lack of really first class artists who are forced to sell under a name that happens to be the fashion in order to sell anything at all. Since it is the method

* Seven Kilns of Enshu were Shidoro in Totomi, Zeze in Omi, Agano in Buzen, Tokatori in Chikuzen, Asahi in Yamashiro, Kosobe in Settsu rnd Akahada in Yamato.

of training artists to make them copy great masters and since the subjects are conventional ones, it may not be difficult to make these copies that are so common everywhere in the country, but as Rikyu laid down, this kind of expertise is the business of the dealers who make money out of it, and not of men of taste who should not be concerned at all with the age or genuineness of a thing but only with its fitness and real beauty. Teaism is far removed from any connexion with commerce. Liability to forgery is the defect of the Japanese or Chinese painting in particular, for if it were not for the conventional subject and the desire to stick to the known beautiful treatment of a theme rather than try something new merely for the sake of seeming original, the picture or screen would not fit into its surroundings as successfully or repeat the feeling of a well-expressed esthetic conception as finely as it does. And the Japanese owner does not have the picture always before him either, so it matters even less to what period it

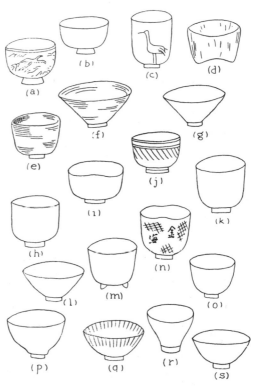

Tea-bowls.

(a) Unkaku. (b) Botode. (c) Gohon-tachizuru. (d) Korai. (e) and (f) Hakeme. (g) Ido. (h) Onte. (i) Gosho-maru. (j) Irobo. (k) Gomokai. (l) Katade. (m) Wari-kodai. (n) Kinkai. (o) Goki. (p) Totoya. (q) Koyomite. (r) Kohiki. (s) Soba.

A large Tea-bowl is used for Koi-cha and a smaller one for Usucha, while the shallow type is preferred for the summer and the deep for winter use.

really belongs. And all this applies even more forcibly to the writings that the Tea Masters love to hang in the Tea-room than to paintings, for they are if anything more difficult to criticize, and those esthetes may be wise who are content to collect the writings of their friends or of living writers who do the work before their eyes, if they wish to be quite sure of the absolute authenticity of everything they possess.

It is perhaps characteristic of the Japanese writer on this theme that he expresses sympathy with the skilful forger as a man who, unable through unlucky chance to work happily under his own name, is driven by hard necessity to sign the name of a famous artist with tears. Another unworthy side of this attitude of connoisseurship is the censoriousness of some Tea Masters well expressed by the saying, " Wait till a Tea Master gets outside your gate." (O Chajin no kado-guchi.) This kind of Chajin is ready enough with praise and compliment when he is your guest, but as soon as he is out in the street again he is as full of criticism. " This was not done properly, and that move was not right, and your Tea-bowl is a forgery and your picture not likely to be genuine, and so forth." This kind of thing shows that he does not understand the spirit of Cha-no-yu at all, for the quality and value of the utensils have nothing to do with it. It goes without saying that tea may taste as well in a bowl that cost ten sen as in one that cost a thousand yen, while the novelty is over with the first use in both cases. Moreover if you have one utensil of very great value all the rest of the equipage must match it. A Tea-bowl of great value beside a cheap Caddy would upset the balance of things and look ridiculous, for in Teaism all things should be in proportion. If one has a thousand yen to spend on tea-utensils it would be easy to get a comparatively large number of interesting and inexpensive things so that pleasure could be given to a great many guests by their variety, and at the same time to avoid any feeling of envy and covetousness that may arise when people are shown things of great value and rarity. Especially as this value was made in the first place by the skill or ingenuity of some Master in choosing them. The last thing that a Cha-no-yu meeting ought to be is an exhibition of curiosities. *The diversion and interest of the Way of Tea do not lie in the utensils but in the Way itself.* If people are always worrying themselves about the value and rarity of their utensils, Cha-no-yu is likely to become a source of annoyance rather than of pleasure. So everything should be in proportion to the means of the host. But whatever kind of material or style there should be beauty and order and cleanliness. A golden kettle if clean and in order is not necessarily wrong, for a millionaire, and in his case it is nothing to boast of. But incidentally iron is quite as beautiful as gold, and usually admits of more interesting work. And it is quite as incorrect to criticize the host's skill or want of it as it is his utensils. For Cha-no-yu is not an accomplishment like dancing or acting, but a Way of Courtesy or code of manners for receiving and entertaining guests. And if people think too much about the manner of performing the various actions they will be in danger of forgetting the real object of them. They may either be anxious about making a mistake or else be proud of making a show of their skill. What is natural is best both in utensils and behaviour.

As an old verse says;

> " *Leave it as it is*
> *Just as the woodman cuts it,*
> *The wooden lattice.*
> *For sure as it is lacquered*
> *'Twill peel and look unsightly.*"

There is a quaint story of the odd monk Ikkyu of the Daitokuji and the Tea Master Shūkō. When Shūkō went to study the Zen philosophy under him Ikkyu made tea for him, but when he took the bowl and was going to drink it, Ikkyu knocked it out of his hand with his iron Nyoi sceptre. This was too much for Shūkō, who started up from his seat, whereupon Ikkyu shouted out " Drink it up ! " Shūkō then saw the point and, quite equal to the occasion, retorted " Willows are green and flowers red." " Good," said Ikkyu, quite satisfied that the other understood. Which is, being interpreted, things must remain as they are, for the nature of phenomena cannot be changed any more than spilt tea can be drunk.

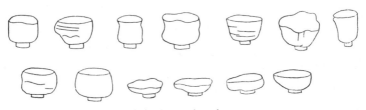

Tea-bowls of various shapes.

Teaism is often reproached with setting a standard of oddness and archaism. Brinkley's criticism is : " To it (Cha-no-yu) also must be ascribed a conservatism which cramped the genius of her artists, a false standard which confused beauty and archaism and an influence which contributed largely to the formalism that constitutes a distinct blemish in her character." But this should not be attributed to the standards of the Way itself as interpreted by its best Masters and formulated by Rikyu, but to the usual lack of enterprise and originality that cause slavish adherence to the acts or words of a Master when the reasons are imperfectly understood. For instance Tamaki Issei cites the case of the two kinds of Tea-shelves, the square and the one with rounded corners. The use of the latter arose from the Tea principle of economy, for mice having gnawed one corner of one of these shelves, the other was rounded off as well so that it could still be used and not thrown away. The people continued to make this kind purposely. The same reason underlies the use of cracked and mended utensils. It was thought better not to discard them, and from this some came to have a preference for them, hence the saying that Chajin prefer old and cracked pots and pay a lot of money for them. Again, pieces of pottery that have been accidentally damaged or misshapen in the process of firing were used for reasons of economy too, and this led to some Chajin making collections of them and caring for nothing that was not odd. But if Cha-no-yu was thus indirectly responsible for some confusion of the piquant and the eccentric, it may have at least helped to prevent that content with dull repetition of form and crude and unmeaning colour and design that characterize so much of western craft and art. And the true spirit of Cha-no-yu was never lost, though at some ages rather overlaid, as may be noted in the stories of the Chajin of various periods.

A story given in the *Sado Yokan* illustrates the pitfalls of the ardent collector. One of these saw in a curio-shop a quaint looking utensil encrusted with oyster shells and much weathered by sea-water, evidently of considerable age, and at once seized on it as a fine addition to his collection. He took it home and put it in his tokonoma with flowers arranged in it and waited for some of his friends to drop in and admire it and envy the lucky possessor. Before long one did come and he showed his find to him with great pride But the guest said nothing though his face assumed a very curious expression. The host was distinctly perplexed and after he had gone began to make investigations with the result that he discovered that his cherished flower vase was nothing but a Chinese chamber-pot.

The standard work on the connoisseurship of Tea Utensils is the *Meibutsuki* of Matsudaira Morimura, Lord of Toba and Rōju to the Shogun Yoshimune, poet and statesman, who gives in it a careful description of all the finest specimens with their history and measurements which he borrowed from the Daimyos of his day for this purpose. It was compiled between the years 1704 and 1715. He divides them into three classes, those of the Higashiyama age and the period before Rikyu, which he calls Dai-Meibutsu or Great Masterpieces, those of the time of Rikyu which are styled Meibutsu or Masterpieces, and those selected after this era by Kobori Enshu, which are described as Chuko Meibutsu or Masterpieces of the Revival or later period. Matsudaira Fumai, Lord of Izumo, was the first to catalogue Tea-caddies correctly under the heads of Dai-Meibutsu and Chuko Meibutsu.

There had been classifications before this, for in the Higashi-yama era Sōami made a catalogue of Chinese utensils called *Gundai Kensa Sōchō*, and later on in the Momoyama period Yamagami Sōji, Tea Master to Takeda Shingen made another called *Chaki Meibutsu-shu* containing the names of Writings, Tea-caddies and Tea-jars. Sōji was a contemporary and pupil of Rikyu, and got his nose cut off and was exiled because he made the careless blunder of confusing Formal and Informal when serving Tea to Hideyoshi.

Kobori Enshu's work was styled *Enshu Goshu Juhappin*, or Collection of Eighteen Classes, and contained descriptions illustrations and measurements of Tea-caddies of Japanese make divided in this way. Most of the great Meibutsu still surviving come from the collection made by Hideyoshi, to whom to a large extent their preservation is therefore due. Had he not been such a lover of Tea it is possible that many of them might have been lost instead of passing directly from his hands into those of the Tokugawas and their great vassals. After the fall of Osaka castle many Tea-caddies were raked out of its ashes, among them the famous Tsukumo Nasu, one of the greatest treasures of the Empire. " Hideyoshi may indeed be regarded as the tutelary deity of Teaism since without his support and patronage it might not have been so easy for the age to produce so great a master as Rikyu." (Takahashi.) One might add that Hideyoshi knew not only how to produce him but also how to make an appropriate end of him.

FURUTA ORIBE AND KOBORI ENSHU

These two masters have had more influence on Teaism perhaps than anyone else after Rikyu, the former being the teacher of the latter.

Furuta Shigeyoshi was the son of one Shigesada, called also Kan-ami who was in the service of Hideyoshi and was fond of Tea-ceremony. He had been a priest originally, but returned to the world and was given an income of thirty koku by Hideyoshi and the title of Gemba-no-sho. His son Shigenari became a pupil of Rikyu and also entered the service of the Taiko after his father's death, being given the title of Oribe-no-sho and succeeding Rikyu as Chief Tea Master. He continued the simple and severe style of Rikyu as well as he could, perhaps, but the times had changed and the country had become less dominated by the stern simplicity that was inevitable when the daimyos and their retainers spent so much of their time in the field. But their jealousies were as active as ever, and there was as much need of the Tea-spirit to soften their asperities as before. Still Oribe was hardly the character to lead such an endeavour, and the Way of Tea was probably not much the loser when he and a group of friends were " granted death " by Ieyasu as a reward for an attempt at revolt in the Summer Campaign before Osaka in 1615. The reason for this rebellion is said to have been the irritation of Oribe at an acid but well-deserved criticism by Ieyasu of his rather childish behaviour in the field. As a critic observes, " Oribe may have been learned in the Way of Tea, but he had little knowledge of the Way of the Warrior and none at all of that of Common Sense." (Sado ni akiraka naredomo, Budo ni utoku, Jindo ni kurashi.)

After the death of Oribe his place as Supreme Tea Master was taken by Kobori Totomi-no-kami Masakazu, usually known as Kobori Enshu. His father Kobori Masatsugu of Omi held the office of Bugyu of Fushimi, and the son took service under Ieyasu and received a fief of 10,000 koku in Totomi and the lower fifth Court Rank. His *nom-de-plume* was Sōhō. He was a good poet, painter and calligraphist and a great friend of the artist Takimoto Shokwado, and was also famous for his skill in flower-arrangement, one of the schools of which is called after him. He retired in his latter days to a hut which he built at Murasakino and died in 1648 at the age of sixty-nine. Like Oribe, Kobori Enshu did not depart from the tradition of Rikyu. But the country had now settled down under the Tokugawa rule and tendencies in the direction of luxury and convention began to show themselves so that he could not follow Rikyu as closely as he wished. But he was very emphatic in his denial of any inclination to break away from the teachings of the Master or found a new school. "Rikyu was the founder of Teaism," he said, in answer to the criticism that his teaching was different, "and as long as there are devotees of Cha-no-yu they will follow him. If any do not they will be wrong. Even his writings are not inferior to those of the great Zen Masters. There may of course arise some little variation in the details of tea-room and utensils, as, for instance, though the pillars of a room remain unchanged the position of the windows and doors and the style of the walls may be slightly altered. But such progress is not only found in Tea but in everything. Rikyu came at exactly the right time, and set the limits of the way of Tea precisely where they should be, in order to keep this Way undefield, and this he did by the authority of his own genius. As for people like Oribe and myself, we are by no means able to attain to this. All we can do is to associate ourselves with all sorts and conditions of people on terms of equality and try to lead them in the way of good taste, using the general principles of the Tea-room and Rōji as temporary expedients, for we are military men first of all and our lives are at the mercy of any hazard. We hope that we follow our master Rikyu, and can only feel ashamed when critics say that other teachers do differently. But in having no originality we must expect to be regarded as different from Rikyu."

On another occasion the same critic (Tachibanaya Sogen) observed that the judgment of Enshu might perhaps be superior to that of Rikyu, since everyone agreed that the things that Enshu praised were good, whereas opinions differed about the things that Rikyu favoured. "That may seem a compliment to me," replied Enshu, "but in fact it is only an ignorant view. Rikyu decided that certain vessels were interesting and beautiful and satisfying on his own initiative and authority, and used them for Cha-no-yu and gave names to them, and his judgment was not only accepted in his day but is still praised as a criterion. This is because of Rikyu's great merit as a Tea Master, and not because of the age or value of the vessels. Articles that are so transformed by virtue of the Master's praise are famous and precious indeed. But as for me I don't possess the capacity of giving real value to anything on the authority of my own taste. When noblemen bring things to me and ask for an opinion I don't care to offend them and so am inclined to say what they like to hear. But this kind of consideration of people's feelings is not in accordance with the best traditions of Tea. There is a difference of Heaven and Earth between Rikyu's lofty principles and mine."

So Enshu, the last of the Five Great Masters was responsible, partly through the influence of his master Iemitsu, for a return to the originally rather plutocratic Shōin style of Teaism. In this he was consistently opposed by Sen Sōtan who carried on the simple Rikyu tradition of the house in Kyoto, and these two styles have continued to the present day and still exist. But it is to be noted that, since the Enshu style was that in favour with the Daimyos and military class generally, the greater number of famous Tea-rooms and gardens that have come down to us are of this type and those representing the Sōan style are comparatively few. They may, of course, be seen in the houses of Sen which have never altered.

THE RETIRED LIFE

The inclination for a life of retirement was partly the product of the fierce struggles of the military class for material advantages and posthumous glory. Their contempt for life and readiness to throw it away in the pursuit of domination or a splendid memory led to an emphasizing of its vanity and transitoriness through the vicissitudes and tragedies thus evoked. And the result of this was the development on one hand of a greedy instinct to make the most of every opportunity for material enjoyment while it lasted, and on the other of a desire to escape from the ruthless struggle and lead a secluded life devoted to literary diversions and the meditative pleasures of nature.

This custom of retirement had been in existence ever since Buddhism was introduced into Japan, inspired by the contempt of this world of impermanence taught by its philosophy. The " Shukke " or hermit is a familiar figure in the middle ages of Japan and is represented in literature by the well known works of Kamo no Chōmei and Yoshida Kenko, the *Hōjōki* and the *Tsure-zure Gusa,* of the twelfth and the thirteenth centuries as well as by the writings of Saigyo Hōshi. The Kyogen or Comic Interludes know him well too, for there he is often held up to ridicule. Not unnaturally it became the fashion for poets and literary men to retire from the world, and when so recognised it became a regular way of making a living, and did not prevent them from enjoying some of the solaces of society either, for unlike the earlier " Shukke " these amateur recluses were not always unaccompanied by wife or family. In fact, since they were separated from society only in so far as they were not reckoned as belonging to any particular stratum of it, they were free to mix with people of all ranks from the lowest to the highest, and sometimes even penetrated to the forbidden precincts of the Imperial Court, as in the case of Botanka Shōhaku.

And no doubt this would be as refreshing to the noble of high degree, thus set free to mix with less conventional characters than those found among the aristocracy, as it would be to the commoner also able to meet interesting people otherwise debarred from his society.

As time went on these dilettanti recluses lost their Buddhist inspiration and came more under the influence of Chinese feeling as set forth in the Taoist idea of the hermit or "Sennin" familiar to Japanese scholars from the pages of Lao-tz' and Chuang-tz'. They did not regard the world as impermament and evil in theory, but rather wished to be free from the bonds of society and its competition and wander at leisure among the beauties of nature.

Thus there came to be a type of recluse who, while not actually separating himself from society, thought little of it, and refused to take either it or himself seriously. They liked to pose as hermits or pilgrims to a certain extent, and to divert themselves by reading poetry and the classics and visiting famous scenes.

It was in the same spirit that people took to Cha-no-yu. It was a way of abstracting themselves for a while from the bother and stress of everyday life. It was becoming a recluse for an hour or two, and though it may owe its simplicity to its plebeian associations, (i.e. when reformed by Rikyu) when it became a convention and an art, this art was one of simplicity and rusticity to which the use of the words "Wabi" solitary, and "Sabi" mellow by use, bear witness.

The changes and upheavals that accompanied the beginning of the Tokugawa era again emphasized the desire for retirement among many who were disappointed in their expectations of rank and property and who were otherwise embittered by failure. A good example is Kinoshita Katsutoshi (1568-1649) Lord of Wakasa, 80,000 koku, one of Hideyoshi's captains, who was dispossessed by Ieyasu for fighting against him and retired to Kyoto and took the name of Chōshō, devoting himself to poetry and literature. His work *Higashi-yama Sangeki* is modelled on the *Hōjōki* of Kamo Chōmei, but it is noticeable that now it is a Chinese flavour that it exhibits and not a Buddhist, i.e. instead of volumes of the *Ōjō-shu*, a Buddhist collection, he speaks of having the anthology of *Tō-sha-ryo*, and instead of the "origoto" and "tsugibiwa" the musical instruments patronised by Chōmei, he has a "Koto" in reference apparently to the "Stringless Koto" of Emmei.

Since the revival of the study of Chinese literature and philosophy was a characteristic of this period, for Fujiwara Seikwa had introduced the Sung philosophy which was to become the official school under his pupil Hayashi Razan, the outlook on nature of the retired man of the day became exceedingly Sinicised and he saw and described Japanese scenery almost entirely through Chinese spectacles, and this literary view of ordinary life became a further assistance in separating him from the mundane affairs that surrounded him. Lao-tz' and Chuang-tz' were no less popular than before, and the early Tokugawa Japanese recluse liked to fancy himself a kind of Taoist Rishi or Chao Fu (a legendary Chinese hermit who retired and lived in a tree to be aloof from the world) rather than a Buddhist S'ramanera as had formerly been the case.

However, these recluses came to find out that retiring did not relieve them of their own personality, and since it was peace of mind they sought, it was necessary to find some means of transcending their own ego or they could not attain it. This being so, it would

be as easy to transcend oneself in the world as out of it, because
the real cause of the unquiet mind is not the environment itself but
the attachment to phenomena leading to regret and sorrow at changes
in them.

But it is as easy to be attached to a hut in the wilderness as
to anything else, as Chōmei observes in the Hōjōki, or to the literary
life of a Chinese hermit.   In fact poetry and literature and all the
other affectations may be regarded as only further incitements to
attachment.   Moreover one needed a certain amount of leisure and
means for life even in the wilderness, and so it was largely people
who did not need to get their living who practised it.   It was
a kind of luxury, and people who could not afford it had to
remain in the world willy nilly.   They were then faced with the
necessity of attaining this peace of mind in ordinary life, and if this
could be accomplished then there was no need for any one to shun
the world at all.   But temperamentally people in Japan were inclined
to look on the world as a vale of tears owing to the severe struggle
for life in it, and this view had been reinforced by Buddhist and
Chinese thought so they could not bring themselves to regard their
duty in life as ordained from on high and to look on the fulfilment
of it as a source of happiness.   Some praised a wandering life like
that of the beggar Rakuami, a mendicant flute player who is the
hero of one of the Kyogen, as the ideal, while others thought to
amuse themselves with the changing aspect of the seasons.   But since
they could not get away from the incidents of everyday life they had
to adopt a casual attitude in regard to them, if they wished to avoid
being involved in anxiety, and ended in adopting a point of view
that refused to take anything seriously.   And so they lived their
ordinary life with the mind of a recluse, but a somewhat humorous
one.

So, like the mendicant Rakuami in the *Tokaido Meishoki*,
wandering along the busy highway, looking into the houses, listening
to the out-of-tune flute playing of the blind minstrels, and strolling
about the quarters of the dancers and strumpets, they found a
whimsical sort of interest in all the varied phenomena of life, letting
themselves be moved to sadness or amusement or anger or fear or
regret as the case might be, but soon passing on and forgetting it
all in the next mild sensation, and all the while looking on themselves as odd sort of creatures not to be taken seriously.   " This
fleeting world is nothing but a puppet show," as Sōin puts it.   And
this spirit forms a considerable element in the Japanese character.
It was a very convenient one too in the Tokugawa age, when society
was so rigidly ordered that failures and non-conforming spirits had
a hard time and had perforce to seek solace in some such philosophy.

Then again, this world of strife for place and power tended to
be a materialistic one and was so stigmatized by the satiric thinkers.
" Love is a dirty sort of business," " Man is nothing but an animal
who eats his way through life."   And it seemed doubly funny that
people should be so blind as to think these dirty and commonplace
things fair and splendid and worth striving for.   Strip men of their

fine clothes and ceremonial deportment and how ridiculous they were! This is a view that the Haikaishi continually reveal in their epigrams. But people with these views were not ordinary of course,—for the average man was content as elsewhere to go on grovelling,—but sophisticated and sensitive men of letters, and for some reason or other it never occurred to them to try and improve matters. They were content either to spurn the world and to go into retirement or to remain in it with a sardonic smile. As for the average man of the military class, he made the best of it. He would have as merry a time as he could while it lasted, for he never knew when he might be called on to die. And this reckless disposition did not change in a time of peace such as was the age of Tokugawa. And it is this view of life that produced the expression " Ukiyo " " This fleeting World " that we hear so often in the West nowadays in connexion with Art and Colour Prints, with all that it implied of reckless gaiety and enjoyment. The words " Ukiyo-no-suke," " Ukiyo-bo " and " Ukiyo-jin " were coined to designate one who was typical of this spirit. Hence the words " Ukiyo Monogatari " or " Tales of this Fleeting World," Ukiyogurui " Fleeting World Madness," " Ukiyo-asobi " " Fleeting World Dalliance," " Ukiyo-bushi " " Fleeting World Songs," " Ukiyo-kōji " " Fleeting World Lane," and many other such terms characteristic of the literature of the Kwambun and Genroku periods (late 17th and early 18th century), while it followed that Ukiyo-e were the pictures that illustrated this transient world of dance and song and revel. This expression thus means more than merely genre pictures. It signifies a world of lurid enjoyment snatched wildly against a black and threatening background.

> " *Consoling ourselves with drinking and dancing,*
> *it is but for a moment :*
> *What does it matter if we spend our all?*
> *An inch before us is the darkness.*
> *We are like a gourd bobbing up and down on the water.*"

> " *With this wretched body of five feet odd,*
> *Let us enjoy the moon while we may.*
> *An inch before us is nought but blackness.*"

Ko-kon I-kyoku-shu.

Man cannot go any farther. This fleeting world is but a temporary lodging. This spirit is just the opposite of the older Buddhist view of the world as a place to be avoided with all its delights, for it is nothing but a determination to enjoy all material pleasures to the utmost instead of fleeing from them. But the sense of sadness is not lost. " In all amusement there is sadness." " A perilous thing is this life of ours " ; are characteristic expressions of its devotees. The Japanese could not be thorough-going materialists it seems. It was the ineradicable legacy of their long history of upheaval and strife and calamity.

DAZAI JUN ON CHA-NO-YU*

When you offer anyone tea you gather in a little hut only six feet square. The meal is not allowed to be served by others, the host must do it himself. And he pours out the liquor and rinses out and wipes the cups when it is drunk, and puts them away. When they have finished this light meal they go out and rinse their mouths and after a while come in again, when the host makes tea with his own hands and serves it to them. It is made in one bowl and the chief guest takes a sip and passes it to the second and so the three, or it may be four, of them drink it, the last one drinking up all there is left. The Tea-bowl is then handed to the chief guest who takes it and examines it carefully and praises its admirable make, after which he hands it to the next, who passes it on to the last, and he hands it back the host. Then all the guests together return thanks and bow. They then ask to see the bag of the Tea-bowl and then the Tea-caddy and its bag and after that the Tea-spoon, and though they may be nothing out of the ordinary it is the correct thing to ask to be permitted to examine them. And since there is a proper way to arrange the ashes in the hearth the guests approach and examine this too, and of course praise the elegance of it all. And so too when the host arranges flowers in the vase. In fact everything the host does they inspect and then praise. It seems the extreme of flattery. As to the style of the Tea-room, it is now rather smaller than the traditional dimensions of the cell of the recluse Vimalakirti, and as the windows are small too it does not get much light. In summer it is extremely hot, and the aperture through which the guests enter is like that of a dog-kennel and they have to wriggle in through it. The room is stuffy and equally unbearable in winter. As to the meal one gets on these occasions, since the host has taken so much trouble about it the guest must eat everything up whether it is to his taste or not, and that is rather an infliction, I think it a shame too to praise utensils that are quite ordinary as if they were rarities. And though it is well that tasteful people should like their house and furniture to be elegant and wish to avoid monotony and symmetry, yet Tea Masters seem to me to go to an extreme in making the pillars of their rooms so small and the frames of their shoji so slight that they look as though they would blow away. And these pillars and the beams of the rooms are always of natural wood with the bark on and oddly shaped and crooked. In everything they like to make an appearance of poverty and scantiness.

In our country the monks of the Five Temples of the Zen Sect brought Tea from China in the Kamakura age, and it seems to have become known to some extent, but hardly very fashionable. It was not till the Muromachi Shogun Yoshimasa took a fancy to it and

---

* Dazai Jun was a famous Confucian scholar, pupil of Ogyu Sorai and author of many works. He died in 1747 aet. 67.

The Confucians were on the side of pedagoguery and disliked the neglect of social distinctions practised by the Tea lovers. Their point of view was that of the English Classical Scholar who declared that "a knowledge of Latin and Greek not only raises one above the common herd but not infrequently leads to positions of considerable emolument."

made it his chief diversion at all hours, and had his Cha-no-yu parties
in the Ginkakuji, that it became the rage. But Yoshimasa was by
temperament luxurious and his Tea-room and its appurtenances were
like him, very ornate and elaborate, whereas the present-day Chajin
looks to Rikyu as his model. Rikyu was a Zen priest and inculcated
simplicity and economy in everything, and his Tea-room was a tiny
thatched hut, and he induced the great nobles to leave their lofty
halls and find it pleasant to meet their friends in this little room
and there make tea with their own hands. And it was because of
this Zen feeling that they disliked rich food and any elaboration, and
kept all the utensils and furniture rough and simple.

Now there may be a reason for the wealthy thus amusing themselves by imitating the poor. But what pleasure can the really poor
find in imitating those who are still poorer? It does not seem to
me at all wise of the rich to invite the poor to take tea with them
merely as an amusement.

Personally I think tea is well enough served after a good meal
and in a spacious room, in separate cups and with new utensils. I
would keep it in caddies of modern ware or in lacquer containers
or boxes made of silver or tin. And I prefer a silver tea-spoon.
The Way of Tea seems to me rather an objectionable one.—*Doku-go*.

A CRITICISM OF CHA-NO-YU FROM THE "KOKORO-NO-SOSHI" OF MATSUDAIRA SADANOBU[*]

Making Tea is a very worshipful performance, I can tell you.
The host invites his guests and comes to meet them with an important
and knowing air. Then it is " This scroll is by Kyōdō. I gave a
huge sum for it. This kettle is an Ashiya. It cost me I don't know
how much. This Tea-bowl was picked up cheap it is true, but I
don't suppose there is another like it. And as I am an adept at
the Zen philosophy, why should I need a famous teacher? You just
take a little tea, and ladle up the water,—so—and then put it into
the kettle—and it will croon its pine-breeze song, and a wonderful
peace steals over you, and over your guests too—if they are the
right sort of people."

Chajin are liable to a number of complaints such as blindness,
a slandering tongue, curio-mania, garden-mania, building-mania, swelled
head, sycophancy, argumentativeness, over-eating and drinking, obsession with technique and cleanliness, stinginess, introversion, covetousness and dilettantism.—Tanaka Sensho, *Chazen Ichimi*.

OBSERVATIONS OF MATSUDAIRA FUMAI[†] ON CHA-NO-YU

" People may ridicule Tea Masters and say that they only care
for what is odd and crooked, and are always looking for old crocks
and spend a lot of money on some curious utensil that they then

---

[*] Matsudaira Sadanobu (1758–1829) one of the greatest statesmen of Tokugawa days, was
minister to the Shogun Ienari. An able administrator and economist, he was also an author,
and is well known as Gaku-ō, the name he took on retirement in 1812.
[†] Matsudaira Fumai Harusato, lord of the province of Izumo, flourished c. 1800, the most
famous Chajin of his day.

proceed to use for making Tea. But the fact is that there is a very good reason for using old Tea-bowls and utensils. When vessels of pottery and lacquer are new they have an earthy or lacquery taste which must disappear with use before tea made with them gives out its proper taste. As to the extravagance of spending money on these things, well, all man wants is food and furniture and utensils, and they do not fall from heaven or well out of the ground, and if his expenditure is according to his means there is nothing to complain about. Only Tea must not be allowed to degenerate into a mere display of curios and so encourage a spirit of covetousness that is entirely alien from its true meaning.

" Teaism means contentment. The art of being contented with the unsatisfying. So it was that Rikyu said that it began in luxury in the days of Ashikaga Yoshimasa and continued more or less as a kind of ostentation even to his time, so he reformed it and instituted Wabi-no-Cha-no-yu or Austere Teaism. One may call Cha-no-yu a kind of Hōben or Pious Device for securing this contentment through the use of discrimination or fastidiousness. Because one must have the discrimination to enjoy making tea in an atmosphere of the severest simplicity, using only bare necessities. So to live contentedly and joyfully with bare necessities is Teaism. We may go so far as to say that one who cannot do this is not a man at all. I fear there are more who understand the form of Cha-no-yu than its inner spirit. Fewer still, perhaps, who, understanding this, carry it into their everyday life as they should do. There may be scarcely one in ten thousand. Those who keep their Teaism for the Tea-room only are not properly educated in it. For what is a Tea-room but a shelter from the rain? Those who cannot practise Cha-no-yu without requiring any other reason for enjoying it than the thing itself should give it up."

THE TEA MAXIMS OF NAMBŌ SŌKEI AND RIKYU

The guests shall assemble in the waiting place and when all are ready shall announce their arrival by striking a board.

As to ablutions, the most essential thing in the Way of Tea is that the mind shall be cleansed of all ill-feeling.

The host shall come out and greet the guests, after which they shall enter the Tea-room. If the host is not wealthy and so the utensils are not all they might be and the food is not specially good and the trees and stones in the Rōji just natural, those who cannot appreciate such simple things had better leave at once.

When the water boils audibly like the sound of the breeze in the pines a bell is rung and the guests come in again. If the heat of the fire and of the water are not as they should be it is very reprehensible. Both outside and inside the Tea-room there must be no ordinary tittle-tattle.

The meeting is one of host and guests, so there is no need of flattery. The meeting should not be longer than two hours, but an exception may be made if there is some lofty philosophical discussion.

TEA MAXIMS OF HOSOKAWA TADAOKI

To enter the Nijiri one puts in one's hand and then one's head, and bends down and, kneeling on one knee, slips in sideways.

When the guests have entered the Tea-room they should be silent. If they babble or whisper the host may be embarrassed. Neither should they peep into the cupboard (Dōkō) if there is one.

The most experienced of the guests replies to the host's greeting, and all bow. Those who are inexperienced should say nothing, but must not look awkward or bored. Their demeanour should be natural and self-possessed.

It is the chief guest who praises the utensils and style of the Tea-room. The younger people had better be quiet and look admiring. If the host tells a story or holds forth, even if he is wordy, one must keep one's mind taut as a drawn bow, and sit up with a straight back, not letting it touch the wall behind, and of course showing no sign of impatience in one's face.

The Menu of the Kaiseki should be only soup, two or three dishes of vegetables and Saké. It is unsuitable to the surroundings to have more. Rice cake, bean jelly, cooked chestnuts, boiled mushrooms and so on may be used as side dishes.

THE TEA MAXIMS OF KURODA JŌSUI. WRITTEN UP IN HIS MIZUYA

When you grind tea do so very quietly and carefully and yet not too slowly.

Wash the Tea-bowls and other utensils often so that no dirt may cling to them.

If you take one ladleful of hot water from the Kettle take great care to replace it by another, and so make up for what is lost. Never use it up without replenishing.

These Maxims are not of a school of my own, but are from Rikyu, and so should be observed. Most people are merely careless when they think they are calm, and fussy when they consider themselves expeditious. But everyone can only act according to the capacity that is in him, and though a man's duty may be plain, yet the impurity of covetousness will quickly defile him. And one receives great kindness from parents and superiors in the first place, and then from colleagues and retainers, and if anyone neglects to repay this he will incur the punishment of heaven.

So that I may think of these three maxims every morning and evening when I make my tea I have written them up here.

Keicho 4th year, 1st month. (1600)

JŌSUI.

Be very careful to observe these.

OBITER DICTA OF KOBORI ENSHU

Cha-no-yu is nothing but Loyalty and Filial Piety, doing good work and minding your own business, and particularly keeping on good terms with your old friends. In spring the shelving mists, in summer the cuckoo lurking in the green foliage, in autumn the evening sky with its feeling of solitude, in winter the snow of early dawn, all these things are the essence of Teaism. And don't trouble yourself about rare utensils. Famous antiques are nothing in particular. They were new enough once, and it is only their survival till now that makes them antique. If antiques are ugly they are no use, while new utensils of beautiful form should not be despised. Don't envy people because they have a large number of these things, or be discontented because you have few. You can get the greatest enjoyment out of using even one utensil, and hand it down to your descendants into the bargain. And as to food, even a plain bowl of rice will taste delicious if the host serves it with real cordiality, while the most delicate trout or carp will not please without it. So sitting all day long in the Tea-room with its dewy fence and twining creepers we must quietly await a guest, only taking care that the pine-breeze crooning of the kettle never ceases.

> *Though there be no flowers*
> *Though there be no straw-thatched hut,*
> *Though there be no sea,*
> *Quite a satisfying view*
> *Is the Rōji's evening calm.**

THE MAXIMS OF KOBORI ENSHU

The hearth must never be stepped over.

If anyone goes out of the room he must do it so that it is audible in the next room.

Should there be a large number of guests in a small room there is no objection to the chief guest sitting in the Tokonoma, or the last one in the entrance of the Mizuya.

THE WALL MAXIMS OF KARASU MARU MITSUHIRO[†]

If you keep calm and untroubled by anything in creation, making your friends of the flowers of springtime and the tints of autumn, and taking a drop of liquor when you feel inclined, you need not regard the world as such a bad place. Just sit down quietly and arrange a flower or two, burn a stick of good incense and sip a cup of fine tea, with some old books for company; and if a congenial friend does happen to drop in, you may find it very comforting to

---

* *Hana momiji*
Tomaya mo ura mo
Nakari keri,
Tada mi-wataseba
Rōji no yugure.—Sōkei.
The reference is to the famous verse of Teika quoted below,
Mi-wataseba
Hana mo momiji mo
Nakari keri
Ura no tomaya no
Aki no yugure.

† Karasu Maru Mitsuhiro. Died 1639. A court noble and one of the greatest literary men of his time. Pupil of Hosokawa Yusai for Japanese verse. Rose to be Gon-dainagon of the second rank.

chat with him about all sorts of people from ancient times to the present day. Some say this kind of life is best achieved by retiring to the hills, but however far away you live you will find no peace of mind if you still harbour egoistic thoughts of honour and profit. So you may just as well live right in the middle of the city without changing your style or choosing any particular locality. Monk as monk, and layman as layman, the flowers are bright and the willow is green.

> *Whether you are enlightened or not,*
> *If you regard the mind of all things as the same,*
> *Things are quite well as they are.*

WALL MAXIMS OF THE ZEN PRIEST TAKUAN OSHŌ*

Why does one eat? Merely to satisfy hunger. If one is not hungry there is no need to eat. People have got into the bad habit of saying that they cannot eat unless food is made tasty. This is nothing but a device for preventing hunger. Eating is not a business, and if people cannot dispense with a relish with their food it is simply because they are not hungry. If people were not hungry they would never need to eat at all, and if anyone is really hungry he won't refuse bran much less rice. As Buddha has said " Take food like medicine. What need is there of relish."

THE TEA MAXIMS OF MATSUDAIRA FUMAI

The characteristics of Cha-no-yu should be quiet, reticence and dignity. As to the choice of a picture, it is best to pick one straight off without a lot of fuss and consideration

Skill in Cha-no-yu consists in making guests enjoy themselves. Expertise in serving tea consists in doing it so that there is nothing to notice.

As to the placing of the utensils, care is all it needs.

In the Kaiseki it is only necessary that there should be nothing uneatable. Do not neglect an opportunity for a Cha-no-yu on a snowy morning. Cha-no-yu is like the bamboos dripping with rain. It is like the pine-trees laden with snow.

> *When the land is bare,*
> *And the fields are colourless,*
> *Then the view is best.*
> *Better than the autumn tints*
> *Is this lack of colour scheme.*

The garden of the Yu-in is the best model.

The host should take it for granted that the guests are less expert than himself.

The flowers that are best at twilight are the wistaria and the bottle-gourd, at night the white plum-blossom, and in the morning

---

* Famous as Takuan Oshō was in his day, his name is now only known to the average Japanese as a synonym for the pickled radish he used as a relish for his rice, and which the Zen master is said to have invented.

the convolvulus and the lotus.   For midday there are any number. Only those are acceptable that are known to everyone and that all the poets have sung.   Very artless are those from the kitchen-garden.

To insist too much on the exactly seasonable is a nuisance.

To study to please one's guests is well but to appear to do so is not.

THE TEA MAXIMS OF MATSUDAIRA NARITADA*

In Tea the host is simplicity and the guest elegance.   If all is done in sincerity it is better than a thousand graces.

Two evil things are to force on others what you like yourself, and decry other people's ideas and laud your own.

It is very delightful to hear the naturally elegant words of able people, and just as objectionable to experience the pretentious talk of the would-be clever.

Decent people do not dislike the prosperous and do not speak nothing but ill of them, or envy the wealthy and estimate their possessions and behave in a flattering or boastful manner.   And they don't tell you how they bought some valuable thing cheap or paid a lot for something qnite ordinary.

Though we may like pictures and utensils, if we go to excess we shall lose our will-power.

Don't fancy flowers and things to eat out of their proper season, or like anything because it is different.   This applies to utensils too. In all things that which is without sham and untruth is to be sought.

Natural elegance is the real elegance.   Striving after tastefulness is a sign of a nature shallow as a mountain well.

As I listen to the wind in the pines and sing to the moon under the eaves and try to gain enlightenment I have put down what has come into my mind for my own discipline and instruction.

THE RULES OF ZUIHŌSAI ISSOKU

Tamaki Issei gives a set of instructions drawn up for pupils by his ancestor Zuihōsai Issoku three generations back.

1.   In the Way of Tea man does not live to divert himself with food and clothes alone, but by the principle of Harmony, Reverence, Purity and Calm.

2.   Strive always to cultivate a delicate and fastidious taste.

3.   If you do not develop adroitness of mind and tact you are not likely to be able to utilize the teaching of the Way.

4.   The cleverness of this Way lies in adaptation to circumstances. Let there be no rivalry between different schools.†

---

* Matsudaira Naritada, or Tayasu Chunagon Naritada.   Of the Tayasu branch of the Tokugawa family (Sankyo) contemporary of Ii Naosuke in the 19th century.
   † Tea Masters who know only their own school and take no heed of any other, and who make their pupils buy utensils at a high price because they are indispensable to their style, whereas they could do as well without them, are a great nuisance and no better than curio dealers.—*Umpei Zasshi.*

5. The object of the Way is the appreciation of the charm of applying natural things in a dignified design.
6. The host must strive to give his guest pleasure by his deportment and by the seemly order of things.
7. The guest must fully realize the pains taken by the host, and try to give him as little trouble as possible. The ideal relation between them is a mutual understanding and appreciation that needs no words to express.
8. If both host and guests have the proper understanding they should carry out everything successfully. But this is not easy without both care and study.
9. In case of a sudden hitch or anything happening unexpectedly, if one has not the wit to meet the situation some confusion may be caused, so one should not overlook the most trifling possibility.
10. There have always been jokes against Cha-no-yu, and indeed some of its devotees invite ridicule by their want of tact and wit.

   The above should be carefully borne in mind.

   First month of second year of Bunkyu. (1862)

   ZUIHŌSAI ISSOKU.

An interesting contemporary account of a Cha-no-yu of the time of Hideyoshi is given by the able Jesuit missionary Father Luis Frois* in his *History of Japan*, as follows :

" Among distinguished and wealthy Japanese it is the custom that, if they wish to show especial favour to a guest, they bring out their particular treasures for him to see before his departure. These are the utensils and necessary articles for drinking a certain powdered herb called Cha, which is not only agreeable to the taste of those who are used to it, but also good for their health. And all the utensils needed for this are as it were the jewellery of the Japanese, regarded just as rings, gems, fine necklaces, pearls, rubies and diamonds are with us. And there are also jewellers among them who are very experienced in their knowledge of these things and their value, and who act as agents in buying and selling them, appraising them according to either their material, their shape or their antiquity. So when they invite you to partake of this herb, and the best quality costs some nine or ten cruzados the pound, and show you their famous treasures, they first of all give you a banquet according to their means. And the place where this is done is a special room that is used only for these solemnities, and the cleanliness, good disposition and order of everything is wonderful.

" Now the next day at nine in the morning they sent a messenger for me and I went with a Japanese Brother and another, a wealthy man and a good Christian, who looked after all our affairs, called Cosme Kōzen. We were led along by the side of the living-rooms and then through a little door just big enough for one person to

* Luis Frois, *Geschichte Japans*, ed. Schurhammer and Voretsch. 2. 369.

enter easily. Then through a straight narrow corridor and up a flight of steps made of cedar, that gave one the impression that it was the first time anyone had ever trodden there, and everything of such perfect workmanship that it was impossible to describe it. We then reached a court and then a wider corridor giving on to a room where we were to be served with a meal. It was little larger than the court and to my eyes appeared very remarkable. On one side of it was a sort of cupboard as is usual here, and immediately beside this was a hearth of black colour about a yard in circumference, that shone like the brightest mirror, strange to say, in spite of its pitch-black hue. On it there stood a kettle of pleasing shape on a very beautiful tripod. The ashes on which the glowing charcoal lay looked like finely ground and sifted eggshells. Everything was exquisitely clean and set out with such order as to be beyond description, and this is not perhaps so remarkable seeing that on these occasions they concentrate their attention only on these things. The charcoal is not that which is generally used, but is brought from a long distance and cut up with a handsaw in such a manner that it kindles very quickly and so continues for a long while without going out or emitting smoke. The kettle, so one of my companions told me, Diogo our host had bought by a very fortunate chance for six hundred cruzados, but its value was much greater.

"We sat down on the painfully clean mats that had a surface of the finest texture, and then they began to bring in the food. I don't recommend this food at all, for Japan is a very sterile land, but the service, the order, the cleanliness and the utensils were all worthy of admiration. And I consider it absolutely certain that nowhere can a meal be served with such spotless cleanliness or better order and etiquette than in Japan. So also when there are many people at a meal you do not hear a single word from those who serve it, but all goes off so smoothly and correctly that it is astonishing.

"After the meal we knelt down and thanked our Lord God that the Japanese Christians had such good customs. Then Diogo prepared the Tea and served it with his own hands. This is the powder I spoke of, and it is put into a porcelain vessel with hot water. Then he showed me among many other treasures that he had there a tripod, little more than a span round, on which he placed the lid of the kettle when he took it off. I took it in my hand. It was of iron, and so worn with age in many places that it showed signs of having broken through and been repaired in two. He told me it was one of the most valuable tripods in Japan, and very famous, and that it had cost him a thousand and thirty cruzados but he considered it worth more. All these utensils are kept in fine bags of silk and brocade, each in its own box. He told me that he had more of these treasures, but could not show them now as they were stored away in a place where it was not easy to get at them, but that he would show us them if we came again. However the value of these things is not so remarkable, for there is in Miyako a lord named Sōtai (Matsunaga Hisahide) who has a vessel of pottery no bigger than a pomegranate that is used for this powder-

tea, which is said to be worth twenty-five or thirty thousand cruzados.
It is called Kukumugami.* I don't say it could be sold for so much,
but it is quite likely some Prince might give ten thousand for it.
For there are many of these utensils worth from three to ten thousand
cruzados, and they are quite often bought and sold.   But they are
not sold in any public place, for then they would fetch nothing.   One
must go to the owner and ask him with much ceremony whether he
will be so gracious as to sell the vessel.   And these people consider
some swords as equally valuable.

MASS CELEBRATED IN A TEA-ROOM

"At this time, while Nobunaga was in Miyako, an uncle of the
King of Mikawa (Tokugawa Ieyasu), a Captain of three thousand
men, had taken up his quarters in our church, so that the Father
could no longer stop in it.   So he went to live in the house of an
old Christian, a man of some consequence named So-i Antao, and
there stayed a hundred and twenty days.   The Father felt great
affection for him and his sons, and he on his part, to give the
Father further proof of his joy and contentment, took him into his
Cha-no-yu room, which the Japanese, both Christian and non-Christian,
regard with the greatest reverence, as its purity is their greatest
refreshment on earth.   And there the Christians assembled and the
Father said Mass."

---

* The famous caddy ‘ Tsukumo-gami ’ or ‘ Dishevelled Hair,’ which Matsunaga presented
to Nobunaga.

CHAPTER II

TEA-MASTERS

MURATA SHUKO THE FOUNDER OF THE TEA CEREMONY

Shuko's ordinary name was Murata Mōkichi. He was the son of Moku-ichi Kenko of Nara, and was in his youth a priest of the Shōmeiji, living there in a cell called Hō-rin-an for ten years, but he was so lazy that he was expelled from the temple, so he went to Kyoto and entered the Daitokuji at Murasakino where he studied under Ikkyu Oshō. His great fault was that he was always falling asleep in the daytime as well as at night, to the considerable detriment of his studies, so that some wit observed that if his teacher was Ikkyu (one slumber) the pupil was Hyakkyu (a hundred slumbers). One day he went to a doctor and asked for a prescription to keep him awake and was told that tea was the best stimulant for the mind and recommended to drink it often. So he began to drink the tea of Toga-no-ō and found it very efficacious, and he not only drank it himself, but when anyone came to see him he would offer some with suitable ceremony. When the Shogun Ashikaga Yoshimasa heard of this he was much interested and ordered Shuko to arrange the ceremony for drinking tea. This he did with the assistance of Nō-ami and Sō-ami after comparison and selection of the etiquette already in use.* Yoshimasa was very pleased with his efforts and made him give up his priestly life and build a rustic hut near Sanjo, presenting him with a tablet written by his own hand to put over the gate, on which were the characters " Shu-kō-an-shu " (Pearl-Bright-Cell-Master."

Shuko devoted himself only to the art of cooking a meal and eating it and infusing tea and drinking it, and when he entertained his friends they used to amuse themselves by composing and reciting Japanese verses. All the esthetes of the time were rivals for the honour of his friendship, and Tea became very flourishing. Thus

---

* There was Cha-no-yu before Shuko's time, but it was not properly organized. He drew up the rules for the Formal, Intermediate and Informal styles (Shin, Gyo, So) with the Daisu, and so he is called the Founder of Teaism.

However the Teijo-hakki says that there was nothing that could really be called Cha-no-yu even in Yoshimasa's time The author, a member of the Ise school of Masters of Ceremony, says : " The Shogun retired and amused himself with Tea drinking during the stormy period of Onin (1467–8) and used to make it himself and serve it to his retainers. As it was made by the Shogun himself they each took a mouthful and passed the cup on. This was just as the Cha-bozu did and there was no special ceremony about it. My ancestor Ise-no-kami, who had charge of the etiquette in the days of Yoshimasa, knew nothing of any particular ceremony of Tea that could be taught to the people, neither is there any ancient family record of such a thing. What is now called Cha-no-yu with its various schools is a thing that grew up in the time of Hideyoshi long after Yoshimasa's days. Sen-no-Rikyu in the period of Tensho began it and Kobori Enshu and Katagiri Sekishu carried it on and added to it. Daimyos and such imitate the manner of poor people purposely, and sit in a little hut they call Sukiya, drinking Tea out of dirty old bowls and collecting all sorts of antique vessels, I don't think it at all a proper diversion for samurai to lay aside their swords and make and drink Tea in this way. I consider it a very silly amusement."

Naturally the older schools of manners did not admire what they considered a newer rival.

Shuko is certainly the first in Japan to whom the name of Tea
Master can be given. He died on the fifteenth of May of the second
year of Bunki (1503), at the age of eighty-one. He was buried in
the Shinju-an of the Temple of Daitokuji at Murasakino. The
finished quality of his Tea meetings was not to be found in the
utensils he used or in pictures and writings, and those who came
after him would give much to be able to recapture it.

THE TEN VIRTUES OF TEA

Myō-ei Shonin of Toga-no-ō got some tea plants from Eisai Shōnin
and planted them in Toga-no-ō, and connoisseurs consider this tea
to be the best, wherefore it was that Shukō used it. This Myō-ei
once wrote out what he considered the Ten Virtues of Tea and had
them inscribed on a Kettle. They run thus :

Has the blessing of all the Deities.	Wards off disease.
Promotes filial piety.	Strengthens friendships.
Drives away the Devil.	Disciplines body and mind.
Banishes drowsiness.	Destroys the passions.
Keeps the Five Viscera in harmony.	Gives a peaceful death.

The *Kissa Yōjōki* or " Tea drinking Good for the Health " of
Eisai Zenji, the famous Buddhist scholar and architect who went
to China in 1187, is the first work on Tea written in Japan. It is
a small pamphlet of some twenty printed pages devoted to the virtues
of Tea and of Mulberry Infusion which he strongly recommends for
the Five Diseases, viz. the water-drinking disease, the want of appetite
disease, paralysis, boils and beri-beri. There are two MSS of it,
one dated 1211 and the other 1214. It was in this latter year that
Eisai is said to have cured the Shogun Sanetomo of some malady by
means of Tea, and as a result it became a fashionable remedy. Other
medicines, he observes, cure only one kind of disease, but Tea is a
remedy for all disorders. As the Sung poet says, " The Pest-god
gets out of his chariot to salute the Tea tree." Eisai quotes the
Sonsho Dārani Kyo as declaring that of the Five Viscera the Liver
likes acid taste, the Lungs pungent, the Heart bitter, the Spleen
sweet and the Kidneys salt. Now the Heart is the chief of the Five
Viscera, as Bitter is the chief of the Five Tastes. And since Tea
is the chief of bitter tastes naturally it is best for the Heart.

ASHIKAGA YOSHIMASA ORIGINATES THE FOUR-AND-
A-HALF MAT TEA-ROOM

In the days of Ashikaga Yoshimasa there occurred the wars of
the eras Onin and Bummei (1467-1480), and the Empire was riven
asunder like flax. In the eighth year of Bummei (1477) he handed
over the administration to his son Yoshihisa and retired to his Palace
of Higashiyama to spend his remaining years. One part of his Palace
had two stories : in the upper part there were three rooms, and this
was called the Shinku-den, while the lower, known as the Chō-on-

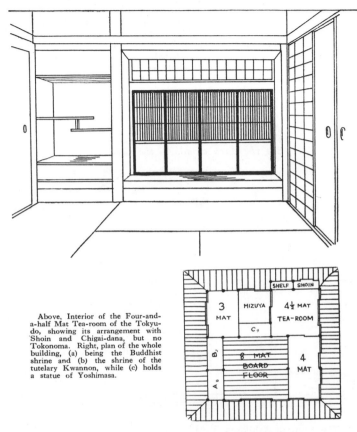

Above, Interior of the Four-and-a-half Mat Tea-room of the Tokyudo, showing its arrangement with Shoin and Chigai-dana, but no Tokonoma. Right, plan of the whole building, (a) being the Buddhist shrine and (b) the shrine of the tutelary Kwannon, while (c) holds a statue of Yoshimasa.

kaku, had four apartments. The garden was most tastefully arranged with a lake and trees, and by comparison with the Kinkakuji or Golden Pavilion on the Northern hills it was called the Ginkakuji or Silver Pavilion, though it never was covered with silver, for even if Yoshimasa meant to do so he died before it was finished. The garden, laid out by Sōami has since been regarded as a model of this type. Yoshimasa's Buddhist Shrine in the same place is a small building called the Tōkyudo in which his favourite Kwannon was installed. Its construction, lighting and detail were intended to give an impression of simplicity, purity and calm. In it is the four-and-a-half mat room known as the Cha-no-yu Chamber which was the first example of this style of Tea-room in the country.

Yoshimasa lived far from the sounds of war and turmoil, devoted to Tea and poetry and giving himself up entirely to the study of the harmony and rhythm of a life of elegance and taste, so that refinement in these things reached its culmination in his day.

So devotees of Tea are reminded that the art was founded in a troubled period of civil war, and when we consider the waning power of the Ashikaga house at this time a pathetic interest is lent to a poem written then by him which still survives:

> *See the moon shine forth*
> *O'er the pine-clad mountain peak*
> *'Neath which stands my cell.*
> *There is nought to trouble me*
> *But the dark clouds in the sky.*

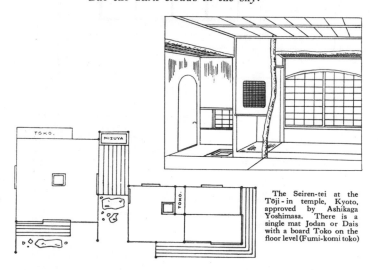

The Seiren-tei at the Tōji-in temple, Kyoto, approved by Ashikaga Yoshimasa. There is a single mat Jodan or Dais with a board Toko on the floor level (Fumi-komi toko)

The Shogun Ashikaga Yoshimasa once invited the Three Kwan-ryo—Hosokawa, Shiba and Hatakeyama—to a Tea after he had taken counsel with them on a certain occasion, and though it was one of the points of etiquette that no one should take part with a sword in his belt, yet an old retainer of Hosokawa named Mibuchi Yamato-no-Kami Harukazu came wearing one sword. He was immediately bidden to leave it outside by Yoshimasa, but instead of acceding he replied, " Pray allow me to retain it since I have my Lord to guard." Harukazu did not understand the spirit of Tea very well, perhaps, but he thoroughly understood that of Loyalty.

That such precautions were not always unnecessary the case of Gamo Shirobyoye bears witness. When Gamo Ujisato died his son Hideyuki was quite young, and Watari Hachiemon looked after the administration on his behalf, and at the same time tried to lead the young lord into evil ways. This enraged Gamo Shirobyoye and he invited Hachiemon to a tea and assassinated him in the tea-room, which was by no means always a very safe place during this period of Civil Wars, whatever it may have become later on.

TAKENO SHŌ-Ō

Takeno Shō-ō's real name was Nakamura Shinshiro, and he was a descendant of Takeda Izu-no-Kami Nobumitsu. His father Nobuhisa lost his father Nakakiyo and also his fortune in the war of Ōnin, and was left without any patron, and so, after wandering about for some time eventually found his way to Sakai in the province of Izumi and became a tradesman.

Shō-ō went to Kyoto when he was a boy and was a retainer of the Udaijin Kimiyori for fourteen years, when he was presented at Court and given the lower grade of the Lower Fifth Rank and the title of Inaba-no-Kami. He studied Japanese verse under Nishi-Sanjo Shōyuin Sanetaka, and since he lived next door to the Ebisu-do in Shijō street he took the pen-name of Daikoku-an.* He also studied the Zen philosophy under Futsu Kokushi and in this connexion took the title of Ikkan Kōji.

Since Tea was very much the fashion at the time he took lessons in it from Sōgō and Sōchin and became such a master that he was considered the greatest adept since Shukō.

The name Takeno was taken by him in reference to the family of Takeda of Kai, so renowned in war, from which he borrowed the first syllable.

> "When the seed was sown
> We may call it Takeda
> From that race I sprang.
> But that field is now laid waste
> So I style it Takeno,"†

is the verse he made to explain this change.

In due time he gave up his appointment and went to a place called Henomatsu in Sakai, where he lived in retirement, diverting himself with esthetic pleasures far from the turmoil of ordinary life. The sights and sounds of nature were all he needed. The long flight of the wild geese in the autumn sky, and the spring flowers when the winter was done. The voice of the stag calling to his mate mingling with the quiet pine-rhythm murmur of the water in his kettle filled his heart with serene content.

North of Henomatsu lived Araki Dōchin, and one day, when he was sitting beside Shō-ō's hearth and the pair of them were discussing the beautiful, he quoted the lines of Kyōgoku Kōmon Teika:

> "When the landscape lies
> Without any flower of spring

---

* Ebisu and Daikoku, the two Gods of Luck, are always associated. They sit together in the Japanese kitchen as tutelary deities.
† Ta (modified to "da"=Cultivated ricefields. No=Moorland.

> *Any autumn tint*
> *On the shore a straw-thatched hut*
> *Limned against the sunset gold.*"*

Shō-ō clapped his hands. "That's just it," he exclaimed, "the secret of Teaism lies only in realizing the calm serenity of such a scene." And he took up his brush and wrote the lines down and stuck them upon the wall of the Tea-room as the best expression of the pith of Teaism.

SHŌ-Ō DIVINES THE INTENTION OF HIS HOST.

Shō-ō was once invited to a Cha-no-yu by a wealthy man of Sakai, and it was the beginning of autumn. When he reached the house and entered the Rōji he turned to his companions and said, "I see his idea. You will find that he has Eikei's verse hung in his Tokonoma to-day." The others did not understand what he meant, but when they entered the Tea-room sure enough there was the verse as he had predicted.

> *"What a lonely sight*
> *When the clover-grass grows long*
> *Round our dwelling-place*
> *Not a trace of humankind*
> *Truly an autumnal scene.*"†

It was written on fine Ogura paper and mounted as a kakemono. The other guests were naturally astonished at his insight and asked him how he was able to know that it would be so. "I knew that our host was no novice at Cha-no-yu," said Shō-ō, "and I noticed that for to-day's meeting he had not swept away the fallen leaves or removed the withered grasses. He had just left the garden as it was and this lent it a most desolate and melancholy air, so that immediately that verse came to my mind, and I imagined he would use it in the tokonoma to-day . . . especially as I had heard that he had lately bought it."

"Well," replied his pupils, "it is really wonderful what sense of fitness our host has, and how exactly the master's mind is in tune with it."

---

* Mi-wataseba
Hana mo momiji-mo
Nakarikeri
Ura no tomaya no
Aki no yugure

Kyōgoku Kōmon Teika or Fujiwara Sadaie (1162–1241), was the son of the famous Fujiwara Shunzei or Toshinari. He held the Court offices of Sangi, Jibu Kyo and Gon-Chunagon. Like his father, he was an eminent poet and was appointed by the Emperor Go-Tōba to collaborate in the compilation of the Anthology called Shin-Kokon-Waka-shu. He was also the compiler of the Hyakunin Isshu or Hundred Poems. At the end of his life he retired to a little cottage on Ogura-yama near Saga, west of Kyoto, when he was known as Kyōgoku Dainagon.

† Yae mugura
Shigeru yado no
Sabishisa-ni
Hito koso mienu
Aki wa ki ni keri.

This seems to have been the first time that this Ogura paper was used in the Tea-ceremony, but as this anecdote was associated with it, it soon became the fashion, while the 'Clover-grass' kakemono was the more prized.[*]

The secret of a successful Tea lies in this harmony of the feeling of host and guests. The host should adapt himself to the temperament of the guests and the guests should be able to add to their enjoyment by an understanding appreciation of the pains the host has taken to entertain them.

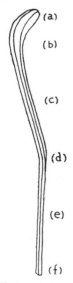

Chashaku or Tea-spoon.

(a) Dew-drop   (b) Scoop
(c) Groove   (d) Knot
(e) Grasp   (f) Butt

This Ogura paper was originally in the possession of Kitabatake, Governor of Ise, who had a pair of screens on which a hundred pieces of it, inscribed with verses, were mounted. When Sōchō, pupil of Sōgi, went down to Ise he was presented with these screens, and when he went away he took one with him and left the other behind. This one was burnt soon after, so only the one in his possession remained, and on this there were only thirty verses. According to the Rōjin Zatsuwa it was Shō-ō who had the two verses entitled Ama-no-hara and Yae-mugura (clover-grass) mounted on Kakemono, but in the above story it seems to have been the wealthy host of Shō-ō who had this done.

Shō-ō was once going to a Cha-no-yu with Rikyu when he caught sight of a flower vase with two handles in a curio shop. He thought he would go in and buy it on his way back and did so only to find that Rikyu had forestalled him. Being invited to a Tea some while after by Rikyu it occurred to him that this vase would be used, and so it turned out, for there it stood in the Tokonoma, but with one of its handles broken off. "Ah," he said, "then I shall have no need of the hammer I brought in my sleeve to knock it off, for I could not bear the idea of it being used with both."[†]

ICHIRO AND IKKYŪ.

There was an odd hermit who lived in Sakai in Izumi named Ichiro (One Way), who excelled in both Chinese and Japanese verse. One day the famous priest Ikkyū came to see him and remarked:

---

[*] This kind of device is only effective the first time. Repetition spoils it.

[†] When his younger sister was married to Hisada Gyōbu, Rikyu made a tea-spoon which he named 'O-furisode' and gave it to her as a wedding present. It was because he was not very prosperous at this time that he gave it instead of a trousseau. Gyōbu's son Sō-ei studied tea under Rikyu and founded the Hisada School. The tea-spoon 'O-furisode' is still preserved in his family.

" The Way is Universal; why then have you styled yourself One Way?" "Rest is Universal, isn't it," replied Ichiro, "then why do you style yourself One Rest (Ikkyu)?" This Ichiro had a kettle of which he was very fond, and which he called "The Handy Pot." He used it for making his tea as well as for boiling his food. This is the comic verse he made about it:

> *"Good old Handy Pot !*
> *Though your mouth sticks out so far*
> *Prithee do not tell*
> *All the various kinds of food,*
> *You so kindly cook for me."*

He made a window in his garden wall and hung up a bamboo curtain in front of it. Through this he used to receive the offerings of those who felt inclined to make them, and so he lived. But the small boys of the village threw horse-dung and straw horse-shoes through it for sport, whereupon the hermit exclaimed sadly; "Ah! this is a degenerate age! I will have no more to do with it." And after this he took no more food, so that he died. Truly he was an unworldly fellow.

This "Handy Pot" of his afterwards came into the possession of Hosokawa Katsumoto, and is no doubt the one that after many changes of ownership at last came into the hands of the hermit Zensuke of Awataguchi and was smashed by him rather than Hideyoshi should get it as he so much desired.

MIYOSHI JIKKYU.

Miyoshi Buzen-no-Kami Motoyasu took the name of Jikkyu when he retired from the world and became Nyudo. He learned Tea from Takeno Shō-ō and became a great adept. In the third year of Eiroku (1561) Hatakeyama Owari-no-Kami Takamasa attacked the castle of Kishiwada which he was holding, with a great force of fifteen thousand men, so Jikkyu, who had only eight thousand, came forth and took up a position at Kumeda. Then in the third month the warrior-priests of Negoro came up against them and Shinohara Ukyo-no-Shin Nagafusa assaulted them and broke their army, while his younger brother Yamashiro-no-Kami Yasunaga also went out to the attack, leaving Jikkyu with only a hundred men under his own banner. Jikkyu was bold enough, but no great strategist, and when his men told him that they thought it would be advantageous to fight with the river Kume in front of them rather than behind, he replied: "To be too far to the front is no bad thing, but it looks very ugly to retreat. If I don't win this fight I'll never take up a tea whisk again." And he remained where he was. Takamasa, taking advantage of this mistake, immediately attacked, and though Jikkyu encouraged his men and fought most boldly, the odds were too much for him. So taking the tea-spoon named 'Asaji,' which he greatly prized, he broke it in two, and then drew his sword, a fine blade by Mitsutada, and slew himself.   A certain Sakyo, priest of Negoro, took his head.

SEN NO RIKYU.

Sen no Rikyu was a native of Imaichi in the province of Izumi. His grandfather's name was Sen-ami, artist, and contemporary and intimate of Ashikaga Yoshimasa.   His father was called Tanaka Yōhei, whose ' Gō ' was Mozuya Sōjitsu and his trade name Naya. The business of his family was that of wholesale fish dealer, and evidently it was not at all poor.   Rikyu changed his name from Tanaka to Sen after his grandfather and first used the title of Sōeki, as well as the style Fushin-an and the 'Saigo' Hōsensai.   The origin of the name Rikyu Kōji by which he is generally known is that when he was commanded by Hideyoshi to make Tea before the Emperor Go Yōzei, since he was not of rank to appear at Court, he was bidden to retire and adopt the style of a Zen monk taking thus the title ' Kōji ' (Sanskrit Kulapati) ' Enlightened Recluse.'   So his Zen Master Kōkei Osho of the Daitokuji suggested the name Rikyu from the phrase Mei Ri tomo ni Kyu su, 名利共に休す, i. e.   " Fame and Profit are both dispensed with."   And this title was given him by Imperial Edict.

At the age of seventeen he was attracted to Teaism and attached himself to Kitamuki Dōchin of Henomatsu to study it.   By the time he was nineteen he showed very conspicuous ability, and his master Dōchin, who was a friend of Shō-ō, one day remarked to him that he had a pupil named Sen Yojiro who was very enthusiastic and able as well as being a good talker.   'Ah yes,' replied Shō-ō, 'he is one who knows how to drink Tea.'   After this he studied also under Shō-ō and from him received the tradition of the· use of the Daisu which Shō-ō had from Sōgō who had it from Dokan who received it from Shukō.   After some time he became recognized as the greatest authority of the day.

He became known to Nobunaga and was often invited to his castle of Azuchi, and after his death entered the service of Hideyoshi who gave him an income of three thousand koku.   He became a great favourite of the Taiko and accompanied him everywhere.

Hideyoshi was very much interested in the Tea philosophy and ordered Rikyu to revise its rules.   So he selected what was best from the old tradition and arranged the etiquette in harmony with the highest standard, and in consequence of this improvement he has come to be known as the second Shukō, his Master Shō-ō being called the father of the Revival Period and Rikyu the founder of the Complete Art.

From this time onward Tea became more and more the fashion, and all ranks of society .from Court Nobles and Daimyos to Samurai and Commoners were numbered among his pupils, and deferred to his judgment in everything that pertained to the connoisseurship of paintings and writings and the proper choice of utensils.

The principles of Tea as taught by Rikyu are comprised in the four expressions Harmony, Reverence, Purity, Calm. Luxury and Ostentation were to be strenuously avoided.*

Once a certain person came to Rikyu and asked him what were the mysteries of Tea. " You place the charcoal so that the water boils properly and you make the tea to bring out the proper taste. You arrange the flowers as they appear when they are growing. In summer you suggest coolness and in winter cosiness. There is no other secret," replied the Master.

> "Tea is nought but this.
> First you make the water boil,
> Then infuse the tea.
> Then you drink it properly.
> That is all you need to know."

" All that I know already," replied the other with an air of disgust. "Well, if there is any one who knows it already I shall be very pleased to become his pupil," returned Rikyu.

"What Rikyu says is very true," remarked Shorei Osho, his Zen Master who happened to be there at the time, " as Su Wu once replied to the poet Po-chu-i concerning the saying, 'do not any evil, but practise every kind of virtue,' it is a thing that every child of three knows but a philosopher of eighty cannot carry out." When the enquirer considered this his displeasure changed to admiration.

Shō-ō once passed by Rikyu's house and noticed him sprinkling water outside the front gate. He stopped to look, struck by the tasteful way in which he was doing it. Asking the name of the host he was told it was Sen Yōjiro, and so they became acquainted. " If I had not a previous engagement I should like to look round at the Mukuge (Rose of Sharon) in your garden," he said, " and take a cup of tea." So he was invited for the next morning, but when he went and opened the door of the Rōji there was not a sign of the flowers

---

* Wa Kei Sei Jaku 和敬清寂 was adapted by Rikyu from the Kin Kei Sei Jaku of Shukō. Kin 匤 means Respect, Jap., Tsutsushimu.

Wa and Kei, Harmony and Reverence, are equally important in Confucianism and Zen, but Sei and Jaku are qualities rather peculiar to Japanese taste and on which the special qualities of Teaism are founded. Purity is the special requirement also of the Shinto Deities and the washing of hands before entering the Sukiya is comparable to the same ablution before a shrine. The simplicity and style of the utensils used also suggest those used in offerings to the Kami. So everything should suggest purity, the aspect of the Rōji to the eye, the plashing of the water in the Tsukubae to the ear, the scent of the incense and fragrance of the Tea to the nose, and the simple taste of the plain dishes to the tongue.

Kei or Respect is the sentiment with which the Zen monk was taught to regard his food. In Tea this is extended to the utensils and the picture, the flower vase and all other utensils as well as, of course, to the guest. " In the West," observes Takahashi, " Love is regarded as the most important thing in life, but according to Buddhist philosophy both Love and Hate are merely the two extremes of one sentiment of Attachment, and it is Reverence that is the first of virtues." Reverence naturally expresses itself in Etiquette. Jaku means here rather more than calm or imperturbability. It is the opposite of showiness and brilliance and has much the same force as Sabi.

It is not always possible to be in harmony with everybody, and Rikyu himself was on distant terms with Imai Sōkyu. This did not, however, prevent his recommending Nobunaga to buy from Imai a Katatsuki Tea-caddy which he considered to be the best obtainable. But when Imai sent him a complimentary present as was the custom on the completion of the bargain Rikyu returned it. " My recommendation was on account of the excellence of the Tea-caddy and nothing more," he said. " So let our relations continue as before."

he had noticed the day before. He was at first inclined to go home again without even entering the Tea-room and had turned round to do so, but on second thoughts he proceeded, and when he did enter there in the Tokonoma hung a flower vase with one Mukuge blossom, the pick of the whole garden. The same story is told of Hideyoshi and the Morning-glory.

RIKYU AND THE DAISU.

Oda Nobunaga ordered Rikyu to make Tea for him and he used the Daisu in a way that was quite new, so that Nobunaga questioned

Daisu.

him about it, but approved when Rikyu explained in detail why he did not adhere to the older methods. Afterwards Hideyoshi summoned Rikyu and asked him to teach him the way of making Tea with the Daisu, and made him swear that he would not transmit the secret to anyone else except with his permission, so afterwards he made Tea with the hearth on ordinary occasions. Those who were allowed to receive this secret tradition were called the 'Seven Masters of the Daisu' (Daisu no shichi nin shu). They were the Kwampaku Toyotomi Hidetsugu, Gamō Ujisato, Hosokawa Sansai, Kimura Hitachi-no-suke, Takayama Ukon, Seta Kamon, Shibayama Kemmotsu. (*Shinsho*.)

The luxurious style of Cha-no-yu in vogue until the days of Shō-ō and Rikyu is called Shō-in or Reception Room style because given in such an apartment. The Daisu was used for it and is so still. The simple and democratic modification of this came to be known as the Sō-an or Thatched Cottage Style.

The main idea of Teaism is a quiet simplicity (Wabi), and a mellow experienced taste (Sabi).* Luxury and gorgeousness are quite alien to it. So Sen Rikyu was always saying " People like expensive utensils because their minds run to covetousness and avarice. A chipped earthenware mortar, if suited to the occasion, is entirely in harmony with the Tea spirit. He expressed his meaning in these verses :

> *If you have one pot*
> *And can make your tea in it*
> *That will do quite well.*
> *How much does he lack himself*
> *Who must have a lot of things.*

---

* Sabi=mellowed by use, patinated by age, reticent and lacking in the assertiveness of the new. Brinkley maintains that it meant 'rusty,' another kind of sabi, and was originally applied as a comic epithet, but this does not seem so likely. It is applied also to the voice of a singer.

> If you have no pot
> Take a saucepan and in that
> Boil your hot water.
> Even so your tea may be
> Quite the best in all Japan.

> Though I tell you this
> Do not go and hide away
> Things you now possess.
> To pretend you have them not
> Is affected elegance.

> He who hesitates
> Saying that he has no flowers
> Let him go and see
> The spring herbage that 'mid snow
> Shows upon the mountain side.*

Rikyu bade his pupils always keep these verses in mind.   It was in the Tea itself that he was interested and not so much in the utensils.

Once he went to a reception at Hideyoshi's Palace of Juraku and there found all the great vassals and distinguished men of the day intently engaged in examining a collection of Tea vessels that was on view in one of the apartments.   For a while he listened quietly but heard only such observations as 'Ah, that is an antique and must be very valuable,' or 'That looks new.   I don't expect it is worth much.'   So seeing that their criticism was no more than an appraising of values he interrupted them with, ' Really Sirs, this is most unbecoming talk.   The connoisseurship of Tea vessels consists in judging whether they are interesting and suitable for their purpose or not, and whether they combine well or badly with each other and has nothing to do with their age at all.   That is the business of curio dealers and ought to be beneath the notice of men of taste.'

Rikyu did not particularly value antiques.   He had his Tea-bowls made by contemporary potters such as Chosuke and Jokei and his kettles by craftsmen like Yojiro Yaemon and Toemon.   He did not necessarily require them to copy old models but had the utensils shaped according to his fancy.   His flower vases and Tea-spoons he made himself of bamboo.   Neither did he care anything for things that were difficult to obtain.   He got his writings done for him by the artists of the day.   So the criticism of Dazai Shundai and others that Tea people only like old or odd looking things certainly could not be applied to him.

---

* Kama hitotsu
Moteba Cha-no-you wa
Naru mono wo
Yorozu no dōgu
Konomu hakanasa.

Kama nakuba
Nabeyu nari tomo
Suku naraba
Kore zo Cha-no-yu no
Nihon Ichi nari.

Kaku ieba
Aru dōgu wo mo
Oshikakushi
Naki mane wo suru
Hito mo hakanashi.

Hana wo nomi
Matsuran hito ni
Yamazato no
Yukima no kusa no
Hana wo misebaya.

Rikyu himself once bought a writing of the priest Mitsuan for two hundred kwan and had a Cha-no-yu in its honour to which he invited Kitamuki Dochin and another priest.   But neither of them seemed to admire it and Rikyu asked them the reason.   ' Because it isn't genuine,' was the reply.   Whereupon he immediately burnt it lest anyone else would be taken in.

VERSES OF SEN-NO-RIKYU.

Though I sweep and sweep,
Everywhere my garden path,
Though invisible
On the slim pine needles still
Specks of dirt may yet be found.

When below the eaves,
The moon's flood of silver light
Chequers all the room,
There's no need to be abashed
If our heart is pure and clear.

When you hear the splash
Of the water drops that fall
Into the stone bowl
You will feel that all the dust
Of your mind is washed away.

In my little hut,
Whether people come or not
It is all the same.
In my heart there is no stir
Of attraction or disgust.

What have I to give?
To my guests for their repast
If I don't rely
On the monkeys of the vale
For the fruits they bring to me.

There is no fixed rule
As to when the window should
Closed or open be.
It depends on how the moon
Or the snow their shadows cast.

Flowers of hill or dale.
Put them in a simple vase
Full or brimming o'er.
But when you're arranging them
You must slip your heart in too.

Every morn and eve
When I sweep the Dewy Path
All is calm and still.
Though it seems a guest is there
No one comes to lift the latch.

Many though there be,
Who with words or even hands
Know the Way of Tea.
Few there are or none at all,
Who can serve it from the heart.

If I look upon,
The still mirror of my heart
What there do I see?
Is it the same mind it was
Yesterday, or is it changed?

Though invisible
There's a thing that should be swept
With our busy broom.
'Tis the dirt that ever clings
To the impure human heart.

Though you wipe your hands
And brush off the dust and dirt
From the tea vessels.
What's the use of all this fuss
If the heart is still impure?

Since the Dewy Path
Is a way that lies outside
This most impure world.
Shall we not on entering it
Cleanse our hearts from earthly mire?

When we leave behind
The Three Worlds' Abodes of Fire,
Storm and Passion tossed,
Entering the Dewy Path
Through the pines a pure breeze blows.

Just a little space
Cut off by surrounding screens
From the larger hall.
But within we are apart
From the common Fleeting World.

In the Dewy Path
And the Tea-room's calm retreat
Host and guests have met.
Not an inharmonious note
Should disturb their quiet zest.

On a Chinese stand
Vessels all of various shapes
Made of gourds are seen
'Tis a feast that we receive
Both from China and Japan.

Just a simple shelf
Hanging from the corner wall
By a plain bamboo.
All we need in such a world
Are these artless simple things.

Take a 'Go' bamboo
Split it up and from the joints
You can fabricate
All the things that you will need
For the use of Cha-no-yu.

When you take a sip
From the bowl of powder Tea
There within it lies
Clear reflected in its depths
Blue of sky and grey of sea.

What a lot of things
Just as though by sleight of hand
Can be done with you.
Everything you can include
In your maw O double shelf.

I am never tired
Of this simple straw-thatched hut.
Wrought of plain round wood
Does its middle pillar stand
Just exactly to my mind.

The following selection from the Hundred Rules of Rikyu, preserved at Ura Senge, will further elucidate his views:

If any one wishes to enter the Way of Tea he must be his own
teacher.

It is only by careful observation that one learns. He is a fool
who gives his opinion without suitable experience.

No pains must be spared in helping anyone anxious to learn.

One who is ashamed to show ignorance will never be any good.

To become expert one needs first love, second dexterity and
then perseverance.

In putting down a utensil after using it, do so regretfully as if
you loved it.

When you give anyone flowers they must not be fully open, for
it is impolite to the recipient.*

---

* Cf. the proverb, Sake wa horo-yoi, hana wa hankai. Liquor, one sheet in the wind,
flowers, half open.

When you take Tea from the Caddy be careful to do it according to the principle of Jo-chu-ge. That is to say in three scoops, first a little, then a little more, and then at last the largest amount.

When you take out hot water with the ladle be sure to hold it straight so that the circle of liquid is preserved (that is, so that it does not spill).

If you give a Cha-no-yu to guests who are on their way back from a flower-viewing, don't use any picture of birds and flowers or put flowers in the Tokonoma. Repetition is always irritating, and the same thing applies to snow viewing when snow landscapes or things connected with snow are to be avoided. On such occasions Cha-no-yu should be of the impromptu type so that the idea of entertainment be not too obvious. Indeed it is best if the guests are not formally invited at all, but just asked to drop in casually, preparations having been quietly made beforehand.

With the hearth the charcoal basket and dust box should be made of a gourd, the incense burner of pottery and the incense Neri-ko. But with the Furo one should use the vegetable-basket type of charcoal basket with metal hibashi, the incense burner should be of lacquer and the incense Byaku-dan.

The reason is that the Furo came first from China and therefore the earliest type of charcoal basket and the utensils that are of Chinese origin are in keeping, while with the hearth, which is Japanese, the later inventions of the same country are suitable.

When a set of three Kakemono is to be hung, first hang the centre one, then the right hand one (on the side of the beginning of the writing), then that on the left (where it ends). In the same way a six-fold screen is opened in the middle first, then right and then left.

However well charcoal is laid it is no good if the kettle won't boil. Though the make-up of the charcoal under the Furo cannot be inspected like that on the hearth, it should be done in the same spirit as if it could.

Kettles have all sorts of names and shapes, but after all they are all kettles.

Utensils must be put down each exactly in its proper place, and their bags with their seams on the lines of the mats.

Utensils that are moved, like the Caddy, must take their position from the one that is at rest. For instance, if the whisk is used and put down and the caddy taken up it must be put down again at a proper distance from the whisk so that no unnecessary movement need be made.

When you handle any utensil take it up lightly but put it down heavily.

Koi-cha must be hot and without froth or lumps.

Take up the Mizusashi by its middle sideways, but lay the Tea-spoon straight across the top of it.

If the lacquered Natsume has a pattern or characters on it see to it that they are in order and correspond both on lid and body and are not crooked.

In handling a Katatsuki there is no need to put the fingers underneath it, for it is higher than it is wide.

But with Bunrin, Nasu, Maru-tsubo and Taikai the fingers should be placed beneath them.   In handling the Taikai put the thumb on its neck.

From a narrow mouthed Caddy the tea is to be drawn (kumu), while from a wide mouthed one it is to be scooped (sukuu).

With a deep Ido Tea-bowl wipe the bottom and then the sides in one movement, so that there be no need to put the hand in a second time when it might be soiled again.

If a guest is asked to put on some charcoal he must be careful not to put on the incense, just as he must leave the host to put in the water if he is asked to arrange flowers, for putting the finishing touch should be considered the prerogative of the host, and the guest should never seem to usurp his functions.

In putting on charcoal don't let two pieces 'scissor' the trivet, or form a cross, or let any piece stick out beyond the edge of the hearth, and be careful that the whole arrangement is evenly distributed, not too little on one side and too much on the other.

Always remove any burnt-out piece of white charcoal and replace it.   In the first place because it tends to put out the fire, and in the second because since it is regarded as being a fire-extinguisher it suggests conflagrations and so is ill-omened.

That the sentiments expressed by Sen-no-Rikyu in verse and otherwise were already current in some circles in the thirteenth century may be seen from the following passages from the *Tsure-zure Gusa* of Yoshida Kenko, a fastidious Worldly Wiseman of a Buddhist recluse who himself died in 1350 aged sixty-six or thereabout.

The Court Noble Taira no Nobutoki, telling tales of the past in his old age, used to relate how Saimyoji Nyudo (the Regent Hojo Tokiyori's name after retirement) once sent for him in the evening, and he said he would go at once. His ceremonial dress was missing, and while he was doing one thing or another, a second message came, saying, "Is it that you have no dress of ceremony? If so, being nigh time, it does not matter what you wear, but come quickly."   So he put on a crumpled robe, and went in his indoor clothes.   When he arrived his host brought out a wine-vessel and earthenware wine-cups, saying, "I asked for you because it would be lonely drinking this wine alone.   There is no food to eat with it. All the people in the house will have gone to bed, but please go and see if you can find something suitable anywhere you like."   So he took a taper and searched in every corner, till, on a shelf in the kitchen he found a small earthenware bowl with a little bean sauce at the bottom.   He went back and said, "I have found this."   The Nyudo said "That will do splendidly."   So they drank several cups together with great gusto and were very merry.   (*Tsure-zure Gusa*, Sec. 215.)

When the present Palace was completed, it was inspected by those versed in ancient customs and they had no fault to find.   The day for His Majesty's removal to the new Palace was drawing near, when Her Highness Genki-mon-in very admirably pointed out that the comb-shaped openings in the wall of the old Kanin-den were round and without edging. The fact being that it was a mistake to have made them foliated and edged with wood, they were therefore altered. (*Tsure-zure Gusa*, Sec. 33.)

Uncommon things, with names that sound hard and foreign, and unfamiliar flowers are not at all desirable. Strange and rare things are mostly what amuse people of bad breeding. It is better to be without them. (*Tsure-zure Gusa* of Yoshida Kenko Sec. 139. Cf. also Sec. 116.) In personal names it is a useless thing to use characters which one rarely sees. A desire for curious things, a fondness for uncommon opinions is a sure characteristic of people of shallow understanding.

He who is high in rank should bear himself as if he were of low rank, the sage as if he were a simpleton, the wealthy man as if he were poor, and the man who is well versed in anything as though he knew nothing about it. (Yoshida Kenko quoting from the work *Ichigon Hodan*. *Tsure-zure Gusa*, Sec. 98.)

If you wish to follow the way of Buddha it is only this: Lead a life of leisure and don't take things seriously. That's the main thing.

RIKYU AND DŌ-AN.

Sen Dō-an was Rikyu's eldest son, also his pupil. He took the titles Min-o and Fukyusai. One day when the snow was falling he asked his father to take Tea with him. When Rikyu arrived at his house and entered the Rōji that led to the Tea-room he looked round the garden in front and saw a figure wearing a rain-coat and wide straw hat digging up with a hoe some vegetables that were growing there. Wondering who it could be, he kept his eye on him till he went into the house and then saw that it was Dō-an himself. This excited his interest and he went on to the Tea-room where the usual simple meal was served. In more than usually good spirits he lifted the cover of the soup bowl to find within it a broth of fresh vegetables and Suzuki fish. Immediately his face clouded. " When I came into the Rōji just now and saw you digging up the vegetables in the snow the sight of you in your straw coat and hat struck me as very fitting and elegant. It showed kind solicitude on your part and naturally gave me great pleasure.* But what is this fish doing here? Cordiality is the first principle of Tea, but everything should be unostentatious and in keeping. How ridiculous that a son of mine should do a thing so wanting in understanding."

Dō-an was much embarrassed and apologised profusely, but when he saw Rikyu's meaning a great enlightenment dawned on him and he made much progress in taste as the result of this incident.

---

* The literal meaning of the word 'Chiso,' ordinarily used for any entertainment, is 'Running about' or 'Exertion,' for the proper kind of treatment of a guest consists in exerting oneself to the utmost to welcome him rather than in spending a lot of money for delicacies.

Rikyu once went with Dō-an to see a certain acquantance, and when they came to the fence in the middle of the Rōji, Dō-an pointed out the antique-looking gate, remarking: "That's interesting, it gives the path a solitary appearance." But Rikyu shook his head. "I don't think so," he replied, "this looks as though it had been brought from some mountain temple a long way off and the labour required to bring it must have cost a lot of money. A rough wicket gate made by a craftsman does give a really quiet and lonely look to a garden, but this sort of thing shows us what kind of Tea this gentleman practises."

Rikyu had an acquaintance who lived in a very simple way, and one evening he called to see him. While he was admiring the unaffected style of the furnishing of the room he heard a noise outside and looked out and saw his host go out with a lantern and a bamboo and knock down a citron from a tree which he brought back in his sleeve. Rikyu concluded that he meant this for some sort of relish, and so it proved, for he served citron Misō. He then poured out Saké and with it offered some fine rice-cake which he said came from Osaka. Now that spoiled the whole thing for Rikyu, because it at once suggested the feeling that the unaffected simplicity of the rest was really carefully prepared, so he excused himself by saying he had an appointment in the city and went off without more ado, though his host pressed him to stay.

On the other hand, he was invited once by a certain Sōmu who was a man of taste, and in this case the host came out and told him he had got some fine water and took the kettle off and went into the Mizuya with it. Meanwhile Rikyu went to the hearth and put on some charcoal, and by this time the host came back with the dripping kettle. It was all very naturally done and both of them were quite in accord. Thus one must entertain naturally and without conscious effort. Rules are laid down to be observed to some extent, but one must not take them too seriously. Only a stupid person will glue the bridges of a harp in place.

On one occasion when Hideyoshi had arranged to visit Rikyu, snow began to fall on the evening of the previous day, so the Master immediately went into the garden and laid round cushions on all the stepping-stones, taking them away the next morning before the dawn broke. So when the Taiko arrived the whole garden was covered with a mantle of snow and only the stepping-stones stood out clear to welcome him. Hideyoshi was filled with admiration for the quick wit that prompted this device.

When Hideyoshi was starting for his headquarters in the Korean campaign Rikyu made an arrangement of the thorny 'Kikoku' bush, and everyone immediately took exception to it, exclaiming that thorns were ill-omened in the Tokonoma. But Hosokawa Yusai saw the point at once and murmured the verse, 'Karatachi no sono mi wa yagate Kikoku nari.' Whereupon the rest caught his meaning too and were loud in their admiration of the adroit departure from convention. For 'Karatachi' and 'Kikoku' are different readings of the same word when it is the name of the plant, but the first, with differ-

ent characters can also mean ' Departure for China ' (Kara), and the
second ' Return home.'

There was a Chajin of Sakai who had a Tea-caddy called Sessan
and he used it when Rikyu came. But Rikyu thought nothing of it
so its owner smashed it against the trivet on the hearth. Another
guest took away the pieces and put them together again and gave a
Cha-no-yu to which he invited Rikyu. This time the Master praised
the caddy, so the host returned it to its former owner and told him
to take great care of it. Later on someone bought it for a thousand
pieces of gold, and noticing that the joins were very rough proposed
to have it mended again more neatly and submitted it to Kobori
Enshu for his opinion. " If you do that you will spoil it altogether,"
was his decision, " for that was just why Rikyu liked it."

THE YAE MUGURA KAKEMONO CHANGES HANDS.

Matsunaga Hisahide obtained the famous ' Yae mugura ' kakemono and treasured it very much, giving it the name of Shigeru no
yado, the words of the second line. Everyone who saw it envied
him intensely, and though he was often asked for it he could not
bear to part with it. Eventually, however, he was moved by Rikyu's
admiration and presented it to him. Rikyu was beside himself with
joy, and regarded it as his most precious possession.

Now Tsuda Sōkyu, the father of Kogetsu Osho of the Daitokuji,
was with Imai Sokyu and Rikyu regarded as forming the usual Three
Great Experts of the day, and he too greatly hankered after this
writing. Rikyu was apparently not aware of this and one day invited
him to a Cha-no-yu and hung it in his Tokonoma. Sōkyu went to
inspect the Tokonoma, but scarcely had he glanced at it when with
a loud exclamation he fell back as though in a swoon, and unable to
remain any longer hurried off home and went to bed and stayed there.
When Rikyu heard of this he felt so sorry for him that he went the
very next day and presented him with the writing.

Kamibayashi Chikuan of Uji once gave a Tea Ceremony in the
evening and invited Rikyu, who came attended by all the nobles who
were his pupils. Chikuan was naturally delighted beyond words and
himself made the tea and served it. But his hand trembled and the
tea spoon fell from the caddy, and without stopping to put straight
the tea-whisk which rolled on the mats by his side, kneeling as he
was, he presented the bowl to Rikyu. The others looked at each
other and were just on the point of breaking into smiles when Rikyu
exclaimed : " Splendid ! No one in the Empire could do it better ! "
Greatly surprised, as soon as the meeting was over they asked him
the reason for this high praise.

" Since he invited you all to come this long way just to take one
cup of tea," explained the Master, " his whole mind was concentrated
on giving it to you before the water got cool. So he took no notice
of those slips or accidents but went straight on and finished serving
it."

There is, as the proverb says, a distance of three thousand *ri* between those who know and those who don't.   The others might laugh at a flaw in the ceremony, but Rikyu's deeper insight perceived how praiseworthy was the cause of it.

When Rikyu was quite young he made Tea for Kitamuki Dōchin, and wished to know what the Master really thought of his performance, so he asked a certain doctor who was a friend of his and who also knew Dochin well to make the enquiries it was not quite the thing to make himself.   So the doctor took the first opportunity and put the question to Dochin.   " Indeed, he did very well, very well indeed," was the reply, " I thought it a very fine performance."   " Yes," said the doctor, " but was there no fault in it at all ? "   Dochin hesitated and after some pressing replied, "Well, I don't call it exactly a fault, but there may have been something that might have been better, for he is still quite young."   "Ah," replied the other, " and what was that ? "   " Well, you see," explained Dochin, " he put a lot of Tea into a big Bulge-bottom Chinese Caddy, and when he made it he put large spoonfuls into the Tea-bowl, and that does not look very well."   " Oh, was that it," said the doctor, " and what ought one to do in that case ? "   "Well," replied Dochin, " it would have looked much nicer to put a small amount of tea into a large Tea-caddy, and coax it out gently in small quantities.   But of course an inexperienced person would hardly think of that.   He will make a fine Chajin when he gets a little older."   When the doctor reported this to Rikyu he exclaimed, "Ah, that's interesting.   No, I should never have thought of that." And from that time he began to improve very much.   Of this story the editor observes that many people would think it rather pointless, and by that very fact show themselves deficient in the more delicate Tea taste.

Seto Kamon Masatada of Omi was first a retainer of the house of Hōjō and afterwards served Toyotomi Hideyoshi.   He was Rikyu's pupil in Tea and became so expert that he was numbered among the Seven Masters of the day.   He was once invited to Rikyu's house and after the tea was over he happened to notice a dipper that lay on the shelf and was much taken with its shape, praising it exceedingly.

Rikyu asked what he saw in it, and he replied that it looked a better shape than those commonly used.   " Indeed," said Rikyu, "and why ? "   " It seems to be a bit shorter than usual, and that gives it a very interesting appearance," replied Masatada.   " I should like to have one like it."   Some time after this Masatada invited Rikyu to his house, and when the tea was over and the utensils were being put away, Rikyu remarked "The dipper you used to-day seems a bit too short."   "Ah, but I liked the look of the one I saw at your house so well that I made my own short to match it," replied Masatada.   "Ah," said Rikyu with a sigh, " I am afraid you don't yet understand the real spirit of tea, though I thought you did. I am a little man, as you see, and so I have a small dipper to suit my size.   But you, on the other hand, are a ·big fellow, so it is natural for you to use a larger one. What do you want with a small one?" At this enlightenment dawned suddenly on Masatada, and in future he had a large size dipper made. This is known as the Kamon style and is still in use. Everything should be in proportion.

Chinsei Hachiro Tametomo used a long arrow and Kurō Yoshi-tsune a weak bow. It would have been ridiculous for either to try and use the weapon of the other.

Rikyu criticised a kettle made to the design of Seta Kamon Masatada, saying that the mouth was too wide. " Teaism dislikes anything that looks ample," he observed. " There should always appear to be something lacking. The mouth of this kettle has nothing lacking. Seta Kamon is a little raw yet." (*Chaden-shu*.)

There was a farmer in Rikyu's day named Dōroku who was much given to simple Cha-no-yu, and he absorbed its spirit so much that he used always to clean his farm implements and arrange them carefully after use. He had a valuable old Chinese Tea-caddy, and when he was dying he called his two sons to his bedside and told them that for their simple style of Tea there was no need of such a thing while it might become a source of envy and discord between them after his death, since it had been greatly admired by Shō-ō and Rikyu and would fetch a lot of money. So he broke it before he became a guest in the White Jade Pavilion.

One day Rikyu noticed a bamboo lattice window in which new bamboos had evidently been purposely mixed with the old. " That fellow," he remarked to his son Sōjun, " is trying to be esthetic. Bamboo lattices like that should either be entirely renewed or else left alone. Perhaps if you have a very special guest it is better to renew them." On another occasion too, when he saw a fence made entirely of cedar-bark, he observed. " That's the fussy sort that will soon get tired of it and change it to bamboo and at last come back to plain plaster."

Rikyu's wife Sō-on was just like him, extremely sensitive to form and the fitness of things. When he bought the famous Chidori incense burner from Sōgi for a thousand kwan she asked him to let her look at it and sat down in front of it and gazed at it for some time. At last she said, " I think the feet are a little too high. Don't you think it would look better if they were cut down a bit?" " That is exactly what I was thinking," replied Rikyu. And he sent for the lapidary and had one bu or a tenth of an inch taken off.

HOSOKAWA YŪSAI.

Hosokawa Hyobu-Taiyu Fujitaka Yusai was deeply versed in poetry and the tea philosophy.* He possessed a number of very valu-

---

* " Yūsai was what might be called the walking dictionary of literature to the Ashikaga Shōgun." Tokutomi Sohō : (*Kinsei Nihon Kokunminshi.*)

In the Sekigahara campaign he held the castle of Tanabe in Tamba, his province, with five hundred men for Ieyasu, and there detained a large army for sixty days so that they were un-able to take part in the decisive battle. And so anxious was the Emperor that he or his books might be damaged that he issued an Edict that the castle should be vacated, but not until it had served its purpose. The investing army too sympathised with the old poet who was then 67 so that they were considerate enough to forget to put many bullets into their guns.

able tea vessels, among which the incense burner called 'Chidori' was especially famous. One evening in mid-autumn during the era Bunroku (1592-96) when the full moon had emerged from the peaks of Higashiyama and was shining brightly, Gamō Ujisato said to Sen-no-Rikyu " This is a perfect evening : I wonder how we can make the most of it ? " So the pair of them concluded that they could not do better than visit Fujitaka, and went off to his house. He was delighted to see them and did everything he could to entertain them. There was not a cloud in the sky or a shadow on the moon, and the heavens shone bright in serene purity and their enjoyment of its beauty grew more and more keen till suddenly it occurred to Ujisato to ask their host if he would show them the famous Chidori incense burner, for the occasion seemed to him just the right one. But when he made the request Fujitaka's face at once clouded and he put him off by saying : " To-night is not a suitable time ; I will show it to you on some other occasion." But Ujisato would take no refusal, urging that it would spoil a perfect evening if he did not accede. So Fujitaka reluctantly and with a very displeased look went and got the incense burner, threw the ashes out of it and gave it to them to examine without putting it in its proper place in the alcove as would usually be done. Ujisato took it and examined it carefully, pronouncing it to be indeed a masterpiece, but Fujitaka made no acknowledgment of his praise, but put it away again without a word. Ujisato could not understand his behaviour at all, so when he met Satomura Shōba, a teacher of Japanese verse, he told him all about it and asked him what he thought could be the explanation, if any, of Fujitaka's curious churlishness, so unlike his ordinary courteous behaviour. Shōba looked blank at first, but after considering a while he suddenly smote his knee : "Ah, I have it," he exclaimed, "indeed Yusai is a true poet ! You know the verse of the Retired Emperor Juntoku :

> On Kiyomi beach,
> Where the waves lap listlessly
> 'Neath a cloudy sky;
> See the flock of sea-birds* cast
> Their dark shadow on the moon.

Well, you see he didn't want his ' Chidori ' to cast any shadow on the moon, and so it was that he said that the night was not suitable. How very natural to a poetic mind like his." Ujisato could not repress a sigh of chagrin at his own ignorance. " How in the world should one know a thing like that unless by asking a scholar such as yourself," he replied, " and what learning and acuteness you possess to be able to unravel it. I must confess that I am thoroughly ashamed of my own denseness and ignorance." And henceforth he made a point of cultivating the acquaintance of Fujitaka the more, and found that he profited by it not a little. And it is not only in the matter of Tea that humility is the mother of knowledge.

Sea-birds = Chidori.

ONE VERSION OF THE DEATH OF SEN-NO-RIKYU.

Rikyu had one daughter named Gin-ko, whose early name was O-Mitsu. She was married to Mozuya So-an of Kyoto, but he died and she lived alone as a widow, for though she was quite young she had several children and so determined not to marry again.

Now in the eighteenth year of Tensho (1591) Toyotomi Hideyoshi with Sasa Awaji-no-Kami, Maeba Hannyu and Kinoshita Hansuke, who happened to be his favourites at that time, went out to Higashiyama with a few pages to amuse themselves by hawking. When they were walking from the temple of Nanzenji to Kurodani they met a lady with one or two servants coming from the opposite direction. She had left her carrying chair and was strolling along quietly admiring the Sasankwa bushes that were then in flower. Seeing this, Hansuke hurried forward and beckoned to her with his fan, calling out, " It is his Highness the Taiko; uncover your heads." In great trepidation the servants dropped the carrying chair and prostrated themselves with their foreheads to the earth, while the lady removed her hat and crouched down among the flowers just where she was, for the road was so narrow that there was nothing else to do. So the Taiko passed by and as he did so he scrutinized her closely. What he saw was a lady about thirty attired in a white wadded silk garment with a scarlet dress worn over it, and above this an over-dress of purple figured satin ornamented with the four Chinese characters Flower, Bird, Wind, Moon, done in gold brocade on it, standing under a tree holding the billowing skirts of her dress about her while her long hair flew loose in the wind. So elegant was her appearance that she really looked like a fairy who had strayed from her palace or else one of the goddesses who dwell on the peaks. With his usual susceptibility to beauty Hideyoshi was greatly excited at the vision, and bade one of his pages enquire who she might be. " It is the widow of Mozuya, the daughter of Sen-no-Rikyu," replied one of her servants. "Ah," exclaimed Hideyoshi, " I had heard she was beautiful, but I never expected to see anything like this. When even among the Consorts and Ladies in Waiting at the Imperial Court there is none so lovely." And with many a backward glance he returned to his mansion of Juraku and not long after sent the lady a letter of invitation. She, however, did not respond to his advances. " Since I am still in mourning for my husband and have several children to bring up as well, I pray you hold me excused in this matter," was her answer. Hideyoshi was not at all inclined to accept this rebuff, and sent one Tomita Sakon to Rikyu without delay with the peremptory order, " Let the widow of Mozuya be sent to Juraku at once." But Rikyu was entirely averse to constraining his daughter thus to dishonour her husband's memory, and firmly refused to comply with the demand, returning the very straightforward answer to Hideyoshi, " It is not Rikyu's wish to establish himself in his lord's favour by the sale of his daughter."

Hideyoshi was naturally enraged at this, though he did not

think it politic to do anything just then, but, in the words of the chronicler, as maggots breed in what is rotten, so does slander in decaying friendship, and from this time onward the Taiko's regard for Rikyu became less and less, and his attention to the tales that under the circumstances many were eager to tell him, grew more pronounced. For instance: "We hear that Rikyu has prevailed on

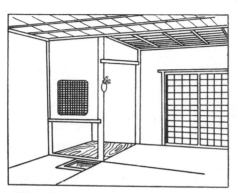

Kōkei Osho, priest of the Daitokuji, to allow a wooden statue of himself to be placed in that temple, and not only is it in a standing attitude wearing a Kosode with the Paulownia crest and a high horned hood on his head tilted to the right, but with sandals on his feet, a staff in his hand and a far-away look in his eyes as he stands gazing loftily into the distance." At this Hideyoshi was very angry. "This is beyond anything," he exclaimed, "How dares he put a statue of

Shuko-in Tea-room in the Daitokuji where Sen-no-Rikyu is said to have committed Seppuku.

himself wearing sandals in the Daitokuji, a temple that is visited by Courtiers of high rank and Imperial Princes, and to which the Emperor himself even deigns on occasion to make an Imperial Progress!* This connoisseur of Tea-vessels makes a great mistake in presuming on my intimacy to attempt such impudent conduct. I never heard of such insolence!" And he ordered him to be confined to his house at Sakai, and on the twenty-eighth day of the second month of the nineteenth year of Tensho (1592) he sent Nakamura Shikibu Shoyu Kazuuji to announce to him that he was required to commit suicide.† Rikyu was by no means surprised at the sentence

---

* Daitokuji or Ryuhōzan of the Rinzai sect of Zen was founded in 1323 by Daito Kokushi, was made chief of the Five Temples in 1334, and is a huge area of 68,400 tsubo, dotted with temples, halls and gardens. Here are the tombs and memorials of many of the great statesmen and soldiers of the Momoyama age as well as those of the house of Sen and other distinguished Tea Masters and Zen Priests. Rikyu, Furuta Oribe and Kobori Enshu all rest here, as well as Katagiri Sekishu, Hosokawa Yūsai, Mori Terumoto, Matsuura Takanobu, Kuroda Nagamasa, Katagiri Katsumoto, Kobayakawa Takakage, Satomura Shoha, Yamasaki Sokan, the priests Ikkyu, Shunoku, Kōkei and Kōgetsu and last but hardly least, Oda Nobunaga, and the mother of Hideyoshi, and some other members of his family. Here more even than in the other great temples of Kyoto are thickly crowded the memories of those who in their day have loved the ways of beauty and philosophy.

† The reason for Hideyoshi's apparently arbitrary order to Rikyu to commit Seppuku has has naturally been much discussed by Japanese historians, without any very definite conclusion perhaps, but it does not seem in accordance with what is known of Hideyoshi's character to suppose that he would have put his old friend and adviser to death for merely this refusal, if he did indeed receive it. Toward the end of his life Hideyoshi became more dangerous to his associates, especially those he suspected of threatening his succession, and for this reason the most drastic of his exterminations was that of his adopted son Hidetsugu and his family. And

for he had been expecting it. Quietly he went into his Tea-room and arranged flowers and made Tea for the last time. After it was finished he gave the Kettle called Amida-do, the Tea-bowl Hachi-biraki and the Stone Lantern to Hosokawa Tadaoki, while the Tea-bowl Orisuji and the Tea-spoon that he had made himself he sent to his pupil Sogan. He then composed two stanzas, one a Gatha in Chinese:

> Man's life is seventy years
> Surrounded by danger he rarely expresses
> Welcome to me is this precious blade,
> Slaying all the Buddhas together.

and a second in Japanese style:

> Now my girded sword,
> That upon my armed side
> Hitherto I've worn,
> Draw I forth, and brandishing
> Fling it in the face of heaven.

And so he cut his abdomen in the form of a cross and died, his age being seventy-one years. Hideyoshi had his head and the statue in the Daitokuji stamped upon and publicly exposed on Modoribashi at Ichijo, where crowds of people flocked to see them. His eldest son Dō-an pre-deceased his father and his daughter Gin-ko concealed herself, but his second son Sōjun stayed in the capital and was pardoned by the government, being allowed to inherit his father's house and stipend.

Rikyu's unhappy end, if it be so considered, was not owing to

---

there is no doubt that, altogether apart from Cha-no-yu, Rikyu was a personality of great sagacity and influence, a power among the great lords who surrounded the Taiko.

As Tokutomi observes, it was not only by virtue of being the first Tea-master in the Empire that he was influential, but because he had the capacity to attain and hold such a position. Fukushima Masanori once asked Hosokawa Tadaoki why he thought so much of one who was no warrior and only wielded a Tea-spoon, and Hosokawa advised him to cultivate the acquaintance of Rikyu himself and then he would find out. He did so, and as result was quite converted and observed that though he would face any foe with equanimity he would not care to oppose this Tea-master. It is evident from contemporary letters that Rikyu's statue in the Daitokuji angered Hideyoshi very much, and we know how violently he resented anything like presumption. His anger blazed up against his brother Hidenaga for daring to sign the peace with Shimazu without first asking his permission, and his old associates, Kato Kiyomasa and Kuroda Josui also had narrow escapes from his wrath that it needed all their capacity to contrive. The latter only did it by retiring from active life altogether and incidentally exchanging his nom-de-plume Josui 'like water' for another, Ensei 'completely round' possibly signifying that this quality was, where Hideyoshi existed, much safer than any degree of angularity. Whether there is any truth in the statement in the diary of Tadaoki that Rikyu used his position as a connoisseur to amass a large fortune is possibly as difficult to ascertain as the credibility of the story that it was because Rikyu refused to poison Ieyasu at his bidding that the Taiko thought it safest to put him out of the way. There is however, little evidence to prove that any of these supposed cases of poisoning, which are rare enough, actually happened; Japanese history seems singularly free from this unpleasant method of removing enemies. Certainly a Tea-master would have good opportunities for this method of putting an enemy away, but there is practically no evidence that they did so. Assassinations have never been rare in Japan, but the dagger seems always to have been de rigeur. One might wonder too whether he and other Cha-no-yu masters were involved in the activities of Christianity, the dangerous thought of that day, which sometimes celebrated its Mass in the Tea-room for the same reason as Hideyoshi held his consultations there. It is to be noted that three of his Seven Disciples, Oda Yuraku, Gamo Ujisato and Takayama Ukon were converts and that Gamo was considered a danger to the Taiko, though he died conveniently young, while Takayama ended his days in exile in Manila. But for some reason or for several Hideyoshi must have considered Rikyu politically dangerous.

his flattery of the great as some have asserted.   It was because he
would not stoop to servile conduct that he offended.   What he really
appreciated was a peaceful and retired life and he cared little for
gain and rewards.   It is characteristic of him that he was often heard
to hum to himself the verse of Jichin Oshō,

> What a pity 'tis,
> That the Pure and Perfect Law
> We should keep unstained,
> Is by men so frequently
> Made a source of worldly gain.

Another verse that has been handed down as made by Rikyu as he
quitted this world runs thus :

> How would this fellow Rikyu rejoice to meet his fate
> If he thought it would be with him as with Michizane.

And he wrote on the outside of the lid of the box that held the Tea-
caddy that he used at his last tea the words " This World," while
inside the lid he wrote in small characters the poem of Izumi
Shikibu.

> What I oft have dreamed,
> Far beyond my troubled life
> In this weary world.
> Now perhaps I may attain
> In the true reality.

ODA NOBUNAGA ENTERTAINS HIS RETAINERS.

On the first day of the New Year of 1569 all the generals and
vassals of Nobunaga from the Imperial Domain, Wakasa, Omi, Ise,
Owari and Mino and the nearer provinces came up to the castle of
Azuchi to pay their respects.   Nobunaga made a special Tea-ceremony
for them to which he invited the following : his son Chujo Nobutada,
Hashiba Chikugo-no-kami Hideyoshi, Takei Hoin Sekian, Hosokawa
Hyobutaiyu Fujitaka, Ichibashi Kurozaemon-no-jo Nagakatsu, Hayashi
Sado-no-kami Michikatsu, Takikawa Sakon-no-Shogen Kazumasu,
Araki Settsu-no-kami Murashige, Niwa Gorozaemon Nagahide, Hase-
gawa Tamba-no-kami and Hasegawa Somon.

The ceremony took place in a Six-mat Tea-room with a four foot
verandah and the Utensil-room on the left side.   In the Tokonoma
hung a set of three kakemonos, the centre having the characters
Manzai, the left the new moon and the right islands and pine trees.
The Tea-vessels were all famous treasures, the flower-vase Tsutsu-
sazae being used and the water-jar Taikai, the Tea-bowl was one
that had belonged to Shuko and the kettle was the Hag's Mouth.

At the hour of the Tiger they all arrived and Nobunaga himself
went to meet them and show them into the Tea-room.   He then
served the Kaiseki or light meal that is customary.   Naturally they

were all exceedingly delighted, and among the number were some who were so moved that they did not know in the least what they had been offered.

As soon as the meal was finished he gave cups to all the lords and high officials and four of them served the Saké. Nobunaga entertained all the rest too and was himself present and received them in audience. The next day he invited all of them to inspect the keep of the castle, and on this occasion Zōni or New Year Soup and choice cakes and sweetmeats were served. " It is only through your assistance and faithful service that I have been able to accomplish what I have," he said, " and therefore I feel the deepest gratitude." Whereat all the company bowed with their heads to the ground.

Again on the fourth day Nobutada held another Cha-no-yu to which were invited Hideyoshi, Sekian, Yukan, Michikatsu, Kazumasu, Tamba-no-kami, Nagakatsu, Nagahide and Sonin. Then were used the Tea-caddies called Hatsubana and Shokwa, a Kakemono of wild geese, the Flower-vase Takeno-ko, the Kettle Fujinami, the Tea-bowl Dosa, the Tray Uchiaka, the Tea-spoon Shutoku, a Charcoal-basket in the form of a gourd used by Shō-ō, and Fire-tongs of Korean work, formerly in the possession of Furuichi Harima-no-kami. All these were utensils that had been presented to Nobunaga during the previous year.

INABA ITTETSU.

Inaba Iyo-no-kami Michitomo was known as Ittetsu after he retired. He was one of the three great men of the province of Mino. He was originally a retainer of Saito Tatsuoki and afterwards joined Nobunaga. But Nobunaga was of a very suspicious disposition, and he could not feel certain that Ittetsu was entirely faithful, so he invited him to a Cha-no-yu to have him assassinated. Ittetsu duly presented himself, and the three other guests entered and greeted him. He then sat down before the Tokonoma, in which was a Kakemono of Chinese verse, and softly murmured the words that were written :

> The clouds lie thick across the peaks of Ts'in,
> My house, where can it be ?
> The snow piles high on the pass of Lan,
> My horse will go no farther.[*]

The other guests asked the meaning of it, whereupon Ittetsu gave them a short sketch of the circumstances of the composition, quoting freely from the context. Nobunaga, who was listening on the other side of the wall, was struck with admiration, and suddenly bursting in exclaimed, " What's this Iyo ? I knew you were a first rate warrior, but I thought that was all. I am amazed to find you are a

---

[*] From a poem of Han Yu of T'ang, the greatest man of letters of his age and one of the most prominent in all Chinese literature. Also known as Han Wen Kung, Han the Prince of Literature, and usually in Japan as Kantaishi. This composition was written on his way into exile in Kwantung.

scholar too." Why should I hide it any longer? This reception was not intended as an ordinary Cha-no-yu but for your assassination. These three guests have each a dirk in his bosom. But now I bear you no more ill-will, so do you remain faithful in future and make good use of your shrewdness." Ittetsu bowed low in his place and replied, " I am most grateful to you for sparing my life, and hence-forth I will give you no cause for complaint. I guessed your intention to-day and determined to account for at least one man. So, as you see, I too came prepared." And he also produced a dirk from his clothes.

SHIBATA KATSUIE OBTAINS THE KETTLE UBAGUCHI.

Shibata Shuri-no-Shin Katsuie was one of Nobunaga's generals. For many years he governed the Hokuriku district, and eventually was allotted the two provinces of Kaga and Echizen. On the twenty-fourth of January of the ninth year of Tensho (1582) Katsuie with his son-in-law Iga-no-kami Kazutoyo and his nephew Sanzaemon Katsunari came up to Azuchi and was received in audience by Nobunaga, when he returned thanks for the gift of the two provinces and offered as a present a sword, a thousand pieces of silver for horses, three hundred ryo of gold, a thousand candles, a thousand bundles of thick paper, a thousand bales of cotton and five hundred lengths of silk. On the twenty-fifth Nobunaga entertained him in appreciation of his great merit and served him with tea with his own hand. Katsuie was deeply moved by his lord's condescension, and after a while said : " It is entirely owing to the martial prowess of my lord that I have obtained the two provinces of Kaga and Echizen. My own small services are of no account. Still, now that the whole Empire comes to incline like a reed in the wind that the waving of your banner moves, and opportunities for proving my loyalty in battle will be few, if you would deign to present me with that Old Hag Mouth Tea Kettle that I have longed for all my life I should feel that in my old age I had nothing more to desire." He spoke with great earnestness, and it was not the first time that he had asked for it, and on a former occasion Nobunaga had promised, " when you have given proof of great loyalty I will consider it." So he thought that this was a very suitable time to present it, and rising with alacrity he went into an inner apartment and brought forth the kettle with his own hand and gave it to Katsuie, murmuring the while this extemporary stanza :

> " Hardly can I bear
> Thus to give away to you
> The Hag's Mouth Kettle.
> 'Tis an old familiar friend
> That long use has never staled."

Katsuie's joy was too deep for words at thus having attained his long cherished wish.

Now this kettle was one of the most precious heirlooms of the house of Oda, and when Nobuhide handed it over to his son Nobunaga he charged him, " This is a great treasure to be kept most carefully; still, even so, where an act of great loyalty to our house is in question, you must do as you think suitable to the occasion."

It is said, " Under the bait there is always a fish and under the reward there is always a corpse," and truly men will always fight to the death where there is something worth having. But there is a limit to fiefs that can be given away though there is no limit to man's boundless desires. So that making such presents as Tea-vessels is a good way of stimulating the courage of retainers and also of keeping leaders in the way they should go.

When Oda Nobunaga was in Kiyosu in the province of Owari he made a tea-room in the castle there that was wrought in very fine taste. On the pillar of the Tokonoma was a knot that looked like a Monkey's face, so that it was called Sarumen - no - Chaseki or the Monkey-face Tea-room. This Tea-room with the Rokusō-an at Nara and the Hassō-an at Osaka are called the Three Famous Tea-rooms of Japan. It is still preserved in the garden of the Commercial Museum of the Province of Aichi in the street Monzen-cho at Nagoya.

YAMASHINA HECHIGWAN.

There was a man named Sakamotoya Hechigwan* who lived in upper Kyoto and was married to a niece of the famous physician Manase Seikei. Originally he styled himself Nyomugwan,† but afterwards changed it to Hechigwan, the character read Hechi being half of the character ' jin ' or ' hito ' which signifies ' man ' so one may take it to mean that that was about all he considered himself to be. When Hideyoshi gave his great Cha-no-yu meeting at Kitano in the tenth month of 1588, Hechigwan set up a great red umbrella nine feet across mounted on a stick seven feet high. The circumference of the handle he surrounded for about two feet by a reed fence in such a way that the rays of the sun were reflected from it and diffused the colour of the umbrella all around. This device pleased Hideyoshi so much that he remitted Hechigwan's taxes as a reward. Another example of Hechigwan's drollery was this. He invited Rikyu to a Cha-no-yu and purposely told him the wrong time. Rikyu arrived at the Tea-room only to find the door shut and no sign of any preparation. So he opened the garden gate and went in to investigate. Now in front of this wicket a hole had been dug and covered with a hurdle over which the earth had been carefully replaced. Rikyu really knew all about it but walked straight on as though he didn't. Naturally the hurdle gave way and he fell into the hole so that his clothes got all soiled with clay. Just then Hechigwan appeared, apparently much astonished, and apologized profusely. He then invited Rikyu to the bathroom where the bath was providentially just

---

* Jap, ノ観.
† Nyomugwan 如夢観 Dream-like appearance.

ready. When he had washed and put on fresh clothes provided by his host he was shown into the Tea-room where Hechigwan treated him with the very greatest consideration, so that the meeting was most enjoyable for both.

Some time afterwards it happened a certain person enquired of Rikyu what he thought of the assertion that Tea involved servility, and the Master quoted his experience with Hechigwan as an example to the contrary. "I had heard of his purpose some time before," he said, "but since it should always be one's aim to conform to the wishes of one's host, I fell into the hole knowingly and thus assured the success of the meeting. Tea is by no means mere obsequious-ness, but there is no Tea where the host and guest are not in harmony with one another." Rikyu's art and his skill in utilising the device of another are well shown in this answer. Hechigwan's intention was to amuse himself at Rikyu's expense, and Rikyu amused himself by the contemplation of this amusement. Rikyu's performance was of a far higher order.

Hiki Hyaku-O once invited Rikyu to tea and served water-melon with sugar over it. Rikyu ate only that part that had no sugar on it and when he got home again said with a smile to his pupils, "Hyaku-O does not understand how to entertain people. He gave me water-melon with sugar over it. Water-melon has its own natural taste. It does not need any other flavour." Rikyu liked the natural and Hyaku-O the artificial. That is the difference between one who has the real Tea spirit and one who has not.

It is said that the great recluse can live the retired life in the city, but most men of taste prefer to retire to quiet and remote spots, and one of the advantages of this is that they are not very liable to the visits of thieves, since the things they treasure are only old pots and pictures and writings. If they had money with them they would attract the attention of the light fingered. There is an example of the poet Botankwa Shohaku who had a hundred pieces of gold stolen while he was living in the Western Hills. Yamashina Hechigwan too once sold his Tea vessels for seventy kwan and kept the money in his cottage. A thief broke in and stole the lot.

So "Safety First" for the man of taste lies in keeping no money in his house. Truly Love and Money are everyone's enemy.

Yamashina Hechigwan and Rikyu were always rivals in Cha-no-yu. Hechigwan was indignant at the way everybody flattered Rikyu, and resented the esteem in which he was held by those in high places. He would often remark: "When Rikyu was young his disposition was warm-hearted, but it is so no longer and he is quite a different person. A man's disposition changes every twenty years. I too from the age of forty felt an inclination to abandon self. Rikyu has only experienced prosperity: he knows nothing of the reverse. The changes of the world and the vicissitudes of life are indeed more rapid than the shallows and deeps of the Asukagawa. Therefore wise men will regard this phenomenal world as nothing but illusion, and wealth and position as mere passing clouds. I don't say that every-one should think thus, but only that those who understand these

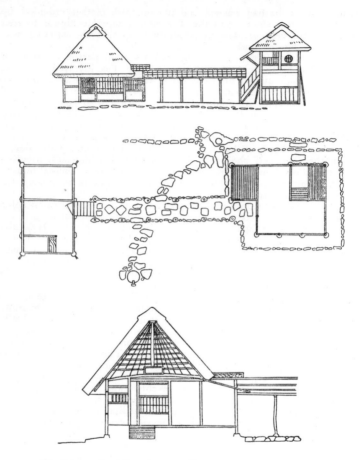

The Shigure-tei and Kasa-chaya, two Tea-rooms connected by a covered way consisting of a roof of bark supported on pillars of natural wood, about twenty-five feet long. The Shigure-tei is two-storied, the upper part used as a Tea-room and the lower as a Machiai. These rooms were formerly in Hideyoshi's palace of Momoyama and were designed by Rikyu, but are now in the Kodaiji, Kyoto. Elevation and plan with section of the Kasa-chaya, so called because the ceiling is constructed like an open umbrella. The Shigure-tei or Autumn Shower Pavilion takes its name from that built by Fujiwara Teika as a resort for viewing the scenery of the showery season and comwosing verse. Cf. the Nō drama entitled Teika.

things will be secure, while those who do not will have trouble in the future. Kamo - no - Chōmei moved his house about like a snail, and I, like a crab, live in a hole that another has made. Why should one trouble about fame and wealth in this transitory life?" And truly he did not value these things, neither did he defer to the rich and influential. At the end of his life he bought in all the poems he had written and burnt them: "So passes my elegance with my life," he remarked, and so died.

It was not so long after Hechigwan made this criticism that Rikyu received from Hideyoshi the order to put an end to himself, though, according to some accounts this was because he opposed Hideyoshi rather than flattered him.

When Hideyoshi was moving to the castle of Fushimi he impressed on each of his personal retainers the necessity of avoiding the use of the word 'Fire' on that day under the threat of a fine if they offended. After a while one of them, Maeba Hannyu, remarked: "That was a very interesting Cha-no-yu that I attended a day or two ago. They used a wooden kettle." "Oh, indeed," said the Taiko, "and how did they prevent the fire burning it."

"Will your Highness be pleased to pay the fine?" immediately retorted Hannyu.

"Dear me, dear me!" exclaimed Hideyoshi, scratching his head in amused vexation.

THE DAWN CHA-NO-YU OF HIDETSUGU.

The Kwampaku Toyotomi Hidetsugu while in Chikuzen obtained a very fine piece of tinted Ogura paper and rebuilt his Tea-room and gave an Inauguration Tea in its honour. Rikyu was the chief guest and there were three others. It was the twenty-first day of the fourth month so the Furo was used according to the summer style. The guests took their seats but there was no light at all in the Tea-room, nothing but the sound of the boiling of the kettle. There was a feeling of unspeakable calm. As he was wondering what the host's intention might be Rikyu suddenly noticed a faint glow on the Shoji behind him and opened it, whereupon the late moon of early dawn threw its beams across the room and illumined the Tokonoma. Moving up closer to inspect it, there hung the famous paper mounted as a Kakemono, and on it was written the verse,

> *When I lift my eyes*
> *To the quarter of the sky*
> *Where the cuckoo cried,*
> *There is nothing to be seen*
> *But the early morning moon.*

Rikyu and his companions sat in silent admiration of the taste and appropriateness of the conception which showed how well their host understood Teaism.[*]

---

[*] This anecdote is also attributed to Hideyoshi in another work, but this version from the *Bizen Rojin Monogatari* seems the more likely one.

HIDEYOSHI'S GOLDEN TEA-ROOM.

Hideyoshi directed his expedition against Korea from the temporary headquarters at Nagoya in Hizen, and here he lived in a very
elegant and tasteful style that was a great contrast to the hard life
and scanty fare of his soldiers in the field.   And rather surprising
was his entertainment of his nobles in a golden Tea-room.   This he
did in the fifth month of the first year of Bunroku (1592) inviting
them in seven parties of six.

The Tea-room was of three mats, and the pillars were all gilt,
as were the sills and lintels, while the walls were of folding gold-
plated boards six feet by five inches, set irregularly.   There were four
Shoji by the verandah and the frames and solid parts of these were
all of gold, and they were covered with silk gauze instead of paper.
The mats were scarlet and their edging was of gold brocade with
a pattern in light green.   They were stuffed with the finest Echizen
cotton wool.   The three foot verandah was of bamboo set in a frame
of round wood with the bark removed.

On the verandah three round seats were placed and on these
three of the guests sat while the other three went inside.   First
Zōni was served and then tea was made.   In the Tokonoma was a
flower arrangement in a turnip-headed arrow mounted on a thin piece
of board.   The stand for the Tea utensils (Daisu), the Tea-cups on
their stands, the square tray, the Tea-caddy, the Kettle and Furo,
the Ladle-rest, the Water-jar and its cover, the Lid-rest, the Tea-
bowl, the Tea-spoon and the gourd-shaped Charcoal-box were all of
gold.   The only articles that were not were the Tea-whisk and the
towel.

This luxury was not exactly inconsistent with Hideyoshi's position seeing that the whole country was at his disposal, but it would
have been out of proportion in anyone else.

HIDEYOSHI ENTERTAINS AT OSAKA CASTLE.

Otomo Yoshishige Lord of Bungo took the name of Sambisai
Sōrin when he retired and became Nyudo.   He was gradually losing
both territory and influence owing to the encroachments of his
neighbour Shimazu Yoshihisa Lord of Satsuma,* and wishing to
obtain the help of Hideyoshi in restoring these, on the fifth day of
the fourth month of the fourteenth year of Tensho (1587) he came up

---

* For further details of this influential and entertaining Daimyo of Kyushu and his dealings
with the Portuguese, his neighbours and others cf. Murdoch, Vol. 2., esp. pp. 74, 77, 102, 104
and 238.   Though Murdoch's view that "In the art of making the best of both worlds old
Otomo proved as incompetent as Omura Sumitada was proficient, . . . King Francis may have
found Heaven, but most of his earthly domains were lost and the house of Otomo all but
ruined in the course of the quest," may be not unjustified. yet he had a very merry and interesting life as well as a lengthy one, with Christianity and Teaism and War and Politics.   He
sent an ambassador and a letter to the Pope in which he observes, "as we are usually at war
and are now aged and weary we cannot ourselves have the honour of coming to the Holy City
to behold your countenance or kiss your feet and receive on our breast the sign of the cross
from your august hand."   According to the Jesuits, says Tokutomi, Sōrin was almost a saint,
but according to his contemporaries he was a rather incompetent general with incomplete control of his passions.

to Osaka and sought an audience through the good offices of Matsui Yukan, bringing a hundred tiger-skins and many other valuable articles as a present. At the hour of the Horse (12 noon) Hideyoshi received him in audience in the reception hall, sitting alone in front while on one side at a respectful distance sat his son Hidenaga, Ukita Hachiro Hideie, Hosokawa Hyobu-no-Taiyu Fujitaka, Hosokawa Tōgoro Hidekazu, Ukita Shichirohyoye Tadaie, and on the other Otomo Sorin in front and Maeda Chikuzen-no-Kami Toshiie, Ankokuji Eikei, Matsui Yukan, and Sen-no-Rikyu a little behind him. First a dinner of Seven, Five and Three, the auspicious number of dishes, was served. This ended Sōrin put forward his petition as follows :   " My family the house of Otomo have since the time of Yoritomo by whom it was conferred on them, held the office of Tandai of Kyushu and have ruled the six provinces of Buzen, Bungo, Chikuzen, Chikugo, Hizen and Higo. Hyuga, Satsuma and Ozumi also should be under my suzerainty, but Shimazu Yoshihisa has taken these three provinces for himself, while Tsukushi, Ryuzōji and Akizuki have each carved out territories for themselves from my land, and with the exception of Tachibana Nyudo Dōsetsu and Takahashi Nyudo Shōun they have all united against us. So Shimazu has become very strong and thinks that if he can subdue the whole of Kyushu he will be able to come up against Kyoto and attempt a decisive battle against you for the sway of the whole Empire ; but I wish your Lordship to attack him first, in which operation I shall be pleased to render all assistance in my power."

" To those who submit to us we give fiefs," replied Hideyoshi, much pleased, " and those who oppose us we conquer one after the other.   The houses of Ōtomo and Mori were for a long time engaged in unseemly strife, it is true, but now we are glad to see that their friendly relations are assured.   Since Shimazu does not obey our commands it naturally follows that we send our armies against him, and as Mori is the nearest we shall cause him to cross over and attack him without delay.'"

The practical business being thus disposed of, Hideyoshi conducted Sōrin to the Golden Chamber.   This was a room of which the walls and ceiling and everything else were all of gold, the frames of the Shoji or sliding doors being of gold and the doors themselves covered with scarlet silk.   The shelves for the tea-utensils had their four supporting pillars of pear-skin gold lacquer and all the metal mounts were of solid gold.   The Kettle and its supporting Brazier, the Incense burner, the Water jar, the Lid-rest, the Dipper-rest, the Slop basin, Tea-Caddy, two Tea-bowls, Tray, Tea-spoon and gourd-shaped Charcoal-container were all of gold.   Only the Charcoal-tongs were of silver, and the hot water Dipper of bamboo.   The Tea-whisk also was of purple bamboo.   Sōrin was naturally amazed.

" I think you are fond of Cha-no-yu, aren't you ? " enquired Hideyoshi.   " Yes, he is quite an adept," replied Rikyu for him. " Then we will give him a cup," said the Taiko.   And Rikyu made

---

* This was the preliminary to the famous campaign of Hideyoshi against Satsuma, the only occasion on which Shimazu's province was conquered.

tea and served it to Sōrin, while Hideyoshi also invited a number of Sōrin's retainers to join them. He then showed them the keep of the castle and gave them tea again in a reception room in it. He also showed them his sleeping chamber.

In it was a raised sleeping-dais about a foot and a half high, seven feet long by four wide, with drapery of scarlet and a pillow of solid gold ornamented with carved work. Next to this were six more sleeping-chambers and in two of them were the jars for keeping the leaf tea, each in a bag of brocade. " Show them my finest jars " ordered Hideyoshi, whereupon Rikyu, Tsuda Sōkyu, Imai Sōkun and Sen Dōan brought out the four tea jars named Shōkwa, Sayo-hime, Nadeshiko and Momoshima, and showed them to Sōrin. He also exhibited the inner apartments and again had tea served to them in an ante-room and presented Sōrin with a short sword of rare make. All the courtiers of Hideyoshi remarked that they never remembered to have seen their Lord in such a gracious mood. After this the visitors were entertained to a feast in Hidenaga's mansion, and when they were preparing to take leave Hidenaga took Sōrin by the hand and said : " The best thing to do is to leave the most private affairs to Sōeki, while I will see to the more public ones. That way you will not go wrong." Sōeki was, of course, Rikyu.

OTOMO SŌRIN AND HIS TEA-CADDIES

The Shogun Ashikaga Yoshiteru once presented Otomo Sōrin with a Katatsuki Tea-caddy. This he in turn gave to Usuki Nyudo Shosatsu, one of his retainers, on account of his knowledge of Cha-no-yu.

In the fourteenth year of Tensho (1586) Shimazu Yoshihisa, lord of Satsuma, made a raid into Bungo and Yoshimune, Sōrin's son, abandoned the castle and fled, whereupon this Katatsuki fell into the hands of Shimazu. On the third month of the following year Yoshi-hisa was retiring to his own province when Saiki Koresada attacked him as he was crossing the Azusa pass on the border of Bungo and Hyuga. The Satsuma men got the worst of it and fell back in haste, and among the baggage the victors captured they found the Tea-caddy. Koresada was immensely pleased to get it, and it eventually found its way into the possession of Tokugawa Ieyasu who prized it greatly and gave it the name of Saiki Katatsuki.

A famous Cha-ire is that called Uesugi Hyotan, the first of the six finest gourd-shaped Meibutsu. Otomo Sōrin, the King Francis Otomo beloved of the Jesuits, had a very high opinion of it, for when Mori Motonari was besieging his younger brother Ouchi Yoshinaga, lord of Yamaguchi, he sent word to Sōrin to ask if he should spare his brother's life or put him to death. " You can put him to death if you like," replied the saintly King Francis, " for I very much wish to have that Hyotan Tea-caddy that is in his possession." So Mori did as suggested and sent Sōrin the desired Cha-ire. It was well for him that Mori himself was no connoisseur.

HIDEYOSHI'S CHA-NO-YU IN THE FIELD

In the twelfth year of Tensho, Toyotomi Hideyoshi was repulsed in the battle of Nagakute in Owari and lost three of his generals, but he paid no attention to this loss but besieged and took all the enemy strongholds in those parts and then started back to the Capital. When about half-way he called Rikyu and said : " Now let us have a Tea-ceremony to liven up our spirits after the strain of this long campaign." So they made tea and the session was just finishing when a messenger came in hurriedly from the front to say that the enemy leader Tokugawa Ieyasu had gone back again to his castle in Owari. " Did you see this yourself ? " enquired Hideyoshi. " I did, with my own eyes," replied the messenger. Hideyoshi turned to Rikyu. " We will have another cup of tea and then we will hurry back to the front," he observed, and in a short time issued orders for the march. He was soon in Ise where he forestalled Ieyasu and came to terms with his ally Oda Nobuo. This was just like Hideyoshi. In the midst of war he never forgot the graces of life, but amid his esthetic diversions he never neglected military necessities.

HIDEYOSHI ENTERTAINS THE CHINESE ENVOYS

After Hideyoshi had been occupied for two years in subduing Korea the Chinese guerilla general Ch'en Wei Ching started negotiations with Konishi Yukinaga who was in command of the advanced post of the Japanese forces and terms of peace were drawn up. Then General Ch'en with the envoy Hsieh Yung Tsu and his subordinate Hsu I Kuan came to the headquarters at Nagoya in Hizen on the fifteenth day of the fifth month of the second year of Bunroku (1594), and informed the Taiko that the Chinese Emperor would affix his seal to the agreement, whereupon Hideyoshi made peace gladly. His great vassals Tokugawa Ieyasu, Maeda Toshiie and Asano Nagamasa took turns to entertain the Chinese guests and then, on the twenty-third day of the fifth month, Hideyoshi received them in audience and drank their health, after which he presented them with swords, wadded garments, hempen summer suits and silver coin and entertained them to a Cha-no-yu in his golden Tea-room.

He himself sat by the side of the Tokonoma while Kyuami made tea and Amako Saburozaemon-no-jo and Mikami Saburo assisted. The great lords and high officers sat on the verandah outside. All the vessels used in the Sukiya were of gold as well as those in the adjoining reception room and in the Tokonoma hung a rare kakemono of Kyōdo's writing which the envoys greatly admired, observing that even in China the work of this master was very rare. When Hideyoshi asked them what artists were most admired in China they replied that Fen Yu Chien came first and then Ma Lin and Mu Ch'i.* So Hideyoshi had the pictures of Evening Rain and The

---

* 芬玉石間, 馬麟, 牧溪.

Bell at Dusk by Yu Chien and Morning Hills and Green Maples
by Ma Lin brought out for their inspection.   The Chinese were
delighted with them and promised that when they got back to their
country they would procure for him the three scrolls of Yu Chien
that were lacking in his set of the Eight Beautiful Scenes of the
Western Lake.   They then praised the scenery of the port of Nagoya
with its splendid bay of calm deep water surrounded by hills.   It
surpassed the ten li scenery of Hsiao-siang, they thought, though it
did not compare with the three hundred li of the Kia Ling river.
So Hideyoshi entertained them in boats on the ninth of the sixth
month, ordering the Nō masters Kwanze and Komparu to attend and
give a performance of their art, and the music and the chanting
echoed over the water and produced so inexpressibly beautiful an effect
that the Dragon Deities of the Sea must have been tempted to
emerge from the waves and take part.

The next day he invited them to take tea in a garden in the
country surrounded by the fresh green of the hills and the murmur
of the mountain streams, far away from everything but the calm of
nature.   Here was a Four-and-a-half Mat Tea-room with the painting
of the Returning Sails by Yu Chien hung in the Tokonoma.   The
Tea vessels were all masterpieces, though simple compared with the
former magnificence.

This time Hideyoshi deigned to serve the tea with his own hands,
using the Temmoku cup on a stand and waiting on the guests himself to their undisguised delight.   In the reception room attached
Yuami made Tea for the feudal lords and high court nobles of his
train.   On the twenty-eighth day the envoys started to return to
China and Hideyoshi made them many presents among which he
included three jars of powder tea for use on the journey and one jar
containing five pounds of fine leaf tea.   This pleased the envoys
exceedingly and they went up to the castle to thank the Taiko
specially for it before setting sail.

HIDEYOSHI'S GREAT CHA-NO-YU AT KITANO*

Toyotomi Hideyoshi, Kwampaku, was a dilettante who always
liked to do things on a large scale.   He conceived the idea of
assembling all the Tea masters in the country and collecting all the
rare tea vessels for a huge Cha-no-yu, and with this object he had
placards erected with inscriptions of two kinds.   The first was a foot
and a half wide, and on a space one foot one inch high within this
was the following inscription :

    " On the first day of the coming tenth month Cha-no-yu will be
    held in the pine woods of Kitano.   Let all, of whatever degree

---

* The Kitano Cha-no-yu was, as usual with Hideyoshi, made an opportunity, not only of
propagating his doctrine of esthetic simplicity and gaining the favour of the people, b..t also of
acquiring some of the finest Tea utensils of his contemporaries.   It was on this occasion that
he was presented with the 'Aburaya Katatsuki,' the property of Aburaya Tsunesaki of Sakai,
and the Kitano Katatsuki, which was given him by the family of Karasu Maru since, as he
went back again specially to look at it a second time, they felt they could hardly do less.   This
Katatsuki was lately bought by a Mitsui from the Sakai family for £ 15,920.

of rank or wealth come and enjoy it.   Everything is to be carried out with an absence of luxury and in the proper spirit of economy.   The Lord Hideyoshi will place on view all the tea vessels that he has collected for several decades, and all are welcome to inspect them.   Tensho 15th year 8th month (1587)."

The other placard was three feet five inches wide and the space of the inscription was one foot five inches high.   The words ran thus :

" From the first to the tenth day of the tenth month Cha-no-yu will be held in the pine woods of Kitano if the weather be suitable, and by favour of his Excellency the Taiko all his famous collection of tea vessels will be displayed for the benefit of connoisseurs.

The devotees, whether rear-vassals, retainers, servants, citizens, farmers or lesser people even, without distinction, should bring a tea-kettle, a bucket and a cup, and if they have no tea, rice powder or other substitute may be used instead.

Two mats are to be spread in the pine woods for the tea, but those whose means do not permit it may use any other straw matting sewn together.

As to dress, guests may wear what they please.

It is unnecessary to say that, according to Japanese custom, all who are interested are welcome, Chinese as well as our own subjects.

The period has been extended from the first to the tenth day so that all from the most distant provinces may be able to attend.

It is out of his great consideration for those of small means that his Excellency makes this proclamation, and he further states that those who do not come shall never afterwards be allowed to use tea-substitute, and this prohibition shall apply even to those who go to visit such people.

To those of small means, even if they do not come from a far province, tea will be presented by favour of His Excellency.

FUKUHARA UMANOSUKE.
NAKAE SHIKIBU-TAIYU.
MIYAGI UKYO-NO-TAIYU.
MAKITA GONNOSUKE.
KINOSHITA TAIZEN-NO-SUKE."

This announcement was placarded throughout the Capital and its suburbs as well as at Nara and Sakai, and all Tea lovers were greatly excited at the opportunity thus provided of seeing the Taiko's treasures as well as of sharing his bounty, while there were not a few who rejoiced at the chance of scoring off the Sakai tea-masters and attracting the attention of Hideyoshi himself, for at this time the men of Sakai had a great reputation for skill in the art, and so were much invited to the houses of the great, and had come rather to despise the people of the Capital in consequence.

And so the meeting was held as arranged, and everywhere in the wide open space under the pines at Ukon-no-baba at Kitano tea-enclosures were made in a setting of plum trees and rocks and pools of water, and all the tea lovers flocked thither and did their utmost to see who could produce the most interesting and recherché effect. The whole extent of the gathering was about a mile square.   Fortunately the day was a fine one, and Hideyoshi with all his nobles and retainers set out at daybreak to find some five hundred and fifty tea-masters assembled, while immense crowds of spectators appeared from all over the country, and the number of the fires that were lighted under the kettles seemed greater than that of the stars in the autumn heaven.

The Taiko was in the highest spirits, and deigned to make tea with his own hands and serve it to his special guests.   They were divided into three parties; first Konoe Nobusuke, Hino Terusuke, Tokugawa Ieyasu, Oda Nobuo and Oda Nobukane; second Toyotomi Hidenaga, Toyotomi Hidetsugu, Maeda Toshiie, Gamo Ujisato and Sen Rikyu; and third, Oda Yuraku, Toyotomi Hidekatsu, Hachiya Yoritaka, Ukita Hideie and Hosokawa Tadaoki.

When this was finished Hideyoshi expressed his intention of going round to see the assembly, and strolled about attended by ten pages-in-waiting.   He first entered the tea-enclosure of Hachiya Dewa-no-kami Yoritaka and took a cup there, after which he invited Hachiya to join him and they went on together.   And as Hachiya was a very merry fellow and never wanting for droll remarks, the whole company soon had sides that ached from laughter.

As they went on they came to a place where a priest of about fifty had hung up a gourd to a branch of a tree and had water boiling beneath it.   Hideyoshi asked for a cup, and the priest replied, with a respectful obeisance, " As your Lordship sees, it is quite ready," and poured out the hot water into a speckless tea-bowl, took down the gourd, and shaking out some tea-substitute from it into the bowl, presented it to the Taiko, who drank it with relish and praised its simple flavour.   This priest turned out to be that odd character Yamashina Hechigwan.   Hideyoshi then proceeded to visit Karasu-maru Asho, and praised a certain famous tea-bowl that he had, when he noticed a bamboo thatched tea-booth next to him and enquired whose it was.   " That is Fukuami's," they replied.   "Ah," laughed the Taiko, " that's the funny fellow who made that odd verse,—how does it run ?

> The man who does not clean his house
> Or plant the gate-way pine,
> Who beats no New Year rice-cake out,
> For him too the New Year will come,
> —Just the same as for anyone else."

And he went in here too.   And so he went round visiting all kinds of people without any respect of rank or possessions until the sun began to sink and he returned to his Palace of Juraku. Very great was the joy and enthusiasm of the people, and the display would have continued for ten days as arranged, but unfortunately a rebellion broke out in Higo, and Hideyoshi had to break up the meeting after one day only, so that all the carefully prepared tea-booths were soon taken down and the glade resumed its wonted quiet. And only the sound of the wind in the pines, which again resumed their sovereignty over the landscape, remained to recall the bubbling of a thousand kettles.

NAYA SUKEUEMON PROFITS BY THE SALE OF TEA-JARS

Naya Sukeuemon, a merchant of Sakai in Izumi,* went over to Luchu and the Philippines in the summer of 1594 and returned to Osaka on the 20th of July of the next year.   He then sent as a present to Hideyoshi by the hand of the Daikwan Ishida Mokuemon Shigenari some Chinese umbrellas, a thousand candles and two live musk-rats, and also showed him fifty tea-jars that he had brought back with him.   Hideyoshi was exceedingly pleased.   " I will get my retainers to buy these," he exclaimed and gave orders that they should be displayed in the great chamber of the Nishi-no-Maru.   After consultation with Sen-no-Rikyu they were divided into three classes and prices were affixed, and proclamation was made that those who wanted one would do well to haste and buy.   Naturally there was no lack of bidders, for, as the proverb says, "A stork has but to cry once," and forty-seven were sold immediately.   Then Sukeuemon asked Ishida to take the other three as a present, but Hideyoshi ordered that he should be paid for them handsomely.   And so, by the sale of these fifty jars† Sukeuemon suddenly became a rich man within a week.

AWAGUCHI ZENSUKE REFUSES THE TAIKO'S REQUEST

Hideyoshi was always on the look-out for rare Tea-vessels, and one day he happened to ask Rikyu whether he had seen any interesting Tea-kettles or other things lately.   " Yes," replied Rikyu, "when I was passing by Awataguchi the other day I noticed a beggar using a kettle to boil water for his meal which I recognized as an extremely fine and rare specimen."   "Indeed," replied Hideyoshi, "then you had better go and get it ; you can give him whatever he asks,

---

* Sakai was an oasis untroubled by the disturbances of the time.   With its peculiar independent elected government of the Ten Chief Merchants and the Thirty Aldermen, and its great wealth drawn from the China trade it was the greatest port in the Empire in these days, easily able to hire the best of the unemployed warriors to guard it, and so bid defiance to all the great military lords, even to Nobunaga and his contemporaries.   Naturally its merchant princes bought up the fine specimens of Chinese ceramic and other art that the Ashikagas had imported, and, like Florence and Venice in Italy, its capitalistic calm enabled culture to flourish. It was not unnatural that the Portuguese missionaries of Nobunaga's day did not find it very sympathetic to their propaganda.

† These were the Tea-jars called 'Boioni' by Europeans that were so much sought for by the Japanese traders to the amazement of the merchant and missionary of the day, whose esthetic standards were different. cf. Murdoch, Vol. 2, p. 273.

fief or money or anything." So Rikyu went off to Awataguchi and said to the beggar, " His Excellency wishes to have that kettle of yours. He will grant you whatever you like in return in fief or money, so please hand it over at once." But the beggar burst forth angrily, " I am poor and have nothing at all to my name, and if I give this away how am I to boil my hot water for tea ? Just because I have a good kettle I am subjected to troublesome demands like this ! " And he took up the kettle and flung it down against a stone in the road and smashed it, and, while Rikyu stood stock still in amazement, he was off like the wind. Rikyu then gathered up the two broken halves of the kettle and went back and reported his adventure to the Taiko, but Hideyoshi did not show any sign of anger. " I have no doubt he comes from a province whose lord is my enemy, and whom I may have slain. That kettle may have belonged to a loyal subject." So he had it mended and it was as good as ever, and he also ordered the kettle maker of Ashiya in Chikuzen to cast three more like it, one of which he kept himself and the other two he gave to Rikyu and Hosokawa Yusai.

But when they made enquiries about this odd beggar they found that he was no loyal subject smarting under an injury to his lord, but a certain Tanaka Hyobu-taiyu who had formerly been a member of the Imperial Bodyguard but who had retired to Awataguchi on the Eastern Hills (taking the name of Awataguchi Zensuke), and there made himself a little hut just big enough to sit in, and with only his Tea-kettle for company spent his old age in this carefree manner, perfectly happy in making tea and sharing it with any passer-by and amusing himself by chatting to all and sundry. They were only grooms and palanquin bearers, it is true, but he found their company quite sufficient. He used this kettle to boil his hot water and also to cook his rice, and when he had no more to eat he used to go into the city and beg it. And all who knew him readily gave him what food and money and clothing he needed, for he never went out till he had finished what he had. And so he continued to live without any desire for wealth or position, passing by the affairs of the world unmoved, and was far too profound a devotee of the philosophy of Tea to do anything else but rush away in anger when offered money and rank in exchange for his matchless Tea-kettle.

HINO TERUSUKE SELLS A TEA-CADDY

Hino Dainagon Terusuke was a distinguished pupil of Sen-no-Rikyu, who was known as Yuishin after his retirement. It was he who was the Imperial Envoy who went to the Tōdaiji at Nara when Oda Nobunaga had a piece cut from the famous Ranjatai* incense

---

* Ranjatai 蘭奢待 is the name of the incense wood that formerly belonged to the Emperor Shōmu and is now in the Shōsōin. Its proper name is Ōjukuko 黄熟香, and the name of Ranjatai contains in its three characters the name of the temple Tōdaiji. In the month of September 1466 the Shogun Ashikaga Yoshimasa passed the Tōdaiji on his way to visit the Kasuga Shrine at Nara and on that occasion he took two pieces of Ranjatai an inch square and one piece

in the Shōsōin. Among the treasures of his family was a tea-caddy which was called Hino Katatsuki and which, with a Canton napkin, was one of the famous tea-vessels of the time.

For some reason or other Terusuke was going to sell this to the merchant Daimonjiya Yōshin, but before parting with it he sent for one Eguchi Sensai and said to him, " I have agreed to sell this tea-caddy for fifty pieces of gold, but I don't feel quite happy about it, so perhaps you might see whether Mimasaka Dono would like it. If he would I would let him have it for forty-five pieces."

Mimasaka Dono was Sensai's Lord, Mori Mimasaka-no-kami Tadamasa, so he hurried off and asked him, but unfortunately he could not get together so much money and had to decline, so it was sold to the merchant after all. So scarce, it seems, was gold at this time that though Mori's income as Lord of Mimasaka was some hundred and eighty thousand koku he could not manage to procure forty-five pieces.

MAEDA TOSHIIE ASSISTS EXILED FRIENDS

When Toyotomi Hidetsugu was ordered by his father to go to Koya-san and there commit suicide, Inoko Takumi and Terada Sōyō were sent into exile and all their property was confiscated. Now Dainagon Maeda Toshiie was a friend of both and when he heard of it he felt very sorry for them and took all Takumi's tea-vessels into his own charge, sending his retainer Kamiya Shinano with a present of five pieces of gold for the expenses of their journey. Sōyō had a famous tea-caddy worth, it was said, some sixty or seventy pieces of gold and of this Toshiie also took charge. Soon after the Būgyo, in the course of a strict investigation, came to hear that these things were in Maeda's mansion and enquired the reason. " That tea-caddy is mine," he answered, " for I bought it of Sōyō at a time when he needed money." And the Būgyo said no more since it was Maeda Toshiie. The next year Toshiie obtained a pardon for the two from Hideyoshi and restored Sōyō his tea-caddy and Takumi all his vessels too.

And all agreed that Maeda was as magnanimous as he was influential. As the verse put it:

> When your luck is out
> And your sleeves with tears are wet
> Then you know full well
> Who's your friend and who is not.
> The true self will show itself.

five inches square. The larger piece he presented to the Betto of the shrine while one of the smaller pieces he sent to the Emperor and the other he kept himself. Again on March 28th 1575 Oda Nobunaga asked the permission of the Emperor and took a piece one inch and eight tenths long, and this he divided into three, taking one part himself and dividing the other two among his great vassals and the other nobles. Again in June 1603 Tokugawa Ieyasu sent Honda Masanobu and Okubo Nagayasu and they took a piece one inch eight bu in length. For the fourth time only in its history of more than eleven hundred odd years, in 1878, when the Emperor Meiji proceeded to Nara, he also took a piece of this Ranjatai.

And Maeda had experienced this himself.   For when he fell under the displeasure of Oda Nobunaga, those who had been his friends turned away from him, while his enemies became still more hostile, and it was only Shibata Katsuie and Mori Nagayoshi who stuck to him.

On the ninth of December 1599 Maeda Toshiie invited his son Hizen-no-kami Toshinaga to a tea party.   The other guests were Inoko Takumi, Yamaoka Sōmu and Hijikata Kambei.   When the tea was finished Toshiie put tea into the Tea-caddy called ' Konomura '* and offered it to Toshinaga   " If this comes to you after my death," he said, " you won't feel any more grateful than other sons usually do when they inherit their father's property.   But I should like to witness the pleasure you will feel in receiving it now, so do you take it and show us your skill by serving us from it."   " I am indeed overwhelmed by your kindness," replied Toshinaga, " but though you allow it to be mine, please let it remain in your keeping for the present and then you can use it when you like."   " Oh no," insisted his father, "there is no need of that.   You must take it and keep it, for that is my desire."   And as the others also pressed him to accept this auspicious present, he hesitated no longer, whereupon Toshiie retired into the Mizuya, summoned the official who carried his clothes-box, changed his garments and returned to the Tea-room, to take his seat this time with the guests.   Then Toshinaga served them with tea as host, and acquitted himself most capably in this rôle to his father's great satisfaction."

KOBAYAKAWA TAKAKAGE TESTS THE WIT OF HIS RETAINERS.

Kobayakawa Saemon-no-suke Takakage had among his retainers one who was very well read and quick-witted.   One day Takakage, when walking in his garden, sat down on a tree and put some grass on his head, calling out to his attendants :   "Here! Bring me this!" But they could not understand what it was he wanted.   The quick-witted one, however, went off immediately and soon returned with a cup of tea.   " Now you see why it is," observed Takakage, as the others stared in amazement, " that I have a high opinion of this man. A good general is one who encourages ability of every kind and uses it in its place, and who does not despise any sort of capacity."   This was intended to be a lesson to the others, who had been inclined to be contemptuous of one who shone rather in letters than in military matters.

The Chinese character for ' Tea ' is composed of the three elements ' Grass ' on top of ' Man ' over ' Tree.'†

Kobayakawa Takakage was for a time very fond of Cha-no-yu, but afterwards gave it up.   In explanation of this he once said to

---

* The Tea-caddy ' Konomura ' got its name from Hachiya Sōgō whose trade name was Konomuraya, and who regarded it as his most valuable possession. He was a pupil of Shukō and teacher of Shō-ō.

† There is a fanciful explanation of the character as ' Tree of a person of twenty.' The great Indian physician Jiva, it is said, had a daughter of twenty who died and in his grief he poured out his best remedies on her tomb, from which the Tea plant forthwith sprang up.

a friend. " Cha-no-yu is a very noble and elegant amusement since it inculcates avoidance of the empty vanities of this world and a taste for life spent amid the beauties of nature, leading men to find their pleasure in that artistic detachment of mind that arises from the contemplation of the calmness of cloud and water and the grace of fish and bird ; yet when one comes to examine the ways of the tea-lovers themselves, they seem to think of nothing but the connoisseurship of tea-vessels and their value and how to find bargains in them, and consider it clever to get a high price for things they have picked up for a song, and give themselves fancy names and so on, and the result is a lot of bickering and jealousy and the real meaning of Cha-no-yu is forgotten. Even without that man's mind is liable to be attracted quite enough by material things, so I have determined to forego this pleasure for the future.

At the present day the late Marshal Prince Yamagata seems to have come to much the same conclusion. In the second volume of Takahashi Yoshio's *Kōshin Chadoki* there is an account of the very modest Kyoto villa of the great soldier statesman called Murin-an, which consisted of only an eight mat room with anteroom, a ten mat reception room, a foreign style study for the winter and a three mat daime Tea-room and Mizuya. The late Prince also built in the very fine garden of this villa a copy of the famous Tea-room called En-an and gave a Cha-no-yu to inaugurate it. For this he provided only ordinary utensils such as are used for practice. To this meeting were invited a number of well-known Kyoto Chajin. Since apparently they found nothing much they could say about his Tea utensils some of them fell to discussing famous Tea-things they had seen elsewhere, and the recent sales of such things and the prices paid for them. After they had departed the Prince observed that it appeared he had merely provided them with a place in which to discuss the price of other people's possessions ; not at all a profitable subject to have to listen to. Afterwards he gave no more Cha-no-yu parties for this kind of Chajin.

FURUTA ORIBE AND THE INCENSE

Furuta Oribe-no-Sho Shigenari* was fond of Cha-no-yu from his youth, and became' one of the seven most distinguished pupils of Rikyu who were known as the Seven Sages of Tea. He is the author of a work known as the Hundred Precepts of Teaism. He entered the service of Hideyoshi and acquired the title of Oribe-no-Sho. At the battle of Sekigahara he was at first on the side of Ishida Kazushige, but left him and went over to Tokugawa Ieyasu, and after things had settled down he received a stipend of ten thousand koku. He was famous for his fastidious taste.

He once went to a Cha-no-yu party at the mansion of Yama-

---

* Furuta Oribe : his name is given as Shigekatsu, Shigeyoshi and Shigenari. As the Chief Tea Master of his time he was called ' the Osho (Upadhyaya) of his age.' And Tea Masters continued to be called Osho, though not priests.

saki Sōkan. He stopped on till late in the evening chatting confidentially, and then became sleepy and turned over and dozed on the mats. "Here," said Yamasaki, "let someone bring a wadded garment and put it over him to keep him warm." And a servant brought one on a large tray and gently slipped it over him, and as he did so a heavy scent of rare incense filled the whole room. "Ah," exclaimed Oribe," aroused by the perfume, "Sōkan's taste is not of the best. Fine incense like this should be used sparingly, for the rarer the incense the more rarely should it be used, and no adept at the Incense Ceremony would burn it thus lavishly."

FURUTA SHIGENARI ON THE BATTLE-FIELD

Furuta Oribe-no-Sho Shigenari was in the field in the winter campaign of 1615 at Osaka, and when the battle began at Imafuku on the eastern side of the castle on the twenty-sixth of November he went to visit Satake Ukyo-no-taiyu at his headquarters there. Happening to notice a barricade made of bamboos, his curiosity was immediately aroused, and muttering to himself, "H'm, I wonder if any of these bamboos would make a good tea-spoon," he poked his head out to look round, when a chance bullet happened to hit it. Shigenari sprang back in astonishment and taking out a purple tea-napkin from his bosom wiped away the blood. "Just what you might expect from a Tea-Master," was the comment of the spectators.

The next day he went and saw Ieyasu at his camp at Chausuyama. "I got this wound at the front, you see, with Satake's army," he observed, pluming himself on his exploit. But Ieyasu, who had already heard all about it, took no notice and spoke of other matters. When he took his departure rather ill at ease, Ieyasu, looking after him, observed drily, "That Oribe is the sort of fellow who will die from a fish-bone stuck in his throat."

When someone was kind enough to repeat this to Shigenari he was very angry. "What does he mean by holding me up to ridicule before everybody?" he exclaimed. "That's a thing I won't forget either in this world or the next." And the next year when the summer campaign against the city was beginning he made secret overtures to the enemy with his pupil Kimura Sōki and others to set fire to the Capital and abduct the person of the Emperor. But the affair was discovered and he and his son were ordered to put an end to themselves, while Sōki and twenty-four accomplices suffered the same penalty.

Though a sage in Tea he was no soldier and lacking in humanity. It was one of Oribe's habits to cut up valuable antiques and patch a piece of one on to a piece of another and so use them. And people thought this was tasteful and some imitated. One day Okawachi Kimbei Mototsuna, who was the father of that Matsudaira Idzu-no-kami commonly known as 'Wise Idzu,' remarked to some one, "Misfortune will befall Oribe some day: death, I expect." And when his plot was found out and he and his son were condemned, people were very surprised and asked Mototsuna how he knew that Oribe would be so unfortunate. "For this reason," answered Mototsuna, "ancient and valuable treasures are things that have had to pass through many vicissitudes and consequently many have been destroyed, and those that have survived have only done so through the protection of the Gods and Buddhas. How then can a person who cuts and mutilates them merely for his own amusement escape the anger of these Deities? It is natural to suppose that he would not pass through life unscathed."

KURODA JOSUI UNDERSTANDS THE MEANING OF CHA-NO-YU

Kuroda Kampei Yoshitaka, known as Josui after his retirement,[*] was a great strategist under Hideyoshi. He often deplored the fashion for Cha-no-yu that prevailed in the Taiko's circle, saying, "Tea making is no business for warriors. It's very risky for host and guests to huddle into a little room like that unarmed." But

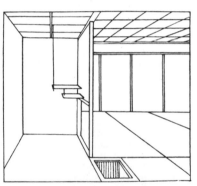

Tea-room of the Ryūkōin at the Daitokuji built for Kuroda Jōsui by his son Nagamasa, showing middle pillar and double shelf.

one day Hideyoshi invited him to a Tea, and as it was not possible for him to decline his Lord's order he entered the Tea-room very reluctantly. Soon Hideyoshi came in, but he did not proceed to serve tea. He sat down close up to Kuroda and in a low voice began to discuss certain confidential military affairs. When he had finished he remarked, "This is one advantage of Cha-no-yu. If I had invited you to meet me somewhere on the quiet, suspicions would very likely have been aroused and something untoward might have resulted. But since it is Cha-no-yu there is no fear of that. What do you think?" "Ah," replied Kuroda, "I should never have thought of that. Now I see that a great general never likes anything without a very good reason. Now I understand

---

[*] Also known to the Portuguese missionaries as 'the virtuous Simon Kondera,' from his earlier name Kodera. He was a Christian among other things, and when he died both Buddhist and Shinto as well as Christian services were held. But his tomb is Buddhist and bears the posthumous name Ryūko-in-ensei-jōsui-dai-kōji, Great Enlightened Recluse, round and clear like water, in the Mansion of Dragon Light. His pen name Josui, 'Like Water,' refers to the Chinese saying that water adapts itself to the shape of the vessel that contains it, and signifies his great admiration for that quality of which he was a most eminent exponent. He was perhaps the greatest military expert of his time, and it was largely by his diplomacy that Ieyasu was able to be sure of his ground at Sekigahara. With Konishi Yukinaga he led the van of Hideyoshi's Korean campaign. Cf. his famous *Tea Maxims*.

the real meaning of Cha-no-yu." And from that day he too began to study it and ended by becoming an expert.

This was a case of Hideyoshi's using tea for his own purposes as he used everything. Both he and Kuroda were merely abusing it, for Cha-no-yu has no affinities with politics or militarism and knows no distinction of rank. It is said that the subject of Hideyoshi's conference on this occasion was the punishment of the Kwampaku Hidetsugu.

ODA YŪRAKU'S MISTAKE

Oda Gengoro Nagamasu was the younger brother of Oda Nobunaga, and a disciple of Sen-no-Rikyu. He took the title of Yūraku-ken Jō-an on his retirement. He was a famous tea-master and became the founder of the Yūraku School of Tea, being known after his death as Cha-no-Sosho (Chief Tea Master). One day he went to visit Rikyu and found the Master fitting a lid to a Tea-caddy. He selected an old one and observed to Yūraku that this suited much better than the larger sized one it already had. Yūraku expressed his admiration. Some time after this Yūraku fitted an old lid to one of his own tea-caddies and showed it to Rikyu for his approval. " I don't think much of your discrimination," was the comment. . "A new lid would suit this one better. A stork's bill does not fit a duck's neck. Mere imitation without regard for what is harmonious is quite contrary to the spirit of Teaism."

ODA YŪRAKU'S DAWN TEA

Once when Oda Yūraku was in Osaka he invited a few friends to Cha-no-yu. They were men of high rank, and he wished to let them see the effect of the garden with the stone lanterns lighted, so he asked them to come very early, before it was light. Thus' they braved the dim bleak air of early morning and knocked at his door some time before dawn. A distinguished-looking man greeted them. " Yūraku is greatly obliged to you for coming at this unseasonable hour, but will you kindly excuse him for a while, for he is an old man and is still in bed. As there is yet no fire in the hearth, will you come this way and sit down and rest yourselves." And he led the way through to an Arbour in the Inner Rōji. There was no moon and the dawn had not yet broken. The light of the stone lanterns shone faintly and the wind sounded loudly in the pines. A lonely and eerie feeling brooded over everything and the guests shivered in tune with it, when suddenly there was a sound of someone clearing his throat, and as they wondered what it might mean there followed the twang of the tuning of a Biwa, and then came the opening words of the ‘ Imperial Progress to Ohara ’ from the *Heike Monogatari*. " In the spring tide of the second year of the era of Bunji, His Imperial Majesty the Retired Emperor Go-Shirakawa made up his August Mind to visit the Former Empress Kenrei-mon-in in her solitary dwelling." And with such feeling and power was it chanted that they could not restrain their tears, and sat spell-bound in ecstasy until at last it came to an end, and as it did so the dawn broke. Then, as they were expressing their admiration and regretting that it was so soon over, the gate of the Rōji opened and Yūraku's voice was heard. "Ah, pray excuse an old man for over-sleeping! How very kind of you to venture. I am afraid you must find it very cold." The taste and tact he showed here were worthy of the highest traditions of Tea, for the singing transported them in spirit to the lonely temple amid the rugged hills.

Oda Yūraku gave a Cha-no-yu on the 14th of the 10th month of Keicho 16 (1612). Hino Nyudō Yuishin and Yamana Nyudō Zenko assisted. The Narashiba Katatsuki was used for Koicha and the Shii Katatsuki for Usucha. The Kakemono was by Kyōdo and the Flower Vase was an antique bronze one. Yūraku made the Tea and Toku-gawa Ieyasu arranged the flowers. (*Sumpu Seiji Roku.*)

After the fall of the castle of Osaka, Oda Yūraku went and lived in retirement on Higashiyama outside Kyoto in order to divert him-self with Cha-no-yu. Thus he came to buy a writing by Sō-hō the founder of the temple of Daitokuji at Murasakino, from Sō-chō, a priest of this same temple, for the large sum of fifty pieces of gold; and this scroll he valued very greatly, but there were some critics who happened to examine it who said it was not genuine. Others, how-ever, declared that it was no forgery, and before long the question was widely discussed everywhere and became a great problem. Though many priestly connoisseurs assured him that it was a good one, since the eminent critics Egetsu and Taku-an were against it he decided to appeal to the authorities. But the Shoshidai in Kyoto, Itakura Iga-no-kami Katsushige and the officials under him did not care to do anything, since this was hardly the kind of case they were qualified to decide.

Now it happened that the Shogun Tokugawa Hidetada was in Kyoto about this time, and when he heard it he signified his inten-tion of dealing with it himself. So he ordered many genuine works of Sō-hō to be sent for from the Daitokuji and placed beside Yūraku's specimen, so that they could be compared minutely. And when this was done many doubtful points became apparent. Then the great Kangakusha Hayashi Dōshun was called in consultation and he gave it as his opinion that there were faulty characters in it and that it certainly was not the work of Sō-hō. Then the Shogun pronounced judgment : " To defraud people by forgeries of works of art is un-worthy of a priest of Buddha. Let Sō-chō be unfrocked and expelled from the gate of the temple."

Sō-hō is also known as Myō-chō. He was a native of Isei district of Harima province, and was said to have been born in response to a prayer that his parents offered before the Kwannon of Shosha-san. He was an intelligent and beautiful child and it is related of him that when he was seven years old, seeing some one polishing a sword, he observed, " The efficacy of a sword lies in its not being efficient.

Yabuuchi Shochi's three mat Daime Tea-room at Nishi-no-Doin, Kyoto.

Do you know that?" And the other could find no answer. This kind of expression is characteristic of Tea and Zen. Sō-hō became a monk at the age of eleven and eventually became the founder of the Daitokuji.

YABUUCHI SHŌCHI AND THE INCENSE-BURNER

Yabuuchi Shōchi was one of Sen-no-Rikyu's best pupils. He had many names, for he was known as Sōchusai, Kenchu, Enan and Insai. At the request of Rōnyo Shōnin he went and lived at the Hongwanji. As the house of Sen was in the north of Kyoto and Yabuuchi in the south the former was commonly known as the Upper School and the latter as the Lower. Now Shōchi had an incense burner called Shimei which he used as a brazier for lighting his pipe. And it chanced that he produced it one day when a certain priest named Rōkan came to see him. Rōkan took it into his hands admiring it and smoothing it caressingly and eventually he said: "Why is it that you use such a precious thing as a brazier?" Shōchi laughed. "It is because I use it in this way that you notice it and think so much of it. If I put it in the Tokonoma and used it as an incense-burner you would take it for granted." It needs taste to use a thing naturally as Shōchi did. For one must know when to stop. If a thing is used too much it loses power to attract and becomes dead. In painting a tiger one must be careful not to paint it like a cat.

The house of Yabuuchi never became attached to any great family, but remained ordinary Tea masters. Consequently the same misfortune did not befall them as happened to Rikyu, though they remained comparatively little known. But on the other hand this family collected and still possesses an unrivalled collection of famous Tea utensils formerly belonging to Ashikaga Yoshimasa, Hideyoshi, Hidenaga, Rikyu, Oribe and so on, such as no other school has retained. In their Buddhist Shrine is a figure of Daruma brought from China by Eisai Zenji, supported on each side by statues of Shōchi Kenchu and Rikyu. And in the hood on the head of Rikyu there is a lock of hair which he himself gave to his friend Kenchu before he died. The Yabuuchi house have always been in close connexion with the Higashi Hongwanji temple and have been instructors to those of the Lord Abbots and high priests who were interested in Cha-no-yu.

Once Rikyu dropped in unexpectedly on his friend Yabuuchi Shōchi, and Tsubouchi had no flower for his Tokonoma, so he immediately went out to his vegetable garden and got a piece of Himeuri which he put into a vase. Rikyu was so pleased that he named the vase Himeuri in honour of the occasion, and it is still among the treasures of the house of Yabuuchi.

Speaking of incense-burners, there was in Nagasaki a woman who cast very fine ones in metal. She had learned the art from her father and behaved herself just like a man. She liked men's company, had a frank and lively nature and was fond of liquor.

She never had any money, but that did not trouble her. If any-one ordered an incense-burner and paid, it might be twenty or thirty pieces of gold, she would spend it in fish and drink and invite all the neighbourhood, and they would go on feasting and guzzling for days before she would even think about starting the work. The Bugyo of Nagasaki once ordered one, and six months went by with-out any sign of it. Then, as his term of òffice was nearly due to expire he pressed her to hurry and she promised it for just before his departure, but still nothing happened. One day she stood for hours with a big iron tube in her hand blowing up the fire and staring into it thinking hard for an idea for this incense-burner, but as none came to her she suddenly seized an axe and smashed it into frag-ments at one blow. And the Bugyo had to go back without it after all. The name of this woman craftsman was Kamejo (Madame Tortoise).

SHIMAI SŌSHITSU

Shimai Shōshitsu was a wealthy merchant of Hakata. His name was Shigekatsu and his ordinary name Tokudaiyu. When he retired he called himself Kyuhakuken Tan-Ō. He traded with Chosen, China, the Philippines and Siam and was a great friend of the well known merchants Kamiya Sōtan, Suetsugu and Sotoku, two of whom were known with him as the Three Hakata Merchant Princes.

Sōshitsu studied Tea under Sen-no-Rikyu and Tsuda Sōkyu and Zen philosophy under the famous priests Kōkei and Kōgetsu of the Daitokuji, and became a great adept at both. He was received in the highest circles both of rank and letters. In the tenth year of Tensho (1583) he went up to the Capital on the first day of the sixth month and paid his respects to Oda Nobunaga at the Honnōji where he was entertained to Cha-no-yu. This night happened to be the one on which Akechi Mitsuhide made his sudden attack on his Lord, and Nobunaga immediately rushed out of the Tea-room to lead his men. But though the whole mansion was thrown into an uproar like hell let loose, Sōshitsu and the others sat calmly in the tea-room, and when the clash of swords and the sound of the war-cries drew nearer and nearer, until they were right round them, the dignity and quiet deliberateness of the Tea-master did not leave them and still they remained unmoved. Soon all was over and Nobunaga put an end to himself and the flames of the burning mansion crept on towards the Tea-room. Sōshitsu took from the Tokonoma a scroll of the Thousand Character Classic written by Kūkai, and, putting it into his bosom, took refuge with Sōtan in the priests' residence of the Honnōji. It was solely owing to the presence of mind of Sōshitsu that this precious writing survived.*

---

* After Nobunaga's death two Tea-caddies were recovered from the ashes of the Tea-room in which he had been when the attack was made. One, of Chinese ware, was repaired by Kobori Enshu with lacquer, for it had been split by the heat, and is known as Honnōji Bunrin. The other was a Ko-Seto Cha-ire afterwards named Enjobo. Both were acquired by Matsu-daira Fumai and are still in the possession of his house.

SHIMAI SŌSHITSU AND THE NARASHIBA TEA-CADDY

All Tea enthusiasts envied Shimai Sōshitsu his possession of the Narashiba Tea-caddy, which was one of the treasures of Matsuura Shikibu-kyo Hōin Shigenobu.* Otomo Sōrin, Lord of Bungo, offered him four hundred kan of silver and the Shiga tea-jar in exchange for it, but he refused. Akizuki Chikuzen-no-kami Tanezane, Lord of the castle of Akizuki, also sent a messenger to him asking for it and threatening that if he did not let him have it he would bring an army against Hakata and take it by force. But again he quietly declined. Then Hideyoshi came to hear of its fame and sent a request for it through Rikyu, Sōshitsu's master. But even this did not move him.

In the eighth month of the fourteenth year of Tensho (1587) Hideyoshi started out on his campaign to subdue Shimazu Yoshihisa, Lord of Satsuma, and his advance-guard under Mori Terumoto arrived at Hakata on the twenty-fourth, where Yoshihisa's men made a stand against him and in the fight the city was set on fire. Meanwhile the Taiko's main army had come round by sea, and Yoshihisa's troops, seeing they could do nothing more, retreated. Now Akizuki Tanezane was with Yoshihisa on this occasion, but when he saw the strength of the army of Hideyoshi, he thought it would be wiser to go over to him. So with the intention of using Sōshitsu as a go-between to treat with the Taiko through Rikyu or Ishida Kazushige, he arranged for a Cha-no-yu party to be held at the merchant's house, at which he was able to say what he wanted secretly. But as he was leaving he managed to put the Narashiba tea-caddy into his pocket without anybody noticing it, his plan being to obtain the favour of Hideyoshi by presenting it to him.

Now when Sōshitsu found this out afterwards, he did not show any great attachment for the tea-caddy or any resentment against Tanezane. But he set fire to the tea-room and gave out that the famous treasure had been burnt. This he did as the result of careful consideration. Meanwhile Hideyoshi advanced and laid siege to the castle of Akizuki. Tanezane did not resist, but went out to meet him with the Narashiba tea-caddy and surrendered himself and it. Hideyoshi accepted both.

When the war was over Hideyoshi came to Hakozaki, and Sōshitsu presented a gift of purple and fresh fish as a congratulation on his victory. The Taiko ordered the rebuilding of the burnt streets and also told Rikyu to invite him to Cha-no-yu, but he declined this honour on plea of illness. Hideyoshi then returned in triumph to Osaka and after a while he sent a message to Sōshitsu, bidding him come to see him there for, he said, " I have a magnificent tea-caddy that I want to show you now I have returned home safely."

---

* Matsuura Shigenobu, the first of the name, who died in 1614 aet. 66. the 'old King Foyne' of the English letters. Matsuura Shigenobu II died in 1703 aged 80. It was this latter, usually known as Chinshin (the other reading of Shigenobu), who founded the Chinshin school of Tea.

Sōshitsu guessed that he wanted to question him about this Narashiba. " I know he thinks I gave it to Tanezane rather than to him and he wants to taunt me with it; but if I tell him that Tanezane stole it I myself may get off scatheless but his fief will probably be confiscated and he will be a laughingstock ever after. That is why I declined to go at Hakozaki, but now he has summoned me thus to Osaka there is no help for it, I must go perforce." So he made up his mind to bear the brunt of it himself and went to Osaka, where the Taiko received him most cordially, and, as he had expected, showed him the Tea-caddy. " How's this, Hakata Bozu? This rare treasure has fallen into my hands unexpectedly, you see. Isn't it the one that was stolen from you a while ago?" Sōshitsu was amazed at Hideyoshi's almost uncanny acumen in divining exactly what had happened.

But he answered without hesitation, " That must be a little joke of your Lordship. That tea-caddy was burnt with my tea-room some time ago. This is certainly the tea-caddy called 'Hatsubana' which was presented by the Lord Tokugawa." Hideyoshi guessed his meaning by this reply, and admiring his tact and loyalty, pressed him no farther. Tanezane also heard of it before long and felt heartily ashamed of his conduct.

This Narashiba tea-caddy was made of fine green paste with light brown glaze run over about half of it. It had two lines at the mouth and a thick band round the middle, and the bottom was marked with 'string cutting.'

SŌSHITSU AND THE KOREAN EXPEDITION

In the third month of the eighteenth year of Tensho (1591) with a view to beginning his subjugation of Korea, Hideyoshi sent a secret message to Sōshitsu that, since he had long had a branch house in Korea, he had better go there and under cover of a business tour carefully observe the geography of the country.

Since Sōshitsu was a man of affairs who was not in any way lacking in daring and endurance, he accepted at once and before he went Kobayakawa Takakage, Lord of Najima in Chikuzen, gave a Cha-no-yu party to speed him, which Kuroda Jōsui also attended. On the fifteenth day of the sixth month he set out from Hakata with Saito Denuemon, Motoyama Uemon, and a certain Shima who was a retainer of Kobayakawa. They soon arrived at Fusan in Korea, and then, accompanied by a retainer of Sō Yoshitomo, Lord of Tsushima, they disguised themselves as Koreans and wandered all over the peninsula making careful observations as they went. After six months they came back safely and reported everything they had seen minutely to Ishida Kazushige and Masuda Nagamori who were then in Hakata. These two returned and reported it to Hideyoshi, who ordered Sōshitsu to go to Osaka to see him personally. When he arrived, Ishida got hold of him beforehand and said, " The country has not yet recovered from the effects of the wars here, and now if an army be sent abroad the hardships of the farmers will be much greater. We have all given this advice, but his Lordship takes no notice; but he will trust what you say, so pray tell him of all the difficulties of this expedition when you see him and so try to turn him from it." Sōshitsu quite sympathised with this view himself, but he knew how hard it was to move the Taiko when he had once determined on a thing. So when he was summoned into his presence he simply reported all the results of the information he had gathered. Hideyoshi was delighted. "Ah," he exclaimed, "my plans are quite ready. We will soon start, and after crushing Korea we will then overwhelm the four hundred odd provinces of China. What d'you say, Hakata Bōzu, will you guide us?"

"Please excuse me," replied Sōshitsu, "this may be a brave and gallant expedition in its way, but the expense will be great and the profit small, and even though it is your Lordship, I don't think a losing business is any good, so would not it be better to give it up?"

Hideyoshi flew into a rage at once. "This is beyond anything," he burst out, "that a mere tradesman like you should dare to dictate to the Kwampaku. Here, let someone take the head off this confounded Bōzu!" And he stamped on the floor and left the room. Kazushige and Nagamori and all the rest who were there were much astonished, and with Rikyu and Imai Sōkyu they had some trouble in calming the anger of Hideyoshi.

Later on next year, when the campaign began, Tokugawa Ieyasu passed through Hakata on his way to Nagoya in Hizen, and Sōshitsu gave him all the information he needed about Korea, Honda Masazumi sitting by them and writing it all down. Sōshitsu also gave Ieyasu a map he had made of Korea and promised to visit him at his house. On the day after Ieyasu and Uesugi Kagekatsu with all their great vassals went to Sōshitsu's house in Hamaguchi Machi. Before the gate were hung two wide curtains with his crest on them while within the rooms were all hung with purple damask. In the Tokonoma was a pair of pictures of wind-blown bamboos by Yang Chia Sung of T'ang. The floor of the reception room was spread with leopard skins, while gold screens stood around the walls and the choicest works of art of China and Japan were displayed everywhere. After a repast of the most costly delicacies they were invited into the tea-room, which was also furnished with utensils of the greatest rarity and interest. Sōshitsu and Sōtan were by no means ordinary merchants or ordinary Chajin. They were men who were ready to make the greatest sacrifices for their country. They might be styled warrior merchants or warrior Chajin with equal truth.

At this time the places where Cha-no-yu was most flourishing were Sakai in the East and Hakata in the West. The spirit of Sakai was esoteric and calm, that of Hakata dignified and magnificent. Rikyu and Sōkyu were typical of the East, Sōshitsu and Sōtan of the West. Of Hideyoshi it might be said that he was inclined to make the East his teacher and the West his friend.

KAMIYA SŌTAN

Kamiya Sōtan was another great merchant of Hakata. He had a Tea-caddy called Hakata Bunrin which was as famous as Sōshitsu's Narashiba. Hideyoshi coveted this also and tried to get it through the good offices of Rikyu, but Sōtan declined to part with it.

When Hideyoshi invited Sōshitsu to Cha-no-yu at Hakozaki after he had received this Narashiba from Akizuki Tanezane, Sōtan had been invited with him, and since Sōshitsu declined on the plea of illness Sōtan went alone. Hosokawa Yusai and Sen-no-Rikyu were also there. "Ah, Tsukushi Bozu, so you've come, have you," said Hideyoshi, " and how about Hakata Bozu ? " for so he always called these two. " Sōshitsu is ill, my lord," replied Sōtan. " What's the matter with him ? " enquired Hideyoshi. " The Narashiba disease, I think," was the ready answer. A smile spread over Hideyoshi's face. "Ah, Hakata Bozu is a sharp fellow ! I've got something here I wanted to show him but he seems to have smelt it out and kept away. You'd better take care that your Bunrin isn't stolen too." "Exactly," thought Sōtan to himself, and tapping his neck he replied, " I'll stake this that it isn't stolen." Hideyoshi looked at Rikyu and laughed. Sōtan had obtained through his trading a lot of knowledge of the Southern Barbarians as the Portuguese and Spanish were then called, and Hideyoshi thought of giving him a province in Kyushu as commander of the front gate of the Empire. So he said to him one day, "You would make a good warrior, I think ; I will give you a province in Kyushu." "Oh no, thank you, your Lordship," replied Sōtan very decidedly, " I am a merchant. That is enough. I don't want to be a soldier."

KAMIYA SŌTAN ENTERTAINS HIDEYOSHI[*]

In the tenth month of the first year of Bunroku (1592) Hideyoshi arrived at Hakata in the course of his Korean campaign and Kamiya Sōtan invited him to his residence in Naraya Machi. Since Sōtan was descended from the house of Sugawara his gate curtain had on it the Umebachi or conventionalised plum-blossom familiar on all Tenjin Shrines. In a large Tokonoma twelve feet long hung a pair of pictures of bamboos in black and white by T'an Shih Jui of T'ang

---

[*] Sometimes European wine was used at Cha-no-yu. Tokutomi quotes an instance from the Sōtan Nikki. " On the ninth of the second month of the year 1600, Ishida Mitsunari entertained Ukite Hideie, Date Masamune, Konishi Yukinaga and himself (Kamiya Sōtan). They used the Daisu. The Tea-bowl and Tea-caddy were of modern pottery and the other utensils ready-made. It was late at night before they went home. They discussed all manner of things and a lot of curious objects were brought out for inspection. They drank grape wine and five-coloured liquor. It came from Nagasaki." *Kinsei Nihon Kokuminshi*. As Tokutomi observes, Nagasaki was the headquarters of the foreign drink trade as well as of Christianity.

As to the *Sōtan Nikki* or Memoirs of Kamiya Sōtan, some scholars doubt its authenticity, but according to Takahashi Tatsuo the descriptions of Cha-no-yu and the details of the famous vessels given in it are certainly accurate, and he therefore thinks that, even if not written by Sōtan himself, it is more than probable that its facts are reliable to the extent of the author's knowledge.

that he had received from Hideyoshi, and in a smaller Tokonoma beside it a horizontal picture of cocks and grapes by Yün Wai of T'ang, an heirloom of his family, beside many other valuable antiques. There were kneeling-cushions for the guests of Yamato brocade, and two pairs of screens with wild geese among reeds by Kano Moto-nobu stood round the walls. A leopard-skin was placed in the seat of honour for Hideyoshi. The tea-room was of two mats. On the hearth was the kettle called 'Johari' or 'World-reflecting' and on the dais the great jar called ' Omokage ' or ' Vision.' In the Tokonoma hung a small scroll of ' Evening Rain on the Hsiao Hsiang River,' and beside it stood the renowned Bunrin tea jar. All the houses adjoining for some distance had been taken by Sōtan also and were draped with his crested curtains and exquisitely furnished inside for the reception of the generals of the Taiko's train. Hideyoshi with Ōda Yuraku entered and took his seat in the place prepared for him, while Odera Kyumu, Nakayama Yamashiro-no-kami and Sōbon retired into the room behind. Tokugawa Ieyasu and some ten other nobles with him were received in the great reception room and in the neighbouring houses, and the number that sat down to the splendid banquet that Sōtan provided was more than five hundred in all. When Hideyoshi had received Sōtan and his wife in audience refreshments were offered and he entered the tea-room with Ōda Yuraku and Sōbon, and Sōtan served them with tea. The Taiko looked long and intently at the picture and the Bunrin tea jar and then turned to Yuraku and observed : " These things don't look quite right. It would be better to alter the Tokonoma and put a shelf by the side of it." Then turning to Sōtan, " That's the sort of thing Soeki and Sokyu would have said." And he went on to converse about various things in high good humour ; then suddenly, unable to repress his admiration for the scroll of evening rain, he asked Sōtan point blank, " I say, Bōzu, will you let me have this picture ? "

" This picture was brought from China by my great grandfather Jūtei who went there in the era Bummei (1469-87) and it came into his hands in rather a remarkable manner. Higashiyama Dono and Ouchi Dono often requested him to let them have it, but he would never part with it, so, though I greatly desire to accede to any wish your Lordship may express, it would seem disrespectful to my ancestor should I lightly give it away. I might however be able to exchange it for something, if your lordship has anything of equal value you would like to give me for it." When Sōtan calmly made this proposal Hideyoshi seemed not at all offended, but after considering for a while slapped his knee and exclaimed, " Yes, I have. There's that big picture of the 'Ships returning from a Far-off Shore': But, I say, Bōzu, have you got a Toko in your house large enough to hang it ? " This picture was one of the masterpieces of Mu Ch'i of T'ang and had more than three hundred ships painted on a surface nine feet wide. So Hideyoshi got the picture of even-ing rain and rejoiced as at the possession of the jade-stone of Pien Ho that was worth fifteen cities. Moreover, Sōtan presented him with ten rolls of fine damask and three pounds of rare incense as well, while the Taiko gave in return a hundred pieces of silver, and a set of gold screens painted with plum trees under snow by Sanraku. So the entertainment came to an end most successfully and Hideyoshi took his leave in great delight. Sōtan and his wife saw him off at the gate, but as he was getting into his palanquin he seemed to to hesitate as though there was something he had forgotten. The fact was that he had arranged with Sōbon beforehand to make off with the Bunrin Tea-caddy while Sōtan and his wife were both at the gate and the Tea-room was left unguarded.* And this Sōtan had foreseen.

"Ah, your lordship," he suggested most courteously, " have you forgotten something? Is it this, I wonder?" And he pushed back the upper part of his costume and showed the Bunrin hanging round his neck. " I have not neglected your lordship's advice to take care of it." Hideyoshi laughed heartily, " Yes, you're a sharp fellow, Tsukushi Bōzu," he said, as he got into his palanquin. Sōtan came with him part of the way and when they came to the shore at Sumiyoshi-mura the Taiko stopped and talked over the affairs of the province with him, and with the final advice, " You put as much money as you can into trade at Nagoya," he hurried on to that city. Probably this Tsukushi Bōzu was the only man in the Empire who would have stood up to the Taiko in this way. Sōtan afterwards took Hideyoshi's advice and made a shelf by the side of the Toko for the Bunrin caddy, and this style of Tokonoma is called Bunrin Toko after it. This Tea-room is now in the grounds of Hiraoka Ryosuke of Tenjin Machi in Hakata.

KAMIYA SŌTAN GIVES AWAY THE HAKATA BUNRIN

When Kuroda Nagamasa was given the fief of Chikuzen, Kamiya Sōtan became very friendly with him. Nagamasa, who was now getting old, also coveted this Tea-caddy and one day Sōtan thought to himself, " Having a famous treasure like this in one's family is a great responsibility. If I have a descendant who cannot live up to it, it may be the cause of a great misfortune to my house. So when his lordship returns home I will give it to him." On the fourth day of the eighth month of Genna (1624) Nagamasa suddenly fell ill at the temple of Ho-onji at Kyoto on his way home, and Sōtan blamed himself for not remembering to carry out his intention. " Chi of Yen Liang in China hung up a precious sword on the grave of his lord Hsu. I may not have the wisdom of Chi, but I must not forget his example." And he put on his dress of ceremony and taking the Tea-caddy went up and presented it to the new lord Uemon-no-suke Tadayuki, the son of Nagamasa. Tadayuki was overjoyed at this and

---

* The story of Hideyoshi trying to steal the Bunrin Cha-ire with Sōbon's (or, according to another version, Ishida's) assistance may not be very creditable, but of course had he succeeded he would have made a present quite adequate to the occasion. And moreover it must be remembered that he could at any time have found some pretext for taking it by force.

offered him a present of three thousand pieces of gold and a fief of the value of five hundred koku. But this Sōtan refused to accept. "A fief," he explained respectfully, " is a thing that a merchant does not want, and I wish to make this present without any return."

The remarkable circumstances attending the possession of the painting and the Bunrin Tea-caddy by his family to which Sōtan alluded are as follows. His great-grandfather Jūtei was encouraged to trade with China by Ouchi Yoshioki and opened a branch house in Ning-Po with great success. This business was in charge of a manager who married a Chinese wife. After a while things went badly and he lost so heavily that he made up his mind to commit suicide in atonement for his mistakes. When his wife heard of it she thought that she was to blame for it and presented him with the picture of ' Evening Rain ' and the Bunrin Tea-caddy, which were hereditary treasures in her family, as some kind of compensation. These were really cherished possessions of the Imperial House of T'ang, for one of her ancestors had accompanied Yang Kuei Fei when she fled and was put to death at Ma-Wei, and rescued these things which were with her and had them sent back to his house. The manager brought them home with him and presented them to Jūtei who was so delighted with them that he not only entirely overlooked his mistakes but again entrusted him with a large capital which he took back to Ning-Po and used most successfully so that the business flourished again. He afterwards brought back his Chinese wife to Hakata.

HOSOKAWA TADAOKI AND IEYASU

The Kwampaku Toyotomi Hidetsugu had lent money secretly to the Daimyos in order to attach them to his side, and when his plot against Hideyoshi failed a number of bonds with their signatures were discovered. Then Ishida Jibushoyu went to the Daimyos concerned and told them to pay these amounts quickly or he would show the documents to Hideyoshi which would mean their ruin. So they all ran round in great perturbation trying to raise money to redeem their debts. Now Hosokawa Tadaoki was one of them, for he had borrowed a hundred pieces of gold, and he tried to borrow the amount from various sources, but as money happened to be rather scarce just then, he found no little difficulty. Now fortunately Tadaoki's veteran Councillor Matsui Sado-no-kami Yasuyuki was very friendly with Honda Sado-no-kami Masanobu, Councillor to Tokugawa Ieyasu, and when he sounded him about a loan, Masanobu asked Ieyasu what he thought, and he very readily consented. So Honda introduced Matsui into the presence of Ieyasu. " This is quite a serious matter," said Ieyasu, " and I fear your master must have been rather troubled about it. However, I think I can arrange something." He then told Honda to bring a certain armour box, giving him the number of it, and when it was brought he produced a key from his purse and told him to open it. " Under the helmet

and also under the body armour you will find a packet of money,"
he observed, and when Honda took out the two packets and opened
them he found the date written on them showing that they were put
there when Ieyasu was at Suruga. "They have been there a long
time. That's thirty years ago," said Ieyasu as he handed them to
Yasuyuki, "and there are a hundred pieces in the packets, so that
should relieve your difficulties."

The Councillor thanked him very gratefully and told him that
he would proceed to his fief and inform his master who would send
an acknowledgement to Ieyasu at once. "Oh, no," replied Ieyasu,
"there is no need of that. I purposely avoided sending to him
directly. That's why I had this money taken out of the armour box
on the quiet, so that nobody should know anything about it. There
is no need to say anything more." And so Tadaoki escaped from
an awkward situation.*

Some time after this Tadaoki happened to come up to Fushimi
on duty and passing before the front gate of the mansion of Ieyasu
he saw a retainer of his, Yamaoka Dōami, going in to pay a visit,
whereupon he went in also and asked Dōami to introduce him.
Ieyasu was very pleased to see him and asked them into the reception room. "I have never so far had the honour of calling on you,"
said Tadaoki, "but as I happened to see my retainer coming in I
suddenly made up my mind to come too. It has long been my wish
to be your guest at Cha-no-yu, so perhaps it is not too much to
hope that it may now be fulfilled."

Now Tadaoki was one of the seven chief disciples of Rikyu and
a very accomplished Tea Master, so Ieyasu turned to Dōami and
said, "Etchu Dono is one of our greatest exponents of Cha-no-yu,
so it will be a great honour for me to entertain him. But please
assist me, as I am not such an expert." But Tadaoki replied that
he would rather they were quite alone. To this Ieyasu objected that
it would be easier for him if Dōami were present too, but still
Tadaoki insisted, whereupon Dōami perceived that he had some good
reason and took his leave. When they were by themselves Tadaoki
requested that Honda Masanobu might be called and soon he appeared
in the Tea-room. "Some time ago," said Tadaoki ˙to them, "my
retainer made a request to you for assistance which you were kind
enough to give, thus enabling me to escape a great danger. This
service I shall certainly never forget, and to-day I have come to thank
you and to assure you that I shall not overlook any way of repaying
you. This is all I wish to say now and perhaps it is not advisable
that I come again for some time." And he took his leave.

Now this was the time when Ishida Kazushige was making his
plans to overthrow Ieyasu, and Tadaoki, while appearing to have
nothing at all to do with Ieyasu, was working very vigorously on

---

* When Hideyoshi pardoned Hosokawa on this occasion he gave him the Cha-ire called
Ari-ake as a consolation for having 'gated' him while under suspicion. Afterwards Tadaoki
again became hard up and pawned it for fifty pieces of gold and it got into the hands of
Ankokuji-Eikei, then taking the name of Ankokuji Katatsuki. It was given by him to Tsuda
Koheiji Hidemasa and from him stolen by Hosokawa.

his behalf in secret.   Therefore he chose the Tea-room as a suitably
private place for this meeting.

Ishida also did not overlook this use of Cha-no-yu, for he sent
a Tea Master round to the various Daimyo to stay in each fief for
a while as Instructor, and then move on with his seditious information
elsewhere. (Cf. Watanabe Sōan.)

NAGAI NAOKATSU AND II NAOMASA

Nagai Ukondaiyu Naokatsu was a retainer of Tokugawa Ieyasu.
His original name was Osada, but as he thought it ill-omened he
changed it to Nagai.   He took the head of Ikeda Shōnyu at the
battle of Nagakude.

After the battle of Sekigahara, Ii Naomasa and Honda Tadakatsu were indignant at the smallness of their rewards and sent back
to Ieyasu the documents they had received from him granting them
increases in their fiefs.*   When Naokatsu heard of it he said to
Naomasa : " You are one of the pillars of the Tokugawa house ; it
is not becoming of you to seem so greedy of large revenues.   You
certainly ought to receive the increase politely."   " You don't know
what you are talking about," answered Naomasa, " Here are lords
who have given comparatively little assistance lately getting large
fiefs and provinces, while we, who have fought for our chief ever
since he was only a small Daimyo in Mikawa, are given small
pittances like these.   Who wouldn't resent such poor recognition of
their services ? "

" I don't see that," replied Naokatsu, " for retainers like ourselves should not grumble whatever they are told to do.   As for these
other lords, they owe their positions and their allegiance to someone
else, but without their forces, however valiantly we might have
fought, there would have been little chance of this success.   But
when you think of the large number of men you were given the
honour of commanding, I don't see how you can complain that your
merit was not recognised.   However brave you may be you could
have done little without the armies entrusted to you."   At this
Naomasa lost his temper and replied.   " Why, you don't compare
yourself to me, do you ? "   " What a stupid remark," returned Nagai
with a sarcastic smile, " If I had been entrusted by our lord with
as many men as you were, there is no reason to think I should have
done any worse.   All I have to regret is that I had not the scope
to do more.   But I thought you had more sense and I am really
sorry that I have been friendly with you thus far.   In future I shall
not trouble you further."   And he got up and went out.   Naomasa
said nothing but sat meditating for some time, after which he came
to the conclusion that he was in the wrong, for it was not the way
of a loyal retainer to boast of his deeds or appear desirous of

---

* Honda Tadakatsu received the fief of Kuwana, 150,000 koku, and Ii Naomasa received
Sawayama 180,000 koku, after Sekigahara. Compared with e.g. Kuroda's 520,000 koku at Fukuoka and Fukushima's 498,000 at Hiroshima this may have seemed small.

rewards. So he went to Honda and told him that he would agree to receive the award if he would do so too, and Honda agreed, so they both presented themselves before Ieyasu and told him that they were willing to receive the fiefs that he had offered them and with which they had formerly declared themselves discontented. Ieyasu commended their decision as a wise one and handed them the documents. Then Naomasa paid a visit to Nagai Naokatsu, carrying in his sleeve the Bunrin Tea-caddy which he valued highly. " I am ashamed of what I said the other day," he said. " You are a real friend and I must apologize and can only hope our relations will be as cordial as ever. This Tea-caddy is the greatest treasure of our house, which I value as I do my life, and I wish you to accept it as a token of my respect and affection, which nothing else will so well express." Naokatsu was very glad to hear that his advice had been taken and assured him that their friendship would be in no way affected, for he esteemed him as much as ever, but as for the Tea-caddy he declared that he had done nothing that he should be given such a famous masterpiece and many times firmly refused to take it. However at last Naomasa insisted on leaving it with him and took his departure saying, " I leave it with you as a pledge of my sincerity." And it long remained the great treasure of the house of Nagai.

THE TEA-JARS OF TOKUGAWA IEYASU

Tokugawa Ieyasu had eleven Tea-jars that he kept in the tower of his castle of Fushimi, near Kyoto, and over each of them he posted a guard of two men. He appointed one Mitsui Yoshimasa to be captain of this 'Tea Guard,' and cautioned him to be extremely vigilant. And that the men might not be tempted to relax, he supplied them with a canteen of their own and boards and men for the games of Gō, Chess and Backgammon.

After a day or two he sent a messenger with orders that two of the jars should be brought to him. Shortly after he himself appeared and inspected the guard, and after greeting them cordially he viewed the jars. " But I gave eleven into your charge," he said to Mitsui, " and there are only nine. Where are the other two ? " " I have just handed them over to the messenger your lordship sent," was the answer. " I appointed you to this position because you had already proved yourself a careful and devoted officer," replied Ieyasu severely, " and if I had really intended the jars to be brought I should have given you orders to go with the messenger yourself. It was extremely careless of you to hand them over to him in this way without any further inquiry."

Ieyasu had a famous Tea-jar called Dai Rosun or Great Luzon which he always used for the New Year Tea Ceremony, and this became a tradition in the family. In the great conflagration of 1657, when the Castle of Edo was burnt, more than half of the treasures of the Shogun that were in the storehouses were destroyed, but fortunately this jar was in the Tea-room, and an ancestor of Ikeda Tango-no-kami, who was then an ordinary page, ran out with it and was able to save it, for which exploit he was promoted to be chief of the pages.

IEYASU ENTERTAINS HIDEYOSHI

Tokugawa Ieyasu and Maeda Toshiie were once entertained at the castle of Fushimi by Hideyoshi, and as they were leaving he said to Ieyasu, " I am now going to the Juraku Palace and to-morrow on my way back I will pay you a visit." So Ieyasu told his retainers that he would just serve him with a very simple Cha-no-yu, for he would certainly have had his fill of rich food at the Juraku, and bade them sweep the garden and clean the Tea-room while he opened a fresh jar of tea and told his Tea Master to grind it.

The next day he came back quickly after attending on Hideyoshi at the Juraku Palace and immediately inspected the tea but found only a very little. Sharply he asked the Tea Master the reason and the answer was that Mizuno Kemmotsu, Ieyasu's favourite page, had drunk up the rest in spite of being told that it was required for distinguished guests. So Ieyasu perforce opened another jar and told them to grind some more, whereupon one of his retainers, Kagatsume Haito, objected that there would not be time before Hideyoshi arrived, and he would probably be irritated if kept waiting, so it would be the lesser evil to serve what little there was. " Perhaps you may think you are imitating my example by giving this thrifty advice," replied Ieyasu, " but even if he is offended at the delay it would be a much graver discourtesy to serve him someone else's leavings. You have yet very much to learn."

TOKUGAWA IEYASU GIVES HIS TEA VESSELS TO HIS SON

When Tokugawa Ieyasu retired he went to live at Shizuoka. On the thirteenth day of the third month of the seventeenth year of Keicho (1612) the Shogun Hidetada went down from Yedo to visit him. On the twenty-sixth day Ieyasu invited him to a Cha-no-yu, the other guests being Hino Dainagon Nyudo Yuishin and Kyogoku Wakasa-no-kami Tadataka. Afterwards, when Hidetada went up to the main castle to express his thanks for the entertainment, his father brought out the famous ' Narashiba ' and ' Nage-zukin,' and told him to take whichever he pleased. The Shogun chose ' Nage-zukin ' and went off with it to the western tower, where his apartments were, in great delight. After he had gone his retainers said to Ieyasu, " His Highness is indeed very pleased." " Yes," said the old Shogun with a smile, "you had better go and ask him to serve you tea from that Nage-zukin," and then, looking round them quietly, he proceeded to give his reason for what he had done. " People like to have children so that they can hand over their affairs to them as soon as may be, and when they have assured themselves that everything is going on well they can take their ease without anxiety for the rest of their days. Still one must be careful in doing this that children are capable and of a suitably mature age and must also especially consider the attitude of the outside world and the state of the times. It may also be well to satisfy one's child by handing over treasured heirlooms of the family to him before he succeeds. For it is considered rather a fine thing that a man should give up everything to his son and retire and live by himself without any encumbering property at all. And though everyone praises this detached and superior attitude, there are not a few fathers who prefer to keep their treasures with them and give them to the heir one by one. Since I was young myself I have watched the ways of parents and children, and noticed that though there has been affection on one side and filial feeling on the other, yet after the father has retired their relations have often become strained. Their affection for each other may be the same as before, but as the parent grows older he is inclined to worry the child, forgetting that he is now grown up, while the child on his part comes to neglect the infirmities of the parent, and so estrangement may come about, and even become noticeable to outsiders. But if a father gives his son the family heirlooms one by one, even if the son does not seem very devoted, people's suspicions will be allayed. For parents ought always to try and prevent their children getting a name for unfilial conduct."

This Tea-caddy was called 'Nage-zukin' or 'Throw-down-cap,' because when its owner brought it to Shuko for his opinion, the Master was so struck with admiration at it that he instinctively took off the skull-cap he happened to be wearing and threw it on the ground.

GAMO UJISATO

Gamo Hida-no-kami Ujisato was Oda Nobunaga's son-in-law In his early years he studied Confucian and Buddhist philosophy under Nankwa Oshō, and Japanese poetry under Sanjo-nishi Ufu, Sōyō and Shōba, while for Cha-no-yu he became a disciple of Rikyu and gave himself up to it with such enthusiasm that he promised to be one of the greatest authorities. But Saito Kuranosuke Toshikazu, the father of Kasuga-no-Tsubone,* had little use for such things, and many times he rebuked Ujisato for wasting his time on useless accomplishments. "A soldier should not allow anything to interfere with his profession," he declared emphatically ; but Ujisato would not listen. Some time after this Ujisato took part in the siege of the castle of Kwannonji under Nobunaga, and Saito Kuranosuke rode over to where he was stationed and gave him such good advice as to how to ambush and take in flank a strong party of the enemy who

---

* Kasuga-no-Tsubone was the foster-mother of the Shogun Iemitsu and the most influential figure at his Court.

sallied out from the castle and attacked the besiegers, that he defeated the attempt with heavy loss and received great praise from Nobunaga, who presented him with a valuable sword by Kunitoshi. He therefore reflected that there was much truth in what Saito said, and gave himself up whole-heartedly to a military career. And with such success that he became Lord of Aizu with an income of a million koku. But he did not give up Cha-no-yu altogether, and even with the little spare time he gave to it he was good enough to be reckoned among the 'Seven Disciples' of Rikyu.*

ISHIDA KAZUSHIGE

When Toyotomi Hideyoshi was Lord of the Castle of Nagahama he went out hunting in the neighbourhood, and after a whole day spent on horseback he became exceedingly thirsty. Coming to a little temple in the hills called Kwannonji, he sat down on the verandah of the guest room and called out loudly to attract attention. The priest soon appeared, and seeing it was the Feudal Lord bowed low before him. "Well, your reverence," said Hideyoshi, "I want a cup of tea." The priest replied that it should be brought immediately and summoned an acolyte to make it. The acolyte, who was an extremely comely youth, filled a large tea-bowl with rather tepid tea, placed it on a stand, put the napkin by it and offered it to Hideyoshi. Draining it at one draught, he exclaimed: "Ah! that's good. Another, please." This time the acolyte served a cup containing not half as much as the first, but the tea was much hotter. Hideyoshi appreciated his intelligence and asked for another to see what he would do. Sure enough he was presented with a very small deep cup but containing a little very hot tea, and he was so pleased at this insight that he called the youth to him and asked his name. "My name is Sakichi," was the reply, "and I am the second son of Sagoemon, a farmer of the village of Ishida in the province of Gōshu." Much taken with his prompt and clear answer as well as with his looks and intelligence, Hideyoshi persuaded the priest to let him go with him to Nagahama and become one of his pages. He was then thirteen years old. This youth was later on to become Ishida Jibushoyu Kazushige, Chief of the Five Bugyo. To such a high position may one rise by care in serving a cup of tea.

Ishida Kazushige was well known for the simplicity of his life. For when he was Chief of the Five Bugyo and by far the greatest Lord in the Empire, his residence at the Castle of Sawayama was entirely plain and unadorned. The walls were of rough plaster left in an unfinished state, and boarded inside. The shōji and fusuma were covered with plain white paper, the garden was planted with

---

* The 'Seven Disciples' were Oda Yuraku, Hosokawa Sansai Tadaoki, Gamo Hida-no-kami Ujisato, Araki Settsu-no-kami Murashige, Seta Kamon Masatada, Shibayama Kenmotsu, and Takayama Ukon Tomoyuki.
† Or Mitsunari.

the most ordinary trees, and the stone water-basin had nothing remarkable about it. This simple house, austere as a tea-room, and very different from those of most of the Feudal Lords, in itself suggested that its owner was no ordinary man.

HOSOKAWA TADAOKI

Hosokawa Etchu-no-kami Tadaoki was a great Tea Master as his father Fujitaka had been before him, and was known to possess a fine collection of rare tea-vessels. In the time of the Shogun Iemitsu the Tairo Hotta Kaga-no-kami Masamori, a lord of great influence in all things, enquired through a third party whether he might see the famous possessions of the house of Hosokawa. Tadaoki gladly consented and invited him on a fixed day, and after serving his guest with a feast of the best that he could provide, said : "And now I will show you my things (dōgu)." And he brought out and displayed all his most valuable armour, swords and bows and arrows and suchlike things, but not a single tea vessel did he show. This was not at all what Masamori had expected, and he was not best pleased, but he allowed nothing of this to appear in his face, and went away apparently delighted, after thanking his host profusely. But afterwards he again sent the third party to Tadaoki and asked him why it was that he had not brought out any of his famous tea vessels. " Oh," said Tadaoki, " Masamori said that he wished to see my most cherished possessions (dōgu), and what should this mean in a military family but the weapons and accoutrements of one's hereditary profession ? "

The same story is told of Fujitaka, father of Tadaoki, the guest in this case being Gamo Ujisato. The word 'dōgu' is a very comprehensive one and means the instruments or utensils used by anyone for the business or diversion in which he may be engaged. What Masamori meant was Chadogu.

Hosokawa Yūsai Fujitaka and his son Sansai Tadaoki once appeared in the presence of Hideyoshi on the occasion of a tea ceremony or some such entertainment, when the Taiko suddenly broke into impromptu verse :

> " See the Narrow Rivers* twain
> Flowing hither in their course."

Without hesitation Yūsai continued :

> " 'Tis the rain that falls
> In the two ruts that are made
> By your Lordship's August Car."

" Bravo ! " cried the Taiko, clapping his hands with pleasure at the happy conceit.

Hosokawa Etchu-no-kami Tadaoki was lord of Kokura in Buzen and had an income of three hundred and ninety-nine thousand koku.

---

* Hosokawa = Narrow river.

He often asked leave to retire on account of ill health, but was not allowed. At length on the twenty-fifth day of the twelfth month of the sixth year of Genna (1621) permission was given him, and he became Nyudo and took the name Sansai Sōryu. But the Shogun Hidetada still continued to treat him with the same favour as heretofore, and would often invite him to Cha-no-yu and have long talks with him.

The year after his retirement Tadaoki asked permission to go back to his province, and the Shogun invited him to a special audience and addressed him thus: "Your loyal service to the Empire and to your Lord has been most meritorious and assuredly deserves a fitting reward, and I would have given you great fiefs and higher rank. But since you have now insisted on retiring this is no longer possible, so I present you with this famous painting instead, as a mark of my great esteem." And he gave him a written scroll by Bussho Tokko of Sung, besides a considerable amount of silver and silk.

Now this writing of Bussho Tokko was the one known as 'the writing of the handing over of the money' because it was sent by Tokko the priest of Ikuozan in China to Taira-no-Shigemori on the occasion of his sending by the hand of one Myōten the sum of a thousand two hundred ryo of gold, with orders that two hundred be given to the priests of Ikuozan and a thousand presented to the Emperor of China, that a small temple might be built in which prayers might be offered for his attainment of Buddhahood. It was therefore a treasure of unsurpassed value in the Empire, and Tadaoki's joy at receiving it can be imagined. He felt he had been given something of greater worth than a fief of a hundred thousand koku. Moreover the gratitude of the Shogun did not stop even there, for he granted Tadaoki the privilege of riding in his palanquin right up to the entrance of the Palace when he came to pay his respects.

This writing was about one foot five inches wide by nine long. It was originally in the possession of the Ashikaga Shoguns Yoshimitsu and Yoshimasa, and was given by the latter to Hosokawa Mochikata.

Hosokawa Tadaoki was accustomed to send his retainers to Nagasaki whenever a foreign ship came in, to buy rarities, and it happened that one year he had sent a certain Okutsu Yagoemon with a companion for this purpose, when some fine incense wood came into the market. There were two pieces, one large log and another smaller one. Yagoemon determined to buy the larger piece of the two. Now a retainer of Date Mutsu-no-kami Masamune also set his mind on the same piece, and a competition started between the two of them as to which should get it. They bid against each other higher and higher and it seemed as though they would go to any price in their determination to secure it for their lords. When Yagoemon's companion saw how things were going he objected strongly, "What is the use of this competition? You may have to pay some huge price for it. And big log or small, they are both the same tree. Let him have the big one and we will take the small, and that will do quite well." " No, no, that won't do," replied Yagoemon, " it is not only a question of having a thing I intend to buy carried off by someone else, but if I give way because I am afraid of the high price it will not only be to my own discredit, but it will reflect on the reputation of our lord. So I will get that big log whatever price I have to pay." The other returned a sharp answer and high words followed, with the result that Yagoemon ended by cutting down his companion and then buying the big log as he had intended. He then returned to Kumamoto and explaining everything in detail to his lord, concluded his report by saying, "And now I am ready to put an end to myself properly by seppuku."

" Cutting down your companion in the course of the discharge of your duty to me does not necessitate seppuku," replied Tadaoki. Then, calling the son of the head man he said, " Both the dead and the living did what they did as faithful retainers. No resentment must therefore be borne." And he made him exchange the cup of reconciliation with Yagoemon there in his presence. And both of them continued in his service in peace. But in the twelfth month of the second year of Shōhō (1646) Tadaoki died in a ripe old age, and on the third anniversary of his death Yagoemon calmly put an end to his life by seppuku at Funaoka in Kyoto. And there is his tomb to this day. As to the rare incense that Yagoemon thus obtained, Tadaoki regarded it as the greatest of treasures and gave it the name ' Hatsu-ne ' or ' First Note.' This name is taken from the famous verse that declares the cuckoo's note to be so fascinating that one always feels as though hearing it for the first time.

In the days of Tokugawa Iemitsu, Hosokawa Etchu-no-kami Tadaoki was the only remaining Tea Master who had received the tradition direct from Rikyu, and consequently he was much in demand as a teacher among all the daimyos who were interested in Tea. He always began his instruction with this warning : " You must remember that it is your military prowess that has obtained your fiefs and honours. Do not then neglect this your main business. It may be well enough to occupy any spare time you may have with Cha-no-yu, but never let a diversion take the place of the serious work of life.

TADAOKI SELLS HIS TEA VESSELS

In the third year of Kwan-ei (1627) there was a great drought in the province of Buzen that lasted from spring till autumn, so that all the crops failed and the people were reduced to extremities. The officials asked what they should do, for there was not only the calamity of this year to consider, but there was no hope for the next. " This is no ordinary case," replied Tadaoki, " I must sell my tea utensils to raise money to help the people." So he got together all the tea things that he had inherited from his father Yūsai, and handed them over to one of his chief retainers, telling him to hurry to Kyoto and turn them into money. " If possible I should have liked to put them in pawn to tide over this emergency," he remarked, " but I doubt if that can be done successfully, so get the best price you can and sell the lot."

As soon as Tadaoki's retainer made his mission known "in the capital there was no lack of wealthy collectors to bid for his master's famous treasures, but, thinking it almost certain that difficulties of some sort would arise if such rarities were disposed of privately he determined to put them up for public sale, and with this intention approached the Shoshidai Itakura Suwo-no-kami Shigemune. " To any help I can give you about the pedigree of these tea vessels you are very welcome," replied Shigemune, " but I don't think there will be any difficulty in the case of the possessions of such a famous family. Let those who want them bid for them openly, and when the transaction is all finished and the money paid, I should like to be permitted to view them myself; for though I have often heard of them I have never seen them, and this will be a lucky opportunity." So they were all sold by auction to the highest bidders, and Tadaoki took the money to Osaka and bought rice and wheat and distributed it to the people of his province. And all admitted that he was a model feudal lord. Six years afterwards, when Kato Higo-no-kami Tadahiro had his fiefs confiscated he received the castle town of Kumamoto in Higo.

Hosokawa Tadaoki had a particularly valuable tea caddy which a certain person took a great fancy to and bought of him for a sword of Aoi make and a thousand pieces of silver. It afterwards became known therefore as the Aoi tea caddy. Tadaoki was criticized for being grasping in this transaction, but the buyer came to the conclusion that he had not given enough, and added another thousand pieces of silver. This too Tadaoki did not refuse. " I don't care much about money," he said, "and if anyone is very anxious for anything I have, I leave the question of price entirely to them, and let them have it because I think it is not right to withhold it."

In the family of Hosokawa there was a Katatsuki Tea-caddy that somehow found its way into the possession of Ankokuji Eikei. Now before the battle of Sekigahara, Tokugawa Ieyasu was in Koyama arranging for the campaign against the west, and Tsuda Kōheiji happened to be there with him. Ieyasu asked him what reward he would like in the event of the campaign proving successful. Koheiji replied that the success was not in any doubt, but that he did not particularly wish for anything. " There is no one who does not wish for anything," replied Ieyasu, "please speak out." "Well, then," said Koheiji, " I should like Ankokuji Eikei's Katatsuki Tea-caddy." " There will be no difficulty about that," answered Ieyasu. And sure enough when the battle was won and the spoils of the enemy confiscated, he sent the Tea-caddy to Koheiji. When Hosokawa Yusai, who was an intimate friend of his, came to hear of it, he was consumed with envy and offered to buy it for a huge sum. But Koheiji said he wanted no large sum of money but would be very pleased if his friend would accept it, and sent it to him. Yusai was immensely delighted and sent five hundred pieces of gold as a return present.

He gave it the name of Nakayama, and regarded it as one of his chief treasures.* When his son sold his Tea-things to help his people, this Nakayama caddy was sold for a thousand eight hundred pieces of gold to Sakai Kunaidaiyu Tadakatsu through the good offices of Doi Oi-no-kami Toshikatsu, and this sum also was spent on the work of relief.

Since after the battle of Sekigahara, Hosokawa Sansai Tadaoki had rendered the greatest services to the house of Tokugawa, he was treated with the greatest favour by the three Shoguns Ieyasu, Hidetada and Iemitsu. On the second day of the tenth month of the second year of Kanei (1625), he was received in audience by Iemitsu on the occasion of his return to his province. He once more greeted the former Shogun Hidetada and was presented by him with some medicine for the journey and handed a valuable short sword by Shimizu Toshiro. " When we were both young men in the service of the Taiko Hideyoshi I remember that you said that if you had this sword at your side, and were able to make tea in the Tea-caddy of Rikyu called Bulge-bottom, life would have no more to offer you, so now gird it on, and make your tea as you wish." It seems that Tadaoki had already obtained the Tea-caddy, and he left Hidetada's presence overcome by gratitude at his thoughtful consideration. (*Tokugawa Jikki.*) In the ninth year of Kwanei (1633) it was that he retired and handed over his fief to his son, and again in the eleventh month of the nineteenth year (1643) he had audience with Iemitsu when leaving Edo for his province, and the Shogun invited him to Cha-no-yu. On this occasion Iemitsu had two scrolls produced, one a rare writing and the other a joint composition of Shunzei and Teika, and through Sakai Tadakatsu addressed him as follows ; " It is entirely owing to the great merit of you Tadaoki that your son Tadatoshi has been permitted to inherit your great fief. And though you have retired we trust that you will take care of your health and live long yet to be of some service to the Empire. These two Kakemono are things that we greatly value, but on account of your exceptionally distinguished services we wish you to choose whichever of them you like best as a present." Tadaoki chose the one with the Japanese poems of Shunzei and Teika, saying that he had on a former occasion been favoured with the Chinese writing called that of the "Handing over of the Money," and Iemitsu took it and graciously presented it to him with his own hand.

When Sen-no-Rikyu fell under the displeasure of Hideyoshi, Hosokawa Yusai and his son Sansai repeatedly pleaded with the Taiko on his behalf, but to no effect. And when Rikyu was ordered to remain in confinement in his house at Sakai these two and Furuta

---

* Another version of how he got it differs somewhat. Tsuda Koheiji Koan, retainer of Takigawa Kazumasu, amused himself with Cha-no-yu when he retired. He had a famous Tea Caddy called Nakayama that had formerly belonged to Hosokawa Sansai. Hosokawa wanted it back but did not like to ask for it, but one day he asked to see it and then slipped it into his sleeve when Koan's back was turned and left the Tea-room quoting to the other guests the line " *Inochi nari keri sayo no nakayama* " (...my life this Nakayama). When they told the host he only smiled, observing that he had been overreached and there was nothing else to be done. But the next day Hosokawa sent 200 pieces of gold with saké and fish and cloth as a complimentary present, whereat Koan smiled again, and when his retainers asked if he might keep it he said he saw no objection.

Oribe were the only visitors he had, for his former friends and pupils all forsook him. Even after his death these two continued to maintain to Hideyoshi that he had been guiltless of any offence, though the Taiko would not have it.

WATANABE SŌAN

Watanabe Sōan, otherwise known as Mōzuya, was a Tea Master of Sakai in Izumi. He was a great favourite of Ishida Kazushige, and just before the battle of Sekigahara, when Ishida advanced to Ōgaki, on the tenth day of the ninth month, Sōan came into his camp to wish him good luck. Ishida was delighted to see him, and in the course of the interview said : " You may remember when some time after the death of the Taiko, we were having a meal together and at the end the page came to serve Saké and I put out my rice bowl absent-mindedly. The page reminded me that it was Saké he had brought and I then took my wine cup, quite overcome by shame. I was extremely put out at what you must have thought of me as well as humiliated at being, without doubt, the object of the page's amusement. Well, now there is no reason why I should not confess to you that this absent-mindedness of mine was owing to my being, even then, entirely preoccupied with these plans about the Empire. As I was ceaselessly scheming and planning to meet this crisis, I became quite unaware of my surroundings and forgot even about my meals, so you can understand my strange and abrupt behaviour. Well, you know that Tea-caddy called Kan Katatsuki that I bought of you some years ago. I wish to return it to you now, for if I should fall in the coming fight, it might easily get burnt or lost, and it would be an exceedingly great pity that anything should happen to so rare a thing. So do you take it away with you and make your tea with it every day in memory of me. And if my luck should be good you can give it me back and I will pay you for it again." So Sōan agreed to take it with him, though he professed himself convinced that Ishida would be successful, and returned again to Sakai.

Now after Kazushige's death Ieyasu was searching for this Tea-caddy and some one told him that it had been given by him to Sōan. So he at once sent to Sakai for the Tea Master, but he had already disappeared and no one knew in the least where he was. Ieyasu then had his portrait sent all round the Empire and had a strict search made for him. Now in Fukuoka in Chikuzen there was a certain priest who was a great adept at Tea. He lived in a poor, but very neat hut, and was evidently an esthete of no ordinary kind, so that all sorts of people were anxious to become his pupils for Cha-no-yu.

And Kuroda Nagamasa, who had greatly distinguished himself in the fight at Sekigahara, obtained the fief of Chikuzen and made Fukuoka his capital. So when he heard of this monk he sent for him without delay and when he entered his presence immediately said to him, " You are Sōan of Sakai, I think. And that being so you have the two Tea-caddies called Mōzuya Katatsuki and Sōan Katatsuki in your possession." "It is as you say," replied the monk, "I am Sōan, and these tea utensils belong to Kazushige," and he told Kuroda without hesitation how they had been given to him by Ishida on the eve of Sekigahara with instructions to keep them if he should be killed. "Well, you must hand them over," replied Kuroda," for they may be liable to confiscation." Sōan laughed. "I may perhaps regret parting with them," he said ruefully, "but it cannot be avoided. Moreover, since I sold them to Kazushige and received the money for them I cannot say that they are really mine, so there is no question of refusal." And he took them from his bosom and gave them to Kuroda and they were forwarded to Edo, together with an exact account of Sōan's speech and behaviour. "He seems to be an honest fellow," was the comment of Ieyasu, "and I think what he says is true. As he has done no harm Kuroda may deal kindly with him." So Kuroda gladly took him into his service and gave him an allowance.

Sōan had been very useful to Ishida in communicating with the daimyos who were favourable to his cause. For in order not to rouse any suspicion and also to prevent any leakage of his plans, he pretended that his Tea Master, Watanabe Sōan, had incurred his displeasure in some way, and expelled him from his province. Sōan fled to Aizu where he communicated the plans to Uesugi Kagekatsu, who signified his assent and took him into his service. When Ishida heard of this he pretended to complain to Kagekatsu of his employing a man he had punished. and Uesugi also sent him away. He then went to Mito and told Satake Yoshinobu all about it. Turned out by him too he went in turn to Komatsu in Kaga and Kita-no-sho in Echizen, by which journeys Niwa Nagashige and Aoki Kazunori were apprised of Ishida's designs. At last he found his way back to Sawayama and reported to Ishida.

Yet another Tea Master, Imai Sokun of Sakai, was equally useful to Ieyasu, for it was he who was the go-between who arranged the political marriages between the Tokugawa relations and those of other great lords that were the cause of the rupture between Ishida and Ieyasu as being contrary to the late Hideyoshi's covenant.

KAMIBAYASHI CHIKUAN

Kamibayashi Masashige who called himself Chikuan was a man of Uji. In the second year of Genki (1572) he went to Okazaki and there was, at his own request, taken into the service of Ieyasu and and received a hundred koku. He was ordered to cultivate tea there, but he took part in the battle of Nagakute, where he did valiantly, taking two enemy heads, for which he was presented with a spear and a letter of thanks. Afterwards when Ieyasu removed to Shizuoka Chikuan wished to go with him, but Ieyasu ordered him to stay at Uji and cultivate tea to send to him, presenting him with a residence and several tea plantations.

But in the fifth year of Keicho (1600) when Ishida Kazushige laid siege to Fushimi, Chikuan hurried there with thirteen retainers and a hundred and thirty-two men, and sought out the commander Torii Hikoemon Mototada. " I am under a deep debt of gratitude to Ieyasu, and I wish to pay it here with my life." But Mototada refused. " You are only a tea merchant. What have you to do with sieges ? You had better go back to Uji and keep out of danger." " Oh, you think I am just an ordinary merchant, do you ? And if I do save my life by shamelessly neglecting my obligations, what will it be worth ? All right then, I'll go and make tea in hell." And he drew his sword and was just about to cut himself open when Mototada, struck by his firm resolve, stopped him and gave him the required permission. Then Chikuan, much pleased, collected a number of tea bags and made them into a banner, and binding a red towel round his head led his men into the castle.

Now Kobayakawa Chunagon Hideaki had arrived with his men outside the castle and he sent a messenger to the defender : " It is a secret order from the East that the castle should be given up. So open the gates at once ! " When they heard this those in the castle could not be certain whether it was true or false, and were about evenly divided, when Chikuan broke in : " The best thing is for some-one to go out to them and find out. It is out of the question for Hikozaemon to go, for he is in charge of the garrison, and it will hardly be well for any of the others to leave the castle either, but it doesn't matter at all what happens to an old monk like myself, so I will go out and see if I can find out the truth." The others agreed and Chikuan went out to Hideaki's camp, and that captain again told him that it was a secret order from the Tokugawa headquarters that the castle was to be given up, so they had better be quick and open the gates. " In that case," replied Chikuan, " you must have a note of hand duly signed." " Oh, no," was the answer, " there is no need of that." " Unless we have a duly signed order," said Chikuan, " we cannot hand over the castle." And he went back again and told the others and they determined unanimously to stand a siege. After a while the enemy brought up a large army to the assault, and though the defenders made a fierce and valiant resistance, they were unable to hold out, and the castle at length fell on the last day of the eighth month. Chikuan fought bravely with his men to the end, and when he could do no more he fell at the foot of the drum tower, and Suzuki Zempachi, a retainer of Nabeshima Shinano-no-kami Naoshige, took his head, which had the honour of being gibbetted with those of Mototada and his three commanders. Truly the chivalry of this Tea Master was even more fragrant than his tea.

THE CASE OF KANZAKI CHIKUGOKU

Kanzaki Chikugoku was Tea Master to Torii Mototada, and when the castle of Fushimi fell and his lord put an end to himself, he flung himself into the thick of the enemy, intending to die with him. But in this he did not succeed, for they took him alive and brought him before the commander Ishida Kazushige, who questioned him closely about the taking of the fortress. When he had related all he had seen, Ishida expressed his great admiration for the splendid bravery of Mototada and then added, " and it would be a pity if his son Shintaro Tadamasa should not hear the whole story of his father's valiant end; so do you haste down to the East country and tell them the tale without delay." And he set him free and provided him with horses, and he went down to Yahagi in Shimosa and there related how Mototada and his men had held the castle and had died when it fell.

TODO TAKATORA'S GOLDEN TEA KETTLE

Todo Izumi-no-kami Takatora had a golden tea kettle, the lid of which somehow got lost; and though his servants searched for it everywhere they could not find it. When they told Takatora he ordered them to get another one made. " It will cost a great amount to make one of pure gold," the craftsman objected when given the order, " but if you make it of copper gilt it can be done for a tenth of the sum." " Make it of pure gold as before," said Takatora when this was reported to him, " for it is not impossible that this one may be lost like the first, and if it should be found not to be pure gold, then the reputation of the kettle itself will suffer and people will think that is only gilt too. One cannot be too careful about the repute of one's family treasures."

KATO KIYOMASA AND THE BROKEN TEA BOWL

Once when Kato Kiyomasa was going to give a party for Cha-no-yu he brought out a famous Tea-bowl and put it in the Tokonoma. This bowl his pages took up and passed round to examine it, when one of them let it drop and broke it. They were much dismayed at this accident, but as befitted the sons of distinguished warriors they bound themselves not to reveal the culprit whatever might happen. After a while Kiyomasa came in and when he saw the broken bowl his face darkened. " Who broke that ? " he demanded, " you must know, so you had better say." But no one answered a word. Kato's expression grew more fierce, " You young men are a lot of cowards. Behaviour like this is a slur on the name of your fathers, however brave they may be ! "

Then one of the pages named Kato Heizaburo, a boy of fourteen, looking straight into the face of Kiyomasa, asked him ; " And why is it that you say we are cowards who bring shame on our fathers' name ? " " The reason you will not tell the name of the one who broke the tea bowl is because you are afraid he will be condemned to commit seppuku, I suppose," retorted Kiyomasa, growing even more wroth, " and what is a coward but one who fears for his life ? "

" Among us," replied Heizaburo calmly, " there is not one who is afraid to die. But the reason why we do not wish to say who broke the Tea-bowl is because we do not think it right that one of ourselves, who certainly is of some use, should suffer anything on account of a Tea-bowl however famous, which can well be done without. Please consider the matter well. In keeping the peace of the Empire of what use can a tea utensil be ? But if an enemy should attack us now we should at once hasten to repel him and to protect our province, holding our lives of no account whatever and willingly throwing them away in defence of our lord and his domains. So however great a treasure a Tea-bowl may be, is it in reason to consider it worth the life of even one of us ? " " That's true," admitted Kiyomasa, overcome with admiration at this clear and logical defence, " you are a fine lot of young fellows. You may become even better warriors than your fathers but you certainly will not be worse. Yes, you are well worthy of my trust." And he said no more about the Tea-bowl or the one who had broken it.

Kato Kiyomasa was no one-sided warrior. There still exists an invitation that he sent to Hori Kyutaro Hidemasa asking him to come to a Cha-no-yu.* It runs as follows :

" I am afraid you must be finding this rainy season very wearisome. I have lately obtained from the province of Aki a very interesting landscape by Sesshu which seems to be genuine, so I am giving a Cha-no-yu party at my country house at Saga so that a few friends may see it, and I should be very pleased if you would honour me with your company

> " *The moon shines bright*
> *Yet o'er its silver mirror*
> *A shade may pass.*
> *So our fair name*
> *In this world's murky courses*
> *May suffer autumn changes.*

" First day of the fifth month.

Higo-no-kami Kiyomasa.

" To Hori Kyutaro Dono."†

Kato Kiyomasa once went to a Cha-no-yu given by Kanamori Sōwa and praised him very highly. He went on to explain that he had not gone as a Tea Connoisseur but to examine the alertness and deportment of the host, and he had been watching to see if he could catch him off his guard and relaxed, so that it would be possible to aim a spear at him with any chance of success, but had to confess that he found no such opportunity.

---

* Murdoch quite overlooks this side of Kato's character, cf. his dictum, " Kato's mental horizon was strictly bounded by the claims of war, of administration, and the statecraft these involved."

† This letter came into the possession of Count Katsu Awa, who kept it hung up in his study that he called the Kaishu Library. He often used to say that if a warrior like Kiyomasa, born in such an age of war and confusion, could preserve a mind so detached and calm, anyone living in a time of peace and quietness such as the present ought to be ashamed of himself if he allowed his mind to be unsettled and agitated. And Katsu Awa was a man of the same type as Kiyomasa.

Some say that he really meant to assassinate Rikyu fearing the influence the Tea Master had with Hideyoshi.*

ASANO NAGAMASA

Asano Sakyo-no-taiyu Yukinaga had a detached Tea-room next to his reception room which he afterwards pulled down: his retainer Asano Naizen then got the timbers of it and built another room with them, and when it was finished he and Hori Mimasaka-no-kami Chikayoshi invited Yukinaga's father Danjo-no-Shohitsu Nagamasa to a Cha-no-yu to celebrate the occasion. When Nagamasa arrived Naizen went out to meet him and ushered him into this new room which was called 'Kusari-no-ma,' or 'Chain Room,' and the guest, looking round at the room and its furnishings, noticed that everything showed signs of extravagant expenditure. " Look here, Naizen," he said somewhat severely, " this room is quite out of proportion to an income of fifteen hundred koku. Ostentation is very offensive to me, and an entertainment in these surroundings will not give me any pleasure. If you wish to show me real hospitality you will serve it in your ordinary room." " I shall be most pleased to do whatever you wish," replied Naizen, distinctly abashed. " Well, in that case," returned Nagamasa, " you will pull this room down immediately." And calling his retainers and those of Chikayoshi, he told them to go into the Rōji and take it down. So they tucked up their hakamas and soon had it dismantled, whereupon he proceeded into the older reception room and was there served with tea much to his satisfaction, after which he departed in a very good humour and much pleased with everything. When this was reported afterwards to Ieyasu and Hidetada, they both expressed their approval of what Nagamasa had done. " These young men," said the Shōgun, " are apt to be extravagant, and that is just the kind of sharp lesson they need."

UEDA MONDO SHIGEYASU†

Ueda Mondo Shigeyasu was a retainer of Niwa Goroemon Nagahide, and at the age of sixteen he distinguished himself as a soldier by cutting down the famous champion Oda Nobuzumi. Being an old friend of Asano Yukinaga, when this captain received the fief of Wakayama in Kishu, he was persuaded to take service under him and was allotted an allowance of ten thousand koku. He had become very well known for his knowledge of Cha-no-yu, and now proceeded to retire and take the name of Sōkō. It happened that the castle of Wakayama was then being repaired, and all the retainers, great and small, turned out to assist in the work. Shigeyasu was especially to the fore, as, clad in a persimmon-coloured cotton haori with a huge rudder on it as a crest, and with a towel dyed with shibu‡ round his

---

* Sen Rikyu is said on one occasion to have warded off with the ladle a sword cut suddenly aimed at him while he was making tea.

† Instead of striking a wooden board or bell, Ueda Mondo once fired a blank charge from a small culverin to inform his guests that he was ready for them, while Taga Sakon, finding himself without flowers, once put a helmet in the Tokonoma instead. Once in a way such a thing may be permissible.

‡ Shibu = Persimmon juice.

head, he took his stand on a big stone and acted as leader in the rhythm of the chanties which the men sang as they worked. When they saw this the younger samurai laughed derisively. " Ah," they jeered, " our master is a great lord indeed, for he has a tea-page of ten thousand koku ! " And this jape was bandied about among them till it became the talk of the whole clan and eventually came to the ears of the daimyo himself. Yukinaga was not pleased, and took the first opportunity to present Shigeyasu with a short sword in the presence of all the retainers. " I have heard that these fellows have been repeating some witticism about you lately, but you need not worry about that," he said ; " when next there is some real fighting to do, see what you can accomplish with this." " I am overcome with gratitude at your condescension," replied Shigeyasu, " and when the time comes I will requite it by dipping this sword in blood in your service." But the young samurai still jeered and said, " Sōkō says he will dip his present in blood, and it may be he will, but it will be the blood of a cat or a rat."

Some time after this Yukinaga died and his younger brother Tajima-no-kami Nagaakira succeeded as head of the clan, and he too retained the services of Shigeyasu. Then the Summer Campaign* at Osaka started in the first year of Genna (1615) and Ban Danuemon, one of the leaders in that castle, led an army of twenty thousand men against Kishu. To counter this attack Nagaakira sent out a force of his own of which one Kameda Ōsumi and Shigeyasu led the van. On the twenty-ninth day of the fourth month the two forces met at Kashii in Izumi and there was a stiff fight, both sides sustaining about equal loss. Shigeyasu, who was then sixty-seven years old, was wielding his spear with all the vigour of a young man when he was opposed by one Yamagata Saburoemon, a fighter of some renown, who aimed a powerful thrust at him. Shigeyasu deflected the spear so that it only pierced the air, while with a great shout he drove his own weapon straight through the helmet of his adversary. Then another of the enemy force, a stout soldier named Sakata Shōsaburo, calling out his titles, rushed at him to avenge his fellow clansman. Shigeyasu avoided his thrust and again put in his own point, but unfortunately for him the spear broke off short at the head. Flinging away the shaft he at once grappled with Sakata, but the latter was a man of great weight and strength and bore him down and would perhaps have had his head, when two of the Kishu men came up and pulled him off, whereupon Shigeyasu, immediately drawing the short sword he was wearing, struck it into his adversary's body and then, springing up with a shout, with a neat sweep took off his head. And this was the short sword that Yukinaga had given him. After this they had no difficulty in repelling the attack, and when this was done Shigeyasu returned to their headquarters and received the congratulations of his lord. Standing up before the whole assembled clan, Shigeyasu exclaimed, " How now you fellows ? You derided me as a tea-page of ten thousand koku and declared that my sword would only be wet with the blood of a cat or a mouse, and how has it

_____

* I.e. of Tokugawa Ieyasu against Hideyori, son and successor of Toyotomi Hideyoshi.

turned out? You, who have never known anything about Tea, but have devoted yourselves to the martial arts alone, are not only less distinguished than a Tea Master like myself, but have done practically nothing at all ! "

After the fall of Osaka castle Osumi and Shigeyasu with their lord Nagaakira were presented to the Shogun Ieyasu, who congratulated them on their exploits and their lord on having such worthy retainers. Afterwards they were entertained to tea by Hidetada and presented with valuable swords.

Once when Ueda Shigeyasu was riding along under a hot fire of arrows and bullets, he noticed a particularly beautiful bamboo in a thicket beside the road. Calmly he dismounted and cut it, and as he took it the enemy charged down on him, whereupon he nimbly sprang upon his horse again and rode on without the least agitation.

KONOE OZAN'S READY WIT

Ōzan was the name taken by Konoe Kwampaku Nobuhiro when he retired. He was most famous as a calligraphist and was founder of the style of writing known as the Konoe-ryu. He and Honami Kōetsu and Shōkwado Shōjō were known as the Sampitsu, or Three Pens of their age. Nobuhiro was also fond of Tea. Once with Shigenoi Gon-Dainagon Sueyoshi he was invited to a Cha-no-yu party by Fukushima Masanori, and they were waiting in the arbour for the summons to the Tea-room when Masanori himself came in to welcome them. As he entered by the middle gate he caught in a spider's web that happened to be there, but brushed it away with his hand and greeted his guests and then went into the Tea-room. Now Masanori was well known for his quick temper, and Sueyoshi felt very uncomfortable at the reflexion that he would almost certainly put to death the servant responsible for the cleaning, but still he could think of no way to prevent it. When they entered the Tea-room, however, Ōzan began : " While we were in the waiting arbour a spider dropped down from one of the pine trees, and we looked to see what he was going to do. Well, he went over to the middle gate and darted about hither and thither very smartly, and before we were aware of it he had spun a fine web. His adroitness was really most wonderful and we were so interested that we did not notice the flight of time till you came. It really seemed as though you had told him to do it." This droll speech convulsed the host and guests with laughter and naturally the servant did not suffer.

On another occasion Ōzan was invited to tea by the Kyoto Shoshidai Itakura Suwo-no-kami Shigemune, who was a good friend of his, and when he got to his mansion he found Shigemune grinding tea in a mortar. " Ah," he said, " as he bowed his greeting, " I thought I would serve some Koi-cha to-day, but indeed you have come before I have had time to prepare it. Well now, how would you like to take a turn at it yourself, just out of curiosity ? " And he went to put in some more. But Ōzan stopped him. " Ah, Suwo," he rejoined, " I suppose it is a trick of yours to be able to say you have some tea that was ground by the Kwampaku, isn't it?" " You are not far wrong," admitted Shigemune with a grin, scratching his head.

In the possession of the house of Konoe is the famous censer called ' Mono ka wa.' It originally belonged to Ashikaga Yoshimasa and later was obtained by the Kwampaku Masaie. On the top it has a cock and hen done in silver, and inside the lid is a bell-tower. There is a silver ring on each side with a cord attached. At the attachment of the ring on one side is the word Mono and on the other the words Ka Wa.

The reference is to the well known verse of Matsuyoi-no-ko-jiju or ' The Eve-awaiting Maid.'

> *When we keep our tryst*
> *'Tis the temple bell at eve*
> *That we love to hear.*
> *Nothing think we of the cock*
> *Who will part us with the dawn,*

which is given in the third chapter of the second book of the *Heike Monogatari.**

NAGAI DŌKYU'S GOOD LUCK

Nagai Zenzaemon, called Dōkyu, a feudatory of the Tokugawa house, was well known to fame in the field, but for some reason after the fight at Odawara he took service first with Gamo Ujisato and after his death with Uesugi Kagekatsu, eventually retiring to Fukaya in Kazusa. An old friend sent him a fine Seto Tea-caddy of which he thought a great deal, but unfortunately one day his waiting maid dropped it and broke it. Naturally he was irritated and scolded her, and wishing to make amends she went and brought him a little pot that she had in her toilet case and asked him to use that instead. Dōkyu rather reluctantly took it as a token of her regret, but attached no particular value to it. Some little time after this the great Tea Master Kobori Masakazu happened to pay him a visit and noticed the pot. Gazing at it in amazement he told Dōkyu that it was a rare one indeed, for it was undoubtedly a genuine Chinese specimen of a ' Katatsuki.' Dōkyu was highly delighted and gave it the name of Nagai Katatsuki. It afterwards became one of the treasures of the Tokugawa family.

Another story is also told of a piece of good luck that befell Dōkyu, this time in the matter of a sword. He was invited by Itakura Katsushige, who was a friend of his, to go up to Kyoto when Ieyasu was proceeding thither and on his way he fell in with a Rōnin at Nagoya in Owari. Wishing to see a relative at Atsuta, near here, he left his baggage with the Rōnin and hurried on there, but when he returned he found that the other had decamped, taking with him Nagai's sword, in exchange for which he had left his own, an ill-conditioned looking rusty weapon. As there was nothing else for it

* For this episode see my translation in *Selections from the Heike Monogatari*. p. 74.

he girt this on and proceeded to the Capital. When he got there Itakura told him that they were clearing out the prison a bit in anticipation of the arrival of the Shōgun, and therefore orders had been given to sharpen a score or so of swords. Thinking this a good opportunity to get an edge put on his own for nothing, he took it to Honami, the sword connoisseur, who examined it and remarked that it looked as if it would cut very well. Since there were several criminals yet to be executed, he had the sword tried on one of them, and it cut through his neck like a cucumber. When they polished it and inspected the tang of the blade they found the name of Masamune on it, and Honami certified it as being a genuine specimen. Nagai was naturally pleased at his find and eventually presented it to the Shogun, in whose family it is known as Nagai Masamune.

NABESHIMA NAOSHIGE'S KAKEMONO

Nabeshima Naoshige had a fine specimen of the writing of Kyōdo mounted as a kakemono, and one day his son Motoshige was looking for it but could not find it. When he asked his father, he said he did not know where it had got to, and showed no particular interest in it.

"But," urged the son, "this is one of the most valuable pictures in existence, is it not?" "Oh," replied the father, "these things are just the fashions of the period. I have better things to leave you than that. I have the retainers I have trained. That is much more important."

HIDETADA'S ESCAPE

Okubo Sagami-no-kami Tadachika was a pupil of Furuta Oribe and was much given to Cha-no-yu when he had any time. He happened to be sent to Kyoto by Tokugawa Ieyasu in charge of his son Hidetada in the fourth year of Bunroku (1596). Now when Hidetsugu, the adopted son of the Taiko, fell under the suspicion of his father, he tried to get hold of Hidetada as a hostage to procure the support of Ieyasu. So one morning he sent a messenger at dawn asking him to come to an early Tea at his house. Tadachika suspected his design and saw the messenger himself, telling him that unfortunately his master was given to sleeping late and as it would of course be improper to rouse him, would he wait a while. As soon as the messenger had gone back again he sent Doi Toshikatsu with Hidetada to Fushimi, staying behind himself. When the messenger came again, after keeping him waiting some time he told him he was very sorry but he found that his master had already gone to Fushimi for an early Tea, but owing to his habit of sleeping late he had only just discovered this, for he thought he was still in bed. As it was noon by the time the messenger returned to Hidetsugu, there was nothing more to be done. So did Tadachika use Cha-no-yu to foil a plot against his lord.

DATE MASAMUNE

When Hideyoshi was besieging Odawara, Date Masamune made up his mind to surrender, and rode in to Sagami with about ten retainers, leaving them there and going on to the Taiko's camp alone. When he arrived there Hideyoshi refused to see him for some time, as a mark of his displeasure at Masamune's dilatoriness. Hearing that Sen-no-Rikyu was in the camp, Date resorted to him and studied Cha-no-yu. When the Taiko heard about this he seemed surprised that, since he came from a far and rather wild country, for he was lord of Sendai in Mutsu, he was so far polished that he cared about the elegant arts, and in consequence he determined to receive him.

Masamune was renowned for his unbending disposition as well as for his boldness and originality. More than anything else he despised being taken aback or losing self-control. One of his eyes had been in some way injured and hung out on his cheek, the appearance of his face in consequence being by no means pleasant. So one of his friends recommended him to cut it out, because if he came to grapple with an enemy on the battle-field it might be seized and he would be in a very awkward position. Date accordingly took the short knife from his sword scabbard and cut it out, but as he did so he gave an involuntary exclamation. "That will never do," said his companion, "if you have no more self-control than that you will never become a great general." Masamune felt very much ashamed of himself and swore that it should never occur again. Once he was admiring a famous Tea bowl, turning it over caressingly in his hands, when it almost fell to the ground and he gave an involuntary start. "Ah," he said, "though I have learned never to flinch on any occasion in battle, not to speak of other occasions, yet I find myself starting like this from fear of smashing a Tea bowl because it may be worth a thousand kwan. This will never do!" And he took the bowl and flung it down on the stones, smashing it into a hundred fragments.

Date Masamune was once invited to a Cha-no-yu by Tokugawa Ieyasu. The latter did not see that the lid of the kettle was very hot, and went to take it off, when a jet of steam shot out and he involuntarily drew back his hand, whereupon Date burst out laughing. But Ieyasu quietly took the scalding hot lid into his hand and kept it there and went on to make the tea, with the remark, "It would need more than steam to make me drop anything."

On another occasion he was invited by Sakai Sanuki-no-kami Tadakatsu, one of Ieyasu's Rōju. The tea spoon was one made by Sen-no-Rikyu, and Date took it in his hand and looking at it remarked, "It is rather a silly thing," and snapped it in two. Tadakatsu was naturally very surprised at this, but showed no sign of it and continued as though nothing had occurred. When Masamune went home again he sent Tadakatsu a tea spoon by Shō-ō with this note, "Very many thanks for your kind entertainment, which I enjoyed so much that I was unable to control myself and did a very clumsy thing, so I hope you will accept this as a slight token of my regret."

These audacious pranks were characteristic of the ' One - eyed Dragon' as Date was usually called, but would have been neither safe nor advisable for anyone else to imitate.

But Masamune was most punctilious about ceremony when occasion demanded it, for once when the Shogun Iemitsu, wishing to show him especial favour, invited him to the Castle to a Tea Ceremony, before he entered the Shogun's presence one of the officials, Sakuma Shogen, met him in the outer Tea Utensil Chamber and placed before him a Tea-caddy in a box which Iemitsu wished to present to him. But Date would not receive it and after three refusals Sakuma took it back again to his master. " Quite right," said the Shōgun, " leave it here," and when Date was ushered into his presence he took the box out of his sleeve and gave it to him with his own hand. Masamune thanked him most respectfully and said : " When Sakuma brought me this just now I declined, because I did not think it proper to receive a present from the Shōgun on the mats of the Utensil Chamber." Iemitsu was very pleased with this courtly speech and the fine discrimination it revealed.

During the protracted negociations that took place during the Winter Campaign before Osaka Castle the Commanders of the various armies used to foregather and while away the time by Incense Smelling Competitions for prizes. Date Masamune happened to drop in during one of these meetings and was induced to take part. The other generals contributed bows and arrows and horse trappings and saddles and other equally valuable things as prizes, but Masamune only offered the gourd he had hanging at his side. The others laughed at this and no one was at all anxious to receive it, but eventually a retainer of the host took it. But when the party was over and Masamune was about to go back to his quarters he took the horse he had been riding and gave it to this man. " There," he said " a horse has come out of the gourd."* And those who had been so amused at first were now rather envious.

KATAGIRI SADAAKI

Katagiri Iwami-no-kami Sadaaki† was the son of Shuzen-no-kami Sadataka, and received the fief of Koizumi in Izumi with an income of ten thousand koku. He was the pupil of Kuwayama Sōsen for Cha-no-yu and took the titles of Sōkan, Nokai-an and Fuhyōken. He is the founder of the school called Sekishu-ryu.

He was a descendant of the great Master Takeno Shō-ō, for his father Sadataka married the daughter of Imai Sōkun who was a grandchild in the female line of Shō-ō. Sōkun's daughter was very good-looking and was sought in marriage by Ono Shuri-no-suke

---

* This is a proverbial saying signifying something surprising.
† Usually called Katagiri Sekishu. Sekishu=Iwami.

Harunaga's* younger brother Shume Harufusa, but he refused and married her to Sadataka. So Sadaaki was descended from Shō-ō if he was her real son. Sadaaki was famous for his taste and the fineness of his discrimination in details. There was once a question of cookery and he gave this pronouncement: " If you want a simple meal in good taste you will have to prepare an elaborate one and then make a selection from that. If you begin by thinking that anything will do for a light meal the result is not likely to be very interesting."

Sadaaki had a fine piece of Chinese pottery that he used as the firepot of his tobacco box, and one of his friends remarked that he thought it was a pity to treat it so familiarly and asked why he did not rather use it as an incense-burner. " That is just where the true spirit of Tea is shown," replied Sadaaki, " for it is because it is used as a fire-pot that people admire it. It is a first-class fire-pot but it would be a second-class incense-burner. Why murder a utensil by taking away its right place in the scheme of things? The important thing is to make things live as fully as possible. It is just the same as with people. A fool may be useful and a sage useless. It all depends on the suitability of their employment."

Katagiri Sadaaki was especially distinguished as a connoisseur of antiques as well as for his deep knowledge of Tea Philosophy, and was appointed Tea Master to the Shogun Ietsuna. Once when on his way to Edo from his fief of Koizumi he noticed in a posting inn where he was staying one night a chamber-pot of what seemed unusual quality. He had it cleaned carefully and then examined it and found that it was indeed a fine piece, so he intimated that he wished to buy it.

" It may be, as your lordship says, a fine piece," replied the host, " but as it has been used for such a purpose it can have no value at all. If you wish to have it I shall be pleased to present it to you, but I could not think of taking anything for it." " But it is quite unreasonable," said Sadaaki, " to get things from people for nothing," and so, after some pressing, he made him take something for it and then ordered his attendants to break it in pieces. They were naturally a little surprised, so he explained, " This is a genuine piece of old Chinese pottery, and if a connoisseur happens to see it he will certainly buy it and in all probability say it was a water jar and sell it at a high price. And the buyer, having parted with a large sum for it, and quite unaware of its former uncleanness, will look on it as a great treasure and treat it accordingly, and it is to prevent a thing so unbecoming that I am now having it broken."†

There is a case of a curious old Chinese vessel dug out of the ground at a place where Gyogi Bosatsu lived and so called Gyogi-yaki. It has a pointed bottom and will not stand up, so that it cannot be used as a Tea-caddy. It is said to be used as a hanging flower vase.

---

* Ono Harunaga, Councillor of Toyotomi Hideyori.
† A similar story is told of Matsudaira Fumai.

TOKUGAWA YORINOBU

Kii Dainagon Yorinobu, son of Ieyasu and ancestor of the Tokugawa lords of Kishu, was very like his father in his disposition. He was most of all interested in military affairs, but also he studied Tea under Furuta Oribe and Oda Yuraku, and Nō drama under Kwanze Kokusetsu and Komparu Taiyu, and became most expert in both. He was very fond of impressing on his vassals that "the business of samurai is the management of men. They should not allow themselves to be diverted from it by things. Those who do are big fools. They should always remember the verse:

> *The true samurai,*
> *When the cherry-viewing's o'er*
> *And he turns back home*
> *Should be quite as pleased to see*
> *By the road the sicklewort."*

TOKUGAWA YORINOBU CONCEALS A MISTAKE BY HIS CLEVERNESS

Tokugawa Yorinobu had a kakemono of the writing of Kyōdo that was one of the treasures of the Empire,* and the Rōju† expressed a wish to be allowed to see it. Yorinobu gladly assented and appointed a day on which he would receive them at a Cha-no-yu at his detached residence by the Akasaka Gate. At the time arranged they all presented themselves and were received at the gate of the inner Rōji by Miura Nagato-no-kami Tametoki as the representative of the host and conducted to the Tea-room. Yorinobu was just going through to meet them by the entrance from the residence, when he passed through the adjoining reception room and noticed the famous picture taken out of its box and lying on the shelf of the chigai-dana there. In astonishment he called the Dōgu-Bugyo, the official in charge of the tea utensils, and Sen Sosa, the Master of Tea, and questioned them about it. They explained that a mistake had been made and another kakemono hung in the Tea-room instead. Yorinobu reproved them sharply, but it seemed that the hitch could not well be corrected, when their lord's quickness found a way out of the difficulty. Without the least flurry or hesitation he sent Watanabe Wakasa-no-kami Naotsuna with this message to the waiting guests. "Since the kakemono that I am about to show you was given to me by Gongen Sama‡ with his own hand, it would not be proper to

---

* The reason for Kyōdō's writing being so much prized was this. Before Shuko was entrusted by the Shogun Yoshimasa with the preparation of the rules of Tea it is related that he made Tea for his master the great Zen priest Ikkyu of the Daitokuji and asked for his opinion about it. "Tea opens the eyes of the mind," said Ikkyu, "and therefore is a great help in Zen meditation." And he presented him with a writing by Kyōdō Zenji of the Keizanji in China, which was one of his most cherished possessions, and Shuko hung it up in his cell and drank his tea in front of it. (*Cha-no-yu Shiori.*)

† Rōju=The Shogun's Council.

‡ Gongen Sama=Tokugawa Ieyasu.

have it hanging in the Tokonoma as usual. I will therefore bring it in and hang it ceremonially myself, and since it would not look well to receive you in a room with an empty Tokonoma, I have hung another picture there for the time." All the Rōju bowed assent to this, considering it a very proper sentiment. Naotsuna then announced: "The Master of Tea will enter and remove the kakemono," and Sen Sōsa came in with the notched bamboo used for this purpose and took down the picture. Then Yorinobu himself entered quietly with the famous Kyōdo in his left hand and the bamboo in his right and hung it in its place, after which he proceeded to serve them with tea. And in all this his demeanour was so calm and unruffled and natural that no one suspected that it was an unrehearsed incident.

Now Hosokawa Tadaoki had been a fellow student of Cha-no-yu with Yorinobu when they were young as had also Sanada Nobuyuki, Tachibana Muneshige and Date Masamune, and when he was old Tadaoki asked Watanabe Naotsuna, Yorinobu's chief retainer, if he could manage to arrange for him to see this famous writing of Kyōdo, for he was now leaving the city for his own province, and as he was now old and infirm it was doubtful if he would live to come up again. Yorinobu willingly assented and fixed a day to receive him, but when Tadaoki arrived and was shown into the Tea-room he was surprised and disappointed to see another writing by Seishun, and not the Kyōdo he was expecting. However, he showed no sign of what he felt in his face, and when Yorinobu served him the tea he said in explanation: "I am very sorry that I have not got here the writing that you came especially to see. I did not tell you before because I feared you would not come if I did, but I hope you will forgive the deceit." Tadaoki certainly had been looking forward to seeing it, but he answered cheerfully enough, "Oh, that's of no consequence. I will see it another time."

After some further conversation he rose and left the Tea-room and as he was just entering the corridor between the Black reception room and the White Wood reception room, Watanabe Naotsuna appeared at the door with a box from which he produced the famous Kyōdo writing and presented it to Tadaoki, kneeling as he did so.

Tadaoki squatted down where he was and Watanabe said: "When you told me lately that you did not think your age would allow you to come again to Edo and so you wished to see this Kyōdo now, I thought it was rather an ill-omened speech, and so in order to suggest instead a happy augury for the future we did not show you the picture. That we will do properly when next you come to Edo and we welcome you in good health and spirits. All the same, if you would care to look at it informally I will hang it up in this room, for that is why I brought it here." This speech and its sentiment pleased Tadaoki immensely and he took the writing and handed it back as it was without looking at it with the answer: "I can hardly find words suitable to reply to your most kind and graceful suggestion. This shall certainly not be the last time I come to Edo, and I will as surely give myself the pleasure of visiting you and inspecting this picture." And he was as good as his word, for the next year he came up again and Yorinobu invited him and they spent a most enjoyable time with the Kyōdo in the place of honour.

Tokugawa Yorinobu had a Katatsuki Tea-caddy that was presented to him by his father Ieyasu and was considered to be one of the three first treasures of the Empire, and he naturally took great care of it and valued it highly. Once at the time of the Midsummer Airing of the storehouses a certain Ando Hikoshiro Shigeyoshi approached the official in charge and asked him to allow him to see this famous Tea-caddy on the quiet. This Shigeyoshi was the son of Ando Tatewaki Naotsugu, but was a great tippler and on this occasion also he was very drunk and exhaled the odour of saké like a cloud. Consequently the official feared that something untoward might happen and tried to put him off. " This is not quite the proper place for you," he said " it would be better if you went away." But, with the persistence of the drunken, Shigeyoshi would not be denied. " That I should be a retainer of this house and never have seen this famous treasure is very shameful for me," he insisted, " and when I meet the retainers of other families and they ask me if I have seen it and I have to say no, then it makes me feel a great fool. Pray stretch a point and let me have a look at it." The official did not like to refuse any longer, so impressing on him that he must not say anything about it, he took him into a room and was going to show it to him when Shigeyoshi, who was so drunk that he could not walk steadily, suddenly fell over on top of the Tea-caddy and the hilt of his sword struck it and broke it.

The official in great consternation went to his father Naotsugu and told him all about it, and he also in his turn was greatly troubled and repeated the tale to Miura Nagato-no-kami Tametoki the Karo of Yorinobu. When he reported it to his lord, Yorinobu said, "Have you the fragments?" and being told that they had, he ordered, "Then stick them together with lacquer." As he said no more Tametoki asked what kind of reprimand should be administered to Shigeyoshi. Yorinobu smiled. " Even if the Tea-caddy is one of the three treasures of the Empire and was presented to me by my father it will not shoot an arrow or a bullet on the battlefield or wield a spear or a halberd. And if you proclaim there, ' Make way for one of the Three Treasures of the Empire! ' I don't think anyone will be very frightened. Shigeyoshi may be a great tippler, but he is a man you can rely on in a fight, so let him alone." Shigeyoshi eventually fell fighting fiercely in the Summer Campaign at Osaka. And since at this time Yorinobu was not more than fourteen years old his discrimination was remarkable for his age.

Tokugawa Yorinobu had in his garden a stone lantern made by Kobori Enshu, and Sakai Tadakatsu, hearing of this, asked if he could see it. Yorinobu assented and immediately ordered his landscape gardeners Yamamoto Dōshaku and Kamada Teiun to put the garden in order and make some alterations in it. Now the Tea Master of the Kishu house, Sen Sosa, happened to be indisposed, and Senga Dōen was also unable to be in attendance, so that the two gardeners Dōshaku and Teiun had to see to the arrangement of the lantern by themselves. When they had examined it they went to the Bugyo Kageyama Uemon and told him that they thought the sun and moon shaped windows in the sides of the head were too small for the present taste and requested that he would have them enlarged. The Bugyo gave no particular thought to the affair but ordered a stone mason to make the windows larger according to the design of the gardeners, and when this had been done and the lantern put in the proper position he reported on it to his lord.

Yorinobu came out and inspected it, and when he saw the windows he at once asked the Bugyo what was the meaning of it. " That was done to the design of Dōshaku and Teiun," replied that official. Yorinobu's face suddenly hardened. " What is the use of a Bugyo, then?" he demanded. " If they did say it was to be done, why was I not told about it? You have allowed a splendid stone lantern like this to be damaged so that it is no longer of any use. I never heard anything like the insolent clumsiness of these two gardeners who dare to alter the work of a master like Kobori Enshu. And I have arranged for the Lord Sakai to come and see it soon. It will be difficult to alter it in so short a time." And laying his hand on his sword he ejaculated; " Uemon, you dolt, what is the use of you?" And the Bugyo, springing back in dismay, flung himself to the ground and crouched with his forehead to the earth. But Yorinobu shut his eyes and thought deeply for a while. Then he summoned Kano Gorozaemon Naotsune and put the question to him, " You see this fine lantern is unfortunately damaged in this way. Well, when I went up to Kyoto with my father I ordered this lantern from Kobori Enshu, and thinking that it would be as well to have two, I brought one down here with me, and the other I had put into a bamboo thicket in the detached residence at Kogawa in Kishu. Now what do you think? Can we get that one brought here in time?" " Indeed you showed great foresight in having two made, my lord," answered Naotsune, "and it is by no means impossible to get it here if you use a whale-boat and picked men." So they sent a fleet messenger to Kishu and the officials there put the stone lantern into a whale-boat in charge of the best seamen they could find and sent it to Edo. The sailors plied the oars by night and day and fortunately the weather was favourable so that it was not long before they landed it at Hatcho-bori, and there Sosa had it put into a cart and brought to the Akasaka residence. There Yorinobu came out and inspected it, and as it had been in the bamboo thicket for more than twenty years exposed to all the rain and dew, it had acquired a fine mellow antique appearance and become overgrown with fine moss so that it might have been of any age, and was in every way far more interesting than the other. Yorinobu was naturally delighted and so were Sosa, Naotsune and Dōen, for had it not been for their master's foresight the retainers' energy would have been of little use. Sakai Tadakatsu came in due time and was overcome with admiration at the appearance of the lantern.

The Tea shelf called Matsu-no-ki-dai was a great treasure of the

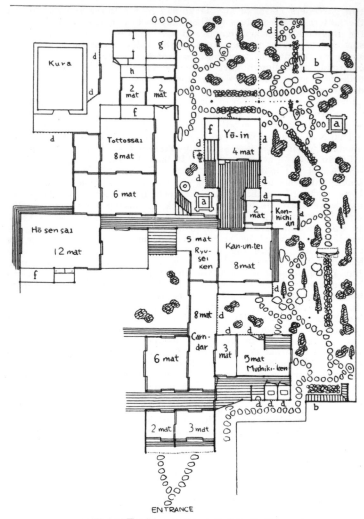

Plan of Ura Senge in Ogawa Kashira, Kyoto.

(a) Well. (b) Waiting Arbour. (c) Tsukubae Basin. (d) Lattice Window.
(e) Setsuin. (f) Tokonoma. (g) Rikyu shrine. (h) Butsudan.

Here is the Konnichi-an to which Sen Sōshitsu I the founder of this branch retired, taking the name of Ura or Rear Senge because it was behind the Fushin-an where Sōsa or Omote or Front Senge lived. Yū-in means 'Further Retirement' and was the Tea-room he made in which to spend his last days. The other rooms are named after the other Masters of the house.

Kishu house handed down from Yorinobu's father Ieyasu. One day Mito Komon Yorifusa and Owari Asho Mitsutomo, the heads of the other two chief Tokugawa houses, came to visit Yorinobu. Yorifusa was his younger brother and Mitsutomo his nephew. After some conversation the two asked him if they could see this famous heirloom and he replied that he would be most pleased to show it to them, but that it was not correct to bring out a thing like that quite casually, so he would let them see it properly in a Cha-no-yu. He then called his Tea Master Sen Sōsa and he served the tea from the precious shelf. When he had finished, Yorinobu said, "Allow me to introduce to you Sen Sōsa, grandson of the great Sen Rikyu, and like him also a great Tea Master, of whom you may have heard."

"The fame of Sen Sōsa has already reached our ears," said the two great lords, greeting him politely, "he is, as you say, a great Tea Master. We are pleased to meet him." Sōsa was so overcome by the courtesy extended to him by the three greatest daimyos in the Empire that he could hardly restrain his feelings as he bowed low and retired.

It was once reported to Yorinobu that a certain retainer of his whose income was only three hundred koku had paid three ryo of gold for a kakemono. Considering the expenditure excessive he ordered the Metsuke* to investigate. These officials told him that they found that the report was quite true, upon which Yorinobu questioned them about the condition of his horses and men, his arms and his military reputation. His horses, retainers and arms, they told him, were all in good order and above the average in quality, while he was himself a soldier of outstanding ability and keenness. "In that case," said Yorinobu, "he is quite justified in spending some time and money on pictures and Cha-no-yu. If he has a guest from another province it would be strange if he had nothing in his tokonoma or only some religious text. I do not mind anyone buying pictures or writings as long as he does his duty as a soldier. Only he should not go to excess." So this retainer's soldierly qualities probably saved his neck.

An instance to the contrary was that of Imagawa Ujizane lord of Suruga who neglected the military arts for Cha-no-yu and other amusements. One of his officers, a certain Mitamura, gave three thousand kwamme for a Tea-bowl, and his lord praised his taste, observing that such a thing was more meritorious than seven exploits in battle. Needless to say the Imagawa clan soon came to the ground.

When Yorinobu retired and handed over the headship of the family to his son the Chunagon Mitsusada, he left his famous tea utensils and arms to his second son Yorizumi. His Councillor Watanabe Naotsuna complained that this did not seem fair, especially in the case of the tea utensils, because the head of the clan would have the important guests to entertain. "Perhaps so," replied Yorinobu with a laugh, "But the younger son will probably be hard up for money

---

* Metsuke = Censors.

and will then ask his elder brother to assist him. And should this assistance be difficult to obtain, he can anyhow get money advanced on these treasures, and thus they will return to the main family while Yorizumi will get the money."

ITAKURA SHIGEMUNE GRINDS HIS OWN TEA.

The Kyoto Shoshidai* Itakura Suwo-no-kami Shigemune was very fond of Cha-no-yu, and used to grind his own tea while sitting in the Court as judge. And the reason was this. He once asked a friend of his who was his companion in Cha-no-yu, a tea merchant named Eiki, to tell him frankly what was the public opinion about him. " Well," said Eiki, " they say that you get irritated with those who don't give their evidence very clearly and scold them, and so people are afraid to bring law suits before you and if they do the truth does not come out."

"Ah, I am glad you have told me that," replied Shigemune " for now I consider it I have fallen into the habit of speaking sharply to people in this way, and no doubt humble folk and those who are not ready in speech get flurried and are unable to put their case in the best light. I will see to it that this does not occur in future." So after this he had a tea mill placed before him in court and in front of it the paper-covered Shoji were drawn to, and Shigemune sat behind them and ground the tea and thus kept his mind calm while he heard the cases. And he could easily see whether his composure was ruffled or not by looking at the tea, which would not fall evenly ground to the proper consistency if he got excited. And so justice was done impartially and people went away from his court satisfied.

In the third year of Keian (1651) Itakura Shigemune retired and was received by the Shogun Iemitsu. The Shogun ordered Matsudaira Nobutsuna to take two bags of the finest tea from the two tea jars called Sutego and Nue and to have them conveyed to Shigemune by the hand of Kuse Yamato-no-kami Hiroyuki, with the message that he had heard that Shigemune liked Tea now that he was growing old and that this was a fine variety and he hoped he would enjoy it. Shigemune was overjoyed at the honour, and wishing to have it handed down for posterity he prevailed on Hayashi Doshun to give it a place in his historical records.

TACHIBANA MUNESHIGE.

Tachibana Sakon-no-Shogen Muneshige was a great favourite of the Shogun Iemitsu, and was one of his Twelve Companions. He was an esthete as well as a warrior, and when he retired he made a fine villa for himself in the Shitaya quarter of Edo with hills, a lake, and a waterfall where he could enjoy fine scenery and the pleasant companionshi⸜ of fish and birds. In the fifteenth year of

---

Shoshidai = Shogun's Governor in Kyoto.

Kwanei (1639) the Shogun paid a visit to this villa and was entertained to a very exquisite lunch, after which tea was served. Then the Shogun went for a walk in the garden and shot two wild geese with his gun and also took another with his hawk. These birds Muneshige straightway had cooked and served to Iemitsu, who was much pleased by these attentions. Muneshige also presented the Shogun with a famous sword by Norishige and in return received from him a short blade by Norikuni of Awataguchi and five silk-wadded garments. Two years afterwards Iemitsu again paid him a visit and on this occasion was most gracefully entertained by the old esthete, and when he took his leave he presented him with a very fine Tea-caddy called Seto-no-Ō-katatsuki. This made three great treasures which the house of Tachibana possessed. The first was a banner which was given to their ancestor Otomo Buzen-no-kami Yoshinao by Yoritomo in the year 1197 when he went down to the Dazaifu, while the second was a short sword by Yoshimitsu and a fan which were given to Sakon-no-Shogen Sadanori, descended in the seventh generation from the above Yoshinao, by the Ashikaga Shogun Takauji in the year 1338 when he cut off the head of Yuki Hangwan Chikamitsu and brought it on the fan for Takauji's inspection. So when this Tea-caddy, presented by Iemitsu, was added, the Tachibana house could boast of the gifts of three great Shoguns of the Minamoto family, a thing that very few other noble families could do.

THE SIMPLE TEA OF DOI TOSHIKATSU.

Doi Oi-no-kami Toshikatsu was well known for his love of simplicity and his hatred of display. He was Tairo or President of the Rōju and his reputation for sagacity was high. One day he asked his fellow members of the Rōju if they would honour him by taking tea at his house. They said they would be delighted and he fixed a day on which they all presented themselves at his mansion by Kanda Bashi. They were first shown into the reception chamber and then into the tea-room, and while they were wondering what kind of entertainment they would receive, the question was soon solved by the entrance of Toshikatsu with a small Jubako or lacquer box containing five dried rice-cakes, one for each member of the Cabinet, with tooth-picks on the lid of the box, with which they could help themselves, which he offered them and then proceeded to make the tea. And this was all they got. And after they had partaken of it they sat there diverting themselves with talk on all manner of subjects, which cost nothing. And some of them were very satisfied with it all, and some were not.

II NAOTAKA RETURNS A FAMOUS TEA-CADDY.

Ii Kamon-no-kami Naotaka, lord of the castle of Hikone, bought for a thousand pieces of gold from Matsukura Nagato-no-kami Katsuie, lord of the castle of Shimabara, a rare Tea-caddy called Matsukura

Katatsuki. Some time afterwards the Shimabara rebellion took place and Katsuie was condemned to death and his fief confiscated, so that his family was ruined and his wife and several daughters were reduced to great straits and had to go and live in a hovel in a back street in Edo. When Naotaka heard of their ill fortune he at once sent and returned this valuable Tea-caddy, which the lady soon sold to the Maeda house for another thousand pieces of gold so that she and her family were able to live in comfort for the rest of their lives. She must indeed have felt, as the proverb says, like a blind turtle that finds a floating plank. And the real worth of Tea utensils, which have in themselves no intrinsic value, is best brought out by such use.

EVEN KOBORI ENSHU IS NOT INFALLIBLE.*

Kobori Masakazu was a most versatile Tea Master, for besides being most expert in Cha-no-yu he was also a good poet and an eminent connoisseur of pictures, writings and antiques of all kinds. He was instructor in Cha-no-yu to the Shogun Iemitsu who trusted

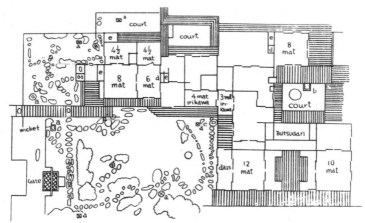

Plan of the Kōhō-an, built by Kobori Enshu, restored by Matsudaira Fumai.

(a) Stone lantern.   (b) Well.   (c) Basin.   (d) Shelf.   (e) Tokonoma.

him in all esthetic affairs, and employed him to design not only his tea rooms but also the gardens of the Western Castle, for which he received an honorarium of a thousand gold pieces. But there was

* Kobori Enshu Masakazu was of the Oda family, born in 1579, and in 1600 given the fief of Komuro in Omi, 12,000 koku. Appointed Bugyo of Fushimi in 1623 and died in 1647. Buried in the Kōhō-an attached to the Daitokuji, Kyoto.
    Kobori Enshu departed from the simplicity of Rikyu and was famed for his connoisseurship. He tried to make Teaism interesting to the dilettante, especially the noble dilettante. With him Tea began to be diseased. (*Cha-fu.*)

one occasion when even he was at fault.   In the year 1630 the ex-Shogun Hidetada requested him to design a study next to his living rooms, and when it was finished and he came to inspect it, he was surprised to find that it was built exactly like a Tea-room with low eaves and unsuitably odd ceiling, and on far too small a scale to be convenient for its purpose.   So Hidetada ordered it to be altered and the rough plastered walls to be painted with scenes from country life in the four seasons of the year, and pictures of herbs and vegetables in black and white.   And everyone admitted that this treatment was most effective for a study.

On one occasion Kamibayashi Chikuan and two friends came to a Cha-no-yu with Kobori Enshu.   He had been expecting Kuroda Josui, but he was unable to come owing to indisposition.   As they took tea it rained heavily so that it was difficult to go out for the interval.   But when it cleared up there was a great coolness, and they found the Tokonoma simply splashed with water without any flower arrangement at all.   " The trees in the Rōji are dripping so beautifully after the rain," observed their host in explanation, " that no flower would look well after them."

MATSUURA SHIGENOBU.

Matsuura Hizen-no-kami Shigenobu studied Cha-no-yu under Katagiri Iwami-no-kami Tadamasa.   He became a great master and finally founded a school of his own called after him the Chinshin-ryu.   He always impressed on his pupils these principles :   " Tea may be an amusement from one point of view, but you will find that the same principles are implicit in it as in the military art.   Cha-no-yu insists on the unity of things, and also on the most careful attention to details, in that the most unremitting vigilance must be exercised in every small point of the ceremony.   It also taxes the fertility of a man's resources when, as often happens, a situation crops up that is not provided for in the fixed rules.   If you are proficient in these things you are not likely to be found wanting in any military problem."

It was the custom of the Matsuura house to keep a club in the bathroom, and though this was discontinued by Iki-no-kami Kiyoshi, a descendant of Shigenobu, when the residence was altered, it was again restored at the instance of the scholar Hayashi Jussai as a fine example of the ancestral foresight, as was also Kato Kiyomasa's privy with two doors.

IEMITSU AND THE NAGASAKI BUGYO.

Hotta Kaga-no-kami Masamori had a fine Chinese Tea-jar which he prized greatly.   Once when the Shogun Iemitsu honoured him with a visit he showed it to him.   The Shogun's face clouded when he saw it and he immediately sent word to the Gorōju :   " A fine jar like this should have been submitted to me before it was sold.   There

must have been carelessness on the part of the Bugyo of Nagasaki.*
Send at once and investigate."

This was accordingly done immediately and the answer came
back from the officer, " I know nothing at all about Cha-no-yu. But
I have heard that only utensils of crooked and distorted shape are
in demand for it, and normal ones are of no use at all, so I have
always put aside any odd-looking piece for the use of His Highness,
and the symmetrical ones I have passed for sale." When this was
reported to the Rōju they were very perplexed for they thought that
if they repeated this speech to the Shogun he would be even more
enraged ; while on the other hand they did not know what to fabricate
instead. Finally they resolved to tell him, and did so in fear and
trembling. But Iemitsu laughed loudly and clapped his hands when
he heard it. " Yes, yes, that's exactly it," he exclaimed " it's just
because he doesn't know anything about Cha-no-yu that he gives such
an explanation." And he took no action against the Bugyo. The
whole affair is most characteristic of Iemitsu.

On another occasion Iemitsu told Kobori Masakazu that he
particularly wished to see the Tea-caddy called Hakata Bunrin formerly in the possession of Shimai Shōshitsu and now once more in
that of the Kuroda family. Naturally the present head, Kuroda Uemon
Suketada, could hardly refuse the Shogun's request, so he sent the
famous Bunrin to Edo in the charge of a trusted retainer and two
Tea Masters. When Iemitsu saw it he was astonished at its beauty
and exclaimed that three years' revenue of the province of Chikuzen
would not buy it, for there were few treasures in the land like it.
When it was returned and Kobori Enshu reported the opinion of the
Shogun to Kuroda, he treasured it still more, and from that time it
was decreed that it should only be brought out for inspection once
in the lifetime of each lord, on the day that he entered into his
inheritance.†

There is a note after this story to the effect that in the lifetime
of Kuroda Chikuzen-no-kami Nagahiro an exhibition was held at Ueno
at which this Bunrin tea-caddy was shown, and that a certain European, paying no attention to the other exhibits, examined it for three
days in succession with a microscope, and informed its guardian that
he thought it one of the great art treasures of the world. The
guardian, out of curiosity, asked him what he thought it was worth,
and the foreigner told him more than twenty million dollars. The
editor adds that he would like to know who the European critic was.
It would indeed be interesting to know.

It is related of Okubo Hikozaemon Tadanori that on one occasion
he met the procession of the Shogun's tea jars on the road. And
he was one of the Rōju at the time. He refused to get out of the

---

* The port of Nagasaki was under the direct administration of the Shogunate which had the
first choice in the purchase of all imported goods.

† Takahashi Sōan, when recently making a complete survey of all the famous ' Meibutsu'
for his work the 'Taisho Meiki-kwan' and taking photographs of them, was unable to get one
of this Bunrin for it is still only displayed on the occasion of the succession of the heir, and it
was explained to him that some misfortune would happen if they showed it at any other time.
One who saw it when it was on view related that it was put in a row with five others so exactly like it that it was impossible to say which it was.

way as even the greatest lord must do, and when the official in charge challenged him, he enquired: "And what is all this about?" "It is the August Tea of His Highness the Shogun. Get out of the road!" was the reply. "Well, I am the Minister of His Highness the Shogun," answered Okubo, "Is tea more important than man? It is that which should get out of my way, I think."

A similar story is told of the famous literary daimyo Ikeda Shosho Mitsumasa, lord of Bizen. He came upon the August Tea Jars one day on the road, but on this occasion they were not in motion but left on the highway, while their escort sat in a tea-house and rested.

Suddenly some of them ran out shouting: "What do you mean by butting into the August Tea Jars? Do you think we can overlook that sort of thing?" in the hope of getting a bribe to keep quiet. "Overlooking the August Tea Jars and leaving them in the road and then making a fuss because I come up to them is a pretty kind of conduct," retorted Mitsumasa; "I will lay a complaint against you in Edo for treating them with disrespect." Whereat the officials climbed down in a hurry and apologized profusely.

HOTTA MASAMORI.

Hotta Kaga-no-kami Masamori lord of Sakura was giving a Cha-no-yu to some friends, and when the Tea-caddy was taken out of its bag and put in its place the chief guest got up and went out into the garden and washed his hands, and then came back and bowed low to the Tea-caddy. "How remarkable!" he said, "This is a famous piece from the house of Sansai." The Sansai he referred to was Hosokawa Sansai Tadaoki. "That's very strange," said his host, "I have no recollection of getting such a thing." "Well, there's no doubt about it," insisted the other. So Masamori called the official who had charged of the tea utensils and asked him how it came to be there. He explained that it came from a box of pottery and tea things of which they were accustomed to receive two every year as a present from the lord of Higo. Still Masamori was perplexed, but after thinking a while he suddenly exclaimed, "Ah, I see it now. It is about the matter of Suga Daizen. He has put this valuable heirloom in the box of new pottery as a thank-offering to show his gratitude for the settlement of that case." Now Suga Daizen was a Karo or Councillor of the Higo clan. And when the former lord Mitsunao died, the heir Tsunatoshi was a minor and Suga Daizen abused his position and acted haughtily and oppressively to the people and paid no attention to their complaints, till his fellow Councillors remonstrated with him, but to no effect, when at last they appealed to the authorities against him and both sides appeared before the tribunal of the Bakufu. Now Suga Daizen was a plausible and eloquent man, and accustomed to litigation, so he was able to make out a very fair case for himself, while the other Karo found it difficult, for want of these qualities, to bring home their accusations very clearly. So when it came to summing up, the Metsuke Kanematsu

Masanao pronounced that in his opinion there was no case against Daizen. The Rōju were silent and apparently undecided when Masamori said, " Though the Metsuke seems to have made up his mind about it after some investigation, for my part I am undecided." So the Rōju pronounced that they would adjourn the case for a while for further evidence. When they sat again later an important witness came from Higo who was able to give conclusive evidence of Daizen's guilt, and so the matter was disposed of and the affairs of the province put in order. And since this happy result was entirely owing to Masamori's shrewd decision the clan naturally felt very grateful to him and took this way of expressing their feelings.

THE SHOGUN IEMITSU VISITS GAMO TADASATO.

In the first year of Kwanei (1624) the Shogun Iemitsu paid a visit to Gamo Shimozuke-no-kami Tadasato at his residence. He was received by Yorifusa lord of Mito and Tōdō Izumi-no-kami Takatora and other high officers who had previously arrived. Tadasato had built a special gate for the Shogun's reception. Its pillars were gilt and ornamented with wistaria blossoms and the doors were carved with figures of Taoist hermits and Buddhist Arhats. It was considered the finest piece of work of its kind in the city, and proved a great attraction to the people of Edo, who came in a never-ending stream ot see it, so that it was nick-named ' Hi-gurashi Mon ' or ' the All-day-long Gate.' Within the residence were displayed all kinds of rare works of art, each one a masterpiece of either Chinese or Japanese work. There was a writing of the Emperor Hui Tsung of Sung and another of Bodhidharma and many other treasures handed down from the collection of his grandfather Ujisato. In the alcove was a large bronze incense burner diffusing the sweet scent of the rare incense called ' Shiba-bune,' and the banquet that was served to his Highness was of the best that land and sea could produce.

After this repast they went into the garden and sat down to rest on some matting spread out under the cherry trees that were still fragrant with late blossoming flowers. There was a lake of clear water fed by a running stream, its surface a-ripple in the breeze, and beside it a hill with a narrow path winding round it with here and there the print of stags' feet. Everything suggested the deep calm of some mountain valley. By a thicket stood a little tea-house. It was thatched with cryptomeria bark and had pillars of bamboo. From a lion-shaped incense burner was wafted the scent of the incense called ' First Note of the Cuckoo.' Iemitsu sat down to rest for a while here and his eye fell upon a boy in patched working clothes apparently drowsing by the window. It was just what you might see on a country road. The Shogun was very delighted with the natural charm of it all, and asked if he could have a cup of tea, whereon the boy took down a gourd that hung on one of the pillars, poured out some tea-substitute and infused it and served it to Iemitsu, who praised its simple flavour and turned to depart, when the boy plucked him by the sleeve and asked for the tea-money. More pleased than ever, the

Shogun took his purse and gave it to the boy, feeling as though he were taking part in a play. After this incident Tadasato met him and conducted him to the tea-room where Cha-no-yu was given with Yorifusa and Takatora as fellow-guests. After that was a performance of Sarugaku mimes, and after that another more elaborate banquet followed by an illumination of the garden in a most tasteful manner. The Shogun returned to the Castle highly delighted with the entertainment, but what pleased him most in the whole day was the incident of the wayside tea-house.

MORI HIDEMOTO ENTERTAINS IEMITSU

Mori Saisho Hidemoto was one of the closest friends of the Shogun Iemitsu, and hearing that he was well versed in Cha-no-yu, the Shogun signified his intention of paying him a visit at his new mansion at Shinagawa. It was the sixteenth day of the ninth month of the nineteenth year of Kwanei (1643) when his Highness arrived and the sun was shining brightly after a day of autumn rain so that all were in high spirits at the happy omen. The Rōju Sakai Tadakatsu, Hotta Masamori, Matsudaira Nobutsuna and Abe Shigetsugu preceded him in the morning to see that all was in order, while Owari Dainagon Mitsutomo, Mito Saisho Mitsukuni, Maeda Chikuzen-no-kami Mitsutaka, Matsudaira Echigo-no-kami Mitsunaga, Hoshina Higo-no-kami Masayuki, Kato Shikibu-no-shoyu Akinari and Matsudaira Shimosa-no-kami Tadaaki were also in waiting to receive him. Iemitsu came in state accompanied by all his great vassals, and Hidemoto met and greeted him in the great reception hall of the mansion.

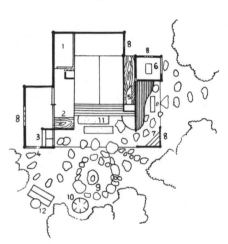

(1) Tokonoma. (2) Board floor. (3) Mizuya. (4) Nijiri-agari. (5) Shelf. (6) Setsuin. (7) Waiting arbour. (8) Windows. (9) Crouching Basin. (10) Lantern. (11) Nobleman's entrance. (12) Garden gate.

Four mat Tea-room called Kansui-an said to have been given by the third Shogun Iemitsu to Okudaira lord of Nakatsu in Kyushu.

At the hour of the Monkey (4 p.m.) he proceeded to the tea-room with Mitsutomo, Mitsukuni, Mitsunaga and Akinari, while Mitsutaka, Masayuki, Tadaaki, Tadakatsu, Masamori, Nobutsuna and Shigetsugu took their seats in the room of the tea utensils, and Miura Shima-no-kami Masatsugu, Naito-Iga-no-kami Tadashige, Ando Ukyo-no-shin Shigenaga, Yagyu Tajima-no-kami Munenori and other great vassals were in waiting in the next chamber. All the other retainers of the Shogun were entertained in the great hall. In all some five hundred people were entertained to a splendid feast served on trays and vessels richly decorated with silver and gold. In the alcove of the tea-room hung a scroll of writing by Nando, and the flower vase was a famous piece called ' Kabura-nashi ' from the collection of Hideyoshi, mounted on a plain stand of thin board, in which the Shogun arranged the flowers with his own hand. After the repast was over Hidemoto made tea. The Kettle was gourd-shaped and the Tea-caddy of Chinese ware, while the Tea-bowl was of black ware with the Tokugawa crest of the marsh-mallow done on it, specially made for the occasion. The tea-scoop was of Rikyu's make, the charcoal box was a gourd, the incense box was clover shaped and of Chinese make, the water-jar was like a ceremonial cap box, the fire-tongs were Chinese and of ivory, the slop jar was shaped like the vizor of a helmet, the lid-rest was fashioned by Shō-ō from a segment of bamboo, and the feather brush was of stork's feathers. The tea over, there was the formal passing round of the charcoal for inspection, and the charcoal boxes used were all of Chinese make.

Afterwards they went into another reception room where many more rarities were displayed. In the alcove was a scroll painting of the Western Lake by Sesshu, and the incense burner was a pair of mandarin ducks of gold on a stand of carved cinnabar lacquer. Among the treasures here were a set of the Ko-kin-shu written by the Shijo Dainagon Kinto and another of the Ro-ei-shu by Yukinari. Music was performed while they were inspecting these and at the end of it the Shogun presented a rare short sword by Samonji to Hidemoto. Hidemoto on his part offered an incense-burner and a bag of aloes incense that had once belonged to Ouchi Yoshitaka, and a sword by Bizen Saburo Kunikiyo.

It was now growing late and the great nobles took leave and departed, while the Shogun went again to the Tea-room with the learned priest Takuan and drank Sake. Just then the full moon rose in the east and Iemitsu in great delight asked Hidemoto for a stanza, whereupon he immediately produced the following ;

> " The rain is over,
> The day is fair, the sun shines ;
> To greet his Highness,
> The mountains do obeisance,
> And doff their cloudy mantles."

When the host had thus celebrated the auspicious weather and also added to the pleasure of his guest, Iemitsu asked Takuan to oblige and he did so in these words ;

> " The dusk approaches.
> We grudge, yet do not grudge it.
> Between the tree trunks

The moon now quickly rising
Floods all the sea with silver."

And this pleased the Shogun even more. Then Hidemoto had a number of tea-utensils, tea-caddies, tea-bowls, incense-burners flower vases, bottles and so on brought out and put on a table on the grass outside the tea-room, and the Shogun first chose from them a couple of incense-burners and Takuan another and a flower vase, after which the retainers in waiting were asked to take their pick while Iemitsu looked on and criticized their connoisseurship. Then it pleased the Shogun that these retainers should engage in a flower-arrangement competition, and a beautiful basket flower vase that had belonged to Shō-ō was brought out, and not until this was over did his Highness return to the Castle in great good humour. This Cha-no-yu was one of the largest and most unique entertainments in the history of Tea, and after it was over people flocked out to view the scene in such numbers that this viewing lasted for a fortnight.

The Tea-room used on this ocasion was made with a ceiling of Chinese material, walls of reeds and wheat straw plaited with rattan bindings and a verandah of green bamboo.

ABE TADAAKI AND THE TEA JAR.

Abe Bungo-no-kami Tadaaki wished to have a wooden box made for a tea jar that he prized very highly, and sent the jar to a carpenter so that it might be fitted. The craftsman set down the jar in his workshop and went on making the box without paying any special attention to it, when his child came in and picked it up and put it over his head for a joke. But when he had got his head into it, it would not come off, and he soon started to howl with fright. This drew his father's attention, and in great surprise he tried to pull the jar away, but it would not move, and the more he struggled with it the tighter it became, till the child was nearly suffocated. The father then desisted and stood resigned with folded hands, only remarking; "What a pity! But what can be done since the jar is such a valuable one?" However, a retainer hurried to his lord and told him. "How foolish!" exclaimed Abe, "why don't you break it at once?" So the retainer ran back and broke the jar and set the child free.

INABA MASANORI.

Inaba Mino-no-kami Masanori lord of Odawara was the son of Tango-no-kami Masakatsu and the grandson of the celebrated Kasuga-no-Tsubone, foster mother of the Shogun Iemitsu, and in the days of Ietsuna he was second only in influence to the 'Geba Shogun' Sakai Uta-no-kami Tadakiyo.* In his domains in the lake Ashinoko at Hakone there was a lot of sunken wood that had been there for centuries, and so far none of the masters of that part of the country

---

* Geba Shogun or Extramural Shogun. Tadakiyo was so nicknamed because of his great influence in affairs and because his mansion was just outside the castle gate by the side of the notice bidding all dismount before entering (Geba).

had cared to get it out because of the expense. But with the aid of that skilled engineer and contractor Kawamura Zuiken, Masanori obtained a great number of fine trunks and transported them to Edo. And the wood was of a very fine grain and beautiful, so Masanori had a tea-room made of it and entertained all the elegants of the capital there and they were very full of its praise. And Masanori had a son-in-law Hotta Bitchu-no-kami Masatoshi, son of Kaga-no-kami Masamori and adopted son of Kasuga-no-Tsubone, who on the twenty-second day of the second month of the tenth year of Kwanbun (1671) was elevated to be one of the Waka-doshiyori.* And in his honour Masanori gave a Tea-ceremony, his son Tango-no-kami Masayuki acting as host. And in the Tea-room was a picture of an ascending and a descending dragon by one of the great Kano Masters, and it was painted with such vigour and life that they seemed to writhe and roar as one looked. And all the guests were loud in their praises of it, and one of them, the Ōmetsuke Ooka Sado-no-kami Tadakatsu, exclaimed ; " Even among the great Kano Masters I doubt whether there are many things as fine. They look just like living dragons." When the tea was over and they adjourned to the reception room and began to chat, Masatoshi remarked quietly to Tadakatsu ; " When you looked at that kakemono just now you said they looked like real dragons ; have you ever seen a real dragon ? " " Why, no," said Tadakatsu, rather taken aback, " I can't say I have. What I meant was that I suppose they would look like that." " Ah, I see," replied Masatoshi, " well, I have seen a real living dragon." " How interesting," said the other guests, " and where was that ? " " My late father," went on Masatoshi with a smile, " owing to the great regard with which his Highness honoured him, rose from very small beginnings to exceedingly high rank and emolument. He was a real ascending dragon. On the other hand my elder brother Kōzuke-no-suke, for a single indiscretion, had his revenues confiscated and his family ended. He was the descending dragon." Whereat the others all applauded his witty remark. Meanwhile Masanori and Masayuki had come in from the tea-room, and Tadakatsu repeated this clever simile of Masatoshi to them, when the latter went on ; " Yes, and when one comes to think of it Masanori is another case of an ascending dragon, though perhaps it is rather rude of me to say so, and he should be careful accordingly." The other guests all looked rather aghast at this, for it is quite against the custom of Cha-no-yu to allow any harsh or discordant speech. But in this case it was for the good of Masanori and it may be that he owed to this timely counsel the preservation his name and fortune by pleading old age and retiring later on.

It is curious to note that Masatoshi himself was an example of a dragon that not only ascended but came down again. For he was appointed Tairo by the Shogun Tsunayoshi and was in high favour with him, so that no one in the Empire could gainsay him, but as the result of his policy of economy he made enemies among the ladies of the Inner Palace and eventually the Shogun also turned against him, so that on the fifteenth day of the eighth month of the first year

---

* Waka-doshiyori.   The Junior Council.

of Teikyo (1684) he received a present of an incense-burner called 'White Jade Cascade' and some rare incense of aloes, it being the custom of the Bakufu to suggest retirement by the present of Tea-utensils. But he considered his responsibility to be too great and would not take the hint and on the twenty-eighth day he was assassinated in the Castle by his relative Inaba Iwami-no-kami Masayasu.* His son Shimosa-no-kami Masanaka was much disliked by the Shogun, who would not receive him and changed his fief to Fukushima, and eventually he died in poverty and obscurity.

TOKUGAWA MITSUKUNI

There was an old man who lived at a place called Kanzaki in the province of Mito who had been fond of Cha-no-yu all his life, and who had always found solace in it if he happened to be lonely. His name was Kuwaya Sanmu, and though he was now over eighty and rather crippled in his movements he still continued to practise his favourite diversion. Now Tokugawa Chunagon Mitsukuni lord of Mito, who had now retired, came to hear of Sanmu, and one day when he happened to be in that part, he called to see him. His dwelling was just a tiny straw-thatched hut, and could hardly be called a Tea-room, for it was merely an ordinary cottage interior rather quaintly arranged, with a hearth cut in the floor, but it sufficed him for his pleasure proceeded from within his own mind. Since the cottage was so small Mitsukuni had to leave his retinue outside and went in with only two attendants. Sanmu tried to sit in the proper ceremonial manner, saying, " I am afraid my old bones won't allow me to sit quite as I ought before a nobleman." But Mitsukuni forbad him, telling him to sit in the most comfortable position. So, again excusing himself, he sat easily like a child and served his lord with tea. Mitsukuni observed that the tea-caddy was an uncommon one and asked him what it was called, " Oh, it has no special name," said Sanmu. " It seems to have a mark like a cloud on its shoulder," said Mitsukuni, " so give it the name ' Yoko-kumo ' ' Cloud-bank '."

When the Tea was over and he returned home Mitsukuni sent a fine Ashiya kettle to the old man as a present.

Tokugawa Mitsukuni had all his life been fond of Cha-no-yu, but when he retired he gave it up, with the remark that that kind of taste gave one too much love for Tea-utensils and such things to be compatible with true detachment of mind.

TOKUGAWA MITSUKUNI AND II NAOZUMI

In the ninth year of Kambun (1670) the Shogun Ietsuna received Tokugawa Mitsukuni and offered him a cup of tea. And Ii Kamon-

---

* This is one explanation of many of Masatoshi's mysterious assassinations. Certainly after the death of his austere minister Tsunayoshi was able to indulge his literary and artistic hobbies without restraint, but Masayasu may have had personal reasons for his action. It was this house of Inaba that in 1919 sold many of its treasures by auction and among them was a tea bowl that brought £16,700, a Shonzui utensil that brought £358, and a green and gold napkin that sold for £700, while the Sakai Bunrin tea caddy went for £311.

no-kami Naozumi, lord of Hikone was in attendance also. Now it is the custom when the Shogun makes tea himself and offers it to anyone, that the cup should not be returned to him, but become the property of the recipient. But on this occasion Mitsukuni was in the fullest of Court Dress and so could not retire with the cup in the proper way, and if he did not do so he could not keep it. Mitsukuni was at a loss what to do, when Naozumi, seeing the point, said to him, " May I have the honour of drinking after you." Mitsukuni was quite pleased at this device and asked the Shogun, and he was pleased to consent. So he passed the tea-bowl on to Naozumi, who put it to his lips and then into his bosom and went out with it."

II NAOMASA AND HIDEYOSHI

There is a story of this Naozumi's grandfather, Ii Hyobu-taiyu Naomasa, that shows the same quick resource. Naomasa had been invited to Cha-no-yu by Hideyoshi, who also invited Ishikawa Hoki-no-kami Kazumasa who was an old friend of Naomasa's, at the same time. But Naomasa turned his back on him and did not say a word, and when they went into the Tea-room and Hideyoshi made tea and offered it to Naomasa, he broke out with : " This fellow Kazumasa is a disloyal coward who has left his former lord and gone over to your side. Pray excuse me from having to sit in the same room with such a man." And he got up and went out, leaving everyone dumb with astonishment. But the real reason was that Naomasa saw that Hideyoshi meant to lay him under an obligation to himself, and took this way of getting out of it.

II NAOTAKA

Ii Kamon-no-kami Naotaka, son of Naomasa, once received a visit from Hoshina Higo-no-kami Masayuki and gave him Tea in the course of which he brought out a utensil that he valued very much and observed : " This was sent me by a certain person, and though I refused it several times he would insist on my having it, and so I gave way in the end. I don't suppose you have anything quite so rare, have you ? "   " I suppose people can see what is in my mind," replied Masayuki, " and as there isn't any inclination for these things there they don't try to press them on me. And they evidently divine your real wishes too."

SAKAI TADAKIYO AND THE KOKURA PAPER

Sakai Uta-no-kami Tadakiyo, lord of Umayabashi in Kozuke, was a devotee of Cha-no-yu and once bought a fine piece of Ogura paper for a large sum which he regarded as a particular treasure. But he was told that there was another piece like it in a certain temple in Kyoto, and was very much astonished, for he declared that it was a piece that was quite unique in the Empire. So he sent to the temple a message that he would like to look at the other piece, and as no one cared to refuse to comply with the wishes of this 'second Shogun' they were not long in forwarding it to him. When he put the two pieces side by side and examined them carefully he found that they did not differ in the least, and it was quite impossible to say which was genuine. Then he found that this other piece had certainly been given to the temple by Hideyoshi, and declared that there could then be no doubt that it was the original. So he tore his own piece into fragments and burnt them, so that there should be no chance of mistake or fraud in the future.

This Sakai Tadakiyo must have collected a great number of rarities in his time. Certainly he was not backward in asking for them. He heard that a relative had an album of six leaves containing the writings of six of the greatest men of the three dynasties Sung, Yuan and Ming which had been presented to his father Sakai Tadakatsu by the King of Korea, so he at once sent and asked him for three of them. Now this relative Sakai Shuri-no-taiyu Tadanao was one of the most altruistic of men, and he immediately sent the whole six to Tadakiyo saying that it would spoil the collection to divide them, and it was not as though they would leave the family, for since they were of one stock it did not matter which branch had the album.

GAMO SATONAGA'S TEA-ROOM

Gamo Genzaemon Satonaga was a page who had risen to become the adopted son of the famous Gamo Ujisato, and after the ruin of that house he took service under Sakai Sanuki-no-kami Tadakatsu at an income of ten thousand koku. Now Tadakatsu was ordered by the Shogun to undertake the repair of one of the stone ramparts of the Castle of Edo, and he appointed Satonaga Bugyo in charge of the work. Then Satonaga proceeded to build a shed for himself from which to supervise it, next to the one that Tadakatsu had. To this he added an entrance porch and made it into a Tea-room. And as he had a large acquaintance among the feudal lords they got into the habit of dropping in there for a cup of tea. Date Masamune was one of the first to do so, and soon the habit became so fashionable that this Tea-room of the Superintendent of Works was never without guests. Now Sakai Tadakatsu was a very strict man and it shows how popular Cha-no-yu must then have been that he permitted this to go on.

KANO TANNYU

This famous artist, the leader of the revival period of the Kano school, was known in his youth as Shirojiro and his first name was Morinobu. It was after he shaved his head and retired that he took the names of Tannyusai and Byakurenshi. He was given the rank of Kunai-kyo. He studied Tea under Kobori Enshu and became one of his most distinguished pupils. His character had all that calm and magnanimity that Cha-no-yu should produce, in illustration of which this anecdote is characteristic. He had a Tea-caddy which he had bought for a large sum, and when his house was burned down in the fire of the third year of Meireki (1658) called the Furi-sode Kwaji, which started from the Hommyoji temple, his servant stole it and ran away to Kyoto and sold it there, giving out to his master that it had been destroyed in the fire with his other possessions. But the theft was afterwards discovered, and Tannyu was able to buy the Tea-caddy back again, which he did very gladly, taking no steps at all against his servant but only rejoicing at the recovery of his treasure, which he proceeded to name 'Miyako-kaeri' or 'Returned from the Capital.' It was this spirit of altruistic calm that led the Shogun Tokugawa Yoshimune to say of him that he was one who had entered into the confines of the Saddharma Pundarika Sutra. Tannyu painted many of the pictures and also made designs for various details in the Tokugawa shrines at Nikko.

Date Masamune once sent for Tannyu to decorate a pair of gold screens seven feet high. The artist said he thought black-and-white sketches would suit them and went home again after considering them carefully. The next morning he came early and made a large quantity of ink into which he dipped a horse-shoe he had brought with him, and then proceeded to make impressions of this all over one of the screens. Then with a large brush he drew a number of lines across them. Meanwhile Masamune had come in to watch his work, and at this he could contain his irritation no longer, and muttering, "What a beastly mess!" he strode away to his own apartments. The retainers told Tannyu he was in a very bad temper indeed. "He shouldn't look on while I am at work, then," replied the painter, "he should wait till it is finished." Then he took up a smaller brush and dashed in touches here and there, and as he did so the prints of the horse-shoe turned into crabs, while the big broad strokes became rushes. He then turned to the other screen and splashed drops of ink all over it, and when he had added a few brush-strokes here and there they became a flight of swallows over willow trees. When Masamune saw the finished work he was as overjoyed at the artist's skill as he had previously been annoyed at the apparent mess he was making of the screens.

HONAMI KŌETSU

Honami Kōetsu was by profession a connoisseur of swords, but he was also a great calligraphist and, as above stated, was reckoned as one of the Three Pens of his time, the others being the Kwampaku Konoe Nobuhiro and Shokwado Shōjō. He was also a great Tea Master and belonged to the Oribe school. He was famous too for his lacquer work and painting as well as for his Tea-bowls.* He received an estate at Takagamine, a village outside Kyoto on the north, hidden away in the hills and at that time much infested by robbers. But after he went to live there they entirely ceased to haunt

---

* Kōetsu learned pottery from Nonko. That is to say he was taught how to fire it by him and then used his kiln; but his work had a freedom and dignity far surpassing that of his master, the result of the expression of the loftiness of his disposition and fastidious taste.

those parts.* When he grew old he built a temple there which he called Ryōjōin, and which is now known as the Kōetsuji, and there spent the rest of his days. He divided all his valuable Tea-utensils among his friends and relatives, and kept only common ones for his own use and with these he was quite content to pass his time diverting himself with Cha-no-yu. When asked why he did this he said that in using valuable things there must always be some anxiety lest they be broken, but one felt quite easy about things that could be replaced at any time. The grace of life lies in quiet simplicity, and real taste in the confines of the perfectly natural.

A wealthy merchant of Osaka, so it is said, asked for the daughter of Kōetsu, but his request had to be declined because there was no dowry to give her. The answer to this was that none was needed if she would bring with her a Tea bowl made by her father. So he made one and she was married into the merchant's family forthwith, but as Kōetsu had no bag for it a piece of one of the girl's dresses was used to wrap it in. Therefore it received the name of ' Ko-sode ' or ' Wadded Garment.' It belongs to the family of Sakai lord of Himeji and its proper name written on the box by Kōetsu is ' Fuji-yama,' not because it has any picture of Fuji on it but because the whiteness of its upper part suggests the snow on that mountain.†

YOSHINO

Yoshino's real name was Toku-ko and she was the daughter of a Ronin of the west country named Matsuda. During the period Genna (1615-1624) she left home and went to Kyoto, where she supported herself by making fans. Meanwhile her parents died, so she had to enter the house of a certain Hikozaemon of the Shimabara quarter and become a singing-girl. Here she took the name of Ukibune and her fame became great. She could write a fine hand and was skilled in playing and singing. Once, on viewing the cherry blossom in the quarter she made this verse, " Even here 'tis Yoshino when the cherry is in bloom," and so she got the nickname of Yoshino. And her charms became more and more famous. Now there was a man named Sano Shōeki. His name was Kiyosada, he was commonly known as Haiya Saburoemon, and he came of a very wealthy merchant family. He was a pupil of Asukai Masaakira, the Court noble, with whom he studied football and verse making, while he learnt Cha-no-yu from Fujibayashi Sōgen. In all these things he excelled. He became acquainted with Yoshino and they fell in love with each other so that at last he bought her out and married her. But when his father Shōyu heard of it he was very angry and disin-

---

* In the first year of Genna (1615), when he was 58 years old.

† Honami Kōetsu, founder of the Kōetsu school of calligraphy and first of the Three Pens of the Kwanei period, in his symbolic paintings is said to be the model of the French ' Art Nouveau.' As a lacquer artist he mixed brilliant gold with dull silver and lead on his writing cases and incense boxes, bringing a feeling of the ' Sabi ' of the Higashiyama age into the gorgeous fashions of Momoyama. But it is not so much the calligraphy, of which he was himself so proud, that is valued at the present day, as the pottery about which, apparently, he cared little. This is now revered as the very summit of his artistic achievement. (*Takahashi Tatsuo*.)

herited him and sent him away. So he went into the country just outside the city and there lived quietly on the proceeds of the sale of his fine Tea-utensils.

One day Shōyu was out for a walk near the city when a shower of rain came on and he took shelter under the eaves of a cottage. The lady of the house, thinking he must be uncomfortable, asked him in and made tea and served it to him. And she did so with much grace and elegance, giving the impression that she was a person of dignity and breeding. " This is a lady of a kind one seldom meets," he thought, as he took his leave and went out when the rain stopped. On his way home he chanced to meet his friend Honami Kōetsu, and in the course of the conversation related his afternoon's experience. " I tell you," he insisted, " there was nothing she lacked. Beauty, character and refinement, she had them all. I wonder who

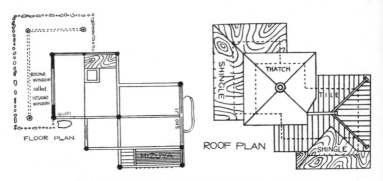

The Ihō-an Tea-room built to Yoshino's design by the Tea Master Risai, formerly at Seiganji Ogawa Kudaru, but now removed to the Kōdaiji, Kyoto.

she can be." Kōetsu clapped his hands. " That is the wife of your son Shōeki. Don't you think you had better give up the idea of disinheriting him?" Shōyu was both surprised and delighted. " So that is the famous Yoshino, is it? Really she is a lady not only of blossom but of fruit as well. No, I don't think she will disgrace our house." And he took back Shōeki and his wife to the family. Not many years afterwards Yoshino became ill and soon died. Her husband was much affected, and made this verse:

> In the Capital
> Where for me the cherry bloomed,
> Now it blooms no more.
> Yoshino is rapt away
> To the mountain-pass of death.

And when her body was burned he mixed the ashes with saké and drank them. Yoshino died on the twenty-fifth day of the eighth month of the eighth year of Kan-ei (1632) aged thirty-one.[*]

After Yoshino had become the wife of Saburoemon she often gave Cha-no-yu parties in her Tea room the Iho-an, and on one of these days snow fell heavily. The guests found that the Kakemono was only a piece of blank paper, and in answer to their question Yoshino answered, " I consider it a great compliment that you have left your tracks on the snow to come to my house to-day, so now will you not increase the obligation by leaving them also on this paper ? " And in the interval they took it out to the Waiting-arbour and wrote poems on it.

Shōeki lived to the age of eighty, dying in the fourth year of Genroku (1692). His Tea-room, popularly known as the Oni-gawara Chaseki or Devil-face Tile Tea-room, from the grotesque tile on it which Shōeki greatly admired, still survives with that of his wife at the Kōdaiji.

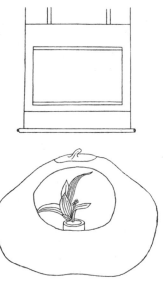

Yoshino's Tokonoma arrangement with blank kakemono and aspidistra in ' Flower Window ' pumpkin vase.

It is in his work the *Nigiwai-gusa* that there is contained the best picture of his friend Kōetsu and his life and tastes.

KURIYAMA DAIZEN PAYS HIS FRIEND'S DEBT WITH A FLOWER VASE

Kuriyama Daizen, an old retainer of Chikuzen, had in his family a flower vase made by Sen-no-Rikyu and inscribed by Hideyoshi himself, which was the envy of all the world of Tea esthetes. Now another retainer of this clan, Hoshino Sōemon, had borrowed three hundred ryo from a wealthy merchant Kawachiya Sanemon of Fukuoka to pay the debts of a relative, from a strong sense of family feeling. When Daizen heard of this he was very anxious to help Sōemon in the matter of this debt, but since he knew that he would never consent, he said nothing. Sōemon was a man who cared very little about wealth, but he had one indulgence and that was growing peonies, and every year he had a splendid show of them in a special part of his garden. Daizen passed his gate one day and stopped his chair and

---

[*] The story of Yoshino and Sano Shōeki has become very well known of late through the very tasteful dramatization of it by Takayasu Gekko in ' Sakura no Shigure ' or ' The Cherry Shower,' one of the most popular plays of the last few years.

enquired if the master was at home, because he would like to see the
peonies. Sōemon soon appeared and was delighted to show them to
him, after which he asked him to come into the reception room. Here
Daizen happened to notice in the Tokonoma a large picture of the
famous scene of the parting of Kusunoki Masashige and his son,

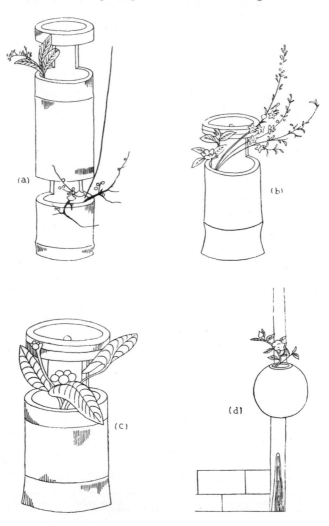

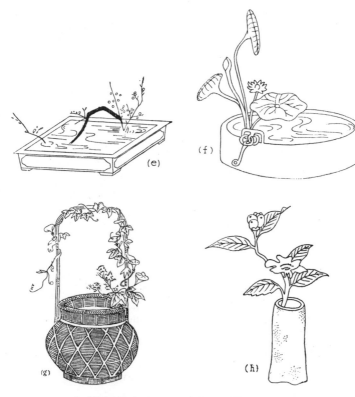

Flower Arrangements suitable for Cha-no-yu.

(a) Flower above and branch of plum blossom below, by Rikyu.
(b) White peach and red camellia in Lion's mouth vase, by Rikyu.
(c) Yellow water-lily (Nuphar Japonicum) in Lion's mouth vase, by Rikyu.
(d) Rose of Sharon (Mukuge) in round pottery vase on Toko pillar, by Sen Sōtan.
(e) Plum branch in 'Suiban' flower vessel for summer use, by Rikyu.
(f) Lotus in horse-trough shaped vessel fixed with a bit, by Rikyu.
(g) Wild chrysanthemum and morning glory in basket, by Kobori Enshu.
(h) Camellia Sasanka in a vase of Shigaraki ware, by Sen Sōtan.

painted by Kano Tennyu. "Ah!" he exclaimed, "there you have the greatest loyalist in our country's history. And a splendid piece of painting too. It would be difficult to find any fault with the force of the brushwork or the skill of the composition. I don't know when I have seen anything I like better." "Well," replied Sōemon, "since you like it so much I hope you will do me the favour of accepting it. I should really be very pleased if you would." "Ten thousand thanks," said Daizen, " I will indeed take advantage of your generosity." And after some more friendly conversation he went off with the picture. The next day Sōemon got a small package from Daizen with a note which read as follows ; " This little thing is a flower vase called Tabi-makura which belonged to Sen Rikyu and I send it as a small return for your kindness of yesterday. Should you not care for it, however, I hope you will give it to anyone you please. For instance there is Kawachiya Sanemon, who I think does business with you, and who is very fond of Cha-no-yu and has often wished to have it. As I hear he has a fine piece of fancy paper which you would much like, it is possible that you might arrange an exchange." Sōemon then saw at once that Daizen had called so that he might have an excuse for taking this graceful way of helping him, and he was very touched at his thoughtfulness. Then he went off at once to Kawachiya, showed him the vase and asked him what he thought of it. " However did you get this," cried Sanemon, " this is Tabi-makura Yamaga, made by Rikyu and signed by Hideyoshi, and owned and greatly prized by Kuriyama Daizen Sama. I have often heard of it, but this is the first time I have ever seen it. It is such a treasure that it is never allowed outside the gate, so how have you managed to get it ? " " Well, however much he may prize it he has been kind enough to give it to me, and as I don't know anything much about Cha-no-yu I am afraid it is quite lost on me, but I understand that you are a Chajin, so if you would like it I might let you have it. What do you say to exchanging it for that bond for three hundred ryo, which I on my part should find much more interesting." " Oh, that's not anything like enough," replied Sanemon in great delight, " I'll give you the bond and another three hundred ryo as well." But Soemon would have none of it. All he would take was the bond, and with it in his pocket he at once went off to the house of Daizen to thank him for his kindness.

AN IMPERIAL TEA-ROOM

Nakatsukasa-kyo Motohito Shinno was the son of the Emperor Reigen,* and became the heir to Arisugawa Masahito Shinno. He was skilled both in verse and calligraphy and held office immediately after the Regent of the Empire. His Highness was also fond of Cha-no-yu and had a tea-room built for him of rather an unusual kind. The fusuma were decorated with paintings of the Kado-matsu or Gateway Pine and other symbols of the New Year with handles of awabi shell,† while the handles of the doors of the tea-cupboard were made in the form of the letter ' No ' the first syllable of ' Noshi ' the symbol that always accompanies a present. When the Dainagon Reizei Tamemura saw it he made the following verse, which greatly pleased his Highness ;

All auspicious things
Portents of a happy age

---

* Reigen Tenno, 1663-1686.   † Awabi. The Sea-ear.

Greet us in this room.
Pine and hanging rope of straw,
Noshi and Awabi too.

The previous Emperor Go-Saiin was also very fond of Cha-no-yu, and had a Tea-bowl called Ido, after Ido Wakasa-no-kami who brought it from Korea in the time of Hideyoshi, which he prized very much, and he often invited the courtiers and gave them tea from it. One day Kwanjuji Dainagon Tsunehiro was his guest and this bowl was used. " I have often heard of this Ido Tea-bowl," he said, " but this is the first time I have had the honour of seeing it. Please allow me to look at it a little more closely." As the Emperor made no objection he got up from his seat and took it with him to the edge of the balustrade of the verandah and was examining it there, when it slipped out of his hand and fell down on to a rock in the garden beneath so that it was smashed to fragments. Seeing that his Majesty naturally looked exceedingly grieved at this mishap, the Dainagon made a low obeisance and said: "It was indeed most clumsy of me to let it drop in this way, but really there is not much harm done. This Ido tea-bowl is a very old one and it is impossible to say how much longer it would last, but anyhow it is not a thing of any public use, so I think it rather fortunate that it has been broken thus." The Emperor evidently thought this was a very right way of looking at it, for the expression of regret left his countenance. No doubt the Dainagon did this purposely, for it is quite contrary to custom in Cha-no-yu to move from one's seat when examining a valuable utensil.

Plan of the Ryokaku-an Tea-room, designed by the famous artist Ogata Korin and formerly in his house, now removed to the Ninnaji Temple Kyoto. Photograph of exterior and Rōji in Harada, *Gardens of Japan*, p. 69.

This Dainagon seems to have been a quaint fellow, for there is a story told of him to the effect that one day he picked up the Kwampaku Konoe Iehiro in his arms when he was a boy of twelve and said to him. " Cucumbers, which are commonly called ' Sekkwan ' or ' Regents ' look sharp enough when they are little, but the bigger they grow the more ordinary they appear. Don't you be a cucumber ! "

THE KWAMPAKU KONOE IEHIRO

Konoe Iehiro was the son of Motohiro and his mother was Tsune-ko Naishinno, daughter of the Emperor Go-Mizu-no-o. He was very skilled in calligraphy and Cha-no-yu, being a disciple of Jiin Ho-Shinno who was a pupil of Furuta Oribe. He often said that the essential spirit of Tea was rather funny, because it was like painting the same thing year in and year out, but all the same in a hundred meetings for Cha-no-yu no two were ever alike.

SEN SŌTAN

Sōtan had a very delightful bamboo Lid-rest made by his grandfather Rikyu. It was cut from a very carefully selected joint and was quite round without any trace of the knot, so that it hardly looked like bamboo at all. In the course of time it took on a beautiful soft brown colour and could hardly be distinguished from lacquer. Maeda Lord of Kaga obtained it from Sōtan and in return gave him a very large sum of money. With it Sōtan constructed a four-and-a-half mat Tea-room in Rikyu's favourite style, which everyone thought an exactly appropriate way of applying the profit that his grandfather's fame had brought him.

Once Kobori Enshu sent a silver Tea-scoop to Sen Sōtan as a present. Sōtan was entertaining some guests when he received it, and after looking at it he took up his writing brush and wrote on the outside of its box the words ' Mizuya yo.' ' For kitchen use.' A very emphatic protest against Enshu's extravagance.

Sen Sōtan once made a flower arrangement with rape. His father Sōjun rebuked him, saying that it suggested manure. Using a thing because it is different is not only wanting in elegance but may also be an offence to guests. This is the meaning of the expression ' The willow is green and the flower bright.' Cf. Wall maxims of Karasu Maru Mitsuhiro.

YAMADA SŌHEN

Yamada Sōhen took a fancy to Cha-no-yu at the age of six. He was first of all a pupil of Kobori Enshu, but afterwards in the fourth year of Shōho (1648) went to study under Sen Sōtan. Here he stayed nine years at the end of which he had become quite familiar with the Rikyu style and received the tea-scoop and inner tradition that made him qualified to teach. Now at this time Cha-no-yu was very popular in Edo, and the Enshu school particularly so. But this school, quite contrary to the ideas of Rikyu, encouraged luxury and connoisseurship and considered that a man was no Tea Master if he did not collect a lot of expensive rarities. Sōtan was very grieved at this

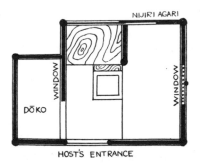

Plan of the Konnichi-an of Sen Sōtan at Ura Senge Ogawa, Kyoto.

tendency and sent a letter to Kobori Enshu remonstrating with him, whereupon this master replied that the matter was not his doing but was by secret order, and its purpose was to keep the peace of the Empire.* So Sōtan made up his mind to teach the correct doctrine of Cha-no-yu in Edo if possible. And it happened that the Rōju Ogasawara Sado-no-kami Nagashige, in the hope of reforming Edo society somewhat, called Sōtan and consulted him about it He said that he himself was unfortunately now too old to do anything much, but when pressed in the matter he made over his tea-room the Fushin-an to Sōhen and put them at Ogasawara's disposal. So Sōhen came down to Edo and taught the true school of Rikyu and soon became quite fashionable among the feudal lords. And thus it happened that among others Kira Kozuke-no-suke Yoshinaka came to be connected with him and this connexion was utilized by Ōtaka Gengo.

OTAKA GENGO USES CHA-NO-YU TO SPY ON KIRA KOZUKE-NO-SUKE

When the Rōnin of Akō under Oishi Kura-no-suke were trying to find a way of killing Kira Yoshinaka to avenge their lord, they were at first unable to learn much about his affairs owing to the strictness of the precautions taken by his retainers. But it chanced that one of them, Horibe Yasubei Taketsune, went to see a friend of his, a Shinto priest named Hagura Itsuki at his house in Zaimoku-cho in Sanjikken-bori, and in the course of the conversation Itsuki said quite casually, " Yes, the landlord of this house is a man named Nakashima Gorosaku, and he is studying Cha-no-yu under the Master Yamada Sōhen. And Sōhen has lately become acquainted with Kira Kozuke-no-suke Dono, and so Gorosaku has sometimes been with him to meetings for Cha-no-yu at Kira's mansion." Taketsune seized on this piece of information as a heaven-sent clue, and hurried away to repeat it immediately to Oishi Yoshio. He too was extremely pleased, and they quickly called one of their companions named Ōtaka Gengo Tadao, who fortunately was fond of Tea, and arranged a plan with him. So Gengo altered his appearance and dressed himself as a merchant, and on the nineteenth day of the eleventh month of the fifteenth year of Genroku (1703) he betook himself to the house of Sōhen at Takahashi in Fukagawa. Here he told the Tea Master that he was a cloth-merchant of Kyoto named Shimbei who had come up to Edo since he was patronized by some Daimyo, and wished to have the honour of taking lessons in Cha-no-yu from such a famous teacher. At the same time he offered an entrance fee of a thousand hiki† with the proper ceremony. Yamada was suitably impressed by his manners and evident means and made no difficulty about acceding to his request. So Gengo began to go to his house regularly and soon by attentions and presents managed to ingratiate himself with the Master.

---

* *I.e.* To make the feudal lords spend money that they might have no resources for use against the Shogunate. The same result was aimed at in granting them expensive honours, such as building part of the Nikko Shrines or some other temples.

† One hiki=¼ of a sen, so that this would be about two yen fifty, at that time perhaps equivalent to about thirty shillings.

He was thus able to learn a good deal about the arrangements of the household of Kira Yoshinaka, and had hopes of going there to a Cha-no-yu meeting with Sōhen. On the third of the twelfth month he was at Sōhen's house for a lesson, and on leaving asked if he should come on the sixth as usual. But the master told him that on that day he had an engagement to go to a Morning Tea at Kira's mansion, so he would ask him to come another time. Gengo was very pleased to hear this, and went off and told Oishi Yoshio. "If he has a Tea on the morning of the sixth," said the leader, "there is no doubt but that he will be at home on the evening of the fifth. So we will make the attack at that time. But we must enquire further so as to be quite certain. So Gengo tried to get more information, and on the fifth he went to see Nakashima Gorosaku who told him he had just heard from Yamada that the meeting had been put off at the last moment for some reason or other, and this news Gengo lost no time in transmitting again to Oishi, who also deferred the attack. They afterwards heard that the Cha-no-yu had been fixed for the eleventh, but again it was put off.

Gengo then heard from Yamada that on the night of the fourteenth day there would be held at Kira's mansion a Cha-no-yu meeting to speed the parting year, and when he reported this to Oishi he was told that another of the Rōnin, Yokogawa Kampei Munetoshi, had heard the same thing from an acquaintance he had made, a priest of Hayashi-machi in Honjo, who was also a Tea-companion of Kira Yoshinaka. So they arranged that the attack should be made on this night. However Gengo was determined to make sure if possible that there was no chance of further postponement, so on the thirteenth he went to Yamada and told him that, though he had looked forward to spending all that year in Edo, he had just had an urgent message requiring him to return to Kyoto, and would have to start immediately, but before he went he wished to give a small farewell party for the Master, and though it was extremely short notice he hoped that there was nothing to prevent him doing him the honour to-morrow, the fourteenth. To this Yamada replied that he was extremely sorry to hear that he was going so soon, and also hoped that he would not be offended with him for being unable to accept his kind invitation, for the fact was that he had already accepted one from Kira Yoshinaka to be present at his Cha-no-yu meeting on that date; and, as he knew, that kind of engagement could not be put off without great discourtesy. So he was afraid he must decline.

That was all Gengo wanted to hear, so, after politely telling Yamada that if that were so the fifteenth would do as well, he hurried off and told Oishi, and he informed the Rōnin, so that the attack was carried out with the success that their careful preparations deserved.

YOKOGAWA KAMPEI

When Yokogawa Kampei heard that there was a priest in Hayashi-machi who was also a Tea Master and who often went to Kira's mansion for Cha-no-yu, he soon made it his business to become acquainted with him, and they became friends. Now this priest was quite illiterate, and it happened one day when Kampei was there, that a note came for him and he asked Kampei to read it out. When he took it he at once noticed that it had on the back the name of Saito Kunai, Kira's Karo, and when he opened it with quite suppressed excitement, he read : " As on the fourteenth day of this month we shall have an evening meeting for Cha-no-yu, all other engagements for that day must be refused."

When Kampei saw this he considered that Kira was now practically secured, and gladly wrote an answer for the priest accepting the invitation. And not only so, but as his man, who did these errands for him, happened to be out, he offered to take the note himself and went off with it to Kira's mansion. Here he pretended not to know his way about, and managed to wander into various parts of the house inadvertently before he delivered the reply. He then made his way to Oishi and told him all that he had found out. It was just then that Gengo also brought the information he had got from Sōhen.

CONCERNING KIRA KOZUKE-NO-SUKE YOSHINAKA

Kira Kozuke-no-suke Yoshinaka received his instruction in Cha-no-yu from Sen Sōtan and became quite expert as far as knowledge of the ceremony went, but since his character was arrogant and self-willed, he was deficient in the real spirit of Tea, and rather apt to be discourteous. It is related that he was once invited to a meeting by Tsugaru Etchu-no-kami Nobumasa lord of Hirosaki, the other guests being one of the retainers of that clan and one of the Shogun's Tea Masters. At the meal that preceded the Tea-ceremony Yoshinaka did not eat any of the rice that was served, and the others, noticing this, asked him why. " The rest of the cookery is all right, but the rice is too bad to eat. I will take something else." Now the officer who was superintending the kitchen arrangements that day was a quick-tempered man, and when he heard this he flew into a great rage : " Kozuke-no-suke Dono is no better than some animal," he ejaculated. " It is a natural human feeling to praise anything that is given you even if it is bad, and what sort of a creature can it be who will tell you your rice is not fit to eat. Especially in a Daimyo's house, where the rice is most carefully selected and prepared, and only the very best of that is served. If this kind of thing is said it is only natural that I should be scolded by my lord. So I will split Kira's head for him and then cut myself open." And he was just going to rush in when the others threw themselves on him and held him back by force. Then Nobumasa, who had heard all this from the next room, came in and told him that there was no need to be so agitated, for the rice was good enough and the other guests had not complained, and one could not cook fresh rice in a moment, so there was nothing to be done. Then the official calmed down, but had his master scolded him at all the history of Kira might have been different,

After Kira had retired in consequence of the affair with Asano

Naganori he became more and more given up to Cha-no-yu, and would invite to his mansion anyone who was skilled in it without caring in the least about his occupation or social position. But since he was very apprehensive of an attack from the retainers of Asano he took great precautions against it, allowing no tradesmen in his mansion but those who were well known to him and taking no servants save those who were from his own estates, and spending his days sometimes at his own house, sometimes at that of Uesugi, his son, and keeping his movements very secret, so that if it had not been for his devotion to Tea, it might have been difficult to have discovered his whereabouts. But perhaps it may have been some comfort to a Chajin to fall after indulgence in his favourite pastime.

MATSUURA MASASHI MAKES 'NIGHT ATTACK' TEA-SPOON

Matsuura Daizen Masashi was the second son of Matsuura Hizen-no-kami Shigenobu, lord of Hirado, and received an income of ten thousand koku, setting up a branch family and living at Okawabata in Honjo. His father instructed him in Cha-no-yu and he was a great adept. He was sitting in his mansion on the night of the fourteenth day of the twelfth month of the fifteenth year of Genroku when he heard the sound of a drum beaten vigorously somewhere in the neighbourhood and resounding clearly through the frosty air. The samurai on duty called out that there was a fire, for at this time a drum was used to give the fire alarm, and the others began to run about, when Masashi said, " That is no fire alarm. That drum is beaten in the Kōshu style. I wonder what it can be. Run out, some of you, and see." And as he was too interested in the affair to sleep, he took up a piece of bamboo that happened to be by him and pared it into a Tea-spoon. After a while the retainers came back and told him that it was not a fire, but it seemed that the Akō Rōnin were attacking the mansion of Kira Kozuke-no-suke. " Exactly," exclaimed Masashi, " Oishi Kura-no-suke is a disciple of Yamaga Jingozaemon and that is just his style of drum-beating. Certainly Oishi is leading them." And so he gave the Tea-spoon the name of ' Night Attack.' He afterwards presented it to one of his friends. Now Matsuura Oribe-no-sho Nagashi, a descendant in the sixth generation of Masashi, was entertaining Iki-no-kami Kiyoshi, the representative of the main Matsuura house, one evening, and a story-teller named Sekiko was giving recitations of tales of chivalry, when after one of these Kiyoshi said to him ; " It is a tradition that has been handed down in my family that when the Akō Rōnin broke into Kira's mansion the drum was beaten in the Kōshu style. Have you ever heard of it ? "

" Certainly I have," replied Sekiko," and the ancestor of your house at that time was fond of Cha-no-yu, was he not ? " " One cannot be so sure of things that happened a hundred years ago, but his father Shigenobu was a great Chajin, so I suppose the son would be interested in it too." At this reply of the daimyo, Sekiko assumed his professional attitude and began to recite. " I have been greatly favoured by the patronage of Matsudaira Fumai,* lord of Izumo, and have made as many as eleven visits to him. Now on one occasion the Karo of that clan, Ohashi Mōemon Dono, invited the lord Fumai to a Cha-no-yu : and the tea-spoon that was used on that occasion was called 'Night Attack,' and was made by Matsuura Tainyu Dono (Masashi) on the night that the Rōnin attacked the mansion of Kira. Originally it was in the possession of Sumiya Sōzen, but at his request he presented it to Ohashi Mōemon. And this tea-spoon I have myself seen. And Ohashi Dono treasures it exceedingly. Now Matsuura Tainyu was certainly the ancestor of your house." And as they listened both Kiyoshi and Nagashi were deeply impressed with the glamour of these reminiscences of former days.

Yamaga Sōkō, the famous strategist and Confucian scholar, was tactician to Asano Takumi-no-kami lord of Ako from the time Oishi was eight till he was seventeen, and so the military details of the night attack were according to the teaching of his school.

The tradition of the branch family was that it was Masashi who made this Tea-spoon, that of the main house Shigenobu. The story teller seems to confirm the former's case, but Tokutomi in referring to this story, which he regards as correct, attributes it to Shigenobu and gives another name ' Fukushu ' or ' Vendetta ' for the Tea-spoon.

SEN SŌSA III

Sen Sōsa III was the son of Hisada Sōzen. He became a pupil of Sōsa II, married his daughter, and carried on the family. His first ancestor Hisada Gyōbu was Rikyu's brother-in-law. He was Tea Master to the Tokugawa house of Kishu as his predecessors Sōsa I and II had been before him and was of great distinction in his art. He was entitled Gensō Gakugakusai.

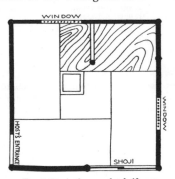

Gensō Sōsa's three-and-a-half mat Tea-room with short four foot Toko-noma on board called Gensō Toko.

In the period Kyōhō (1716-35) he was summoned to Edo and stayed in the Kishu mansion and had to buy Tea-utensils for use there. He got quite ordinary rough things and none of them was anything to look at. One day he said to one of the men-servants " This water-jar is too small. It is a bother to have to fill it so often. Go and get a bigger one." So the man bought a big ordinary kitchen-ware jar costing three hundred mon (three sen), and this he stood beside the Hearth and so used it. And he took a brush and wrote its name

* See pp. 214–216.

'Busho-mono' which means 'Incorrigible.' Sōsa was during this period received in audience by the Shogun Yoshimune, and taught him the way of using the Daisu that was traditional in his family, receiving from him a Tea-bowl as an acknowledgement.

When he had finished his service in Edo he prepared to return to Kyoto, where he usually lived, and the utensils he had been using he gave away to his pupils, letting them choose what each would

(a)

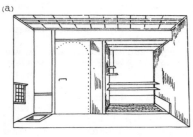

(b)

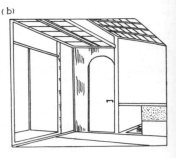

(c)

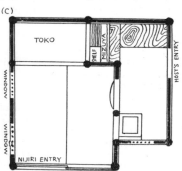

Gensō Sōsa III's arrangement of Mizuya and Tea-room, having the hearth inside the Mizuya but visible through an opening in the wall beside the host's door. The prototype of the modern labour-saving kitchen and dining-room.

(a) interior of Mizuya.
(b) interior of Tea-room.
(c) plan. The Tea-room is of two mats and the Toko 2.5 ft. deep.

have. They made him presents of money in return as the custom was. The one who got the jar called Busho-mono gave the sum of three hundred hiki (seventy-five sen), so Sōsa called the man-servant who had bought it and handed the sum over to him. The servant bowed and thanked him and was going out of the room when Sōsa told him to wait.

"I gave you three hundred mon for the jar," he said, "and I want that back. The rest you can keep." Sending one servant on before him to Kyoto with the news of the honour he had received from the Shogun, he himself followed on with the other, carrying the Shogun's Tea-bowl in a bag hung round his neck. When he arrived he found all his family and friends and pupils waiting for him, and after telling them all about his adventures in Edo he bade them get the Tea-room ready because he was going to have a Cha-no-yu to celebrate the honour the Shogun had done him. So the pupils swept the Rōji and put everything in order, and then they enquired who was to be the guest, so that they might send the invitation. " My wife will be the guest," replied Sōsa. But when they told her she firmly refused the distinction, asking him what had made him think of such a thing. " You must not refuse," said he, " I came into this family from another house, and you are the real representative of that family. It is because of my marriage with you that I have the honour of bearing this name, and it is owing to the virtue of that family name that I

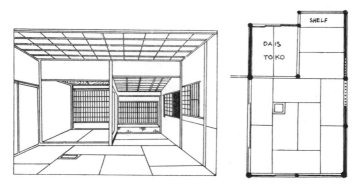

Hiroma, or Large Tea-room with two mat Dais called Zangetsu-tei, in the house of Sen Sōsa.

have received the honour just conferred on me. Therefore it is natural that I should show my gratitude to our ancestors by inviting you, who really represent them, to be my guest on this occasion." So she no longer declined, and when she had changed her dress she took her seat in the Tea-room and Sosa served the tea to her in the Shogun's bowl, after which he put it away most carefully and did not show it even to his pupils.

The Rōju Mizuno Izumi-no-kami Tadayuki had occasion to call on Mizuno Oi-no-kami Tadaaki, Councillor of Kishu, at the mansion of that clan at Joruri-saka in Ichigaya, while Sōsa happened to be there, and Tadaaki asked him to come in and make tea for them. Tadayuki was so much pleased that when he was leaving he invited Sōsa to visit him at his mansion also. " But " he said, " on account of the public position I hold it will be well if you do not do so openly. But come privately when you can spare time, and I shall be very pleased to see you." But this did not appeal to Sōsa at all. " Since you hold the great public position that you do," he answered, " there can be no privacy in your case. Even if it is called private, some-one will know of it. Now I am an unimportant person in myself, but through the merits of my ancestors my name is known far and wide in the Empire. So that if I do come privately the fact will certainly be known. Therefore I would ask you to invite me publicly, and I will report it to my lord and then come. Otherwise I cannot come." And the Rōju departed distinctly crestfallen.

YOSHIMUNE'S SIMPLICITY

The Shogun Tokugawa Yoshimune was of the Kishu house. He was fond of simplicity in all things and hated luxury. One day he happened to stroll casually into the waiting-room of the Sado-bōzu or Tea pages, much to their surprise, whereupon they all fell down with their faces to the ground. " Come," said the Shogun, " I should like some tea." Whereupon they immediately set to work to make it, in some confusion and trepidation, for such easy informality on the part of a Shogun had never been known, and were going to hand it, when made, to a page to convey to His Highness, but Yoshimune remarked : " Oh, it is all right as it is," and he then took the cup from the one who had made it and so drank it. When he looked at the cup he saw it was decorated with the Tokugawa crest in gold. " Aren't there any ordinary ones ? " he said and they took the hint and in future used ordinary Takahara ware.

This Takahara ware was called after its maker Takahara Tōbei, who was brought from the province of Settsu at the recommendation of Katagiri Sekishu in the Genroku period and given a *cho* square of land in Asakusa, opposite the Hongwanji temple. Hence it is also called Asakusa ware. The Tokugawa Shoguns had no kiln of their own.

HOTTA MASASUKE'S GENEROSITY

Hotta Sagami-no-kami Masasuke lord of Sakura in Shimosa was chief of the Rōju under the Shogun Ieshige. The main family of his house was that represented by Hotta Kaga-no-kami Masanobu lord of Miyagawa in Yamashiro, and though it was very poor and insignificant since the confiscation of its revenues in the time of Kōzuke-no-suke Masanobu, Masasuke always showed it the greatest respect. Now this house had a famous Tea-caddy called Kuki Bun-rinro presented to its founder Kaga-no-kami Masamori by the Shogun Iemitsu, which they had greatly valued ever since, and Masasuke once asked if he could see this treasure. " Very sorry," said Masanobu, " but we pawned it once when we were hard up." This grieved Masasuke very much and he soon got a lot of money together and sent and obtained it back again. His retainers naturally thought he would keep it in his own family after this, and said so. " Oh no," he explained, " A treasure is no treasure if it is not in its proper place. It would not be right for me to keep in the branch family a thing that rightly belongs to the main house." And after looking at it carefully he sent a messenger with it to the mansion of Masanobu.

MAKINO SADAHARU'S GENEROSITY

Makino Etchu-no-kami Sadaharu lord of Kasama had a rare Tea-caddy called ' Shirakumo.' It had originally belonged to Hosokawa

Yusai and had been presented to Sadaharu's ancestor Sadamichi by that house on account of the assistance he had given on the occasion of the assassination of Hosokawa Munetaka in the Shogun's Castle by Itakura Shuri Katsukane. But since it was such a famous heirloom in the Hosokawa family it was almost indispensable when they gave any great entertainment, so in the time of Sadaharu they made overtures to him to get it back. If he would be so considerate as to let them have it again they would be delighted to send him ten thousand pieces of gold as some slight recompense, small though that would be.

When his Councillors gave this message to Sadaharu they suggested that it was an opportunity too good to let slip, since the finances of the clan were not at all flourishing. But he replied without hesitation : " If its possession is of such importance to the house of Hosokawa, let it be sent back at once, for it is of no particular consequence to our family whether we have it or not. I may not be very wealthy, but still I am one of the daimyo, and it would be a low action to take money for other people's treasures. I could not think of accepting anything."

MATSUDAIRA NANKAI

Matsudaira Dewa-no-kami Munenobu lord of Izumo was a devotee of Cha-no-yu, but was very much given to luxury. He retired and took the name of Nankai. He was the father of the great Chajin Matsudaira Fumai. There was a priest of his acquaintance who was also fond of Cha-no-yu, and Nankai promised to visit him one day at his country house at Negishi. The priest was highly delighted at the honour, and a day was arranged on which the retired daimyo proceeded to the house. But he found the front gate shut and the house locked up, while the unswept paths showed that no one had been near it for some time. When one of the retainers asked the gate-keeper, he said he knew nothing about it, and another who knew the house found his way round into the Rōji, but that was also neglected-looking and shut up, with the stones covered with fallen leaves, and spiders' webs hanging from the trees. So they told their master that there were no signs of any preparation for them and supposed they must have mistaken the day, and had all turned back to go home when out of a cross street came a man in a wide countryman's hat and straw rain-coat with a fishing-net in his hand accompanied by several servants carrying a big tub. He gave an exclamation of surprise when he saw them, and when Nankai looked at him closely he saw it was their host. " Hullo," said the Daimyo, " we have just been to your house and were going home again on finding you out." " Indeed, I hope you will excuse me," said the priest, looking very much ashamed of himself, " I went out this morning to the Arakawa to catch some carp, but unfortunately I was not very successful and the time went by without my noticing it. It is really a most unpardonable thing to do, but I hope you will at least be pleased to come back and allow me to entertain you as best I can with what I have." So they turned back again and the host went on in front, and passing his own gate led them to a place where there was a Rōji newly made amid clumps of trees and bamboo. Instead of stepping-stones the path was curiously constructed of sand-bags, while the water-basin was a white wood bucket, and the tea-room that stood there was also newly built. Here they found that the hearth was edged with white wood with a kettle hung over it, and the tea-utensils were also made in the shape of round white wood buckets as in the case of the water-jar and slop-bowl, or else of new pottery. The meal was served in bowls of new pottery with lids of unglazed earthenware on trays of fresh white wood, and all the dishes were made of the carp that had just been caught, dressed in various ways. In fact every detail of the entertainment was so novel and unexpected that even one so accustomed to luxury and variety as Nankai could only utter delighted exclamations.

MATSUDAIRA FUMAI

Fumai was the title taken by Matsudaira Dewa-no-kami Harusato, lord of Izumo, after he retired. He was one of the most famous of Tea Masters. One day when out for a walk, he came to a Tea-utensil shop in Shiba and went in to take a rest and look round, and a kettle caught his eye. " Ah, that is a real Ashiya kettle," he exclaimed. The shop-keeper was naturally delighted, and made a box for it and took it to lord Fumai's mansion and asked him to attest its make by writing ' Ashiya kettle ' on the lid. " Oh, all right," said the daimyo, and it was left there. After some time he called again, but Fumai said that though he had once or twice thought of signing it the matter had gone no farther than that and he had not done so. Again and again the tradesman called, but to no purpose, for Fumai wrote nothing at all. The fact was that he had only said it casually, and if he wrote it he would lay himself open to the charge of misleading posterity. However his remark was soon bandied about everywhere and people began to come to the shop to see the famous kettle, and the result was that the business of the shop increased by leaps and bounds. Of such weight in the world of Teaism was the word of this great connoisseur.

These Ashiya kettles were made in the district of Oka in the province of Chikuzen. The first maker seems to have been a Chinese in the Yuan dynasty who was patronized by the Japanese Court and given office and permitted to use the Imperial Chrysanthemum and Paulownia Crests. Some of these crests were designed and drawn by Sesshu. After the era Tensho (1573-91) their quality deteriorated, and after Keicho (1596) it became even worse and they eventually ceased to be made. At the present day the manufacture has been revived and they are said to have some reputation. Next to them came the Tenmei kettles of Kozuke.

It happened that the famous antique dealer Fushimiya of Edo, when on his way from that city to pay a visit to Matsudaira Fumai in Izumo, stopped at a wayside tea-house at Okayama in Bizen to rest a while. After drinking a cup of tea the old woman there offered him he scrutinized the cup carefully and eventually asked for it and went on his way. Now an Osaka artizan who was also an amateur curio-dealer saw this and wondered why he did it, so he asked the old woman of the tea-house if she knew who he was. She did know and told him that he was the most eminent connoisseur of the day, antique dealer by appointment to the Lord of Izumo. When he heard this the Osaka man at once ran after Fushimiya and begged him to sell him the cup, since no doubt anything that attracted such attention from the greatest authority of the day must certainly be well worth having. But Fushimiya only burst out laughing " It's just an ordinary cup of Bizen ware," he explained, " and is not at all valuable. The reason I was looking at it was that the steam seemed to hang about it strangely and I wondered if there wasn't a leak somewhere." However, as he felt a bit flattered that the other should set such value on it merely because his eye lingered on it he let him have it for nothing. The artizan went off overjoyed and took it back to Osaka where he had a brocade bag made for it and a fine box as well, and showed it off proudly to all his acquaintance, but since it was nothing but ordinary Bizen ware they were not very enthusiastic over it. Still he was not discouraged, but spent all his time going about in the hope of finding some rare expert who would appreciate it, and in doing so neglected his business, spent his substance and even sold some property to provide himself with the money to travel. So at last he came to Edo and started to enquire for the shop of Fushimiya, the greatest expert in the land. Arrived there he related all his adventures and asked him if he would not buy it at a proper price. Fushimiya felt sorry for his very odd obsession and gave him a hundred ryo for it, recommending him very seriously to give up his hobby of collecting tea-things and apply himself seriously to his business. Fortunately he took this good advice and went back again to Osaka and did so. But the story soon got wind among the curio dealers and at the next sale they clamoured for this tea cup to be put up. Fushimiya at first refused, telling them very emphatically that it was the man's mood he had bought and not his tea-cup, for that was not a thing one would put up for sale at such a place. However they pressed him so that at last he consented to put it up and so keen were the buyers that two put in a bid of twenty Oban or two hundred ryo simultaneously. This led to a dispute between the two in the course of which the tea-cup got dropped and broken. Fushimiya then took it back and mended it and kept it carefully, until the matter coming to the ears of Matsudaira Fumai, that great Cha-no-yu devotee expressed a wish to see it and Fushimiya rather shamefacedly showed it to him. " As a piece it is not up to much," said he, " but as Chajin prize sentiment and association more than intrinsic value, as a nucleus of these it is most interesting ; " and he wrote on the box himself the name he gave it, which was ' Shikoro-biki ' or ' Gorget-snatcher ' the reference being to the rough warrior Kagekiyo of whom the proverb says that even he could be softened by esthetic sentiment.* And so this worthless crock became one of the most famous pieces in the land, and the compositions both in prose and verse that were written about it would fill several chests.

KOBORI MASAMINE

Kobori Izumi-no-kami Masamine was the great grandson of Kobori Masakazu. In the nineteenth year of Kyōho (1735) he was appointed Bugyo of Fushimi and stayed there some time. While he was there he thought he would like to see the famous garden called the Kyōgokuden, considered the finest in Kyoto, which the Shogun Iemitsu had ordered his ancestor Masakazu to make. It was a very exquisite composition with its hills and lakes and pavilions and plantings of fine old trees, and as Masamine went through it he found nothing that was not exactly right. But on entering the Rōji of the Tea-room he at once asked the attendant if the stepping-stones had not been changed at some time, and the man admitted that they had, but it was some time ago and they were well mossed and looked not at all different from anything else. But it was by walking over them that Masamine concluded they were not put there by his great ancestor, for there was something indefinably inharmonious in their arrangement that made them awkward to the tread.

This Masamine was afterwards made one of the Waka-doshiyori. At that time among the daimyo two houses were employed by the Shogun, that of Yagyu as Fencing-Master and that of Kobori as Tea-Master. And as the first was more honoured than the second in most people's opinion Masamine gave up this hereditary business of his house and ceased to be Chief Tea Master to the house of Tokugawa.

AKIMOTO SUZUTOMO REBUKES HIS RETAINER FOR GIVING TOO LITTLE FOR A TEA-BOWL

Akimoto Tajima-no-kami Suzutomo, who was very fond of Cha-no-yu, was once offered a Tea-bowl by a dealer for a hundred pieces of gold, and remarking that it was a very good one, told his page to buy it at that price. Now the page thought that it was not worth anything very much, but as it was his lord's order there was nothing else but to obey. All the same he thought it likely that he could make the dealer take less, and after a good deal of bargaining he managed to get it for ninety-five. Some time after, when he got an opportunity he told Suzutomo what he had done, and that with a very virtuous look, but, far from commending him, his master burst forth with some heat: " What an ignoramus you are! A Tea-bowl that anyone asks a hundred pieces of gold for can only be a family heirloom, and a thing like that is only sold when the family is pressed

---

* ' Kagekiyo mo hanami no za ni wa Shichibyoe.' ' Even Kagekiyo is called by his first name Shichibyoe at a flower-viewing party.' Basho. This fierce warrior tore off the gorget of Mionoya Juro in the fight on the shore at Yashima in the Gempei war of 1185. Cf. the Nō *Kagekiyo* trans. A. Waley, *Nō Plays*, pp. 123–133.

for money. And in that case they will be hoping to find someone
who will give even a hundred and fifty pieces for it, so what sort of
a fellow is it who does not consider their feelings ? Quite apart from
that a curio that you give a hundred ryo for is something worth
having, but one that has only cost ninety-five gives a mean impression. So never let me see that Tea-bowl again." And he never so
much as looked at it at any time.

SHIBAYAMA MOTOAKI

Shibayama Motoaki was a thoroughly unconventional spirit who
first became a priest and wandered about the country for many years,
living a life of austerity, and teaching and enquiring into the way of
enlightenment.   Later on he became disillusioned as to the efficacy
of the Buddhist priesthood and threw away his stole and went to live
in Kyoto. Here he made a scanty living by selling tea, going out
with his tea-utensils on his shoulder among the crowds that went to
view the cherry blossoms in spring and the maples in autumn. He
was welcomed by all and the people flocked to his stall, giving him
the nickname of ' Baicha-o ' or ' Old Tea-seller.'   Over his stall he
had this quaint notice : ' For the tea you can pay from a hundred
pieces of gold to half a mon.   Or you can have it for nothing.   I
am sorry I cannot let you have it for less.'

His literary name was ' Gekkai ' or ' Moon-on-the-sea.'   In fine
weather he did quite well, but in the rainy season when there was
none to buy his tea he was often almost starving, but yet he never
lost his composure and light-heartedness.   Then a friend of similar
tastes came to his assistance, one Kameda Kyuraku, who, though he
liked Sake rather than tea, was equally a ' companion of the wind
and the moon, and a lover of the rhythm of things.' Gekkai was so
thankful to him that he wrote his thanks in Chinese verse :

> Oh empty was my bamboo flask;
> No tea, no rice had I,
> Among the ruts I struggled on;
> No help did I descry.
> My deepest thanks I offer you
> For succouring my grey hairs,
> Now with full gourd I'll shift to live
> My few remaining years.

Some time after, when his days were indeed coming to an end,
he went to live in complete retirement in Okazaki, shutting himself
up and declining to see anyone. He then burnt all his Tea-vessels
and made this verse ;

> The fires of hell may not be far,
> But still I've some respite.
> The green hills and the soft white clouds
> Will still be my delight.

He died not long after on the sixteenth day of the seventh month of the thirteenth year of Horeki (1763). He was indeed a Taoist Rishi of later days.

In the Ashikaga period priests, or at least tonsured individuals in priestly garb, used to go about selling tea in the street for a sen a cup. Mr. Kumata observes that when a man dressed in Chinese costume with bamboo pipes sold tobacco for a sen a smoke it only provoked mirth. Such a difference is there in dignity between these two herbs. A priest named Tsu-en is associated with the Uji bridge, where he is said to have had a tea-booth by the river and to have given tea to the passers-by to acquire merit. Afterwards a statue of him was put up there by his successors. It is also said that Hideyoshi gave him orders to draw water from the Uji river at the third beam of the bridge and bring it every day to Momoyama, but whether he lived in this period is not clear. There is a Kyogen or Comic Interlude that takes him for its subject, representing him as dying in frantic efforts to make tea for a huge multitude, and parodying the death of Gensammi Yorimasa at the Byodoin.

KAWAKAMI FUHAKU

Kawakami Fuhaku, a retainer of the Daimyo of Shingu in Kishu was a Tea Master who was responsible for a great revival of interest in the Sen school. He was sent to Kyoto when he was a boy of sixteen to study under Sen Joshinsai (Sōsa III) by Naito Awa-no-kami who had taken a fancy to him, but when he came back to Edo with the knowledge he had acquired and set up as a teacher, he got no pupils. Therefore at Naito's suggestion he went back again to study further, and his teacher told him that things were now changed in Edo and something more was needed than the older tradition. So this time he was less exclusive in his learning, with the result that when he went back to Edo he was a great success and soon

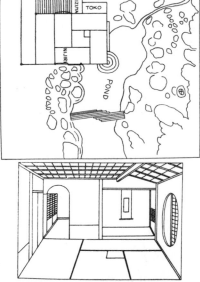

The Shogetsu-tei Tea-room by the pond at Daigo Sambo-in. Plan and Interior.

became the fashion among the feudal lords. Besides, being a Chajin he was also a poet, and, the following anecdote would suggest, of a philosophic temperament.

He had a concubine of seventeen who became intimate with a young man in the neighbourhood, but Fuhaku took no notice. One night she ran away, and Fuhaku, rather concerned, went and examined her belongings and found several pieces of gold in her letter case. At this he looked very grave and sent out people to search for her everywhere. " When young people run away and take money with them," he explained, " there is no need for anxiety, but when they go without it then it is usually tragic. How sad that I could not do something to prevent it." The pair had committed suicide together in the ricefields at Waseda.

IMAI SŌSEN

Imai Sōsen was a pupil of Fuhaku. He was of the province of Shinano, and as this was rather a wild country, the people who came from it to Edo were only fit for men-servants or rice-cleaners. Sōsen had heard of this from the time he was a boy and felt very much ashamed of the bad manners of his countrymen. So he determined that he himself would go there and learn to behave so that he could associate on equal terms with anyone. So after a while he found his way there, and tried to learn Go and Chess and other accomplishments, but he was no good at them, when at last somebody managed to get him a place in the house of Fuhaku as a servant. One day after breakfast Fuhaku came into the kitchen with a tea-bowl in his hand to get some hot water to drink and when he saw Imai he asked him to get it. Sōsen took the tea-bowl, and then, with a ladle, lifted some hot water from the kettle and poured it in, and his deportment was just like that of one who was accustomed to Cha-no-yu. Fuhaku was quite surprised. " Have you studied Cha-no-yu in your province? " he asked. " Oh no," replied Sōsen, " I had never seen it until I came here ; but since then I have looked in on the quiet whenever you have been giving lessons and saw that you always used a ladle in this way, and so I copied it." Fuhaku was much struck by his enthusiasm and also by his good deportment, so he told him that in future he might attend whenever he gave lessons, and also presented him with a Haori, observing that it would not look well if he wore the dress of a servant on these occasions. Sōsen's joy knew no bounds, and he gave himself up to the study with the greatest keenness, and after a while absorbed all that his master had to teach him and became a distinguished exponent of Tea himself.

Sōsen was very severe and exacting in his teaching and this made him unpopular, so that his pupils were few and his income in consequence small. But he would not depart from the way of his master though his purse might suffer. He always impressed on anyone who came for instruction that Cha-no-yu was not just deportment learned for the Tea-room alone, but should be put into practice in everyday life. For instance when one sits down the right big-toe should be underneath and the left above and then one can sit easily for any length of time without discomfort. One should always walk with the same correct carriage whether in a room or out in the street. And one should keep to the left to avoid confusion in the street just as much as in going to the hearth or to one's seat in the Cha-no-ma. In fact there is a correct way of doing all these things and it should always be practised everywhere.

MINE GENWA BUYS A PLUM-TREE.

Mine Genwa was Tea Master to the lord of Izumo. As he was walking in the country one day he saw a fine Plum-tree in bloom in a farmer's garden, and stopped quite a time in front of it, enjoying its beauty and fragrance. After a while he said to the farmer: " I should like to buy this tree." The farmer at first refused to sell it, but as Genwa offered him a very large sum he at last consented. Genwa went off and came back again the next day with food and Sake and sat down and made merry under the plum-tree, and while he was doing so the farmer came and told him that he would dig up the tree carefully the next day so as not to damage the roots and then have it taken to his house. " Oh, no, I don't want it," said Genwa, " let it stay where it is." " Well then," persisted the other, " let me bring you the fruit when it is ripe." " No," replied Genwa, " I have no use for the fruit. All I want is to enjoy the beauty of the flowers. And it wouldn't be fair to do that if they belonged to someone else. So I bought them."

This incident was celebrated by Shiba Kokan in the verse :

One branch full-laden
With thy blossoms I must own
O flow'ring plum-tree.

One might quote as an example of the opposite spirit the popular story of the man who used to eat his rice near an eel-shop so that he might enjoy the smell as a relish, without paying anything. The other noticed this, and presented him with a bill for the smell. Which the niggardly one paid by putting down the money and then pocketing it again, with the remark that the smell of the eels was well paid for by the sight of the money.

But this story in a slightly varied form is found in the collection of the Turkish wit Nasr-ed-din Khoja, and so may not be of Japanese origin. It is also told by Rabelais and included in *Great Short Stories of the World*, (Heinemann) p. 312, "The Roast Meat Seller."

DOI   TOYOTAKA.

Doi Toyotaka was a native of Niigata in Echigo. He learned Tea from Oda Yuraku and was also fond of the Biwa and Incense. He became a retainer of Makino Bingo-no-kami Narisada lord of Yoshida in Mikawa, receiving an income of two hundred koku as

Monogashira (Captain of Infantry), but afterwards retired and went to live at Okazaki near Kyoto, at which time he made this verse:

> *Whether there's a hell*
> *Is a thing I do not know,*
> *Yet if such there be,*
> *'Twill not cost me much, I think,*
> *To boil up my kettle there.*

Doi was rather fond of luxury and was always well dressed, and at the age of ninety he used to go for a walk every day to a tea-house at Kurodani where he would have a meal. He never went without the sum of thirty mon fastened to the top of his staff, which he said was sufficient for one day's expenses. When he started off to go anywhere, which he frequently did quite casually, he always had two ryo in his pocket, which he explained, was for his burial fee. He carried also a paper with these instruction:

"Wherever this old Bōzu happens to die just pitch him into the sea or river or anywhere that is most convenient, but do not take any further trouble about him.

"In the bag round my neck is a rosary and some aloes incense. I want these left with me.

"When this happens please communicate the fact to farmer Shirobei who lives in front of the Torii of Teno at Okazaki."

This old man died on the sixth day of the first month of the seventeenth year of Kyoho (1732), aged ninety-four.

HIJIKATA NUI-NO-SUKE

Hijikata Nui-no-suke was the Karo or Councillor of Mizuno Dewa-no-kami Tadatomo lord of Numazu in Suruga. Mizuno had received as his adopted son Nakatsukasa-no-shō Tadayuki, second son of Tanuma Tonomo-no-kami Okitsugu, lord of Sagara in Totomi, the corrupt statesman who at this time held the Empire in the hollow of his hand, and profited considerably by the connexion, for first of all he was accorded the treatment of a member of the Rōju and afterwards received promotion to that body. His influence and the presents that people made him in consequence were not small. And since those who would obtain the favour of the lord had first to get that of the Karo, Hijikata Nui-no-suke benefited also. One day this Hijikata gave a Cha-no-yu to a certain Hotta, a friend of his, and it was called a ceremony in the most informal style. In the reception room hung a painting by Kano Motonobu and in the Tokonoma in front of it stood an incense-burner made in the form of a rice-bale of gold on which stood a cock of silver. In the next room was a flower vase of silver, it might be three feet long, with a flower arrangement in it, while on the tea-shelf was a feather brush of rare Chinese feathers and a golden tea-caddy engraved with iris by the younger brother of Goto Mitsutaka. Over the hearth was a huge silver kettle and beside it a wonderfully beautiful water-jar of blue-and-white

Nankin ware. When the after-ceremony of the Sumi was performed another golden incense-burner in the form of a tortoise worked by Goto Mitsutaka that had come from the collection of the great Osaka merchant Konoike Zeneimon was brought in a basket by the attendant. And the weight both of this and of the tea-caddy was very considerable, and far too great to make them comfortable to handle. Such was the vulgar and ostentatious Tea of a corrupt age. And if the luxury of the Karo was great, that of the lord was naturally greater, and even that did not compare in any way with that of Tanuma himself.

The Tanumas, Okitsugu and Okitomo were more or less in control of the administration during the time of the Shogun Ieharu (1760-86).

A certain wealthy and ostentatious person built a Tea-room and made the receptacle* of the urinal of the Setsuin of black lacquer, gilt inside. When he gave a Cha-no-yu one of the guests went to use the Setsuin, and being shown there by a retainer as was (and still is) the custom, he drew back on seeing this elaborate arrangement and asked if they would not allow him to use a more ordinary one. Which they did. But the host felt very much ashamed of himself. This might be called the Tanuma style.

YANAGITA SHOGEN AND THE FROG

Yanagita Shōgen was a famous flute-player of Nikko. He was given to Cha-no-yu, and built himself a Tea-room in his house. By the Rōji entrance he made a bamboo sword-rack, and in one of the bamboos of this a tree-frog made his home, and announced his presence by an occasional croak. One day Shōgen took his flute and began to play, when the frog joined in too and apparently tried to tune his voice to the notes. Shōgen noticed this and thought it rather remarkable, so in future he made a point of practising near this place. Sure enough the frog took his part in the duet, quite entering into the spirit of the thing, and as time went on he became more and more skilled in harmonizing his notes to the varied tones of the flute. This pleased Shōgen exceedingly and he gave strict orders to his servants that they were on no account to do anything to disturb the frog.

Lovers of Cha-no-yu should approve of the frog on account of his correct deportment, for his way of sitting is just like that of a Japanese in the attitude of ceremony, as the Haiku of Sōgen attests :

> Hands correctly placed
> Thus you sit and sing your song
> Ceremonious frog !

---

* This receptacle goes by the pleasant name of ' Asagao ' or 'Morning Glory,' from its shape. It is normally of green of grey pottery or celadon.

THE KWANRYO'S BRAZIER.

The Kwanryo of the temple of Chōrakuji on Higashiyama in Kyoto had a brazier of Sentoku bronze that he greatly prized, and which he was always rubbing with a silken cloth and polishing with his sleeve, seldom letting in out of his sight. One day he had a guest to whom he was serving a bowl of Koi-cha, and the two of them were deeply absorbed in some interesting conversation when the guest took the fire-tongs and scraped a hole in the ashes of this precious brazier, in spite of there being a tobacco-box by him, and was just going to spit into it. When the Kwanryo saw this he was greatly taken aback, and, pressing his finger into his forehead, said : " Oh, please wait a moment. There is a spitting-tube in that tobacco-box. Please use that." The guest reddened. " Dear me," he exclaimed, "pray excuse me. The fact is that I have got into the habit of doing this at home and so I went to do it here without thinking." If he had studied Tea he certainly did not put it into practice ordinarily.

When the Kwanryo told this story to another Chajin Yanagisawa Gien, his comment was : " Ah, I wonder whether it is better to press your forehead with your finger, or not to do so."

YANAGISAWA GIEN AND AKISHINO YOHEI

Outside the village of Akishino in the district of Ikoma of the province of Yamato, there is a small temple of Nyo-i-rin Kwannon, and one day when Yanagisawa Gien was crossing over Mt. Ikoma he stopped there for a while to have a smoke and admire the scenery. Here he saw a man blind in one eye whom he supposed to be the caretaker, busily engaged in shaping Sotobas,* and when he hailed him the man put aside his unfinished piece of wood, got up and raked together the ashes on the hearth, put on some shavings, and soon had a kettle boiling over it, whereupon he carefully washed a Tea-bowl stained with much use and made some tea, which he offered to Gien with the remark : " It is some tea I have just got from Osaka. I hope you will enjoy it." Gien drank two or three bowls and the man went on : " This is not my native country. When I was young I spent some twenty years in Kyoto, working at my trade of a joiner, but now I am getting on and my sight is bad, and I have had rather a succession of troubles, so I have come over here at the invitation of a friend, and here I suppose I shall end my days. Well, it seems that Cha-no-yu began by being the diversion of people like me." And he produced another bowl with some cakes. These were nothing else but the buds of the Tatara tree coated in bean-paste and roasted. Yanagisawa thought them very uncommon and had another bowl of tea with them and the old man went on :   "When I was in Kyoto

---

* Sotoba. Wooden lath inscribed with Sanskrit characters set up by a tombstone. From Sanskrit " Stupa."

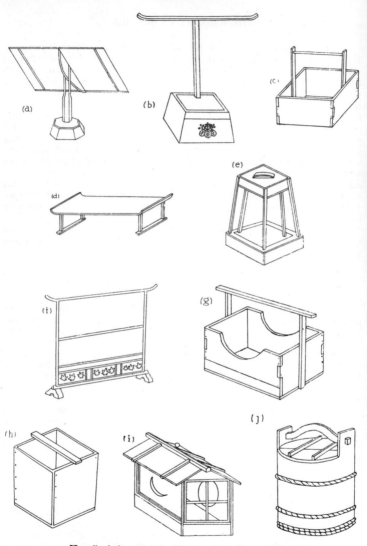

Utensils designed by the Masters of the House of Sen.

(a) Book-rest, by Rikyu. (b) Towel stand, by Rikyu. (c) Ash box, by Rikyu. (d) Writing desk, by Rikyu. (e) Roji lantern. (f) Clothes horse, by Rikyu. (g) Tobacco box, by Sokan. (h) Mizusashi, by Rikyu. (i) Lantern, by Rikyu. (j) Bucket.

I got to know a lot of Tea Masters, and used to be invited to their meetings and studied a bit myself, but it seemed to me that most of them thought Cha-no-yu was something quite apart, for they used to order all sorts of complicated things to be made for it.   There was a man who took a great fancy to a Tea-room called the 'something-or-other-An' on Higashiyama, built by some famous Master, and had one just like it built for himself, and for the floor of the Tokonoma, he ordered a piece of wood with seven knots in it.   When I askèd him why seven, he said because the original room had seven.   I thought this the funniest thing on earth, because the only reason the great Master had knots in the floor was that when he built it he could not get any wood without them, and however much a man may admire a Master and wish to follow him, this blind imitation can hardly be called handing on his tradition, it is rather exposing his shortcomings in public.   I take it the Way of Tea does not so much enjoin people to be clean as recommend them not to be dirty, and that its entertainment consists in making up for what is lacking in one's equipment by some ingenious contrivance. The interest lies in things being a little deficient or imperfect, and a superfluity is always tasteless.   People get into habits, unfortunately, and though a man may fancy all sorts of different things you can't call him really a man of taste until he has got rid of them.   Unless a man understands ordinary logic but yet is not bound by it, you can't call him a real Tea Master but only a man who fancies Teaism."   Gien was astonished and charmed at this elegant discourse and thought he would like to take the man home with him and employ him.   Then he said : " Well, can you write me something as a souvenir of this pleasant meeting ? "   But he could not write.   So he asked for one of the Sotobas instead.   "Ah, that's an ill-omened present," was the reply, " but I think I have something."   And he looked in a box and found a piece of paper with some writing on it.   Gien looked at it and read : " It may be fragile, but better make a thing of earthenware than of wood.   Don't make anything of metal that you can make of pottery.   What you make of wood, make of wood, and what you make of pottery make of pottery.   Only make of metal what can't be made of anything else.   Never make anything of metal that can be made of wood or earthenware because you think you will make money by it.—Akishino Yohei."

YODOYA TATSUGORŌ

Yodoya Tatsugorō was a great merchant of Osaka.   He was very extravagant and ostentatious in his life as well as very dis-sipated, and spent most of his time in the company of strumpets, without caring what people thought of him or what the effect might be on his family.   Now this grieved his mother very much and she enlisted the services of a kind old physician she knew, and whether through his representations or not Tatsugorō gave up his dissipation. His mother was naturally overjoyed and sent the doctor as a present with her warmest thanks a very valuable tea-caddy which had been a long time in the family. But he knew nothing of Cha-no-yu and sold it to a dealer, and after that it changed hands until it came into the possession of one of the officials of the Bakufu.

Now this tea-caddy had been the subject of investigation at the court some time before, so the official immediately ordered an inquiry as to where it had come from. It was not long before it was traced to Yodoya. "For saying that you knew nothing of this last year when enquiry was made, and thus deceiving the Government, you are guilty of contempt of Court," was the decision of the authorities, and Yodoya was brought up for examination. As a result he was convicted of extravagance and presumption and sentenced to be expelled from the Three Cities and to have all his property confiscated.* This consisted of 1,120,000 ryo of gold, 8,500 kwamme of silver, landed property and bonds worth many tens of thousands of ryo, eighteen ships of more than a thousand koku burden, and more treasures and rarities than were easily counted.

Among these valuables were especially remarkable : a golden kettle ; a pair of golden storks ; ten great branches of coral ; four tiles from the Kanyo Palace† ; three verses of Teika on fine paper ; a set of coral curtains ; sixteen sparrows of silver and gold ; three golden tea-bowls ; twenty trays of aloe-wood ; three thousand four hundred fine kakemonos of paintings and writings ; fifteen silver ricebowls ; thirty golden Buddhas ; a 'Gō' board and pieces of gold and silver ; twenty-eight glass Shōji ; a hundred sticks of pure gold ; seven hundred swords ; thirty-seven spears and halberds ; a hundred and fifty rugs ; forty-eight carpets ; and several hundred famous tea-utensils.

KAWACHIYA TAROBEI

Kawachiya Tarobei was another great Osaka merchant, generally known as Kawataro. He had immense wealth and was a great spendthrift, but was also a very droll and humorous fellow and liked to fling away money like water on some mad prank, so that his odd escapades were the talk of the countryside. Once when the lord of Kishu was passing through Osaka, Tarobei went out to meet him and offer him tea. The Daimyo liked the water with which it was made very much and asked him if he would send him a little.‡ He meant perhaps a couple of bottles to use for his own tea. "Oh,

---

* This confiscation took place in 1707 towards the end of the Shogunate of Tsunayoshi and shortly after the gay Genroku era. Cf. Murdoch, *History of Japan*, vol. iii. p. 207.

† Kanyo, i.e. Han Yang, the capital of the Chinese Emperor Shih Huang Ti of Ts'in, died B.C. 206. His palace of A Fang Kung was said to have been tiled with emeralds.

‡ The best water for tea was that drawn from the stream as it ran under the Uji bridge by the third pillar from the west. Other parts of the Uji river were not so good because of the pools and shallows. In Osaka, tea lovers liked to get water from what were called the Four Noted Places. The water of these four spots was especially good for Sake brewing too. They are : the water of the well Horii in the temple of Sennichi ; the water of Akitaya at Dotombori ; the water of Atago in Jurakumachi ; and that of Tenjin in the shrine of Temmano-Tenjin.

certainly, my lord," replied Tarobei, " I shall be delighted to have the honour of sending you some."

The Daimyo nodded his thanks and passed on, and soon after reached his province. Then one day not long afterwards, one of his retainers came to him and said, " The water sent by Kawachiya Tarobei, the citizen of Osaka, has arrived as he promised. What shall we do about it? " "Oh, just take it in," replied the Daimyo. "But," said the retainer, " there is such an immense quantity that the question is where to put it." In great astonishment the lord went up to the castle tower and looked out and saw a long line of coolies carrying buckets of water, it seemed hundreds and thousands of them, stretching away into the distance like a trail of ants. "Ah, this is one of that fellow Kawataro's little jokes," exclaimed he as he gazed in amazement at the sight. And to astonish one of the lords of the Three Great Families was just about Kawataro's idea of a little joke. But what was not the least strange thing about him was that when he had beggared his family in one generation by a succession of jokes of this kind, far from being in any way troubled about it, he seemed to regard it as the biggest joke of the lot. He had, at any rate, more reason for satisfaction than Yodoya, who was beggared by the government. Also he was a real Chajin.

TOKUGAWA IENARI

On one occasion, when the Shogun Ienari was arranging flowers with his suite he presented each of his chamberlains and gentlemen in waiting with a vase selected according to their rank from a number he had by him made of odds and ends of old pieces of wood and bamboo roots, which he had arranged in the order of their worth. But in the distribution he happened to overlook a certain attendant of low rank, and the chamberlains, noticing this, mentioned it to his Highness.

Looking round to see if there was anything left, the vase standing in the Tokonoma of the room caught the Shogun's eye. "As there is unfortunately nothing better, give him that," he said, and they took the flowers out of it and did so. It was a very splendid piece made of solid silver, and the Shogun's thus judging it of little account, and preferring the beauty of the simple and natural, greatly impressed the Courtiers.

KATSUSHIKA GOMBEI AND CHA-NO-YU

Gombei was the Mura-osa or head of the village of Katsushika near Edo, and as his people were offering a great Kagura to the Shrine of Ise, he went up there with thirteen others to superintend it. When they arrived they were fêted by one of the priests attached to the shrine, and after a good feast they were ushered into the Tea-room where the priest made tea and set the bowl before Gombei as being the chief of the guests.   Now Gombei had never before had any experience of Cha-no-yu and did not in the least know what to do, but he had heard that it was the custom to pass round the bowl, and now he looked at it and wondered how that could be made to go round fourteen people.   As he was considering the matter, the priest put the cakes before him and asked him to help himself, as usual, when Gombei in a flutter seized the bowl and drained the contents and set it down again.   The priest then took it back, rinsed it and filled it and again set it before him.   As he did so he asked him again to help himself to cake, so Gombei did so and once more drained the tea-bowl, whereupon the priest again rinsed and filled and set it before him.   This time he hesitated and "Oh, thank you very much, but I have had enough."   "Then please pass it to your neighbour," replied the priest quietly, and then Gombei perceived that the tea was to be passed on in this way and managed to get through without any more mishaps.   But when he got out of the room he drew a sigh of relief and when he retired that night he observed : " I think we had better hurry off early to-morrow in case there should be any more Cha-no-yu."

When he arrived home again, he related his experience to Yanagisawa Gien, who was an acquaintance of his, and told him how ashamed he felt of his ignorance, and he thought he had better study Tea-ceremony lest something of the kind should happen again.

"But that would be very silly," said Gien, "You were born a farmer, and if you know all about farming, you have nothing to be ashamed of.   Cha-no-yu is the diversion of esthetes and retired people. There's no need for farmers and wardsmen to bother themselves about it.   Of course, if they like to do so after they have retired and become Inkyo, that's all right, but if you begin to study tea and all the village follows your example, farming will get neglected and what will happen to the crops ?   If in a province, a hundred farm and fifty divert themselves, people will soon go hungry, but if there are only ten who amuse themselves for a hundred who follow the plough, then the province will be prosperous enough."   And Gombei took his advice and gave up the idea of Cha-no-yu.

II NAOSUKE*

Ii Kamon-no-kami Naosuke, lord of Hikone, belonged to the main Sekishu school of Tea, but eventually made a school of his own.   What he considered especially important was its disregard of social distinctions.   He used to say in explaining it : " No man is really worthy of either honour or contempt, but in the world as it is there are grades in society which are necessary for order and must be strictly preserved.   It is only in the Tea-room that no notice

---

* Ii Naosuke, Kamon-no-kami, 1815–1860, one of the ablest of the Japanese statesmen, was Tairō or Chief Minister to the Shogun Iesada and his successor Iemochi.   He insisted on signing the treaties with the U.S.A. in 1858 and afterwards with England and France, and dealt severely with the anti-foreign party who opposed this policy, and as a result he was assassinated in 1860 by samurai of the Mito clan, whose head, lord Nariaki, he had offended.

is taken of rank or birth. This is a most attractive feature of it, that the order of precedence is merely according to the degree of skill or the order of arrival. When Rikyu gave a Cha-no-yu party and the tradesman Zeniya Sōnō was the principal guest, the daimyo Kimura Hitachi-no-suke happened to come and ask to be allowed to take part. He was given the lowest seat and the ceremony proceeded thus. The reason I find Cha-no-yu so interesting is just because it is so out of the ordinary. It is a world of its own and the only one where you may find a wardman occupying the highest place and a Daimyo the lowest."

Naosuke entertained all sorts of people quite regardless of their means or position and a certain plasterer named Rihachi was not seldom his guest. Naturally he practised the simplest style and heartily disliked any other. Once when he was invited to Cha-no-yu by Tayasu Chunagon Yoshiyori, he remarked to one of his household officers when he came back that evidently Tayasu did not understand the real meaning of Tea judging by what he saw and heard there, for it was what you called 'Seken-cha' or 'Society Tea,' a type that was not only boring to him personally but, he considered, was responsible for getting the Way into disrepute generally.

Naosuke made a verse which he considered expressed the Four Principles of Tea.

> By the river bank
> See the weeping willow stand,
> All its pliant boughs
> Quivering in the slightest breeze
> Mirror'd in the placid depths.

SHIBATA ZESHIN

Shibata Zeshin, one of the greatest artists of modern times, was a native of Edo and lived on the Ishigari embankment in Shimo-Heiemon Cho in Asakusa. Since he lived opposite to Yanagihara, he took the name of Tairyukyo which has just that meaning. He studied Cha-no-yu under Yoshida Sō-i, and made a large collection of fine utensils. When he was twenty-five years old, he went to the temple of Tofukuji near Kyoto and saw the treasures of one of its halls called Sanshōji. Among these was a picture of the sixteen Rakan by Li Lung Mien, and before this Zeshin became a fixture, gazing abstractedly at it like one in a trance. When the priest at last interrupted him, he exclaimed : " This is one of the world's masterpieces ! What amazing talent these Chinese have ! Words fail one before such work." Seeing that he had such a genuine admiration for it, the priest allowed him to copy it and Zeshin gladly took the opportunity.

Twenty-five years after this, a certain Hashimoto Sōjun came as a visiting priest to the temple of Kaizenji in Asakusa, and meeting Zeshin happened to remark that the treasures of the Sanshōji were to be sold. Zeshin immediately asked if the picture by Li Lung

Mien was for sale too, and the other replied that it was and that it was regarded as the most valuable of all. As soon as Zeshin heard this, he immediately sold all his cherished Tea-utensils, and as he considered that not enough he put his wife's clothes in pawn and borrowed from the moneylenders till he had got together two hundred and fifty pieces of gold.

Then he hurried off to Kyoto and managed to secure the Sixteen Rakan he admired so much, as well as another of Shaka Muni supported by the eighteen Heavenly Kings. Then he gave himself up to self-forgetful meditation on these inspired paintings. entirely oblivious of everything, though his family had hardly anything to eat and the duns were continually at his door, and when one of his household remarked what a pity it was to have parted with some of his fine Tea-utensils, he only remarked: " Well, that's my Teaism. What is there to regret ? " Zeshin's favourite saying was this: "Neglect your work and it will deteriorate and become a business, and then if you don't avoid commonplace patrons you will become commonplace yourself."

CHAPTER III

SCHOOLS OF TEA

Twenty-four schools of Cha-no-yu are given by Yasuoka as the principal ones, though there exist a few more. They are as follows:

	Founder	
Mizuho		Tamaki Ittotsu
Yabuuchi	,,	Yabuuchi Shochi Kenchu
Oribe	,,	Furuta Oribe Shigenari
Nambo	,,	Nambo Sōkei
Yuraku	,,	Oda Yuraku
Sansai	,,	Hosokawa Tadaoki
Sekishu	,,	Katagiri Sadaaki
Enshu	,,	Kobori Masakazu
Sōwa	,,	Kanamori Sōwa
Hisada	,,	Hisada Sōzen
Sadaoki	,,	Oda Sadaoki
Sōhen	,,	Yamada Sōhen
Fusai	,,	Sugiki Fusai
Matsuo	,,	Matsuo Sōji
Hayami	,,	Hayami Sōtatsu
Yōken	,,	Fujimura Yōken
Fuhaku	,,	Kawakami Fuhaku
Chinshin	,,	Matsuura Shigenobu
Ikei	,,	Ikei Oshō
Unshu	,,	Matsudaira Fumai
Enjōbō	,,	Enjōbō Sōen
Isa	,,	Isa Kotaku
Abe	,,	Abe Kyuha
Ōguchi	,,	Ōguchi Joken

The chief schools of Omote and Ura Senge, deriving from Sosa and Soshitsu, the second and third sons of Sōtan, the grandson of Rikyu and after him the figure in the family, both carry on the same tradition and are in no way to be regarded as greater or lesser, but only as perhaps differing in emphasis on certain details. The names 'Front' and 'Rear' Senge refer only to the position of their residences, the Konnichi-an of Sōshitsu being behind the Fushin-an of Sōsa opposite to the Honnōji. Rikyu's elder son Dō-an did not succeed on account of his lameness, and the Tea-room he contrived was arranged to conceal this defect. His school descends through Katagiri Sekishu, Matsuura Chinshin and Matsudaira Fumai, Daimyo styles carried on by their Tea Masters rather than themselves, while from it derives the Isa school which officiated in the Shogun's Tea-rooms. In early days, the Yabuuchi school was known as the Lower School as distinguished from the two schools of Sen who lived in the Upper Town and so were together called the Upper School.

The Fuhaku School was called the Senge of Edo because it carried on their tradition there as opposed to Enshu who represented the Oribe or more elaborate manner. All these various schools that again divided later on are like the sects of Zen or Shinshu Buddhism in that they have their origin only in family history and not in any conflicting convictions.

Matsudaira Fumai once said : "In the construction of Tea-rooms and their gardens there is no one like Sōtan, while Enshu is supreme in the connoisseurship of utensils and knowledge of painting and calligraphy, and Sekishu holds most faithfully to the details of the ancient tradition. If these three were combined you would have the perfect Tea-master.

It is said that Nambo Sōkei had a most retentive memory and wrote down his reminiscences of Rikyu's teaching in three hundred chapters. But Rikyu told him he had better burn them, for the more mysterious a principle was the more it was respected, and there would be more harm than good in thus revealing everything to posterity. At first, Sōkei intended to follow his advice, but afterwards thought it a pity to destroy what he had so industriously accumulated, and only hid his book at the bottom of a chest, thinking it did not matter as long as no one knew of it. But after his death, it came into the hands of Dōan, Rikyu's eldest son, and then passed to his pupil Kuwayama Sakon, eventually reaching Katagiri Sekishu. He gave it to his favourite pupil, the priest Ikei of the Tōkaiji at Shinagawa, and so it was that this house of Ikei came to be considered the true representative of the Rikyu tradition in the Kwanto and became Sukiya-gashira or Tea Masters-in-chief to the Shogun. The possession of this document seems to have given them authority beyond that of the main houses of Sen and those of Oribe, Yabuuchi and Yamada, who were all at this period rather in a state of eclipse. This is evident from the fact that the great Master Matsudaira Fumai chose to identify himself with this school.

A glance at his fellow pupils will show that then as now all classes were represented among those who learned from even the most fashionable teacher.

Isa Kotaku III

Isa Kotaku IV	Shiina Chuemon, Cabinet-maker to the Shogun	Fujimori Tōgen, Bag-maker to the Shogun	Mizumura Jimbei, Townsman of Edo
Kitamura Hikozo, City Councillor of Edo	Matsudaira Keizan, Daimyo	Niwa Kaga-no-kami, Daimyo	Matsudaira Dewa-no-kami, Lord Fumai, Daimyo
Itō Chōdaiyu, Retainer of Matsudaira Fumai	Ochi Sōtaku, Tea Master to Matsudaira Shimosa-no-kami		

The following is the genealogy of the Masters of the house of Ura Senge as given in the Tettchu Chawa of Sasaki Sammi.

Title	Saigo	Gago	Date of death	Age
Rikyu	Hosensai	Fushinan	2. 28. 1591	70
Dōan	Ittossai	Fukyusai	2. 26. 1608	62
Sōjun		Shōan	9. 7. 1614	69
Sōtan	Tottossai	Konnichian	12. 19. 1658	81
Sōshitsu		Rōgetsuan	1. 23. 1698	76
Sōshitsu	Fukyusai		5. 14. 1714	32
Sōan	Rokkansai		8. 28. 1727	33
Sōkan	Saisaisai		3. 2. 1734	25
Sōshitsu	Yugensai	Butsubutsuken	2. 2. 1772	53
Genshitsu	Fukensai	Kanun	9. 26. 1801	56
Sōshitsu	Nintokusai		8. 24. 1827	57
Sōshitsu	Gengensai		7. 11. 1878	68
Genshitsu	Yuimyōsai	Yuiken	12. 8. 1918	65
Sōshitsu	Ennōsai	Tettchu	8. 5. 1925	53
Sōshitsu	Tantansai	Baishian	Present Head	

Since Dōan is not included officially the present head of the family Sen Tantansai Soshitsu VII is reckoned as the fourteenth generation from Rikyu.

The 'Gago' is the 'elegant' or literary name taken by anyone in Japan, but the 'Saigo' or name ending in 'Sai' is rather used by devotees of Tea and Flowers, and derives from Zen Buddhism, for the meaning of Sai is 'abstention,' i.e. from a meat diet. Thus as associated with the Zen monastery it came to signify 'living a life of leisured and scholarly dignity,' hence the other meaning of sai, room for such a life, library.

SOME CHARACTERISTIC NAMES OF TEA-ROOMS

Fushin-an.	Doubting Hut.	不	審 庵
Mugai-an.	Introvert Hut.	無	外 庵
Kō-an.	Bamboo Thicket Hut.	篁	庵
Sekika-an.	Beautiful Evening Hut.	夕	佳 庵
Mokurai-an.	Silent Thunder Hut.	默	雷 庵
Shinju-an.	Pearl Hut.	眞	珠 庵
Tokyu-do.	East Seeking Hall.	東	求 堂
Tsusen-in.	Hall frequented by Rishi.	通	仙 院
Ihō-an.	Bequeath Perfume Hut.	遺	芳 庵
Shigure-tei.	Shower Arbour.	時	雨 亭
Kasa-tei.	Umbrella Arbour.	傘	亭
Chinryu-tei.	Pillow Stream Arbour.	枕	流 亭
Shūhō-an.	Gather Perfume Hut.	集	芳 庵
Myōgi-an.	Wondrous Joy Hut.	妙	喜 庵
Gishō-in.	Beneficent Brightness Hall.	慈	照 院
Konnichi-an.	To-day Hut.	今	日 庵
Yu-in.	Further Retirement.	又	隱
Mushiki-ken.	No Colour House.	無	色 軒
Kanun-tei.	Cold Cloud Arbour.	寒	雲 亭

Shūkō-in.	Gather Brightness Hall.	集	光		院庵
En-an.	Swallow Hut.	燕			庵
Seiren-tei.	Clear Wavelets Arbour.	清	漣		亭
Taiku-an.	Great Emptiness Hut.	大	虚		庵
Shō-an.	Pine Hut.	松			庵
Shogetsu-tei.	Pine Moon Arbour.	松	月		亭
Jisso-an.	Real Appearance Hut.	實	相		庵
Issui-an.	One Sleep Hut.	一	睡		庵
Shingetsu-an.	Heart Moon Hut.	心	月		庵
Shōkin-tei.	Pine Lute Hut.	松	琴		亭
Busho-an.	Caressing Pine Hut.	撫	松		庵
Kōhō-an.	Lone Mugwort Hut.	孤	逢		庵
Ichimoku-an.	One Tree Hut.	一	木		庵
Murin-an.	Neighbourless Hut.	無	隣		庵
Shibukami-an.	Shibu Paper Hut.	澁	紙		庵
Fukō-an.	Hut of Indifference.	不	顧		庵
Bōji-tei.	Forgotten Path Arbour.	忘	路		亭
Yūgetsu-an.	Dim Moon Hut.	幽	月		庵
Yuishiki-an.	Enlightenment Hut.	唯	識		庵
Ryōkaku-tei.	Distant Emptiness Arbour.	遼	廓		亭
Setsu-an.	Hut of Clumsiness.	拙			庵
Maboroshi-an.	Hut of Illusion.	幻			庵
Kigyu-an.	Ride Cow Hut.	騎	午		庵
Yūgeki-an.	Secluded Quiet Hut.	幽	間		庵
Koshiba-an.	Little Brushwood Hut.	小	柴		庵
Karo-an.	What a Mean Hut!	何	陋		庵
Yamasato.	Mountain Village.	山			里
Shuun-an.	Massed Cloud Hut.	集	雲		庵
Hasso-an.	Eight Window Hut.	八	窓		庵
Rokuso-an.	Six Window Hut.	六	窓		庵
Tengo-an.	Varied Meeting Hut.	轉	合		庵
Sunsho-an.	Inch Pine Hut.	寸	松		庵
Kansui-an.	Cold Green Hut.	寒	翠		庵

PROGRAMME OF A CHA-NO-YU PARTY

Taisho tenth year, twelfth month, twenty-sixth day. Evening Tea.
Guests.　Takahashi Sōan, Kato Masayoshi, Yoshida Fūken,
　　　　Masuda Takime, Aoki Rōdō.

Tea-room.	Three-mat-and-a-half of the style approved by Genso.
Tokonoma.	A Writing by Seigan.
Incense burner.	Blue-and-white porcelain.
Feather brush.	Storks feathers.
Ash scoop.	Mulberry handled fire tongs.
Kettle.	Ashiya. Monkey-patterned-wide-mouth.
Charcoal basket.	Bamboo plaited vegetable basket type.
Ash vessel.	Yakenuki. by Nonko.

KAISEKI

Soup.	Minced duck with Deutzia.
Roast.	Haze fish with laminaria in Kenzan bowls.
Side dish	Haze caviare pickled in Sake lees.
Sake.	Choshi of blue-and-white porcelain with iron lid. Bottles of Chosen Karatsu ware. Cups of Karatsu ware and blue-and-white patterned ware.
Second dish.	Horse-mackerel with Radish salad and carrots, in bowls of Hagi ware.
Broth.	Aralia bud with shredded ginger.
Pickles.	Shin Takuan, in dishes of Imbe ware.
Cakes.	Steamed Manju.

INTERVAL

Tokonoma.	Two sprigs of white ligustrum in single story bamboo vase of Enshu make.
Tea-bowl.	'Amamori.' Box inscribed by Sakamoto Shusai.
Water vessel.	Seto ware, called ' Shiro-kuranushi.'
Lid stand.	Green bamboo.
Tea-caddy.	Sho-o Fubuki Natsume. Bag of Satsuma Kwantung material.
Tea-scoop.	' Mushi-kui.' Made by Rikyu.
Slop bowl.	Lacquered, circular.
Tea.	Hatsu Mukashi.

USU-CHA

Tea-caddy.	Imbe ware wide mouth.
Tea-bowl.	Red Raku ware by Ichinyu. called ' Ka-ai.'
Slop bowl.	Ninsei ware.
Tea-scoop.	Ivory, Rikyu style.
Second Tea-bowl.	Takatori ware.
Water vessel.	An old cloisonné kettle shape with handles.

EXAMPLES OF RIKYU'S MENUS FOR KAISEKI TAKEN
FROM THE NAMBO ROKU

Guests. Shorei Osho. Hosokawa Yusai. Nambo Sokei.
Bean Soup. Boiled Tofu (Bean Curd). Citron Gruel.
Cracknels and Mushrooms.
Second Day of the Eleventh Month.
First Snow.

Guests. Hideyoshi. Two-mat-and-a-half Tea-room.
Miscanthus Soup. Boiled Salmon. Trumpet Seaweed.
Roast Chestnuts. Mushrooms.
First Day of the Tenth Month.

An impromptu Cha-no-yu given to three friends who came in on the twenty-fifth of the twelfth month at a time of great snow :—
Cod Soup.   Namasu (Salad of raw fish and vegetables in vinegar). Awabi (Sea-ear) served on skewers.   Cracknels.   Mushrooms.

On the evening of the fifteenth day of the first month Rikyu entertained Sō-un and two rice-cake dealers named Dōhi and Mata-shichi in a three-mat room.
Broth.   Fish Salad.   Trumpet Seaweed.
Cracknels.   Roast Chestnuts.

When the great Lord Mori Terumoto came by himself Rikyu served :
Broth.   Namasu.
Seaweed.   Mushrooms.

On the thirteenth day of the sixth month Hideyoshi came accompanied by Kuroda Kageyu (Jōsui), Hosokawa Yusai and Imai Sōkyu.
In the Tokonoma was a verse written and composed by himself.
Soup.   A cereal dish.   Namasu.
Sashimi of raw tunny.   Boiled food.
Parched miscanthus.   Chestnuts.

PLATES

Plate 2. Yellow Seto tea bowl. Muromachi period. Collection of Nishida Yoshitaka, Japan.

Plate 3. White Temmoku tea bowl. Muromachi period. Private collection, Japan.

Plate 4. Black Raku tea bowl by Chōjirō. Momoyama period. Collection of Hosokawa Goritsu, Tokyo.

Plate 5. Black Raku tea bowl by Chōjirō. Momoyama period. Itsuo Museum, Osaka.

Plate 6. Bizen tea bowl. Momoyama period. Private collection, Japan.

Plate 7. Shino tea bowl: "Furisode." Early Edo period. Collection of the Seikadō Bunko, Tokyo.

Plate 8. Black Oribe tea bowl. Early Edo period. Itsuo Museum, Osaka.

Plate 9. White Raku tea bowl by Jōkei. Early Edo period. Private collection, Japan.

Plate 10. Tea bowl with fan design by Ninsei (front and back views). Early Edo period. Collection of Tokusawa Kunitaka, Tokyo.

Plate 11 Tea bowl by Ninsei. Early Edo period. Tokyo National Museum.

Plate 12. Raku tea bowl by Kōetsu: "Fujisan." Early Edo period. Collection of Sakai Tadamasa, Tokyo.

Plate 13. Black Raku tea bowl by Chōnyū. Middle Edo period. Tokyo National Museum.

Plate 14. Tea bowl by Kenzan. Middle Edo period. Collection of Takeuchi Zenji, Tokyo.

Plate 15. Karatsu tea bowl. "Edo." Middle Edo period. Collection of Kondō Shigeya.

Plate 16. Hagi tea bowl. Middle Edo period. Courtesy of the Smithsonian Institution, Freer Gallery of Art, Washington, D.C.

Plate 17. Hōraku tea bowl. Late Edo period. Collection of T. Rosenberg, New York.

Plate 18. Teahouse garden with stone lantern and pavement of natural rock and cut granite. Ichi-riki, Gion, Kyoto.

Plate 19. Teahouse courtyard garden with rocks set in moss-covered soil.
Ichi-riki, Gion, Kyoto.

Plate 20. Teahouse garden with bamboo fence and gate. Ura Senge, Kyoto.

Plate 21. Corner of teahouse garden with stone water basin. Shinju-an, Daitokuji, Kyoto.

Plate 22. Corner of teahouse garden with water basin and stone lantern. Shinju-an, Daitokuji, Kyoto.

Plate 23. Teahouse: Shōkintei. Katsura Imperial Villa, Kyoto.

BOOKS CONSULTED

Chado. Takahashi Tatsuo. Tokyo, Ooka Sansho-ten. 1929.
Taisho Kōshin Chado-ki. Takahashi Yoshio. Tokyo, Sōbunsha. 1922.
Chashitsu to Chatei Zukai. Matsumoto Buntaro. Tokyo, Kenchiku Shōin. 1920.
Chado Hokan. Kurokawa Shindo. Tokyo, Chōyōsha. 1917.
Chado Yōkan. Tamaki Issei. Osaka, Maeda Bunshindo. 1916.
Chado Kōgi. Tanaka Tei.
Kwado to Chado. Nakazawa Risui. Tokyo, Nishodo. 1918.
Cha-no-yu Taizen. Korika Kyusai. Tokyo, Hakubunkwan. 1901.
Cha-no-yu no Tebiki. Kōho-an Yūsai, preface by Prince Sanjo. Osaka, Nagura Shobunkwan. 1929.
Chashitsu to Chatei. Yasuoka Katsuya. Tokyo, Suzuki Shoten. 1928.
Cha-no-yu Shiori. Nippon Kasei Kenkyu Kwai. Osaka, Subundo. 1928.
Chawa Bidan. Kumata Sōjiro. Tokyo, Jitsugyo no Nihonsha. 1921.
Cha-no-yu Dokushu Shinan. Izawa Kamakichi. Osaka Sanzosha. 1896.
Cha-no-yu Michi Shirube. Sen Ennosai Sōshitsu. Osaka, Maeda Bunshindo. 1927.
Shinsen Teisakuden. Osaka Shubundo. Reprint. 1894.
Nihon Tōki Zensho. Onishi Ringoro. Tokyo, Shosando. 1918.
Nambo Roku. Nambo Sōkei. 1744. Reprint by Kyoto Kaiekido 1920.
Kōetsu. Edited by the Kōetsu Society, revised by Dr. Miura Shūgo. Kyoto, Soundo. 1921.
Kinsei Nihon Kokuminshi. Tokutomi Iichiro. Tokyo, Minyusha. 1922.
Tokugawa Jikki. Zokkokushi Taikei. Tokyo, Shueisha. 1902.
Nihon Kokumin Taikan. Article Cha-no-yu. Tokyo, Chugai Shōin. 1912.
Bungaku ni arawaretara waga kokumin shiso no kenkyu. Tsuda Sokichi. Tokyo, Rakuyodo. 1917.
Riso no Kaoku. Mihashi Shiro. Tokyo, Okura Shoten. 1913.
Kwansei Enkaku Ryakushi. Tokyo Daigaku. Tokyo. 1900.
Eisai Zenji. Kinomiya Yasuhiko. Tokyo, Shueisha. 1916.
Kōji Ruien. Yugibu. Tokyo, Tsukiji Kappan Seizo. 1908.
Nihon Kenchiku Jidai Yoshiki. Masuyama Shimpei. Kyoto, Heiando. 1921.
Chashitsu Teien Gacho. Okamoto Teikichi. Tokyo, Isseisha. 1917.
Tetchu Chawa. Sasaki Sammi. Kyoto, Chado Gepposha. 1928.
Matsudaira Fumai-den. Takahashi Tatsuo. Tokyo, Keibundo. 1917.
Kwanko Dzusetsu. Ninagawa Noritane. Tokyo. 1877.
Kuroda Jōsui-den. Count Kaneko Kentaro. Tokyo, Hakubunkan. 1917.
Rikyu Hyaku Shu Shikai. Kanazawa Soi. Kyoto, Chado Gepposha. 1927.

In English may be consulted :

The Book of Tea. Okakura Kakuzo.

Japanese Traits and Foreign Influences. Chapter, ' On Teaism.' I. Nitobe.

Japan and China. Vol. 2. Refinements and Pastimes. Cha-no-yu. Vol. 3. do. Incense ceremony. F. Brinkley.

History of Japan. Vol. 3. Appendix. On the Tea plant. E. Kaempfer.

Life of Hideyoshi. Appendix Note 2. W. Dening.

Cha-no-yu. Japan Society Transactions. Vol. V. Harding Smith.

Pottery of Cha-no-yu. Japan Society Transactions. Vol. VI. C. Holme.

Gardens of Japan. Jiro Harada.

Gardens of Japan. J. Conder.

Japanese Homes and their Surroundings. E. S. Morse.

History of Korean Art. A. Eckardt.

Cha-no-yu. Y. Fukukita.

Zen Buddhism. D. T. Suzuki.

INDEX

About the author . . .

A. L. SADLER, M.A., was Professor of Oriental Studies at the University of Sydney from 1922 to 1948, at which time he became emeritus professor. He also served as Professor of Japanese at the Royal Military College of Australia. Among his numerous published works, in addition to the present volume, are *The Life of Tokugawa Ieyasu* (1936), *A Short History of Japanese Architecture* (1941), *Three Military Classics of China* (1944), *A Short History of Japan* (1946), and a number of translations from Japanese literature. His *The Ten Foot Square Hut and Tales of the Heike* (1928) has recently appeared in a reprint version of the same type as the present volume. From the time of his retirement until his death in 1971, he made his home in England.